D0434854

Russell Lack was born in London in 1964 and holds a BA Hons in Philosophy and an MBA from the Norwegian School of Management. He is married to Siv Amundsen. For most of his career he has worked in television, primarily as independent producer, both in the UK and in Sweden, Norway and Denmark. He has also written articles on film, television and music for publications such as *Sight and Sound, The Wire, Film Bulletin, Film Comment* and *Screen International*. He has recently returned to live in London after six years in Scandinavia and is currently working as a senior executive in business affairs for Pearson Television. *Twenty Four Frames Under* is his first book.

RUSSELL LACK **TWENTY FOUR FRAMES UNDER**

SIC • A BURIED HISTORY OF FILM MUSIC

Quartet Books

S

First published in Great Britain by Quartet Books Limited in 1997
A member of the Namara Group
27 Goodge Street
London W1P 2LD

A catalogue record for this book is available from the British Library

ISBN 0 7043 8045 5

Typeset by FSH Ltd, London
Printed and bound in Great Britain by C.P.D. Wales Ltd.

For my parents Roy and Barbara Lack, and for my wife Siv Amundsen Lack whose love, encouragement and insight made this book possible

I wish to thank those many people whose ideas, comments and enthusiams helped me to imagine, to write and to rewrite this text. This book evolved during a five year period from 1992 in which the original scope was changed considerably as new areas of interest and contacts opened up. The rise of the Internet during this period also accelerated the research process and put me in contact with hundreds of people around the world who provided help and advice of many kinds, for which my thanks and apologies for not listing everybody by name. I am also indebted to a number of good friends, old and new who offered support, common sense and humour when the going seemed toughest.

Contents

PART ONE: THE SILENT ERA

FILM MUSIC IN THE SILENT ERA:
AN INTRODUCTION

Film music has been with us from the very beginning of cinema. Even the short one- or two-minute film shows of the 1890s bore a live piano accompaniment. The addition of even the simplest of music served to partition this newly photographed world. Just as the projected moving image fragmented time into so many images per second, so the addition of music served to index that division. Music created an expressive analogue to the eerie silence of the cakewalking ghosts up on the cinema screen. The most fundamental question we can ask about film music is how did it come to be used in the first place?

On a practical level film music not only removed the essential strangeness from these silent projections, it also helped to mask the often horrendous noise made by early projection equipment:

> It [film music] began not as a result of any artistic urge, but from the dire need for something which would drown out the noise made by the projector. For in these times there were as yet no sound-absorbent walls between the projection machine and the auditorium. This painful noise disturbed visual enjoyment to no small extent. Instinctively cinema proprietors had recourse to music, and it was the right way, using an agreeable sound to neutralize one less agreeable.[1]

> Music was employed to cover the uncouth noises of the machines projecting the pictures. There was no thought of its relevancy or irrelevancy to the drama being enacted upon the screen. It was simply to distract attention from this unpleasant and unavoidable concomitant to the picture.[2]

Quite apart from the noise of the projectors, there was also an audience unused to the collective intimacy of a darkened room. Without dialogue to

[1] Kurt London, *Film Music* (London: 1930), p. 23

[2] Frederick Converse, 'Music and the Motion Picture', *Arts*, October 1923

follow, what reason was there to keep quiet during a screening? Modern films such as *Amarcord* (1973) or *Cinema Paradiso* (1988) depict the silent cinema's auditorium as an almost gladiatorial space. In such an arena, the embattled film image vies for attention with an audience lost in its own agenda of squabbles, baiting and heckling:

> Music was needed for its magic. To drown the whirring and the coughing, to bind the separate spectators into one audience. To hypnotize, to make a mood.[3]

Music neutralized not only distracting noises but dramatic and technical flaws within the film itself. Music was deployed for its form rather than its content. Its palliative effects soothed and caressed spectators into suspending disbelief in what they were watching. Without doubt,

> A restlessness would develop were we to witness only the actions, a restlessness dependent upon the potential alertness of our auditory nerves. We should expect sound and none would come. The musical accompaniment of silent films, therefore, simply occupied our attention and prevented the disappointment resultant upon a thwarted expectancy.[4]

> Always while the visual sense was engaged in following the action on the screen, the aural sense was employed in listening to music, the combination being perfect from a physiological stand-point for the reason that when the visual sense is occupied exclusively, it tires more readily than when another sense, the aural sense, is occupied in sympathy with it.[5]

As musical accompaniment was primarily a live spectacle, this meant that critics saw films 'cold' - stripped of their musical armour. They watched in silence, or rather with all the attendant distractions that film music was supposed to drown out. Any film that could survive such a process and still attract positive reviews, as Kevin Brownlow points out,[6] had certainly earned any praise it received.

Even without music, some sort of accompaniment was apparently felt to be necessary. Luis Buñuel tells a story from his youth in the Spanish town of Zaragoza of watching a film which was accompanied by a commentator who would literally explain the screen events to the audience. This task was performed with the aid of a megaphone, and seems to have existed chiefly to

3 Ivor Montagu, *Film World* (London: 1966), p. 59

4 Allardyce Nicoll, *Film & Theatre* (London: 1936), p. 125

5 Welford Beaton, *Know Your Movies* (Hollywood: 1932), p. 82

6 Kevin Brownlow, *The Parade's Gone By* (London: 1968)

bring the largely peasant audience through the complexities of the film's grammar. Not simply who was doing what to whom but to explain why pictures suddenly cut from one scene to another, why whole scenes suddenly shifted, why characters walked out of the edge of one picture only to return from a different edge of a different picture. The man with the megaphone was clearly providing a help to understanding a film in the same way film music has continued to do ever since.

In the period 1906–16 music tended simply to mimic events on screen, tracking the dominant physical movements or the most melodramatic moments. It wasn't particularly subtle. The most extreme examples of a formulaic approach to the portrayal of certain kinds of emotions were the cue music sheets sent out by distributors to the managers of cinemas from about 1909 onwards. These contained specific suggestions for musical sources (usually light nineteenth-century romantic material) that could portray particular types of scenes. This highly conventionalized practice did much to cement ideas over the next two decades (up to the beginning of the sound era in 1926) of how film music should sound and more importantly how it should be used.

Although by no means the only form of accompaniment, the lone piano player endures as a potent symbol of the silent era. The early accompanist laboured hard for poor pay and low social status. The abilities of even the most adroit player were stretched across punishing work schedules, often involving three or four continuous programmes a day of wildly varying accompaniments to the same film. Any drop in quality, however, and the brickbats came thick and fast:

> There is one head under which nearly every moving picture theatre in New York City, in our opinion, is lamentably deficient. We mean the music – the music that accompanies, illustrates, or which is supposed to harmonize with the pictures. The piano and some sound effects are usually considered sufficient; and oh, and oh, the piano and the players we sometimes hear and see! The former is more often than not out of tune, and the latter, though he can strike the key with something like accuracy and precision, if not violence, cannot play music, or, if he can, he does not . . . Half the pianists whom we have heard these last six months deserve to lose their jobs, for if they can play, they either won't or don't. The pianos should be either burnt or put into tune or replaced with better ones. But better still, we think, is our advice, wherever practical, to engage a small orchestra of strings, with the addition of the piano and the sound effects. Of course, this costs money, but we think that the outlay would recoup itself.[7]

7 *Moving Picture World*, 3 July 1909

For the accompaniment to work it had to provide the illusion of a seamless flow of melodies, tremolos and whatever else was required to illustrate the scene. The raw materials were inoffensive, lightweight and reasonably well-known romantic symphonies. To fit disparate sources of music together within the dimension of what was after all a live performance required an intelligence equivalent to at least that of a competent improviser.

It wasn't simply playing skills that varied in quality, but the availability of music itself. Producers and distributors had not yet begun to supply musical cue sheets to theatres showing their products and the choice of musical accompaniment was left pretty much to the theatre's musical director, or more likely the pianist himself. The accompanist's ideal preparation consisted of an initial viewing of the film (a luxury frequently overlooked by distributors anxious to move their prints as quickly as possible between venues) in order to spot the chief points of dramatic action. With these notes the accompanist resorted to the musical catalogues of the larger publishers, companies such as Feist, Ted Snyder, Remick and Witmark. The resulting programmes might include a smattering of contemporary popular songs intermingled with abridgements pillaged from the classics. This technique was therefore highly dependent upon ready access to the publishers' catalogues, notable powers of memory and a fertile musical imagination. Clearly, anything that went before and was printed on a manuscript was deemed to be fair game for musical plunder.

This spirit of adventure was linked closely to the sort of films that were emerging during the first ten years of the twentieth century. The earliest films, typified by Georges Méliès in France and Edwin Porter in America, are simple shot sequences approximating to some sort of narrative. The repetition of close shots on the central characters' faces forcing an identification from shot to shot pretty much removed the need for a live commentary which had been a prominent characteristic of the Magic Lantern spectacles, probably the nearest thing cinema has to a direct ancestor. Once liberated from a live commentary or text, the story is able to become far more fluid, notably in one of the earliest conventions of cinema – the chase sequence.

Clarence E. Sinn writing in the *Moving Picture World* in 1911 emphasizes the importance of selecting the right music to illustrate chase scenes. He recommended the following progression: pianissimo agitato, moving on to forte with a steady increase in tempo, segueing into a fortissimo gallop and concluding with a furioso.[8] Of course these instructions should remain flexible and would naturally be tailored around the action on screen.

8 *Moving Picture World*, 14 January 1911

The chase sequence is important as it illustrates a tendency amongst the early film makers to try to escape from the text-based device of an intertitle card, again a relic from the Magic Lantern days. The 1905 Pathé film *Au Bagne* begins as a series of shots of daily prison life, each described by an intertitle. A prisoner escapes and is pursued by his jailers through a succession of changing location shots cut straight together without resort to intertitles. The innovation of cross-cutting between parallel streams of narrative action freed up the early film and added dimensions of visual rhythm and tempo, thereby creating a narrative space which music was perfectly placed to fill.

On a general level, the evolution of the film image in America and Europe appears to have taken two different paths. In America the tendency was towards faster cutting between shots which were ostensibly rather flat and stage-like, whereas in Europe, particularly in France, the tempo remained somewhat slower although the compositions of each shot tended to involve deeper staging. The fast-cutting fluidity of the early American cinema and the innovation of the chase sequence foreground the cinema's most basic characteristics – temporality and (visual) rhythm. These two qualities are of course fundamental to the perception of music.

Whilst structuralist analysis has tended to see the film's soundtrack as simply being composed of sound effects, dialogue and music, little attempt is made to separate out the very different qualities of each of these. The French composer Pierre Jensen has described music as a 'foreign body' within the picture space[9] and indeed this seems pretty close to the truth. Whilst both dialogue and sound effects are clearly 'owned' in some sense by the events taking place in the picture space, what can we say about the music? Our experience of the world, and our passage through it, is not, as a rule, serenaded by alien melodies that mimic our every waking state.

Though music may be owned in a trivial sense – the diegetic source within a film that is revealed (as the camera pulls back) to come from an element contained in the amplified shot of the original picture space – it is never anchored there by the 'realism' demanded of the other sound elements. Even diegetic source music within a shot sequence hardly ever remains anchored at its point of incidence but is used by the director to provide a convenient abridgement into the next scene. Music has no direct equivalent in the visual space, unlike a sound effect which is an audible record of a visual event. Music has no literal visual referent. As Jensen claims, it is indeed a foreign body.

[9] Pierre Jensen, 'Roundtable on Film Music', *Cinématographie*, no. 62

Perhaps one can say that music has realistic qualities in the way in which it provokes appropriate emotional responses in the spectator. However, this raises the notion of suitability. If music is to be deployed for its emotional effects, then presumably there is some absolute criterion that determines whether a piece is appropriate or not to the mood the director wishes to represent. This line of argument leads towards some serious difficulties, since the emotional content of music is itself a highly contentious issue.

That film music survived its earliest beginnings is due to its effectiveness as a marketing tool and the fact that film was treated as an entertainment form in a similar fashion to various kinds of earlier spectacles. Theatre owners began to realize that when a musical accompaniment was provided (as well, perhaps, as other refinements such as comfortable seating and various supporting attractions to the main film) ticket sales rose accordingly. The cinema was becoming a sensorium and, in the darkness, music (foreign body or not) proved a vital tool in the assault upon the spectator with the offer of transport from the humdrum into the fantastic.

A BRIEF PREHISTORY OF FILM AND FILM MUSIC

There were precedents for the conventions of cinema, of course, and no less for film music, although film represented something of a technological quantum jump forward. The Diorama, the Peep Show and the Magic Lantern were all visual spectacles, but were live events much closer to theatre. Often they consisted of sensationalist presentations of current affairs, or miraculous scientific marvels. Occasionally they carried the promise of faintly salacious material. In essence the Magic Lantern shows offered up easily digestible perspectives upon a world beyond the physical experience of its audience. Within the simple technologies that drove these first mass entertainments are found the raw materials that spawned cinema.

In terms of a quest, the search was for some representation of movement, a decisive step towards the representation of reality. Photography, through the work of pioneers such as Eadweard Muybridge, became a servant of science using inventions such as the Zoopraxiscope to provide new discoveries beyond the perceptual threshold of everyday life. The famous debate over the movement of a horse's legs between Leland Stanford, an American millionaire, and Muybridge was resolved by an experiment which showed that the galloping horse's legs in fact moved rather differently from the ways in which they had been represented in academic painting. In fact the famous French painter Meissonier refused to believe Muybridge's photographic series and accused him of trickery.

The French physiologist Étienne-Jules Marey's government-funded experiments refined Muybridge's work by enhancing the graphic element in order to deliver specific kinds of scientific data. This rationalist application of photography to the analysis of movement led to the development of the 'photographic gun' which used stroboscopic techniques to track movement. These photographs of progressive movement were all captured on a single photographic plate which Marey subsequently replaced with a roll of film.

In October 1888, Marey presented to the French Academy of Sciences a roll of sensitized paper which carried images recorded at a rate of twenty per second. Despite its limitations, Marey's photographic gun was seen by Thomas Edison at the Paris Exhibition in 1889.

Whilst the technological impetus that resulted in the invention of the cinema was scientific, the aesthetic style of the early 'cinema of attractions' was unsurprisingly borrowed from the front-on views of the theatre and of the Magic Lantern shows of the second half of the nineteenth century. Edison's commercial development of the electric light bulb in the late 1870s (astutely capitalizing on existing vacuum-pump technology) was deployed extensively in the larger scale Magic Lantern shows, which underwent progressive degrees of refinement with the introduction of multiple projectors which permitted some semblance of pictorial movement through the adroit use of dissolves, fades and super-imposition. Musical accompaniment was widespread, and often ingenious. Preceding even the Magic Lantern, such singular oddities as the Phantasmagoria may be found which exploited music for dramatic effects. The Phantasmagoria, a miniature theatre based on projection, used an instrument called the Glass Harmonica, invented by Benjamin Franklin to provide the accompaniment to its galleries of Gothic horror. The Glass Harmonica was keyboard-driven, and consisted of a series of glass discs, the edges of which were rubbed by damp pads to produce a sound not unlike the noise made on the rims of glasses filled with different levels of water. Very much a society spectacle of early nineteenth-century Paris, the Phantasmagoria was clearly an effective tool of illusion:

> While several ladies usually had need of smelling salts, only one found herself really ill, and experienced quite a violent nervous crisis. The fault was not due to the phantoms. The sounds of the Harmonica, too sweet and too penetrating, alone were to blame.[1]

Of all these, the Magic Lantern bears the closest resemblance to cinema, Noël Burch describing its role in the subsequent mass acceptance of cinema as 'absolutely crucial'.[2] It was after all a spectacle that was projected, which demanded an attention similar to those early films from its audiences, insisting for its effect upon a darkened auditorium. What sort of material was paraded in this primal darkness? At least in Britain, like so much of Victorian entertainment, the content masqueraded under the guise of education – improvement for the masses.

[1] E. G. Robertson, *Mémoires Récréatifs, Scientifiques et Anecdotiques d'un Physicien Aéranaute* (Paris: 1830), quoted by David Robertson in 'Music of the Shadows', *Griffithiana*, no. 38/39, October 1990

[2] Noël Burch, *Life to Those Shadows* (London: 1990), p. 85

The accompaniment to these educational programmes was primarily the spoken voice; a lecturer (usually not an expert on the show's content) would simply read, from a script, blocks of text selected for each slide. T. C. Hepworth was one of Britain's more successful lanternists, and his approach typifies the instructional tone of much of this activity:

> In composing a lecture which is illustrated by lantern pictures, care must be taken to so arrange it that the pictures come in naturally, and are not dragged in willy nilly, as if they were in stock and must be shown at any price. The views should be the best of their kind, but must be altogether subservient to the text.[3]

His son, Cecil Hepworth, a pioneer of the early British cinema, combined lantern slides with short films. From the early 1900s he describes a typical programme called *The Storm* consisting of six slides and a forty-foot film. Unfortunately his musical memories are not so detailed:

> The sequence opened with a calm and peaceful picture of sea and sky. Soft and gentle music (Schumann, I think). That changed to another seascape, though the clouds looked a little more interesting and the music quickened a bit. At each change the inevitability of the coming gale became more insistent and the music more threatening; until the storm broke with an exciting film of dashing waves bursting into the entrance of a cave, with wild music (by Jensen, I think).[4]

Interestingly, most of the early accounts of the birth of cinema go to great pains clearly to demarcate cinema from its theatrical heritage, while later accounts attempt to integrate the conventions of cinema within a general evolution of drama in all its forms. Cinema was seen in various cloaks of mysticism: 'frozen time', 'plastic shape' and its much strived-for rhythmic unity became the main topics of the first wave of film aesthetics (roughly covering those writings produced between about 1912 and 1925). One of the first to write seriously about cinema was Hugo Münsterberg, whose *The Photoplay: A Psychological Study* was published in 1916. In Münsterberg's history of the cinema, written less than twenty years after its invention, the stage play looms large as the primary aesthetic antecedent. Despite some early years which Münsterberg describes as primarily experiments with the visual field itself and with the technology, the cinema really began to take shape with the development of its narrative function, even if at first that narrative was reliant on the techniques of staged melodrama.

---

[3] T. C. Hepworth, *The Book of the Lantern* (London: 1894), p. 275

[4] Cecil M. Hepworth, *Came the Dawn, Memoirs of a Film Pioneer* (London: 1951), p. 31

RECORDED SOUND SYSTEMS IN THE SILENT ERA

Edison's invention of the phonograph in 1877 was in many senses a catalyst for the rush of technical innovation that led towards the invention of cinema. His two main inventions, the Phonograph and the Kinetophone, dominate the early sound film period. An early review in *Scientific American* confirmed the promise of the phonograph:

> Mr Thomas A. Edison recently came into this office, placed a little machine on our desk, turned a crank, and the machine inquired as to our health, asked how we liked the phonograph, informed us that it was well, and bid us a cordial goodnight. These remarks were not only perfectly audible to ourselves, but to a dozen or more persons gathered around, and they were produced by the aid of no other mechanism than the simple little contrivance.[1]

Contemporary with the earliest screenings in Europe and America was the use of recorded soundtracks. Georges Demenÿ had set the trend by the use of a Chronophotophone to accompany his photographic slide shows in the late 1880s.

Edison himself had seen cinema almost as a by-product of his experiments with sound recording technology. But the editor of *Scientific American* perhaps showed greater prescience than Edison:

> It is already possible by ingenious optical contrivance to throw stereoscopic photographs of people on screen in full view of an audience. Add the talking phonograph to counterfeit their voices, and it would be difficult to carry the illusion of real presence much further.

Despite Edison's penchant for patenting virtually everything that emerged from his notebooks, there were early and numerous imitations of the phonograph. One of the first was British and was developed by

[1] *Scientific American*, 22 December 1877

Wordsworth Donisthorpe after he read a reprint of the *Scientific American* article in the British scientific journal *Nature*. Donisthorpe's confidence was impressive:

> Ingenious as this suggested combination is, I believe I am in a position to cap it. By combining the phonograph with the kinesigraph I will undertake not only to produce a talking picture of Mr Gladstone which, with motionless lips and unchanged expression, shall positively recite his latest anti-Turkish speech in his own voice and tone. Not only this, but the life-size photograph itself shall move and gesticulate precisely as in real life. Surely this is an advance on the *Scientific American*![2]

Unfortunately Donisthorpe's system was not a resounding success. With glass plates used instead of celluloid film, the illusion of movement was impossible to maintain and the Kinesigraph took a fast track to obscurity.

By the early 1900s there was a dazzling array of recorded sound systems on the market in one form or another. In England alone, the following systems competed for what was a relatively small market: the Chrono-megaphone, the Appollogramaphone, the Filmophone, the Replicaphone, the Vivaphone and the Warwick Cinephone. All were phonograph- or recorded-disc-based systems which were synchronized to the moving image with only periodic success; amplification was also problematic. Venues were increasingly cavernous and, naturally, given the small volume of sales generated by the manufacturers the phonograph systems were expensive.

Due to the highly erratic synchronization performance of these myriad systems the nature of what was produced tended towards simple renderings of performance. Very much the 'cinema of attractions' that Tom Gunning has characterized.[3] This type of cinema is primarily exhibitionist in that it presents us with an unambiguous spectacle taken from the world outside the cinema – a magician's act, a vaudeville performance, an illustrated lecture; there is nothing in these films that attempts to construct any kind of fictional space that we as spectators are then drawn into.

In England in 1900 a short film called *Little Tich and His Big Boots* was released and screened with a recorded orchestral score on gramophone disc. In France in 1902, a number of productions were screened with a recorded dialogue track and one, in particular, *The Dress*, with sound effects as well. During the Paris Exposition, a scene with dialogue from *Cyrano de Bergerac* was shown.

[2] *Nature*, 24 January 1878

[3] Tom Gunning, 'The Cinema of Attractions', in *Early Cinema: Space, Frame, Narrative*, ed. Thomas Elsaesser (London: 1990)

Oskar Messter's Biophone system and Léon Gaumont's Chronophono-graph were two of the main competing gramophone-based sound systems in the years leading up to 1913 when Edison unveiled his Kinetophone. Messter alone was estimated to have recorded over five hundred sound films between 1903 and 1913. Many of these were arias from well-known operas or even music-hall acts sung by well-known artists and likely therefore to have been attractive 'fillers' for a distributor to put in a package of programmes for sale to exhibitors.

A typical bill is reported in a Swedish newspaper[4] of 1906 about a show in the town of Norrköping which, out of five films shown, reported that two were music-based – one on an aria, 'Schaukelwaltz', from an opera by Victor Hollaender, and the other on 'The Whistling Bowery Boy', a popular song sung by S. H. Dudley, a music-hall star.

Elsewhere in Sweden, at more or less the same time, reports abounded of new cinemas opening[5] which were equipped to play sound films based on the gramophone. There were also moves into the domestic production of sound films using gramophone synchronization from two fledgeling production companies: A. B. Svensk Kinematigraf and the Montgomery Group. Film catalogues from 1908 show that a number of Swedish-language music subjects were emerging on to the domestic market each month. Inga Berentz was a popular female singer in these films, which were often duets performed with minimal staging direct to camera. Very often, however, the artists appearing in the picture were not those who had performed on the recording. A typical case was a 1908 production by A. B. Svensk Kinematograf of Carl Barcklind's operetta *Bondvisa* in which the composer himself sang but was depicted by Max Mohlin who simply lip-synced his way through the performance.

The opening of *Kärlek*, a recorded vocal performance by Inga Berentz of a song by Björn Halldén at a Stockholm cinema in 1908, was well attended by the press. *Kärlek* was but one part of an evening's programme that included film of the Swedish army on manoeuvres and a melodrama called *The Rose and the Thorn*. Yet the reviews were enthusiastic:

> One sees Miss Berentz enter the stage, clutching the obligatory handkerchief to her fair face and . . . sing! To really sing! With the help of an incredible gramophone synchronized to the pictures and driven by compressed air. The result is an astonishing illusion where one appears to see a popular artist performing in front of one's own eyes.

4 Reported in *Från Filmljud til Lyudfilm* by Jan Olsson (Lund: 1986), p. 44

5 Ibid., p. 47

One of the main reasons for *Kärlek*'s success was that it showed the real artist in performance:

> It's the first time that we have seen a Swedish artist both sing and mime in a cinema, and it is likely that we are seeing the start of a new wave of cinema fever, which will draw the whole of Stockholm to this theatre.[6]

Undoubtedly, these forerunners of the modern music promo were relatively inexpensive ways for producers to make spectacles which would have a strong local appeal. They were simple and fast, as Charles Magnusson, a Swedish producer and engineer who worked on several early Swedish film sound systems, recalled in an interview in 1922:

> How were the singing films made, you ask? It's a simple secret. We bought the gramophone record on which the performer we wanted to film was featured and then we filmed the artist we wanted to perform the piece, getting them to dummy their way through, following the words and music of the [German] original recording. We'd then go out and find some customers willing to pay us the 1 kr per metre we'd ask as against the normal film rate of 12 to 15 øre for non-musical subjects. 1909 was the year of the singing film! They didn't stay in vogue for very long, but whilst they were in they were very popular. We recorded some twenty-five films in that summer alone![7]

Most European countries produced similar repertoires of popular music either mimed or sung by well-known performers.

In America the focus was less on operetta and more on popular musical vaudeville acts. *The Moving Picture World*[8] seems to have approved, however, and predicted in early 1909 that 'speaking films' would soon challenge the popularity of the silent films. As the vast majority of films of this period were of around ten to fifteen minutes in length, and the conventional recording cylinder or disc could hold up to only four minutes of sound material, it must be assumed that the dialogue sections were intermittent high points in an otherwise silent film. Nevertheless the popularity continued and by 1913 the Vi-T-Phone (not related to the Warner Brothers' Vitaphone system) company could announce a catalogue of over a hundred American artists in singing or talking films.

The various phonographic systems competed for dominance until 1913 when Thomas Edison himself unveiled an updated version of his

[6] *Stockholm Tidningar*, 11 November 1908; quoted ibid., p. 64

[7] Quoted in *FilmNyheter*, no. 38, 1922; quoted in Olsson, p. 81

[8] *Moving Picture World*, 16 January 1909

Kinetophone. After an initial success fuelled by impressive American demonstrations, the system proved notoriously unreliable once installed in public theatres – sound lags of ten to twelve seconds seem to have been about average. A fire at Edison's factory in West Orange effectively aborted the experiment and indeed any further attempts, for a while, to unite mechanically the phonograph with the film projector.

New developments were placed on hold during the First World War and were not revived seriously until 1923, with the introduction of the Phonofilm system which, rather than being disc-based, was sound-on-film. The inventor of the Phonofilm process, Lee deForest, was not blessed with entrepreneurial skills and his innovation was dwarfed by the far more successful ERPI system (despite being still sound-on-disc, it did at least synchronize during performance). DeForest's Phonofilm was highly innovative however:

> I have simply photographed the voice on to an ordinary film. It is on the same film
> with the picture, a narrow strip down one side, so narrow that the picture is not
> spoiled.[9]

By 1924 more than thirty theatres in the United States were wired up to take Phonofilm. A small biopic of Abraham Lincoln, *Love's Old Sweet Song*, was followed by *The Covered Wagon*, as demonstrations of Phonofilm's ability to transform the soundtrack. DeForest presented the system to William Fox of Fox Studios, who ordered that sequences from a new Fox production in 1924, *Retribution*, be reshot using the Phonofilm process. The results were not commercially released however. Curiously, deForest himself does not appear to have had much faith in the future of sound films:

> The Phonofilm will never attempt to tell the same form of story adapted for
> pantomime, nor will it draw its talent from the regular motion-picture field.[10]

Fox purchased the patents from deForest in 1925 and the following year bought patents for the USA of the German Tri-Ergon system. The merged technology became known as Movietone from 1927.

Vitaphone, a joint venture between Warner Brothers and Western Electric (two mid-sized-industry players at the time) began in 1925 to develop sound-on-disc film projects, particularly music-based projects. By all accounts the results were impressive, at least in relation to everything that had gone before. Even disregarding his obvious motivation for public

[9] *SMPE Journal*, October 1924

[10] Ibid., p. 17

relations puffery, Harry Warner was still moved:

> I had heard and seen talking pictures so much that I would not have walked across
> the street to look at one. But when I heard a twelve-piece orchestra on the screen at
> the Bell Telephone Laboratories, I could not believe my ears. I walked in back of the
> screen to see if they did not have an orchestra there synchronizing with the picture.
> They all laughed at me. The whole affair was in a 10 x 12ft room. There were a lot
> of bulbs working and things I knew nothing about, but there was not any concealed
> orchestra.[11]

The Vitaphone shorts of this period anticipate the imminent arrival of the sound era. Mainly they were recordings of then popular vaudeville acts, rather similar in many ways to the MTV-style music clip. On 6 August 1926 *Don Juan*, starring John Barrymore, was premièred with a synchronized musical score at the Warner flagship theatre in Los Angeles. This score, played by the New York Philharmonic, was on disc. To prevent the performance slipping out of synchronization, four projectors and disc players were used, each one capable of becoming the 'live' projector/sound system should synchronization fail on any one.

The end of 1926 saw Warners (then on the verge of bankruptcy) acquire a hundred per cent of the Vitaphone system. *The Jazz Singer* was selected to première the new system, even though at the time only a hundred theatres in the US were wired for it. *The Jazz Singer* premièred on 6 October 1927 to lukewarm press reviews, but the four Vitaphone segments of Al Jolson's songs proved very popular. Warner Brothers made further contracts with Jolson to produce musical shorts. The short all-talking comedy *My Wife's Gone Away*, released in December 1928, was a box-office and critical success. Similarly, *Solomon's Children*, another all-talking short, was released in January 1928. *Tenderloin*, a run-of-the-mill, but nevertheless feature-length murder mystery, was released in March 1928 and contained five segments (totalling twelve minutes) in which the actors spoke their lines. The success of *The Jazz Singer* at the box office prompted Warners to transfer entirely to the production of sound films. The long runs enjoyed by the film at key movie theatres throughout the United States were vastly profitable in relation to the earlier practice of hiring a band or orchestra for each performance.

In the few months after *The Jazz Singer*'s première, Warners added musical accompaniments to *When a Man Loves* and then dialogue to *Glorious*

---

[11] Source unknown, quoted in James L. Limbacher, *Four Aspects of the Film* (New York: 1969), p. 207

Betsy, *Midnight Taxi*, *My Man*, *State Street Sadie* and *Women They Talk About*. By the end of 1928 Warners had made five all-talking films: *The Lion and the Mouse*, *The Terror*, *The Home Towners*, *The Singing Fool* and *On Trial*.

Amongst Warners' competitors, it was the Fox corporation who showed the most enthusiasm for sound technology. Their application of Movietone was more in the field of newsreel film and their success was immediate and well planned. Their same-day coverage of Lindbergh's historic flight to Paris on 20 May 1927 presented footage of the take-off, complete with sound, to a packed Roxy Theater in New York. The Fox patent-owned sound system, Movietone, became symbolic of a brave new world of technological triumph and speed of communications. Fox revived earlier silent successes with new synchronized recorded music scores, *Seventh Heaven* and *What Price Glory* being two examples from 1927. Fox competed vigorously with Warners to produce music-based shorts, and had filmed ten by the beginning of 1928. The key to the rapid expansion into sound production by both Warners and Fox was that both were investing heavily in the expansion of their ownership of movie theatres. Each was therefore able to wire up its own theatre with its own sound system.

The larger industry monoliths followed Warners, Western Electric and Fox into the sound era, with each developing (or buying) its own patented sound delivery system for installation in its own cinema chains. RCA exhibited the Photophone system through its recently acquired chain of ex-vaudeville theatres, the Orpheum chain, during the latter half of 1927, with Paramount following a few months later.

The RCA Photophone system premièred late in 1927 with the release of *Wings* from Paramount Studios, different theatres using the sound system in differing ways. In a film about First World War flying aces, the sounds of aircraft were amplified from disc recordings. RCA, buoyed by the success of *Wings*, bought FBO, a production company, and moved into the business of making their own films during 1928 and 1929. These included *The Perfect Crime*, a part-dialogue film with synchronized music score.

Outside the United States, the coming of the sound era signalled a problem in the export of English-language products to countries where English was not the dominant language. With the intertitles of the silent era, export adaptation had simply been a matter of printing local-language title cards for insertion into the prints. However, replacing spoken dialogue or, worse still, a singing performance created problems of a new and challenging nature. Dubbing was technically complicated and expensive, and initial forays by most of the big American companies in this area had proved that dubbed films were not well received in export markets.

A relatively costly although often popular alternative was to produce local-language versions shot back-to-back on location with the original English-language version. Although these versions rarely cost more than thirty per cent of the cost of the original (since sets and technical facilities were amortized), they were still hard pressed to turn a profit in foreign markets. Exceptions there were, however. MGM's Italian version of *Min and Bill* and the French version of *Trader Horn* in 1930 were both highly successful export products.

By 1929, European alternative sound systems had sprung up, and with them monopoly positions on exhibition. Germany led the way in creating a concerted attempt to block what it saw as the excessive US presence in its domestic market. One particular manufacturer–producer, Tobis-Klangfilm, won an appeal to protect its monopoly position of sound hardware in the German movie theatres against a Warner Brothers' film, *The Singing Fool*, that was scheduled to open in Berlin in May 1929. This effectively stopped the import of American products from Warners and the other Hollywood monopolists. Germany was subjected to a boycott (which had also been deployed against France a few months earlier to scupper a particularly fierce quota system), which was overruled by the German government itself, who helped Tobis–Klangfilm to secure injunctions against Western Electric in Germany, Holland, Czechoslovakia, Hungary, Switzerland and Austria. Throughout the first half of the 1930s an uneasy alliance existed between the Hollywood monopolists and the Tobis–Klangfilm corporation in which the world was effectively divided up into territories over which these companies had control over distribution (through paying royalties for whichever sound system was being used in the film) and exhibition (through the retention of monopolistic practices in placing sound systems in theatres).

The sound era arrived not through any kind of stylistic choice on the part of film makers themselves, but through the efficient exploitation of a range of competing technologies, each designed to exclude alternatives.

NON-MUSICAL SOUNDTRACKS IN THE SILENT ERA

An alternative to a musical accompaniment – and even possibly the more successful in terms of entertainment value – was a live spoken accompaniment presented by actors or comedians. This practice spanned the entire length of the silent era but for a number of reasons (primarily expense!) did not become common practice in any one location.

In Italy the comedian Leopold Fregoli began utilizing this method from around 1898. His performances were primarily live spectacles, but he also integrated his own short film sketches into a typical performance. By positioning himself behind the screen Fregoli was able to accompany his own films with either songs or commentaries.

The most sophisticated use of live talking soundtracks was in Japan in the 1900s and 1910s. *Benshi* (speakers or orators) and more specifically *katsuben* (film explainers) were highly talented, lowly paid local wits recruited by owners of local theatres and small embryonic cinemas to provide a live commentary on films of all genres. The practice of using live performers was not confined to mainland Japan but seems also to have been used during these two decades in Korea, Taiwan and amongst the Japanese communities of Los Angeles and San Francisco.[1] However, the practice of using *katsuben* was by far the most dominant, uniquely Japanese aspect of cinema exhibition in Japan up till the 1920s. Although most *katsuben* were male, there were female *katsuben* as well – an employment register from Tokyo in 1920 lists over 750 male *katsuben* in regular employment and ninety female.

Quite why commentary should have been so much more popular in the East than in Europe can be explained partly by the earlier traditions of *etoki* (picture commentary) and the age-old tradition of *bunraku* (puppet drama) which established a precedent for commentators to accompany a

---

[1] J. L. Anderson, 'Spoken Silents in the Japanese Cinema', in *Reframing Japanese Cinema*, eds Arthur Nolletti Jr. and David Desser (Bloomington, Indiana: 1992), pp. 259–311

performance of some kind. *Etoki* was a little different in that the commentator supplied a story or commentary to the gradual unfurling of an illustrated scroll with a story literally unfolding panoramically. As in Europe and the USA, there does seem to have been a passing success with mixed performances of theatre in which interior scenes took place up on the stage as normal but where exterior scenes had been pre-shot on location and were presented to the theatre audience at the appropriate points in the drama. This practice, known in Japan as 'chained drama', seems to have proved more popular than simple films or theatre performances. Prior to the government outlawing 'chained drama' in 1917 (on the pretext that it was too great a fire threat in the small wooden neighbourhood theatres where it so often played), a survey in 1915 found that over one-third of the Japanese public's favourite film stars worked only in chained dramas.

A typical urban theatre that also showed films would house a staff of perhaps seven or eight *katsuben*, plus their apprentices. At the start of a film, perhaps a ten-minute filler on a bill of maybe twenty such films, the *katsube* would mount the stage carrying a placard announcing the title and perhaps the theme of the film, which had probably been imported from Europe or the United States. Sometimes the performer could communicate directly with the projection booth by means of a buzzer; for example, two buzzes might have meant speed up the projector and so forth. The speed of the projector seems to have been treated with more significance in Japan than in the West during this period. In his memoirs, Norimasa Kaeriyama[2] suggests that projectionists often varied the speed of projection in order to add their own dramatic emphasis to the cinematic events. The imperial family should also be projected slowly, Norimasa advises, to show proper respect. The *katsuben* who proved themselves on the local circuit often became a greater attraction than the film itself and, given their celebrity, the well-known *katsuben* were able to interpret a film in any way they chose. Bad melodrama was turned into situationist comedy by an astute commentator who literally redubbed a film live as it was being projected. Good dramas acquired a novelistic depth as characters were effectively foregrounded by an omnipotent (and definitely omnipresent) narrator who interpreted the slightest facial expression and dramatic nuance with the description appropriate to the plot. Interestingly, any form of psychological narration/interpretation does not seem to have been a part of the *katsuben*'s craft; however, without a dramatic precedent to follow (such as the narrative

[2] Ibid., p. 275

practices of *Etoki*, for example) perhaps this is not so surprising.

Katsuben seem almost, in time, to have acquired a similar kind of status to stand-up comics and sometimes toured several towns with their film programme intact. There were even charts of relative popularity published in newspapers. Famous *katsuben* artists released records of their best-known performances, and they were even heard on radio. Until the mid-1930s NHK (Japanese Broadcasting Corporation) regularly broadcast live coverage of a *katsube* at work interpreting the latest foreign film to hit town, thus affording listeners a strange kind of exposure to the first American talkies, whose English-language dialogue was still clearly audible under the *katsube*'s commentary.[3]

The *katsuben* point up the radical separation between Japan and the West in terms of narrative function. Japanese cinema evolved in a quite different way from that of the West, which, with its emphasis on dialogue and conflict, remains locked into a very Aristotelian dramatic tradition. Japanese drama is far closer to what the West thinks of as story-telling, with the narrator occupying the main speaking parts.

The *katsuben* phenomenon peaked in the mid-1920s, at which point there were some seven thousand *katsuben* working throughout the Japanese empire. The talkies came rather late to Japan (1935) and certainly in part this protected the *katsuben* from a rather speedy demise. At their height they even influenced the directors of films: Nomura Hotei, a leading director of silents, claimed that he based the pacing of his 1929 *Haha* on the spoken style of a particular *katsube* he admired. They were ubiquitous for a while in a country with a mainly poor population – cinema tickets in the 1920s cost about one-third of a daily wage and there were very few cinemas (470). Even today amongst the rich countries, Japan has far fewer cinemas per capita than its Western counterparts. By 1940, the number of *katsuben* in regular employment had shrunk to around two thousand.

In both America and Europe the use of lecturers to provide live commentaries seems also to have found some minor success. One of the more notable examples was a faked version of *The Passion Play*, supposedly filmed at Oberammergau in 1898 but in fact shot on a rooftop in New York by Richard Hollaman, who then hired a lecturer sententiously to proclaim its authenticity. In terms of spoken-word commentators leading what constitutes narrative action, it's worth mentioning James Williamson's semi-documentary *Attack on a China Mission Station* of 1899, which re-created a

---

[3] Ibid., p. 280

real incident during the Boxer rebellion, at the time a recent event. It is filmed in a garden in Hove, East Sussex, where Williamson constructs a series of scenes showing the plight of a group of missionaries, which was intended to be accompanied by a spoken commentary. The critic Morton Sopocy suggests that:

> The man who made it could still rely on the circumstance that any ambiguities in the action of his film would be cleared up for its audience in the commentary of the master of ceremonies.[4]

Certainly this kind of implicit reliance on an additional narrative element, the spoken word delivered live to each audience, is a direct hangover from the days of the Magic Lantern shows. A contemporary journal, *The Moving Picture World*, campaigned for the rehabilitation of lecturers into the new art form and demanded a voice that:

> Explains the figures and the plot and brings out by its sound and language the beauties that appear but darkly or not at all until the ear helps the eye.[5]

In Britain the reaction to this kind of narrative cinema was similarly positive. A writer in *The Times Engineering Supplement* in 1910 said:

> It is important to bear in mind that, though this form of entertainment is still in its infancy, the cinematograph is not a mere means of amusement and recreation, but that it is destined to become a most valuable vehicle of instruction and that it will furnish a powerful education medium in the hands of the teacher and the public lecturer.[6]

Despite the fact that it must have been fairly hard to recoup one's costs, by 1908 there were in America no fewer than twelve companies which toured their moving pictures with a company of actors who would speak their lines standing directly behind the screen. In Cincinnati, for example, the Colombia Theater presented a summer season of exactly this type of entertainment:

> The daring idea of having human beings imitate the various sounds which the moving pictures call for and the dialogue to portray each story has made an impression on Colombia audiences and the new name of Advanced Pictorial Vaudeville has been coined for the summer shows. The company of demonstrators

4 Morton Sopocy, 'James A. Williamson: American View', *Cinema Journal*, Fall 1978

5 *Moving Picture World*, 23 January 1909

6 Quoted in Michael Chanan, *The Dream That Kicks* (London: 1980), p. 253

behind the scenes, but close enough to make the figures appear human, are all thoroughly trained in the work and they are all thoroughly acquainted with the pictures before they are presented. This work has injected new life into the picture show. The pictorial demonstrator must be a character artist and impersonator, a versatile vocalist and able to delineate all the sounds which are supposed to emanate from the action on the sheet. Under his magic spell the picture is no longer a picture for it becomes real life.[7]

One of the most inventive pioneers of 'live' film performances was Lyman H. Howe, an American who specialized in drama films with a strong travelogue element which he toured from state to state accompanied by a team of sound effects 'technicians' who would provide additional realism. Howe was generally acknowledged to be a master of his field and reviews were usually favourable:

The Noise portion of the show – the use of stage effects to make the pictures more like real – is the best that has ever been used in Pittsburgh. Conversations of the subjects in the pictures – expressing every emotion as depicted on the faces in the pictures – whirr of machinery, rumble of railroad trains, swish of water in marine scenes, and various other things that help the onlooker to imagine that he is witnessing the real thing instead of a counterfeit presentment, were in evidence.[8]

Howe was clever enough to realize that in order to stay ahead of his rivals he had to invest in quality actors to back his touring film programmes. In 1908 he engaged Maude Anderson, a well-known stage actress:

Her appearance here with the Howe show is significant, since it shows recognition of the importance of having talented artists to carry on the dialogue and unseen acting behind the curtain. If the scene represented is in France, Miss Anderson has a sufficient smattering of the language to carry on the dialogue in that tongue, and so with other lands and their people. Her knowledge of the stage is helpful and often she makes up extemporaneous speeches to go with the pictures as they are shown on the sheet. However, most of the time these behind-the-curtain actors have daily rehearsals to become familiar with the pictures so that they can make them seem lifelike. 'I really like the work,' Miss Anderson said yesterday, 'for there is no jealousy in the company and I don't have to bother with any make up.'[9]

In 1911, Howe's company provided the soundtracks on at least two films

[7] *Cincinnati Commercial Tribune*, 10 June 1908

[8] *Pittsburgh Post*, 21 July 1908

[9] *Cleveland Plain Dealer*, 17 August 1908

for companies other than his own – *The Gray of the Dawn* by Reliance and *Fate* for Rex.

Another travelling showman, George Hale, presented his 'attractions' in a converted railway car which lucratively travelled America and parts of Europe between 1903 and 1910. His films were mainly landscapes, shot in wide angle and projected at the front of an open carriage:

> The size of the screen, the distance of the screen from the car, and the distance of the projector from the screen were intended to provide an image which covered the entire field of vision of the car's occupants and which was life size.[10]

The impression of motion was heightened by the addition of mechanical sound effects resembling the noise of the train. There are strong similarities between this phase of film exhibition and the modern era of theme-park rides such as those of special-effects supremo Douglas Trumbull, whose Trumbull Theater opened in 1993 in the $375 million Luxor Hotel in Las Vegas. Hotel guests can experience a $4 fifteen-minute ride through the past, the present and the future.

Vitagraph's 1910 version of *Uncle Tom's Cabin* utilized a full cast of actors at selected screenings who provided a continuous soundtrack of dialogue, accompanied by a live orchestra. D. W. Griffith used a similar method when touring with the monumental *The Birth of a Nation*. James L. Limbacher quotes a soundman who had participated in one of these presentations:

> I was just a high-school student at the time and I was given the privilege of helping make the sound effects . . . I was given instructions to slap two boards together when a certain red light flashed on. We could see the film through the back of the screen to be sure we got our synchronization correctly. But I was glued to that red light. When it came on, I slammed the two boards together. When I looked at the screen I discovered that I had just shot Abraham Lincoln.[11]

Such enterprises were often advertised in such techno-fetishist terms as 'Humanova', 'Dram-O-Tone' or 'Actologue'. They were expensive to mount and many exhibitors simply reduced costs by cutting back on the number of actors they engaged, to the point where some shows were driven by a single actor attempting to lip-sync for every member of the on-screen cast.

In Europe, speech was used both as commentary and, even within the silent image, as realistic action. In Germaine Dulac's *La Souriente Madame*

10 Raymond Fielding, 'Hale's Tours, Ultra Realism in the pre-1910 Motion Picture', in *The American Cinema* (Washington: 1973)

11 Quoted in James L. Limbacher, *Four Aspects of the Film* (New York: 1969)

Beudet there is a prolonged telephone conversation in which the lead actress can clearly be seen to be reciting some sort of scripted conversation. The resort to intertitles is very limited, yet the sense of the conversation, with its dramatic twists and turns, is clearly illustrated by the actress's facial expressions, and just as significantly by her obvious engagement *prima facie* in some sort of actual dialogue. In Abel Gance's *J'Accuse* a poet is seen reciting extracts from his work which are then summarized as text in intertitles.

While the Futurist art movement left precious little on film during their brief but influential flowering in Europe, they did leave some examples of recorded sound works. These are interesting in that they point up an underexplored link between what we would now term 'performance art' and the more unusual specimens found amongst 'talking soundtracks'. Filippo Marinetti, the leader of the Futurists, had his poem 'Zang Tumb Tuum' recorded in 1924 and again in 1935. This and other Futurist sound works were available as vinyl recordings as late as the 1970s.[12] Marinetti composed five pieces for radio performance in the early 1930s that apparently bear some similarity to the techniques of collage and juxtaposition to be used by Pierre Schaeffer in his work with *musique concrète* some fifteen years later.[13] Marinetti himself predicted:

> Detection, amplification and transfiguration of vibrations given out by materials. As today we listen to the song of a forest or the sea, tomorrow we will be seduced by the vibrations of a diamond or a flower.[14]

Napoléon, Abel Gance's historical epic of 1927, crystallizes many of Gance's earlier experiments with the visual representation of sound sources. When it received its première at the Paris Opéra, actors were employed to recite the principal speeches in synchrony with the projected images beside them. Live re-enactments of speech were complemented by a complete choir. Gance exercised his usual care in selecting music which he knew would take in the visual rhythms which he wished to create in the cutting room. The triptych montages which are some of the film's most memorable sequences were cut to match specific pieces of music, for example 'Auprès de ma blonde', sung by the marching soldiers returning to France.

Another sequence integrates both voice and music and at the same time

[12] *Futurism* (1978), EMI Italiana, Milan 3CO65-17982 and *Musica Futurista* (1980), Cramps Records Collona Multipla 5206308/2

[13] Kevin Concannon, 'Cut and Paste', in *Sound by Artists* (Toronto, 1990), p. 163

[14] Ibid., 164

purports to explain how the revolutionary song 'La Marseillaise' received its first public airing. At a political meeting in Paris at the height of the Revolution a song manuscript is distributed amongst the crowd which contains the text and music for 'La Marseillaise'. Two actors, one playing Danton, one playing Rouget de Lisle, teach the song to the assembled mob. The tempo of the sequence begins slowly with some initial chords from the beginning of the song and close-ups of faces in the crowd. As the song gathers force, the crowd begins to sing and the rhythm of the cuts increases exponentially, cutting back and forth from Danton in the pulpit to close-up superimpositions of successive members of the crowd. The entire sequence is structured musically and in *Auteur de Napoléon*, a documentary about the making of *Napoléon*, Gance explains that creating the central montage sequence of some fifteen seconds' duration involved the editing of ninety-four shots and took nearly two weeks!

ORIGINAL FILM SCORES OF THE CLASSICAL SILENT ERA

As films took up residence in the larger theatres of European capitals it seems clear that organized musical accompaniment was being used regularly. Many theatres employed full-time professional music directors, who may well have featured their own music as accompanying themes, abridging well-known selections. One such director was Herman Finck, a composer of light operettas. In January 1904, the British music trade paper the *Encore* carried the following report:

> The beautiful and very original music which accompanies the *Marie Antoinette* biograph series at the Palace Theatre is from the harmonious pen of Herman Finck, who is, it is whispered, writing a musical comedy.

In America Louis Levy, a musical director active during the years before the First World War, offers the following claim:

> The first real step taken towards the development of a true technique of music for the movies was started by films being given a preview to the conductor (or, as he was sometimes ingloriously known, the 'fitter') with the object of making some attempt at fitting the music to the mood of the film to be shown. Things began to happen immediately this need for such artistic synchronization became apparent.[1]

Original scores in the sense of wholly composed manuscripts were not common, however, in the silent cinema before the early 1920s. Whilst they added immeasurably to the initial prestige and impact that a new production might have in its opening run, once the film began to tour the country, the impracticalities of mounting a special orchestral presentation were not considered worthwhile by producers and exhibitors.

One of the first high-profile original film scores was Camille Saint-Saëns' 1908 score for Pathé's *L'Assassinat du Duc de Guise*, otherwise known as

---

[1] Louis Levy, *Music for the Movies* (London: 1948)

Opus 128 for strings, piano and harmonium. Much was made of the composer's involvement in the production at the time and indeed the film was largely promoted on the basis of Saint-Saëns' score. Interestingly the manuscript reveals just one formal cue, 'l'Assassinat – Presto'. It therefore remains unclear exactly how the score was to have been synchronized in performance with the picture.

The greater part of 'original' music from this period appears in the form of the countless abridgements and variations to be found within volumes of library film music. A notable example would be the large body of work written by Giuseppe Becce[2] in the Kinothek series of mood-music compilations. One might also mention Walter C. Simon, composer of several scores and numerous library pieces for the Kalem music publishing company. One of Simon's more notable efforts was an original soundtrack for a 1911 production with the improbable name of *Arrah-Na-Pough*. In this case, the published score was sold to exhibitors to help cover the costs of engaging Simon.

Even amongst the theatres that utilized the music catalogues as fully as possible, there was always a large amount of refitting to be done with the library pieces, matching them scene by scene to the upcoming attraction. Originality was therefore unavoidable, possibly to the chagrin of the publishers.

The emergence of cue sheets and tailored volumes of library music aimed at the producer and exhibitor represented an important advance in thinking about the exhibition of cinema. It also represented the advent of a new form of synergy between owners of copyright properties such as films and published music which by the 1920s had seen numerous strategies of vertical integration amongst the leading American and European producer conglomerates.[3] Producers after about 1910, obviously anxious to present their product under the best possible circumstances, began to send out to the theatres instructions for the musical accompaniment to their film reels, indicating sources to be included. This growing sophistication created a secondary industry amongst musicians and publishers, the creation of generic score-sheets which attempted to provide appropriate music for any dramatic eventuality.

One of the first to appear was published in 1909 in the *Edison Kinetogram*, a promotional publication for the Edison company. It provided musical cues for seven current Edison productions and consisted simply of a brief

[2] Becce was responsible for incidental abridgements to the 1911 bio-pic *Wagner*

[3] Paul Rotha, *The Film Till Now* (London: 1931), pp. 25–30

29

musical description for each scene. For example, the enticingly titled *Why Girls Leave Home* contained the following instructions:

At opening – popular air

Till second scene – pizzicato

Till view of orchestra seats – regular overture

Till view of stage is shown – waltz time

(Note: Knock on door till girl starts to leave home – 'Home Sweet Home')

Till audience applauds – lively music

Till Act 2 snow scene – plaintive

Till audience applauds – lively music

Till Act 3 bridge scene – pizzicato

Till gallery applauds – lively music

Till Act 4 heroine's home – plaintive music

Till hero bursts through window – lively, work to climax

Till next set, girl's return home – waltz movement.[4]

The general response to these innovations seems to have been highly positive:

Incidental music is claiming the attention of some of the picture manufacturers, notably the Edison and the Vitagraph. Some time ago the Edison Company commenced printing programmes of instrumental music suitable for Edison releases, and recently the Vitagraph Company announced that it would introduce properly arranged piano scores with each film of its manufacture. Now let some enterprising firm send along a prepared programme of sound effects to go with each subject, and another step upward will have been recorded . . . The value of proper incidental music is well illustrated at the Keith & Proctor Union Square House, where the management pays particular attention to this feature. When the Biograph film *In Old Kentucky* was exhibited at that house the applause was more frequent throughout the reel than at the other houses where the same subject was shown, and the difference is attributed to the excellent musical selections that were used . . . Bad judgement in the selection of music may ruin an exhibition as much as a good programme may help it.[5]

These developments, however, were not the same as providing a precisely timed cue sheet with a specific score already selected. That innovation belongs to Max Winkler, a one-time employee in Carl Fischer's sheet music

[4] *Edison Kinetogram*, 15 September 1909

[5] *New York Daily Mirror*, 9 October 1909

store in New York City. Through his extensive knowledge of standard orchestral repertoires Winkler realized that the intensive demand being made on sheet-music suppliers by movie-house orchestras could be increased further if the studios could be persuaded to provide each cinema with the same, highly detailed cue sheets. Winkler pitched his idea to Universal Films by supplying them with a cue sheet for an imaginary film:

Music Cue Sheet

for

The Magic Valley

Selected and Compiled by M. Winkler

Cue

1   Opening – play Minuet No. 2 in G by Beethoven for ninety seconds until title on screen 'Follow me, Dear'

2   Play – 'Dramatic Andante' by Vely for two minutes and ten seconds. Note: play soft during scene where mother enters. Play cue No. 2 until scene 'hero leaving room'

3   Play– 'Love Theme' by Lorenze for one minute and twenty seconds. Note: play soft and slow during conversations until title on screen 'There they go'

4   Play – 'Stampede' by Simon for fifty-five seconds. Note: play fast and decrease or increase speed of galloping in accordance with action on the screen[6]

Winkler's idea was deceptively simple and naturally paved the way for a number of other innovators. For a time Winkler prospered. The overall effect of the introduction of bespoke cue sheets was naturally to increase the demands for new sources of cue music generally and the music publishers were not slow to respond to this new market. In his autobiography, *A Penny from Heaven*, Winkler writes:

In desperation we turned to crime. We began to dismember the great masters. We began to murder the works of Beethoven, Mozart, Grieg, J. S. Bach, Verdi, Bizet, Tchaikovsky and Wagner – everything that wasn't protected by copyright from our pilfering.

Whole passages were lifted from concertos and symphonies, retooled with more literal clues to their sound. Beethoven's 'Sinister Misterioso', Tchaikovsky's 'Weird Moderato' – the list of sonic atrocities was endless. Winkler successfully supplied cue-sheet music to Universal, Triangle,

[6] Max Winkler 'The Origins of Film Music', *Films in Review*, December 1951

Douglas Fairbanks, William S. Hart, Fox and Vitagraph.

Joseph O'Sullivan, the musical director of the Mutual Film Company, was another innovator in the area of cue sheet materials. His process is described in an edition of *Photoplay* from 1918. O'Sullivan would record a live running commentary of a film's plot and actions into a phonograph, which he would then play back, annotating appropriate musical selections using a timer wired up to the phonograph to record the precise duration of each scene. Whilst this process must have proved extremely time-consuming one would at least be left with a very precise blueprint from which to perform a live accompaniment.[7]

Detailed cue sheets were still not a match for the inept musician, and numerous stories survive where at the end of a film anything up to fifteen numbers detailed on the cue sheet remained unplayed due to idiosyncrasies in the accompanist's sense of tempo! Similarly, the more eclectic the cue sheet suggestions, the less likely the sheet music was to be obtainable at short notice, particularly away from the big cities. In general, however, responsibility was shifting on to the producers of films to supply adequate instructions for the music accompanist when sending out their prints for exhibition.

The ultimate evolution of the cue sheet industry was the appearance from 1913 of J. S. Zamecnik's work of classified mood music, *The Sam Fox Moving Picture Music Volumes*, which attempted to provide suitable mood music for most of the common film themes. Titles such as 'Indian Attack', 'Storm Scene', 'Fairy Music' and countless others efficiently indexed the thematic preoccupation of the film industry at the time. Intended for piano rather than orchestra, Zamecnik's several volumes of greatly simplified musical themes provided even the most stunted musical imagination with food for thought. 'Indian Attack', a typical piece dating from 1914, consists of three sixteen-bar phrases in D minor with a repeat, one or all of which can be played with or without repeats depending upon the length of the scene they are intended to cover. Zamecnik's volumes of mood music for piano were subsequently imitated for the orchestra. As the movie houses increased in size and films increased in spectacle so the musical accompaniments grew larger and more sophisticated.

The influence of the cue sheets and library music upon the music played in cinemas was substantial. In addition to increasing the overall quality of repertoire across the length of a performance, it became noticeable that the

[7] *Photoplay*, March 1918

32

styles of linkage between music cue and screen action were becoming much more creative and subtle. The main difficulty with cue sheets was in adapting them for specific performances. This in itself required the expertise of a relatively skilled arranger to prevent a slavish obedience to the cue sheet's suggested timings and to smooth over transitions and create effective resolutions between sections of the cue sheet.

The simplest solution to this long-standing problem was to issue a prearranged score with the print of the film as it was distributed to exhibitors. Surprisingly, this was not a common practice. Pathé issued a piano score in 1910 for its film version of Verdi's *Il Trovatore*. Hailed as a bold innovation within the industry, the sheet music was even made available to the public, but did not appear to find many takers.

Various attempts were made to supply orchestral compilations to specific films. In 1915, Paramount began an alliance with the music publishing company G. Schirmer under the direction of George Beynon, a well-known orchestrator and arranger. Beynon's arrangements were published by Schirmer and distributed with film prints by Paramount. The venture was not a great success and by 1921 was defunct, mainly due to lack of interest by exhibitors, for many of whom the expense of engaging an orchestra was prohibitive in the first place. Subsequent attempts by other publisher-producer alliances failed similarly, at least partly because the early film distributors regarded the exercise as an unnecessary distraction from the business of making a quick profit. Regional variations in censorship also complicated matters as a film's overall running time would obviously be affected by the removal of even small scenes and therefore synchronization with the printed score would have proved difficult for even the most skilled orchestra leaders.

Although they were primarily employed as musical arrangers by the flamboyant theatre owner Samuel 'Roxy' Rothafel, two of the most adept orchestral composers on the American scene during the silent era were Erno Rapee and Hugo Reisenfield. Their original scores and arrangements played in many movie houses outside Rothafel's burgeoning empire. Rapee inserted pieces from his original composition *Diane* into the score he provided for the Fox picture *Seventh Heaven*. Much of his work, however, was more piecemeal:

> Every big feature picture is made up of themes. It is the job of the musical director to embody each theme in his score and combine them so perfectly that the melody slides gracefully from one to another. In my work I first determine the geographic and national atmosphere of the picture, and then I figure out the more important

characters. There must be a musical theme for each character, and one for the entire scenario.[8]

Rapee and Reisenfield built up a vast library of manuscript sources, which were ultimately published as *Rapee's Encyclopedia of Moods and Motives for Motion Pictures*. Despite his relatively high profile as a composer and musical director, Rapee's feeling for the function and form of film music remained generous:

> If you come out of the theatre almost unaware of the musical accompaniment to the picture you have just witnessed, the work of the musical director has been successful. Without music the present day audience would feel utterly lost. With it they should obtain an added satisfaction from the show, and still remain unconscious of the very thing which has produced that satisfaction.[9]

D. W. Griffith's 1915 *The Birth of a Nation* stands out as a paradigm of film-scoring method during the silent era. Whilst not all the music used was original by any means, the film represents a quantum leap forward in both film music design and presentation. This spectacular and controversial film, packed with visual innovation, represents one of the first deliberate attempts to create a score specifically for a single picture. It is no exaggeration to say that, in a film that is itself about the presentation of a particular ideology, the music too assumes an ideological character.

Birth represents a flowering of Griffith's earlier practices of giving music a central function in his films. His earlier films, *Home Sweet Home*, *The Avenging Conscience* and *Escape*, were all made in 1914 and appeared in exhibition with full orchestral accompaniments (usually a ten-piece orchestra). Griffith's main musical collaborator since 1909, Joseph Carl Briel, had been arranging musical accompaniments to Griffith's films on progressively more elaborate scales as the opportunities for increasingly lavish presentations grew with the industry's evolution. Briel had an unusual sympathy with the screen image, a quality unusual amongst composers during the early years of cinema, many of whom regarded the new art form as distinctly philistine.

The Birth of a Nation score can be heard as an aggregate of folk melodies, well-known classical sections (Wagner particularly being a favourite of Griffith, who had studied music at Louisville, Kentucky) and such well-known traditional pieces as 'The Star-Spangled Banner' and 'Dixie'. These

---

[8] Erno Rapee, quoted in Ben Hall's *The Best Remaining Seats* (New York: 1987), p. 176

[9] Ibid., p. 176

disparate sources were welded together into symphonic arrangements. One should bear in mind that symphonic music of any kind was virtually unheard on the West Coast in 1915 and that simply the resolution to 'go symphonic' was notable in itself.

The film itself has over 1,500 scenes, and Briel's score has 214 separate music cues. The opening of *The Birth of a Nation* in the Clunes Auditorium in Los Angeles saw the film accompanied by an orchestra of nearly a hundred musicians and twelve singers. Wagner's 'Ride of the Valkyries', used to illustrate the rampages of the Ku Klux Klan,[10] seemed particularly to catch the public's imagination. The *Chicago Examiner* reported:

> One leaves the play with the strange, weird, melodic calls of Wagner's 'Ride of the Valkyries' and 'Flying Dutchman' ringing in the ears. This is because the call sounded in reeds and trumpets in the rush of the Ku Klux Klan are modifications of these themes. This call is sounded most impressively, and more than any stage mechanism brings right to mind the rush of legions of men. It brings convincingly the idea that these men of the play had an absolute consecration to a cause that they believed to be a holy one.[11]

The moral outrage that greeted *Birth* in the more liberal quarters of America and Europe was certainly justified. The 'ideological' temperament of *Birth* renders it somewhat difficult to access for modern audiences. In terms of musical analysis of the score, however, as well as extensive extracts from contemporary critical notices one should turn to *Film Culture* magazine's special issue on the film.[12]

Birth certainly influenced the development of film orchestras in America and Europe. Their size and popularity swelled in the larger cities as the spectacle of film itself grew in ambition and scope. Griffith's approach to scoring not just *Birth* but many of his later films was decidedly modern. Griffith, together with Briel, pioneered the compilation score, perhaps not so surprising for a director so fond of leitmotif. In an interview in *Photoplay*, Louis F. Gottschalk, one of Griffith's most admired music directors, had this to say about the scoring of *Orphans of the Storm*:

> He [Griffith] labels each important character with what is known as a motif. Griffith

---

[10] Francis Ford Coppola reprised Griffith's use of Wagner in *Apocalypse Now*, lending on ironic undertone as the same piece of music blares from American helicopters strafing Vietnamese villagers all in the cause of locating the perfect surfing beach.

[11] *Chicago Examiner*, 18 July 1915

[12] *Film Culture*, no. 36, Spring–Summer 1966

has learned that his audience has a memory sense of hearing. Not only is Lillian Gish remembered for her face, not only is she the character she represents, but she is also that sweet melody which is always played during her most poignant moments on the screen, and which seems to exhale the simplicity and beauty of her unsuspecting character.[13]

The approach of Griffith to the scoring of *The Birth of a Nation* certainly influenced the composer Victor Herbert's score for the 1916 *The Fall of a Nation*, a propaganda film designed to bring America into the war against Germany. It was directed by Thomas Dixon, whose novel *The Clansman* had been the literary source for *The Birth of a Nation*. Herbert composed several pieces for symphony orchestra designed to fill key scenes in the film, only to find that the realities of the exhibition circuit quickly reduced his intended accompaniment from an orchestra to a single piano once the film left New York City on tour. Herbert became engaged for weeks after his contract had officially finished to make amendments to his score, pruning and reshaping it for different orchestral combinations.

Particularly in Europe, the impact of *The Birth of a Nation* led many leading film makers to see music now as something integrally linked to the experience of cinema. Certain films of Abel Gance reveal both in the composition of narrative and in the director's own preparatory notes a conscious attempt to find a visual equivalence to the power of music. He had, after all, referred to cinema as 'the music of light'. The clearest statement of Gance's musical intent may be found in his 1917 film *La Dixième symphonie*, a film that is itself about the composition of a symphony to be performed in a cinema, framed within a rather flimsy backstage melodrama. Gance's notebooks indicate that he intended to use recorded sound as the accompaniment for this film, yet the final score was a largely original work by Michel-Maurice Levy.

What is interesting about this film is the conscious attempt to overcome any literal diegetic coding and instead to aspire towards music as an absolute entity. Levy's score is symphonic, yet the film is a fragmented series of shots of a symphony being prepared, including moments where the only diegetic source on screen is a solitary piano. The incongruity between on-screen source and the full symphonic sweep of an orchestra that Gance evidently intended to accompany the film points towards a clear break with visual narrative. Music becomes the dominant element, whilst the picture merely illustrates. Perhaps hints is more correct. Where Levy interpolates passages

[13] *Photoplay*, date unknown, quoted by David Robinson in 'Music of the Shadows', *Griffithiana*, no. 38, October 1990

from Beethoven's Ninth Symphony into the score, the on-screen performer's own tinkering undergoes a sea change. Beethoven is clearly represented as the summit of compositional technique and we see, for the first time in the film, into the mind of the on-screen performer. His aspirations as a composer and the emotional impact of the Ninth Symphony redouble his own efforts to create the Tenth Symphony of the title. The resolution of the first shot in the film, of the screen composer's face overlaid with a death mask of Beethoven, is matched by a final shot that introduces Gance himself, as the director and ultimate assembler of this musical palimpsest, thanking the audience for their attention.

Gance's later film *La Roue*, made in 1920, was conceived as a narrative grounded in musical metaphors. Ostensibly a retelling of the myth of Sisyphus updated to the industrial age, the film juggles a patchwork of extracts from Fauré, Saint-Saëns and Massenet, with specially written pieces by Arthur Honegger, which later crystallized into the orchestral piece *Pacific 231*. Honegger's score is primarily designed to capture the dynamism of Gance's montage sequences, particularly an extended sequence of virtuoso cross-cutting illustrating a train in motion. Gance constructed his montage elements by close reference to a rough system of musical notation already worked out by Honegger. The final scoring was then based on these notations. An eyewitness at the original première, Henri Frescourt, himself a director, remembers it as a startling experience:

> Thanks to the marrying of visual and aural rhythms each coinciding with the other, you had the impression that the noise was coming at you from the image. It was not at all music that tried to imitate but a music that suggested, that imposed on the ear the same effect as the impending catastrophe imposed upon the nerves. The commotion of sound translated the turmoil, the toil of the locomotive into heart-rending notes, percussive explosions, breathless cadences. The image–sound complex created a sensation of total unity.[14]

Luis Buñuel used bricolage for his 1930 *L'Age d'or*, using extracts from works by Mozart, Wagner, Beethoven, Mendelssohn and Debussy. The chief feature of Buñuel's approach was his use of selections against the natural feel of each picture sequence. In the 1961 post-synchronization of another silent masterpiece, *Un Chien andalou*, Buñuel simply culled together fragments from two records – one a pathetic movement from Wagner's *Tristan und Isolde*, the other a popular Argentinian tango. Naturally the two sources jar

14 Paul Montel, *La Foi et les Montagnes* (Paris: 1959)

when alternated, which was presumably Buñuel's intention. This is certainly one of the more successful examples of post-synchronization.

Erik Satie's 1924 score for René Clair's short film *Entr'acte* marks a further involvement of a hitherto 'serious' composer in the bric-à-brac world of film music composition. The film itself might be described as a gentle flirtation with Dadaist techniques of juxtaposition and narrative subversion: a vaguely surreal series of events culminating in an out-of-control funeral procession racing through the streets of Paris. The score-sheet Satie wrote for the film bears a marked resemblance to a conventional cue sheet. Unfortunately only a few fragments survive. In any case, Satie seems to have relied on the orchestra conductor Roger Désormière to take care of the finer details of synchronization during the recording itself. The directions for orchestration are simple, and can be likened to the music-hall style Satie played around with elsewhere. Perhaps the only unusual feature is the inclusion of brief percussion solos as bridges with an exaggeration of those instruments' natural dynamics. Again, this points to Satie's fascination with the music-hall and the immediacy of live performance.

Even by Satie's highly mechanical standards, the score is pretty rudimentary. He merely uses eight measures as the unit that most closely matches the average length of a single shot in the film, each of which is designated a phrase which is then repeated eight times. A simple signatory transition bridges each of these units, resulting in a score that is deeply tedious when heard away from the film. However, when paired with Clair's film the music works brilliantly. The funeral procession acquires the unique velocity and rhythm of a machine gradually breaking free of its moorings. Where Clair seeks to subvert the funereal ambience by irreverent cuts to unrelated material, for example a front view from a car as it careers down a narrow mountain road or a roller-coaster ride, Satie concentrates instead upon changes of tempo and rhythm to provide a unity to the parade of juxtaposed imagery. Satie does not seek to illustrate events by mimesis with his score, but to capture the dynamism of cinematic time, with particular reference to cuts between successive shots. This results in a music that is peculiarly self-effacing and perfectly in step with Satie's wider musical philosophy.

Towards the end of his life (he died in 1925, barely a year after the collaboration with René Clair), Satie developed an increasing fascination with music as a form of atmospheric furniture not so dissimilar from the aesthetic of Muzak – *musique d'ameublement*. For Satie music was intended to be heard but not listened to, which presented problems in mounting any sort of public performance of his later 'furniture pieces', as his reputation naturally attracted an audience who listened to his music despite pleas from the composer that it should be ignored. The opportunity to collaborate with Clair on *Entr'acte* must have seemed to Satie a golden opportunity to write music which would be instantly consumed by the image it was supposed to illustrate. Music as collage. Like his earlier piece *Socrates* (a musical setting for a Socratic dialogue written in 1920), the temporal continuity which Satie's score lends to *Entr'acte* satisfies another condition of the composer's ideas about music: that it should be functional. By deliberately denuding his musical ideas, stripping them of both rhetoric and sentimentality, it is possible to see Satie's music as an idealized solution to some of the problems of film-scoring. He had grasped that rhythmic structure was the most fundamental component of film music, since it is this that plays a vital role in our perceptions of musical relationships and thus supplies continuity to the silent film.

Considerations of the sense of duration in film can be found in the various abstract films that emerged in the 1920s. Celebrating the power and spectacle of machinery in motion, these were pure renderings of mechanical movement, the cuts between shots functioning as pointers to the manipulation of cinematic time. The shorts of Hans Richter (*Vormitaggspuk*, *Filmstudie* and *Rhythmus*) appeal directly to the eye of the spectator, moving two-dimensional forms through a three-dimensional space. These remarkable films, however, were never released with any kind of recorded soundtrack, so their impact would have been determined largely by the sounds paired with them during individual screenings. It seems likely, due to the somewhat specialized audiences these films reached, that some attempts would have been made to provide an audio equivalent to the extremities in vision.

The new Soviet school of film-making, whilst not immediately exerting an influence over European and American film makers, was for many held up as a standard of absolute artistic expression. Away from the commercial pressures of the marketplace, the chief exponent of this highly codified form of politicized art was undoubtedly Eisenstein. In terms of film music, his two well-known collaborations were with two established Russian composers, Edmund Meisel and Sergei Prokofiev.

The Battleship Potemkin stands alongside Griffith's *The Birth of a Nation* as a key advance in film technique. It particularly stands out for its stunning original score by Edmund Meisel. *Potemkin* was conceived as a sound film, where music supplied more than simply an illustration of screen content. At the rare showings in the West where the original score was used, the reactions are notable:

The score is as powerful, as vital, as galvanic and electrifying as the film. It is written in the extreme modern vein, cacophonies run riot, harmonies grate, crackle, jar; there are abrupt changes and shifts in the rhythm; tremendous chords crashing down, dizzy flights of runs, snatches of half-forgotten melodies, fragments, a short interpolation of jazz on a piano and a melody in the central portion of the film – when the people of Odessa stand on the steps waving to the sailors on the cruiser *Potemkin* and others go out on fishing boats with provisions for them – that is one of the loveliest I have ever heard. It sings! It soars and endears itself to the heart. It is full of gratitude and the love of man for man. It's one of the warmest, tenderest passages that has found its way into the cinema-music repertoire.[15]

Hanns Eisler, the composer and critic, was less forthcoming about the technical merits of the score but acknowledges its power:

Meisel was only a modest composer, and his score is certainly not a masterpiece; however it was non-commercial at the time it was written, it avoided the neutralizing clichés and preserved a certain striking power, however crude. Nevertheless there is not the slightest indication that its aggressiveness impaired its effectiveness to the public; on the contrary, its effectiveness was enhanced.[16]

The score to *Potemkin*, in stark contrast to the patchwork of interpolations that characterized *The Birth of a Nation*, is a self-contained organic entity. The score, like the thematic content, presents the audience with a rupturing experience that engages the body rather than the mind. One might say that in choosing to utilize folk and popular classical sources for *Birth*, Griffith was seeking to confirm a certain idea of American history through popular music. Eisenstein, in accord with Marxist dialectics, was seeking to announce an end to history, and so to have utilized existing music would have severely compromised his rigidly applied sense of aesthetics. A new score, an original composition, was essential. Only then could music be activated not in the service of images, but as the inner voice of those silent images. Eisenstein based his theory of film music on what he termed 'vertical montage' in which music, sound effects and the visual would be conceived as a gestural composite. He was possibly the first writer and certainly the first film maker to posit an all-encompassing theory about the relationship between the film image and its soundtrack.[17]

The Battleship Potemkin and another silent classic, *October*, were post-

15 *New York Herald Tribune*, 29 April 1928

16 Hanns Eisler, *Composing for the Films* (New York: 1947)

17 S. M. Eisenstein, *The Film Sense* (New York: 1947), p. 74

synchronized many years later in the Soviet Union. Both were originally shot and projected at sixteen frames per second which was necessary to reproduce sound on film, but when post-synchronization took place, it was necessary to increase the number of frames by mechanically reprinting one out of every two frames to arrive at the conventional standard of twenty-four frames per second. As a result of this, movements took on an oddly animated appearance compounded by new scores commemorating the fiftieth anniversary celebrations of the October Revolution.

Eisenstein's theory presents music as a direct counterpoint to the image. When the film image is relatively static, then dynamic properties can flourish on the music track, and conversely when the image is dynamic then the music must remain relatively static. It does seem a little bizarre now to advance such a rigidly confining set of rules for the use of music. Certainly these 'rules' have no unique claim to being the 'truth', but were clearly stated preferences on the part of Eisenstein himself. Christian Metz[18] refers to Eisenstein's 'fanaticism of montage', and although there is some evidence that by the time he had begun work with Prokofiev on *Ivan the Terrible* Eisenstein was placing more compositional value on the individual shot, this did not surface in his theoretical writings.

The score to *Alexander Nevsky* illustrates some of the limitations of the theory of vertical montage, since some of the key central scenes were constructed in this way. Again the film is a dialectical appeal to mass mobilization, but it is also a film about the past history of Russia. Prokofiev's film work is not extensive, which has much to do with the fact that he was highly selective of the projects he chose to associate himself with. He worked on three projects with Eisenstein; one was *Fergana Canal*, which was subsequently abandoned, another was *Ivan the Terrible*, which was produced between 1942 and 1945.

In his biography of Prokofiev, Seroff quotes the composer's reflections upon cinema on a number of occasions. Prokofiev considered that the cinema was:

> A young art that offers the composer interesting possibilities. He should develop them, and not limit himself to writing music and then delivering it to a motion-picture factory, as it were, for others to do the recording.[19]

In preparing the score for *Alexander Nevsky*, Prokofiev sought to update

[18] Christian Metz, *Film Language: A Semiotics of the Cinema* (New York: 1974), p. 32
[19] Victor Seroff, *Sergei Prokofiev: A Soviet Tragedy* (New York: 1968), p. 173

twelfth- and thirteenth-century musical sources, thereby creating a twentieth-century score with the same sort of sonorities. The score subsequently became the composer's Opus 78 Cantata, and perhaps that is how it is better remembered, because although the overall experience of *Alexander Nevsky* is stirring stuff, it is not notably because of the score, at least as it appears on the film's soundtrack. Despite Eisenstein's highly vocal championing of his musical collaborator, some obviously intended resolutions and abridgements have been lost in the flourishes of that famed Eisensteinian montage. The famous 'Battle on the Ice' sequence uses musical devices that come across as clichéd derivatives from an American Western:

> Perhaps the major fault derives from inconsistent design: at one moment Eisenstein took a realistic approach; at another, a symbolic one. Sometimes the music was altered to fit the edited scenes; in other instances Eisenstein choreographed the action to fit the pre-scored music. Musical entrances and exits do not seem motivated by consistent logic, and the result is a lack of musical unity.[20]

the authenticity of silent film scores

Since the majority of silent films were shot without much of a creative consideration for the sounds or music that would eventually accompany them, it is important to make a distinction between those films that are post-synchronized versions of silent films, and those that are post-synchronized versions of sound films that were shot with the intention of being sound-synchronized during their exhibition or 'performance'.

When Charlie Chaplin decided to reissue some of his films with his own musical soundtracks during the 1970s, he unwittingly exposed a dilemma facing restorers and enthusiasts of silent-era film music. His 1923 film *A Woman of Paris* is felt by many critics to be one of the best films of the 1920s. Chaplin's brilliant grasp of editing techniques to reveal a character's innermost intentions, coupled with his decidedly unconventional heroine, make the film visually one of his most adventurous. But Chaplin's self-composed score was not of the same standard. This was revealed in the late 1970s when a new print was pairing a score Chaplin wrote in the 1940s with the film for the first time since its original release. At best it was mechanical,

[20] Douglas Gallez, 'The Prokofiev–Eisenstein Collaboration', *Cinema Journal*, no. 17 (Spring 1978)

at worst entirely superfluous. Written to be played at waltz tempo, Chaplin's score consisted of a key orchestral motif to be repeated throughout the film. At certain points the music overstresses crescendo-style what are in fact subtle dramatic situations. Chaplin's score rendered the film overly sentimental and reduced many of the scenes to pure melodrama. While reflecting Chaplin's uneven career as a film-music composer (his score to *City Lights*, for example, is much more impressive), it also illustrates the difficulty of reuniting films with scores that were composed fifty years before and have been reconstructed from a number of sources or, as in the case of *A Woman of Paris*, in placing a more recently composed score on to an important historical film. Although music was obviously an important part of a film's impact in a cinema, the film as an entity was usually conceived as a completely visual form. The music was often impossible to preserve alongside the visuals since it was unsynchronized and stored on gramophone records.

It is virtually impossible to re-create the atmosphere of a film performance in the silent era, we have simply moved on too far in our expectation and appreciation of a marriage between sound and image. With this in mind, how are we to treat the large collections of silent films that are scattered around the world? In most cases all musical directions and cue sheets have been long lost, yet a modern audience clearly deserves an opportunity to experience these films in something like their original condition. Therefore, in recent years, re-creation and historical authenticity have taken second place to the rehabilitation of silent films with new scores by high-profile modern composers such as Carl Davis. This approach obviously allows the composer a certain degree of latitude and creative integrity, since he is composing a whole piece of music to accompany a cinematic whole. Rather more difficult is a post-synchronization assignment where the composer is being asked to 'fill in the gaps' of a film that has been structurally designed for a specific kind of soundtrack (the score for which in many cases may no longer exist). Carl Davis points up the difference in approach on his collaborations with silent-film experts Kevin Brownlow and David Gill:

Our aim has never been to say to the public, 'Here is the original', our aim is something quite different. But even though the reconstruction of the original scores has never been part of the original premise, I always look at original scores and use aspects of them that I think can work. Our view is that if we find an original score that we think is first-rate, as we have with our latest project [Raymond Bernard's *The Chess Player*], we will use it. So our version of *Broken Blossoms*, while not a reconstruction, uses ninety per cent of the original. But even here my arrangers and I have reorchestrated it. I feel perfectly free to pick and choose. For instance we have the original MGM score for *The Big Parade*. What I discarded and replaced was the stuff that was written by the studio hacks who turned out mood music by the yard. But what I kept was all the documentary music – the American popular songs, war songs, bugle calls and two fabulous French chansons which are indicated in the original score. How I weave them in and out to make a kind of symphonic whole is part of what I do and what I can bring to these films.[21]

In addition to orchestral scoring, one should also mention the progressive influence that jazz was having on film music in America during the silent era. Many American critics found jazz too primitive a form of music to warrant serious critical attention in the 1920s and 1930s and it was not until the late 1930s that jazz began to be discussed seriously in American publications such as *The New Masses*. When critic Olin Downes and composer Elie Siegmeister put together their *Treasury of American Song* in 1940 they did not include any jazz songs because:

Jazz songs are short-lived because they seek only surface entertainment values and are unable to take deep root in human feeling.[22]

The support for jazz as a serious music form tended to come from European critics and composers. Yet many attempts were made during the 1920s to fuse jazz and blues with other more 'sophisticated' forms of music to win over a wider audience, but most were merely adapting some of the token surface aspects of the jazz idiom. It was really the Swing style of the early 1930s that bought jazz over to a wider audience.

Inspired from the virtuoso sources of Jelly Roll Morton, Louis Armstrong and King Oliver, jazz offered a uniquely literal form of illustrating the moving image. The nervy syncopated rhythms and dramatic slides of 1920s jazz marked a considerable departure from earlier forms of theatre music. Films such as *The Girl with a Jazz Heart* (1921), *The House That Jazz Built* (1921), *Children of Jazz* (1923), *His Jazz Bride* (1926) and *Syncopating Sue* (1926) were all variously charged with somehow capturing the essence of the 'jazz life', or at least as it was perceived to be by American movie producers. Although there are no surviving cue sheets from any of these rare films' exhibition tours, it seems highly probable that some sort of

21 Carl Davis, interviewed by Russell Merritt, *Griffithiana*, no. 40/42 (October 1991), p. 169

22 Quoted in Alan H. Levy, *Radical Aesthetics and Music Criticism in America 1930–1950* (New York: 1991), p. 47

jazz-influenced textures would have found their way into the orchestra pit.

The link between the silent and sound eras was the musical short, a form that ensured jazz reached a wider audience since it appeared on so many film programmes as a supporting feature, thus ensuring that jazz influenced more mainstream film music. New York City was the natural home of the first wave of jazz and naturally became the recording centre of America due to the availability of the best musicians, arrangers and conductors.

THE PRESENTATION OF FILM MUSIC IN THE SILENT ERA

By 1910, the number of theatres equipped with more than one projector had grown, with the result that film lengths could actually increase and take advantage of the uninterrupted action now made possible by alternating projectors. The one-minute Lumière attractions of the turn of the century were superseded by films lasting up to an hour or more by 1912 and the advent of the 'epic' format pioneered by D. W. Griffith. An initial development was to utilize music to bridge the gap in a show whilst reels were being changed. However, the real function of music as a provider of continuity was its capacity to maintain a mood throughout the entire length of a film.

> Music is not just sound; it is rhythmical and melodious movement – a meaningful continuity in time. Now this movement not only acts upon our sense organs, causing them to participate in it, but communicates itself to all our simultaneous impressions. Hence, no sooner does music intervene than we perceive structural patterns where there were none before. Confused shifts of positions reveal themselves to be comprehensible gestures; scattered visual data coalesce and follow a definite course. Music makes the silent images partake of its continuity.[1]

> Music is and always must be a vital part of film art . . . Music can make a film less intellectual and more emotional. It can influence the reaction of the audience to any given sequence . . . It can develop rhythmic suggestions from words. It can carry ideas through dissolves and fade-outs.[2]

This desirable effect depended upon some semblance of musical ability in the accompanist. In the years before celluloid carried its own soundtrack, music was primarily a live accompaniment, a patchwork of existing musical fragments welded together by the improvising skills of the pianist or orchestra assigned to each performance. The continuity that music provided was quickly exploited

[1] Siegfried Kracauer, *Theory of Film* (New York: 1965), p. 135

[2] Muir Mathieson, quoted in 'Film Music Forum 1947', British Film Institute

by producers and exhibitors to paste over a film's inherent weaknesses. However, sometimes even the sweetest music could not save a flawed picture. Kurt London[3] remarks that the early years of the American cinema were marked by poor attention to visual rhythms and cuts by directors and editors, resulting in a finished piece that was an accompanist's nightmare. Complaints of 'choppy' or 'illogical' editing were frequently voiced by film composers and musicians.

By 1910 music was the norm rather than the exception in an exhibitor's programme. The first decade of the twentieth century in America and Europe had seen a progressive refinement of accompaniments coupled with a definite upturn in their use. There was no sudden universal shift towards a heightened musical creativity in cinemas, but rather the beginnings of a slow trend which seems to have been catalysed by the advent of the multiple-reel film, particularly in the full-scale multi-reel epics of film makers such as D. W. Griffith whose overweight paeans to Great Moments from American History were conceived as integrated spectacles of image and music. Quality became the central issue.

Gregg Frelinger voiced the feelings of many composers when he wrote to the American magazine *The Moving Picture World* in February 1910:

> The articles which you have recently written are a great source of enlightenment to moving picture theatre managers. If they would insist that their pianists try and conform their music to the picture, it would soon be noticed that the patronage of the theatre would greatly increase in numbers, super-induced by the added enjoyment and pleasure derived by having the picture properly interpreted.[4]

Specialized magazines such as *The Moving Picture World* and *Moving Picture News* began to carry regular columns in which film music was discussed at length, often incorporating suggestions from composers and even readers for musical ideas suitable for adaptation into the latest films of that week or month.

mass exhibition and performance

The music-hall culture that had established itself in Britain during the second half of the nineteenth century as the most popular form of mass entertainment was mirrored in other countries. Thousands of entrepreneurial exhibitors

3 Kurt London, *Film Music* (London: 1936), p. 60

4 *The Moving Picture World*, 26 February 1910

sprang up between 1896 and 1910, of which the Nickelodeon boom in the United States was characteristic. The rise of urban theatrical venues as powerful centres of variety created a network of artists' agencies that allowed, for the first time, an 'entertainment' to be booked in advance by a theatre and for the show to be toured thereafter around the country. This cultural and economic framework undoubtedly helped to spread cinema and facilitated the contractual engagement of musicians across the country. It also serves to illustrate that the first mass audiences for cinema were predominantly the same audiences that had attended the music-halls – the working class and lower middle class – which in turn determined the content and style of those first films.

The public reaction to film was not a uniform experience in all countries. The initial dip in enthusiasm in America at the turn of the century seems to have been a direct result of the product exhibited. Cinema, with its one-minute scenes of everyday life, was exhausting its appeal. Thematic innovation was slow in coming and the integration of films with vaudeville-style variety shows from 1897 onwards (until the rise of the Nickelodeons in 1905) did much to limit the appeal of film. It became just another item on the evening's programme, competing with unionized actors and performers who jealously guarded their place in the limelight. Some early film distributors, however, worked well with vaudeville theatres:

> The Biograph Company, for example, used a complete service approach, providing theatres with projectors, films and operator, and making the movies very similar to any other act on the vaudeville circuit.[5]

With the spread of cheap exhibition equipment, film in America moved out of the theatre and into just about anywhere that would have it: penny arcades, church basements and exhibition tents. With a projection screen, a few chairs, a projector and a mechanical piano, the Nickelodeon was born.

Certainly one element that helped to fuel the Nickelodeon boom was the growing popularity of fictional narratives. This marked a departure from Eisenstein's[6] vision of a theatrical art of 'attractions' marshalled to produce 'sensual or psychological impact' in the spectator. Certainly much of early cinema would have obeyed this principle, offering something more like pictorial confrontation to the audience, rather than diegetic absorption. At any rate, by 1907 there were some three thousand Nickelodeons in America.

[5] Robert C. Allen, 'Contra the Chaser Theory', *Wide Angle*, vol. 3, no. 1, 1979

[6] S. M. Eisenstein, *Notes of a Film Director* (Moscow: 1961), p.16

Three years later the figure had increased to over ten thousand. Cinema had become a fully fledged entertainment.

Mass exhibition and a high turnover of audiences became something of a science, the perfection of an ideal environment in which musical accompaniment was at first an attraction in itself but quickly became an expected part of the evening's entertainment. Put simply, the best musicians attracted the best wages. Exhibitors began to promote the music content of their shows by illustrating the sources used by the accompanist as well as the accompanist's or conductor's pedigree (if distinguished enough) at the start of a programme. This was more than simply a service to the audience, providing a way of differentiating one's own programme from those of one's competitors'. Sometimes the lengths exhibitors went to were excessive:

> Instead of the usual pit in front of and below the stage, the orchestra occupies a place on the stage in an elaborate setting of an Italian garden . . . a floral hedge extends across the front, behind which are three electrical fountains that play continuously during the performance. The whole setting is illuminated by concealed lights, giving a striking and wonderful effect.[7]

William A. Krauth was a conductor and virtuoso violinist at a theatre in Boston who developed a particular trademark by playing a haunting violin solo during key moments in every performance. Usually his repertoire included requests from the audience, which seems to have proved a powerful draw. In order to support his demand for a wage increase, Krauth proved to the manager of the theatre (the Orpheum) that his music increased box-office takings by omitting to play his solo during one performance. The theatre was deluged with letters of complaint as a result. Clearly there was an equivalence between the musical performances and box-office gross.

A further development was the employment of stage singers who led audiences in collective sing-alongs to song sheets projected on to the screen at the start of an evening's programme. This was a short-lived practice and one that seems to have had much to do with the willingness of sheet-music publishers to go to any lengths in order to plug their new releases. The publisher paid for the hire of the singer and cut the exhibitor in on a percentage of the volumes of sheet music sold during the evening. This practice, however, seems to have been linked, at least in the minds of

[7] 'The Evolution of the Picture House', *Cadenza*, January 1915

distributors, to the very music-hall practices they were trying to distance cinema from. It was subsequently discouraged. This innovation, however, produced a small number of films that were made solely to illustrate song titles. One of the first was *Silver Threads among the Gold* in 1911, but this type of production also included D. W. Griffith's 1914 production *Home Sweet Home*.

In 1914 the Strand and Vitograph theatres opened in New York. These two theatres signalled the end of the Nickelodeon era with its ramshackle collections of old chairs and creaking piano. The new breed of movie houses were designed for comfort and deliberately situated in more prosperous parts of town in order to attract a more middle-class audience willing to pay more for a seat. The Strand boasted a thirty-piece orchestra and a pipe organ as well as a quartet of singers. The musical diet was of course the light classical fare that had formerly been sourced by the solitary accompanist. With the swollen accompaniment of a full orchestra, however, these insubstantial short pieces and abridgements acquired an epic character which served well enough to convince the new middle-class patronage that cinema was in some way operating within the wider cultural continuum they had previously accessed through the theatre and concert hall.

Contemporary magazines such as *The Moving Picture World* were instrumental in creating a forum in which film music could be discussed, debated and advanced. One means of advancement was to attempt to attract a better class of accompanist through the lure of higher wages in return for some modicum of demonstrable ability. One exhibitor, Samuel 'Roxy' Rothafel, later to become one of the most renowned movie theatre exhibitors in America, had this to say in an edition of *The Moving Picture World* in 1910:

> I agree that the cost is sometimes large and you may think too that you cannot afford it, but just give it a trial and see for yourself how much better your performance will be, how much better your average will loom up, and the very thing that you were afraid would be an extravagance will turn out to be the best investment you ever made.[8]

The conditions under which the majority of accompanists worked were hard. Shifts were lengthy, programmes incessant and the crowd often not particularly appreciative, even if the trade press was aware of the vital function of music as a presentation tool:

> Moving pictures and music are inseparable. This the public cannot deny. And yet

8 *The Moving Picture World*, 16 April 1910

how little attention and praise the musician at the piano receives. The musician or piano player in a moving picture show must be versatile. He should have accurate knowledge of the tunes of a catalogue of songs that have caught the public fancy. Coupled with this knowledge he must have the power of application. The pianist must be able to quickly change his music to put the interested spectator in the mood the picture demands. He must acquire the ability of being able to play to the correct time in which the figures in the picture dance, if there is a Terpsichorean film. This is no easy matter, as the figures sometimes change the time quite frequently in a picture. The pianist must watch close, because the effect would be rather marred if a two-step were played whilst a Colonial minuet was being executed . . . Music, whilst it may escape the attention of the spectator, has the strange and subtle influence of creating moods, and that is why it is so important in the presentation of the moving picture.[9]

The musicians who stood out were those who provided their audiences with something unique. One approach was to play for laughs. The 'film funner' sought to subvert every scene in a film whether comic or drama with his own brand of musical bricolage. No doubt tedious after two or three performances, this peculiar practice continued for most of the silent era, such performers building their own audiences who would attend shows irrespective of the main attraction simply to see what gags could be pulled by the resident 'funner'. Probably the only interesting aspect of this practice historically is that the 'funners' pioneered the use and deployment of music as imitative of actions on screen, which of course sowed the seeds for many of the basic precepts for accompanying the first popular cartoon films. With a pipe organ the possibilities for 'funning' knew no bounds, since virtually every action could find its wind-driven aural equivalent. This versatility was seized upon by aggressive marketers such as the Wurlitzer company to promote sales of their $20,000 instruments. An alternative approach was for the accompanist to tailor his repertoire to his audience. A middle-class audience in the suburbs would be treated to segues of well-known light classics, whereas a more populist audience would often demand interpolations of currently popular songs to enliven the musical mix. Slides were frequently used to provide an audience with information not only on the musical programme they would hear that evening but also on the accompanist as well.

The accompanist was more than simply a functionary of the theatre, he was a showman. Edith Lang and George West's *Musical Accompaniment of*

[9] *Moving Picture World*, 23 April 1916, quoted in *Sounds for Silents* by Charles Hoffmann (New York: 1970)

Moving Pictures, published in 1920, offered the normally dinner-jacketed accompanists advice on how to present themselves at the beginning of a programme:

> Tuck your music under your arm and walk into the orchestra pit with a firm tread and a confident heart. There is no time now for any misgivings. You have entered an electric atmosphere . . . Seat yourself leisurely and with confidence. Turn on the lights, arrange your music at a satisfactory angle, and you are ready to begin.[10]

Full orchestral accompaniments remained exceptions, however, with the vast majority of film performances between 1910 and the end of the silent era being accompanied by a solitary pianist (usually working desperately long hours!). In 1924, Erno Rapee, an arranger with some of the most successful New York film orchestras, issued *Motion Picture Moods for Pianists and Organists*. Specifically designed for the lone piano player, Rapee's catalogue of fifty-two short pieces was intended to provide at least something for every cinematic eventuality. Rapee edited and indexed selections from the works of (amongst others) Beethoven, Grieg, Tchaikovsky, Brahms and Mendelssohn. Often Rapee selected only a few measures of a specific piece and the problem of creating bridges and links between these disparate sources remained up to the ingenuity of the performing musician.

Clyde Martin, a sound effects expert at the time, explained their impact:

> Sensation is ever a desire of the American public. They delight in being surprised, startled and amused. The drummer of today who can go before an audience and perform in such a manner as to attract special attention to the features of a picture with some particular trap (i.e. a device designed to produce a sound effect) or imitation will soon prove his value.[11]

'Roxy' Rothafel did much to haul film music out of the orchestra pits and into the forefront of an exhibitors' marketing armoury. His own New York theatres included the Strand, which opened in 1914, the Rialto (1916) and the Rivoli (1917). His work culminated with the opening of the Roxy in 1927, his supreme statement as a presenter of musically driven spectacles. The Roxy boasted a 110-piece orchestra, four conductors, three organs and a chorus, as well as numerous vocal soloists. Amongst the ranks of musical directors and conductors were Hugo Reisenfield, Erno Rapee, Frederick

10 Edith Lang and George West, *Musical Accompaniment of Moving Pictures* (Boston: 1920)

11 Clyde Martin, 'Working the Sound Effects', *The Motion Picture World*, 23 September 1911

Stahlberg and Maurice Jacquet. All were respected figures with serious musical pedigrees, yet all found a home within Rothafel's sprawling organization of first-rank movie theatres. Prior to the opening of the Roxy, Rothafel had been manager of the Capitol Theater and evidence of his ability as an imaginative programmer is found in this review from the *New York Evening World*:

> Last night I went to the Capitol Theater, where one of the most elaborate of musical entertainments garnishes the feature film. It is really extraordinary the amount of pains that are taken here to put over the music. The Capitol Orchestra is admirable. It is as large as any of the regular symphonic organizations and better than many of them. But movie fans come to be shown, not merely to be told. So there are dancers to interpret the music, and good ones too.[12]

It was with the opening of the Radio City Music Hall in 1933, a part of the Rockefeller Center in New York, that Rothafel's career came skidding to an abrupt halt. Conceived as a daring piece of modernist design, the Hall consisted of a huge egg-shaped auditorium, capable of holding audiences of up to six thousand people. The theatre boasted an electric rainbow instead of a proscenium arch, which could be 'played' by a 'colour orchestrator'. The main spectacle was to be film but, as with Rothafel's other cinemas, there would be many other acts designed to buoy up the expensive ticket prices and differentiate this from any other cinema. The painter Georgia O'Keefe was hired to paint murals for the Men's Smoking Room and the Ladies' Powder Room and Stuart Davis provided a large mural in the entrance foyer. Throughout the building and design process there had been a long series of disputes and misunderstandings between the many contractors and the building's owners, and as often happens in building projects a mad rush to complete the facilities before opening night. From the start Rothafel conceived the opening night as a gala without film, concentrating instead on the various musical acts and performers he had assembled: Louis Armstrong, expressionist ballet, Rothafel's own Rockettes dancers, Martha Graham and numerous others. The film director Joseph Losey was the assistant stage manager on the opening night:

> The night before the opening, at four o'clock in the morning, we still had not had one complete rehearsal. The gala opening was attended by the Rockefellers in the royal box, and everyone else was there. At two o'clock there was nobody left but the Rockefellers! At three o'clock they had all gone home! The show went on until about

12 *New York Evening World*, 1926, exact date unknown

three thirty. It hadn't been rehearsed, it hadn't been cut, nothing. It was a disaster – absolute disaster.[13]

Rothafel was summarily fired and in less than a year the landlord of the Rockefeller Center, RKO Pictures, was bankrupt. Eventually the Rockefeller family took over control of both the site and RKO Pictures and in an interesting footnote were eventually forced to withdraw the film *Citizen Kane* from its planned première on the demand of William Randolph Hearst, the newspaper baron.

The importance placed by Rothafel on the integration of music into the cinema spectacle remained exceptional throughout the silent era but by the mid-1930s his approach was little more than a curiosity as cinemas became vertically integrated into distribution and exhibition chains controlled by the studios, which favoured a policy of high-turnover admissions and low thresholds of luxury. Rothafel's experiences show, however, that at least for a time there was an enormous appetite for cinematic experiences that bordered on multimedia spectacles. Key weapons in Rothafel's early armoury were the new cinema organs that delivered a variety of sound effects as well as musical sounds. These organs were highly popular for a few years. Probably the zenith of sophistication was reached with the arrival of the pipe organ and finally the grand Wurlitzer. For the not inconsiderable sum of $20,000 a theatre owner could acquire a machine capable of imitating many of the instruments to be found in a full orchestra. An added bonus was a dazzling array of sound effects including such wonders as a lion's roar, rainfall, thunder, winds of various types and an arsenal of gunshot noises. Roughly parallel to the rise of full orchestras in the larger urban movie houses, the organ in its various proprietary guises – Wurlitzer, Moller, Kimball, Barton or Reuter – became an attractive alternative for many theatre owners. Carl Edouarde, musical director of the Mark Strand Theater in New York, had this to say as late as 1921:

> If an exhibitor should be forced to choose between a poor orchestra and a good organist, he should consider it his duty to give the organist the preference. After all, it is quality and not quantity that really counts. Besides it has been my experience that audiences would rather hear music played extremely well than extremely loud.[14]

The inventor of what became subsequently known as the Wurlitzer was a

13 Michel Ciment, *Conversations with Joseph Losey* (London: 1985), quoted in Peter Wollen, *Raiding the Icebox* (London: 1993), p. 61

14 Ben Hall, *The Best Remaining Seats:* (New York: 1987), p. 179

rather eccentric Englishman named Robert Hope-Jones. He adapted the existing pipe organ (to be found in many churches) by, in effect, unifying the pipe system to create many more sound possibilities. The reinvented pipe organ became known as the Hope-Jones Unit Orchestra and the inventor installed a number in theatres along the east coast of America. In 1908, his initially profitable business collapsed and he was bought out by the Wurlitzer company, which promptly excluded him from any active role in further refinements of his invention. By 1914, the new theatres were taking precedence over the humble Nickelodeons (similar trends were taking place in Europe) and cinema was gearing up to reach a mass rather than largely working-class audience. Wurlitzer were doing a roaring trade and Hope-Jones was surplus to requirements. In the same year he committed suicide, again adapting a pipe system, this time, however, to gas himself. A bizarre end to a talented inventor. Hope-Jones' Unit Orchestra opened up the possibilities for smaller theatres to compete with the larger theatres so used to engaging orchestras. Ben Hall's book *The Best Remaining Seats* testifies to the innovations the pipe organ made to the role of the accompanist:

> There was virtually no mood or situation on the silent screen that a quick-thinking and agile organist couldn't heighten with some musical theme and mechanical effect from the Wurlitzer, Hope-Jones Unit Orchestra's bag of tricks . . . no longer was it enough to be able to play gems from Tchaikovsky; you had to know your Irving Berlin, and you had to know how to hit the Jazz Whistle, the Chinese Block, and the Bass Drum in proper sequence when Fatty [Arbuckle] did a pratfall up on the screen . . . you had to be an entertainer, capable of doing an act on your own.[15]

15 Ibid., p. 183

FILM MUSIC AND THE SILENT ERA: CONCLUSIONS

The gamble that Warners had taken with the Vitaphone sound system and its pay-off in the success of *The Jazz Singer* in 1927 did much to change attitudes within the industry about the future of the medium. Synchronized sound systems promised producers and distributors a far greater level of control over their product than ever before. Until the introduction of sound-sync technology, the soundtrack had always been at the mercy of the exhibitor, and in many cases little effort was put into the musical presentations of films running on circuits away from the first division of big city cinemas. This, of course, limited the mass appeal of the medium in many important territories where films were distributed and exhibited.

Producers such as Chaplin and Griffith, who did make serious efforts to improve the musical presentations of their films (by providing copious notes on musical compilation and placement), were few and far between. Sound-sync allowed producers to standardize the music tracks that went out with the film print, thus ensuring at least an improvement in quality. At the same time, the need for intertitles disappeared which, whilst being a blessing for domestic audiences, meant that each film now became a much more local product, and language for the first time became a factor in a film's international appeal. The economic consequences of this were considerable, and were only partly addressed in America by a brief attempt to mass-manufacture different versions of the same film in different languages by producing them back-to-back with the original and simply importing foreign actors.

Whilst certain theatres and musicians attempted to undermine the impact of recorded soundtracks in order to protect their own jobs – the usual argument being that the recorded soundtracks were badly amplified, which was certainly true – other musicians, Erno Rapee for one, felt that orchestras would still be needed to give some important first-run theatres a competitive edge.

Economically, however, the arguments were obvious. Charles M. Berg[1] estimates a fifteen-man orchestra at $60 per man per week as running at $46,800 annually, whereas the cost of installing a sound system in a movie house seating two and a half to three thousand people was no more than $15,000.

Without the introduction of sync-sound, could a cinema grounded upon live-music presentations have survived? The answer would appear to be that it would have, but that its success worldwide would not have been nearly as complete. One should remember that cinema in both Europe and America went through a considerable dip in popularity during the years 1906 to 1912. The subsequent recovery of cinema as a mass entertainment phenomenon seems to have been due mainly to a change in attitude amongst producers, theatre owners and distributors towards the ways in which cinema was presented to its audiences. Irving Thalberg, one of the main producers at MGM during the 1920s, argues that music in the pre-sound era played a crucial role in the development of the film industry:

> There was never a silent film. We'd finish a picture, show it in one of our projection rooms, and come out shattered. It would be awful. We'd have high hopes for the picture, work our heads off on it, and the result was always the same. Then we'd show it in a theatre, with a girl down in the pit pounding away at a piano, and there would be all the difference in the world. Without that music there wouldn't have been a film industry at all.[2]

The end of the Nickelodeon era in America and the tendency during the 1910s towards the building of larger auditoriums seating thousands resulted in a relatively developed exhibition circuit not only in America but also in many other parts of the world by the end of the silent era. Cinemas became temples of entertainment with the film as the central element in a programme that would have included live music, dancing and other spectacles. This is in stark opposition to the earliest sites of cinema where the film became relegated to a fairly lowly place on the programme in order to accommodate bizarre vaudeville performances.

When considering music's role in the success of the silent film one should also bear in mind that, particularly in the early cinema (the 'cinema of attractions'), films were primarily records of events. Whether these attractions were rehearsed performances, documentaries or reconstructions,

---

[1] Charles M. Berg, *Music and the American Silent Film* (New York: 1974), p. 275

[2] Irving Thalberg, *The Wit and the Wisdom of Hollywood*, ed. Max Wilk (New York: 1971), p. 13

they were very much the simulacra of theatrical or variety performances, filmed front on and with no attempt to create any kind of narrative. They were highly repetitive, particularly the trick films, which consisted of subjects or props miraculously appearing or disappearing before the spectator's wearied eye. The 'attractions' were a long way removed from the theatrical and music-hall conventions of melodrama, and therefore any concept of cueing music to signify escalation in dramatic content would have been inappropriate. Even a resort to the model of the Magic Lantern lecture or the slide show, the immediate precursors of cinema, would have been inappropriate since most of these films were about one minute in length. Certainly, some sort of musical accompaniment would have been used with these sorts of early film, but, as I have suggested earlier, these 'spectacle' films gained a musical soundtrack simply because they played alongside more traditional music-hall attractions. Possibly worse, in terms of de-sanctifying the new medium, was that in many cases musical accompaniment was added simply to drown out the noise of the projector. Film needed a narrative technique and found it in stage melodrama and no less in popular nineteenth-century literature such as Dickens.

With the advent of narrative as the dominant form of cinematic entertainment, the case and need for music became more vital. Stage melodrama was a relatively simplistic way of telling a story. The various dramatic twists and turns were signposted heavily, both by conspicuously hammy acting and by music:

> The use of music was neither random nor capricious, but closely related to the nature of the piece and to the effects sought. In many instances music was almost continuous, extending for entire scenes, possibly entire acts.[3]

With stage melodrama as a model, the narrative film was born. Intertitles had their limits (recognized by Carl Mayer and his *Kammerspiel* series of silent films which used no intertitles at all) and music offered a ready passport into the story. The predominant signifier of 'mood' and therefore of a large part of 'silent' film's dramatic impact was music. Music gave an approximation of interior life to a flat projected world, and rescued film from becoming an experience too bizarre for most people to sit through. It could appear to represent, if not actually embody, sadness, happiness, passion, disappointment, almost anything pertinent to drama. It could even represent distant cultures or imaginary landscapes. In the hands of a skilled musical

3 David Meyer, 'C19th Theatre Music', *Theatre Notebook*, vol. 30, no. 3, 1976

accompanist, arranger or conductor, film music became a transport of desires.

The early adoption of music ensured its subsequent commodification as publishing companies fought each other to deposit vast amounts of prearranged cue music at the doors of distributors and theatre owners. Nineteenth-century musical sources were reconfigured into fragments of their former selves to feed a burgeoning new leisure activity. Notions of musical copyright fell by the wayside as live performances at film shows therefore became mass celebrations of well-known or half-remembered repertoires. Those moments are probably the closest that cinema has ever come to being a participatory medium.

The enduring symbol of the silent era, the lone piano player seated in front of the cinema screen, was something akin to a lightning conductor. His performances were close to acts of quotation as diverse musical sources and inspirations were sandwiched together often via improvised abridgements. In live performance the status of the source works was changed for ever. An accompanist was not simply playing a piece derived from Mozart or Grieg, he was 'instancing' it, changing it, intentionally summoning up some part of those works whose emotional impact could work towards the greater impact of the image.

These nineteenth-century musical quotations then were also assertions; they were directions to an audience to feel them in the same way, a deliberate coding of isolated fragments of larger musical works. Film music during the silent era delivered to its audiences a new way of hearing music, something much closer to the spirit of instant replayability offered up by modern playback technology. Due to the speedy adoption by the majority of small cinema owners of the prepared catalogues of mood music sold by publishers such as Sam Fox, certain pieces from the nineteenth-century repertoire came to be widely known as passages tracking a particular kind of cinematic event. These musical passages therefore entered the public imagination in a way not possible prior to the wide availability of gramophones and long-playing records.

To watch a performance of a silent film with a live piano or orchestral accompaniment is to experience 'silent' cinema in its primal and complete form. Perhaps from our present-day perspective it is not so important what is played as long as the mood supplied by the pianist fits the film context. In any case the sound of a solitary piano tends to homogenize all but the most recognizable cues during a film performance. The modern spectator becomes displaced, hypnotized by the absence of synchronicity and by the kudos of the live performance and the apparent freedom of the accompanist to put whatever 'spin' they feel is appropriate on to the performance of whatever music they are using as a base. The accompanist becomes our guide, his performance an assertion, a declaration of values about the cinematic events. The music's impermanence, compared to the durability of the silent image, lends these early instances of film music an archetypal status.

PART TWO: THE SOUND ERA

THE EXPERIENCE OF FILM MUSIC

Music has been made mysterious over the past two hundred years. Philosophers, poets and critics (such as Mallarmé) thought of it as a language, but a language far removed from any references in the everyday world. Nineteenth-century philosophers such as Nietzsche and Schopenhauer believed that music opened up a realm of primordial, intuitive knowledge unattainable via other art forms, since these could only represent such feelings through material forms like writing or painting. Whilst music was often bound up in wider theories about the nature of beauty it was also included in theories of the sublime, a concomitant source of aesthetic satisfaction in much the same way as beauty. The sublime refers traditionally to that which is indisputably great, either mathematically in terms of limitless magnitude or dynamically in terms of limitless power. Music enjoys a special relationship to the experience of the 'sublime' which, in philosophical terms, has been formulated in a number of different ways. The two best known, by the British eighteenth-century philosopher Edmund Burke[1] and by the German Immanuel Kant,[2] differ considerably. Burke's notion of the sublime is sensory and describes our pleasure in experiencing sensory overload as a kind of indigestible threat or terror manifest in certain kinds of sensational stimuli. In Kant's philosophy, the sublime points towards the capacity of the mind to apprehend the limitless or the indeterminable.

As chamber music and symphonies written during the eighteenth century established instrumental music and thus displaced verbal music, so a new kind of aesthetic was needed to accommodate this kind of music. Kevin Barry, in his book *Language, Music and the Sign*, puts it like this:

[1] Edmund Burke, *A Philosophical Enquiry into the Origin of Our Ideas of the Sublime and the Beautiful*, ed. John Boulton (London: 1958)

[2] Paul Crowther, *The Kantian Sublime: From Morality to Art* (Oxford: 1989)

> At the moment when eighteenth-century epistemology noticed that the signs of music evade the categories of distinctness and clarity of ideas, it became possible (1) to locate the significance of music in its composition, in its structure or source; and (2) to locate the significance of music in its emptiness, in its absence of meaning, and therefore in the act of listening, in the energy of mind which its emptiness evokes.[3]

This 'emptiness' becomes the musical sublime, and begins the process of mystification that has continued to the present. Music continues to summon up feelings and ideas which resist concrete analysis. Film music exploits this 'objectless' stimulation, constantly testing our perceptual and imaginative resources. Edmund Burke claimed that the sublime is enhanced by darkness and obscurity, and that it is a solitary experience. At its best, film music explodes the (solitary) viewing experience into something vivid, enlarging the scope of our understanding without necessarily *representing* anything.

Whilst our world has changed immeasurably since Burke wrote his *Philosophical Enquiry*, human nature and our basic perceptual apparatus have not. In introducing an element of shock into the aesthetic agenda, Burke points towards the ungovernable regions of musical sound. Instrumental film music is the nearest that cinema comes to the sublime. The sense of hopelessness we feel at trying to describe music adequately, to pin it down, is bound up with the emotional impact it has upon us. To be presented with this chaos in an artistic form on a soundtrack results in an existential sublime very similar to that outlined by Burke some two hundred years ago.

The act of listening involves a kind of responsive 'journey' within the internal structures of a musical passage where distinctive kinds of tensions and resolutions, expectations and fulfilments meet their muscularly felt equivalents in the body. Musical expectation, like dramatic expectation, is partly learned. We seek to grasp complete forms and we learn what sorts of event constitute complete forms in particular musical and dramatic styles. Our musical expectations mirror our dramatic expectations as each confirms the other in the more formulaic genre movies.

In the early period of cinema, music became quickly rooted in a kind of mimesis. Music tended to track dominant physical action or melodramatic display of emotion. It wasn't particularly subtle. The most extreme examples of a formulaic approach to the portrayal of certain kinds of emotions were the cue music sheets sent out by distributors to cinema managers from about 1909. These contained specific suggestions for musical sources (usually light

[3] Kevin Barry, *Language, Music and the Sign* (Cambridge: 1987), p. 65

nineteenth-century material) that supposedly provided the perfect accompaniments to certain types of scenes. This highly conventionalized practice did much to cement ideas over the next two decades (up till the beginning of the sound era in 1926) of how film music should sound and more importantly how it should be used. Yet this too was the result of a set of musical intuitions that linked music irreducibly to certain emotional states.

An important aspect of musical reception is obviously the private experiences and values that we bring with us as listeners. The idea is that our own autobiographical experiences mediate powerfully in our overall aesthetic experience of any given film. Film becomes a 'mirror' (a term originated by the French psychoanalyst Jacques Lacan but appropriated for film by Christian Metz[4]) of our own accumulated experiences. This idea of aesthetic judgements being part and parcel of our own autobiographical experiences is Freudian in its appeal to preference formation as something symptomatic of an individual's formative experiences. Our musical preferences from the wider field of music are just as likely to be operational when we step inside a cinema but we do not 'choose' the film music we hear since it performs a programmed function, serving a purpose in a way that few other kinds of music do.

Since the music of cinema is so highly programmed and controlled by the film industry's production organizations, it has evolved in something of an aesthetic vacuum and it is only in the last twenty years or so that the 'canon' has opened up to admit any real kind of pluralism. Until the 1970s the vast majority of film music was symphonic, wholly tonal and derived directly or indirectly from the conventional practices that had grown up with cinema, which in turn had derived from practices common in nineteenth-century theatre. Our individual experiences and preferences as viewers are checked in favour of a collective surrender to certain conventions which have now, through the complex figurations of cinematic histories through several decades, taken on something like an archetypal status.

One should never forget how bizarre a phenomenon film music really is. When placed alongside the supposed realism of the photographed image our experience of film music is radically at odds with our experience of the world. Not that this is to claim that the cinema offers up or reflects reality in any way, merely that the film image resembles reality in a way that the soundtrack does not. Our passage through the everyday is not as a rule

4 Christian Metz, *The Imaginary Signifier* (New York: 1974), p. 42

serenaded by alien melodies as satirized in the book *A Voyage to Purilia* by Elmer Rice:

> It is difficult to convey to the terrestrial reader, to whom music is an accidental and occasional phenomenon, the effect of living and moving in a world where melody is as much a condition of life as are light and air. But let the reader try to fancy himself lapped every moment of his existence, waking or sleeping, in liquid swooning sound, forever rising and falling, falling and rising, and wrapping itself around him like a caressing garment. The effect is indescribable. It is like the semi-stupor of a habitual intoxication.[5]

That film music survived its earliest beginnings is due to its effectiveness as a marketing tool and the fact that film was simply treated as a variation of other forms of theatrical entertainment. Even in the most primitive Nickelodeons, theatre owners realized that musical accompaniment (like comfortable seating and refreshments) directly affected ticket sales. Cinema quickly became a sensorium, and in the darkness music proved a vital tool in transporting the spectator from the humdrum into the fantastic.

Much of the historical and theoretical writing about film music has assumed that its incorporation was inevitable. The French structuralist critic Noël Burch claimed in 1969 that the presence of film music during the pre-sound era helped to 'naturalize' the moving image, helping:

> . . . the global process of the naturalization of the film show, just as much as the later close-up, and ultimately synchronized speech.[6]

This is an interesting remark, and seems to assume that cinema needed in some way to imitate or conform to other, earlier popular entertainment such as melodrama or the Magic Lantern shows which used music to heighten dramatic impact. John Huntley remarks that music gave a film a certain 'reality' that helped to compensate for its lack of dialogue.[7]

Yet what could be less 'realistic' than film music? The soundtrack in a film is far more controlled than the visual field. Music, alongside the other elements on the soundtrack, is predisposed in a hierarchy predetermined by the sound editor. Each element of sound is precisely choreographed against all other elements. Sound (at times including music) exists as a counterpoint to the picture space not simply as a double to what is already seen. This is

[5] Elmer Rice, *A Voyage to Purilia* (New York: 1929)

[6] Noël Burch, *Life to These Shadows:* (London: 1990), p. 246

[7] John Huntley, *British Film Music* (London: 1947)

particularly true of sounds heard 'off screen'. One might say that sound elements are in a flux of constant competition whereas visual elements allow the viewer a certain freedom to assign priority within a shot sequence, despite the limits of the visual frame. The status of each sound element in a shot sequence coexists with, competes with and transforms other sound elements across the duration of the film.

Of course both images and soundtracks can be manipulated to deceive. We tend to believe what we see, however. Despite the obvious fact that sounds are anchored to objects, and therefore to causes, in a way that picture elements are not, the soundtrack arrives manipulated and controlled to a degree that seems to engender suspicion of what Metz terms 'aural objects'. Their ontological status is far less durable than that of the visual. 'Noises off' are referred to as 'off' simply because they are not part of the visual field. They can of course never be 'off' since they are always heard:

> The language used by technicians and studios, without realizing it, conceptualizes sound in such a way that makes sense only for the image. we are clear that we are talking about sound, but we are actually thinking of the visual image of the sound's source. This confusion is obviously reinforced by a characteristic of sound that is physical and not social: spatial anchoring of aural events is much more vague and uncertain than that of visual events. The two sensory orders don't have the same relationship to space, sound's relationship being much less precise, restrictive, even when it indicates a general direction (but it rarely indicates a really precise site, which on the contrary is the rule for the visible).[8]

Visual hierarchies are simply the spatial arrangements of elements within shot sequences. This ranges from static 'hierarchies' in which visual objects are presented sequentially in successive but separate shots to more complex tracking shots in which visual objects seem simply to drift conveniently into the compass of the shot.

Musical accompaniment plays a similar role for aural objects as camera movement plays for visual objects. Music in the tracking shot can be seen as a kind of 'continuum' reconciling or 'smoothing' the differences and sound levels of aural objects. Music envelops the visual with a sense of the sublime, the impact of which is absolutely intertwined with the way the music sounds.

How we are influenced by an individual piece of cue music is as much to do with our wider experiences as listeners. We hear far more than simply

[8] Christian Metz, *Aural Objects*, Yale French Studies, vol. 60, 1980, pp. 24–32

film music in our everyday lives and these experiences enter into each new listening experience. This is particularly true when we hear popular songs embedded in a film's soundtrack. Our common-sense notion of memory is that it is a kind of retrieval system which sorts through well-defined sedimented 'images' of the past and sets them out for present attention, but this is naïve. Memory is much more opaque than this, each act of recall being framed and contoured by the interests of the present. Our musical 'framing' process searches out some kind of meaning in the music, a kind of 'redemptive' narrative, which reconnects us with past experiences, overcoming the past's alien character. Music by itself has no content, no entailment. Its force in film is derived from its strong connotational effect; it generates chains of secondary meanings, without necessarily having any one primary meaning or denotation. A piece of music judged by an audience of spectators in a cinema to be 'sad' will be felt as sad in a hundred different ways. The denotation of music is highly ambiguous but is redoubled by the apparently endless play of connotation that marks the experience of listening to music. It is as if we forget that we've forgotten what it is that the music first made us think of.

FILM MUSIC AND NARRATIVE SENSIBILITY

Film music is designed to reinforce our emotional reactions to film scenes. We as an audience have very few interpretative choices: the film we watch arrives fully formed, fully determined. Although quite a lot of work had been done since the 1920s on literary narratives, it was not until the 1950s that a systematic study of film narrative was attempted. Particularly of interest to French *filmologues* of the 1950s, such as Gilbert Cohen-Séat and Gérard Genette, was the role of the primary narration in a film. What kind of a place was the world referred to by the story-teller from whose stand-point we view the film?

The universe that the story takes place in and the inhabitants of the story are all part of the film's diegesis. The diegesis of a film is such that we assume that characters in the story are bound by laws of space and time similar to those that govern our own lives. The film that we watch, even despite the fact that it consists of a lot of edited and spliced together scenes shot in a variety of places and times, somehow hangs together. Characters exit one scene and miraculously enter another with no more apparent trouble than we would have in our own universe. The way our basic psychological processes work allows us to impose our own sense of continuity on the diegesis of a story we are following. Three separate shots of a burning building, a child at an upstairs window and a racing fire engine inevitably lead us to assume that the child is trapped in the burning building and the firemen are going to try to save her.

Film music is one of the most powerful aids we have in entering into the diegesis of a filmed story. Claudia Gorbman[1] defines two main kinds of film music: diegetic film music, which comes from a source that we actually see on screen or understand to be part of the diegetic world, and non-diegetic film music, whose presence is not 'explained' within the film's world – violins shrieking as a woman is murdered in a shower room, for example, in

---

[1] Claudia Gorbman, *Unheard Melodies* (Bloomington, Indiana: 1987)

Alfred Hitchcock's *Psycho*.

Emphasizing the difference between the narrative of film and that of literature, the American critic Noël Burch claims that:

> After 1930, nearly all the main narrative signifiers (with the important exception of music, and the occasional off-screen commentary or title) are diegetic as well, whereas in the classical novel there is usually a great deal of extra-diegetic 'voice over' (explicit commentary from the author, psychological observations, descriptions, etc.).[2]

Whilst music aids our 'reading' of a film's narrative, the use of more and more pre-recorded music, whether classical or pop, over the last thirty years threatens to overwhelm our sense for musical context. Quentin Tarantino has claimed that certain pop songs have been used so successfully in certain movies that in a sense the movie blots out all other associations and 'owns' the song. Judging by the successful soundtrack sales to *Reservoir Dogs* and *Pulp Fiction*, he is very probably right. Fragments of these films become so well known that they are often heard and seen as 'quotations' which hive off the rest of the film.

The whole parade of Vietnam films has, one might argue, reconfigured the anti-establishment themes of numerous 1960s rock and soul songs, transmuting pure pop sound into a sociological jukebox that generates connotations undreamed of by the musicians. The use of pop music, and to a lesser degree 'classical' or concert repertoire, undermines the uniform ways in which we might be supposed to interpret music on the soundtrack.

Brain research[3] indicates that narrative interpretation in film is primarily conducted in the right-brain hemisphere. This is the site of imagery, feeling states, moods and sensations. The left side of the brain tends to be more analytical and often 'tunes out' during passive activity such as watching a film. Film music plays on our intuitions about the emotional content of music, very much a right-brain function. It can be highly directive in its emotional impact, the more so the greater our familiarity with the music on offer. Studies have shown that the degree of familiarity with a piece or type of music affects dramatically the way in which we hear music. In musically naïve listeners, the right-brain hemisphere appears to predominate at the level of melodic appreciation whereas in more musically experienced listeners brain activity seems more resident in the left hemisphere.[4] The musical

---

[2] Noël Burch, *Life to These Shadows* (London: 1990), p. 246

[3] Herbert Krugman, *Electroencephalographic Aspects of Low Involvement Implications for the McLuhan Hypothesis* (New York: 1970)

[4] Thomas Bever and Robert Chiarello, 'Cerebral Dominance in Musicians and Non-musicians', *Science*, vol. 185, 1974, pp. 537–9

intuitions of an experienced listener are able to weave back and forth through the musical surface to arrive at unnotated correspondences and diversions from earlier listening experiences. The greater emphasis being placed by directors and producers on pre-packaged soundtracks made up of 'hits' would also seem to have implications for the way in which we hear this music.

Wagner believed that the music of the future would be closely linked to some kind of dramatic narrative. Music would bring out those details of the drama that could not be spoken or shown. Wagner's ideas were taken up and developed further by a few French film makers in the early 1920s: Louis Delluc, Germaine Dulac, Abel Gance and Jean Epstein. These silent-film makers believed in the evocative and allusive qualities of music as an analogue to highly personal films, conceived as art works and not as commercial pieces of cinema.

Louis Delluc referred to film as 'that prodigious art which lives, like music, off mathematical precision and mystery'.[5] The role of the narrative in these films remains central. Epstein observed that ordinarily feeling can burst out only from a situation, a story.[6] The film makers' concept of *photogénie* (the transformed image through technical and mechanical processes, such as the close-up or editing) bears some similarity to the Wagnerian conception of the orchestra's relationship to the drama, intensifying feelings already latent in the story.

Early film makers, perhaps in an effort to boost the credibility of their new art form, claimed that film was in fact very like music. There were even a number of abstract films made in the silent period which certainly aspired to the condition if not the sound of music. Schoenberg hoped that the planned film of his opera *Die glückliche Hand* should be as sensuous and as absolute as music.[7]

Germaine Dulac was one of the first to experiment with producing photographed interpretations of pieces of music with films such as *Disque 927* (1927), *Arabesque* (1927) and *Variation* (1929). These were apparently of varying quality:

> Her attempt to apply musical time to pictorial time was a real disaster. Mind you, I'm glad she tried it, somebody had to. Her mistake was in confusing aural and visual reception and retention.[8]

[5] Louis Delluc, *Cinéma et Cie* (Paris, 1919), p. 68, quoted in David Bordwell, *The Musical Anthology*, Yale French Studies, 60,1980, p. 144

[6] Jean Epstein, 'Réalisation des Détails', *Cinéma*, no. 45, 1922, p. 12 quoted in Bordwell

[7] Standish Dyer Lowder, 'Structuralism and Movement in Experimental Film and Modern Art 1896–1925', quoted in Bordwell, p. 141

Other abstract film makers have carried on this idea, with film titles such as *Diagonal Symphony*, *Jazz Dance*, *Rhythmus 21*, *Toccata and Fugue*, *Thème et variations* and so forth, leading Frank Lloyd Wright, picking up on these films' non-representational qualities, to refer to this type of abstract cinema as 'icing for an unbaked cake'.[9] Clearly music has a certain architectonic similarity to cinema in that it too is composed of successive hierarchies of forms. Rhythmic and melodic constructions and motivations in music have their equivalence in the construction (or deconstruction) of certain aspects of film form. The question is, which aspects?

A further development of the basic Wagnerian principle was undertaken by Sergei Eisenstein in his later films and writings, particularly those after 1930. Eisenstein focused upon temporality and in particular upon the musical notion of counterpoint as the central aesthetic element in his films. Moving beyond straightforward rhythmic editing, Eisenstein sought to conjure effects not only between image and sound but also between weak accents (visual and aural) and strong ones. In this way, each architectonic element in the film acquires a structural independence. The musical idea of counterpoint allowed Eisenstein to claim that:

> The plot is no more than a device without which one isn't yet capable of telling something to the spectator.[10]

What he meant was that the cinematic form was at least as powerful a determinant of the film's impact as the narrative structure. The soundtrack, particularly the musical soundtrack, becomes a vital element in the construction of the narrative. Counterpoint applied to montage created the appearance of conflict at every level. Montage can be metric, rhythmic, tonal or overtonal. Each type of montage creates collision and conflict;[11] rhythmic montage has the effect of negating metric beats whilst 'tonal' montage creates dissonance, for example. Eisenstein characterized these relationships between image and sound as instances of 'contrapuntal conflict'.[12]

Eisenstein's conception of the absolute parity of narrative material with the structural elements can be paralleled with Schoenberg's twelve-tone compositions begun in the 1910s. Harmony and melody were suddenly less

8 Alain Resnais, interviewed in *Sight & Sound*, Summer 1969

9 John Whitney, 'Moving Pictures and Electronic Music', *Die Reihe*, no. 7, 1965, quoted in Bordwell, p. 142

10 Sergei Eisenstein, 'A Dialectical Approach to Film Form', in *Film Form*, ed. Jay Leyda (New York: 1957), p. 61

11 Bordwell, p. 148

12 Sergei Eisenstein, 'Methods of Montage', in *Film Form*, op cit., p.71, quoted in Bordwell

important than the compositional logic of the piece of music. Serial composition takes the twelve notes of the chromatic scale and arranges them in a fixed order. This ordering then forms the basis for generating harmonies and melodies and remains binding across the whole work. The series becomes a kind of hidden theme and is typically manipulated within a composition in a variety of ways – individual notes may be changed in register by one or more octaves, the series itself may be inverted or reversed or transposed by any given interval. Serialism guarantees a degree of harmonic coherence since the fundamental interval pattern remains always the same.

Serialism is perhaps best thought of not as a style or system but more as a palette of compositional 'suggestions', as Schoenberg himself said: 'One uses the series and then one composes as before.' Serial composers such as Webern used silence as an essential part of the musical palette.

Eisenstein came to see the film as analogous to a piece of music, unencumbered by text. If the narrative was able to aspire to the condition of music, then narrative action would become less of a dominating force in film creation. Visual montages were to be constantly challenged by the music and sound effects on the soundtrack.

In terms of theory, music was far ahead of cinema until at least the mid-1950s. Noël Burch calls serial musical forms the most 'open' in the history of Western composition.[13] He claimed that this openness led to new rhythmical freedoms which are ideally suited to the filmed image:

> Because of the equal presence of all the sound components of a film as they are channelled through the funnel of the loudspeaker in the theatre, an overall musical orchestration of all the distinct elements of the soundtrack seems to be imperative, in somewhat the same manner that the way in which a visual image is perceived demands that constant attention be paid to the total visual composition.[14]

Burch constructs a genealogy of different parameters that would create an open form for cinema. These he constructs in Eisenstein's terms as a series of oppositions: hard vs. soft focus, studio vs. location sound, spatial continuity vs. spatial discontinuity. The open film would seek to combine and recombine these elements in a spirit of play leading to a predetermined end. The problem is in articulating just what sort of end this might be. Burch is vague here, but clearly approves of Fritz Lang's *M* as embodying an open combination of autonomous structural elements which finally

[13] Noël Burch, 'The Structural Use of Sound', in *Theory of Film Practice* (New York: 1973), p. 99

[14] Ibid., p. 92

resolve in the climactic trial scene in which temporal and spatial continuity are preserved.

Burch's theories link 'openness' to a certain kind of 'under-determination' – a vague throwing up of signs and connotations without necessarily generating any kind of thematic message. However, Burch failed to pin his theory convincingly on any real piece of cinema. In nearly every case, what Burch claimed as opposition might just as easily have been taken as accompaniment. Since Burch wrote *Theory of Film Practice* it might be argued that there have emerged film makers capable of taking further in practice what Burch had hinted at in theory.

The Canadian film maker Atom Egoyan has persistently undermined the notion of a linear narrative and often adopts different types of open narratives. Typically these are pieces of recording technology that determine ways of seeing or interpreting: the photograph (*The Adjuster*, 1992), videotape (*Family Viewing*, 1985; *Speaking Parts*, 1987; *The Adjuster*) or a telephone answering machine (*Calendar*, 1994).

Calendar, for example, is on one level the story of a photographer and his wife who travel to Armenia to photograph twelve churches. They hire a native guide to drive them around and the photographer's wife acts as interpreter. At the end of the assignment the photographer has his twelve photographs but has lost his wife to the driver. Everything in the film's narrative is constructed around the twelve calendar months. Back in Canada, the photographer listlessly dates twelve different women from different countries, one each month, each of whom breaks off her dinner with him for no apparent reason other than to make an erotic telephone call to someone else in their own language. Periodically messages are left on the photographer's answering machine from his ex-wife whilst he listens passively adrift in a sea of videotapes of her taken during their trip. Everything about the central character screams alienation, a condition only alleviated through the lens of a video camera or still camera. Egoyan conjures with a dazzling variety of sound sources in his films and these are usually arranged in opposition to the basic narrative, which whilst not exactly linear is at least coherent. With Egoyan's films, the represented content becomes simply one parameter amongst several which seems to travel a good way towards the serialist ideal.

Egoyan is not alone amongst contemporary film makers. One might also consider recent films by Peter Greenaway (*Prospero's Books*, 1991) and Derek Jarman (*Edward II*, 1991) and Jean-Luc Godard's documentary *Histoire(s) du Cinéma* (1993).

Recent narrative theories[15] have analysed the classic Hollywood studio films of the 1940s. Caryl Flinn in *Strains of Utopia* sees in the American studio outputs of the 1930s and 1940s a tendency to treat music as nonrepresentational. Yet, she argues, in such a culturally loaded system as the American film industry, is such a musical neutrality really possible? The problem, Flinn claims, begins with our very notions of the meaning of music. We tend to ascribe to music transcendent properties based on different kinds of utopian idealism. For the aesthete, it's the form of music that gives it its utopian function; for the semiologist, music's existence as a sign system is an instance of its utopianism; for many ordinary listeners music's ability to interact with private memories, transporting us back to 'better times', is another kind of utopianism. The musical outputs of the 1940s studio are linked closely to a nineteenth-century romantic musical tradition. Flinn points out the general preference for musical magnitude and expansiveness. Heavily orchestrated scenes in films such as *King's Row* (1941), *The Sea Hawk* (1940) and *The Adventures of Robin Hood* (1940), coincidentally all scored by Erich Korngold, are musical throwbacks in every sense. The adoption of the Wagnerian leitmotif for dramatic rather than musical purposes eventually became such a commonplace that its effectiveness waned:

> Max Steiner's score for *Gone With the Wind* typifies the classical style, consisting as it does of leitmotifs for Scarlett O'Hara, Rhett Butler, and the other characters within the film. ('Tara's Theme' works in much the same way, although it identifies a place and not a character.) But the score does much more than this. In the early pre-war scenes, it establishes the grandeur of the antebellum South; later it provocatively recalls it, suggesting not only a homesickness for the period but a strength through the sense of identity the past seemed to offer. Just as the plantation home is used metonymically to convey this visually, 'Tara's Theme' appears on the soundtrack when that home appears to be most deeply threatened.[16]

Film music mediates between the different elements on the sound and image track. Although film music is a culturally diverse phenomenon it draws on our common ideas about the emotional content of music. Martin Bernheimer, the music critic for the *Los Angeles Times*, once referred to film music as 'pre-digested', a phrase that captures the accessibility and occasional banality of much film music.

[15] In particular Claudia Gorbman, Kathryn Kalinak and Caryl Flinn

[16] Caryl Flinn, *Strains of Utopia* (New Jersey: 1993)

Leonard Rosenman, one of the more experimental American composers of the 1950s, observes:

> Music for films has all the ingredients that real music has – counterpoint, orchestration, harmony, voice leading, bass line – but it doesn't have the primary ingredient that separates music from non-music. The propulsion is not by musical ideas but by literary ideas.[17]

This literary quality ultimately clashes with the orchestra's 'need' to develop tonal complexity and variation, to differentiate its elements. With composers now working in increasing isolation, the simple underscoring of action has become the standard creative approach, as Amin Bhatia observes:

> The beauty of scoring to film is that form is predefined. You know the exact length of the chase sequence, and all the twists and turns that are defined by the initial attack. Once you settle on an idea, a motif, a fragment, a sound, it's then easy and joyous to put that idea through as many permutations as the scene allows. Therein is the perspiration. The idea itself is ten per cent.[18]

Despite the predominance of underscoring, music still continues to integrate itself into the narrative in complex ways. Luchino Visconti's *Death in Venice* (1971), based upon the novel by Thomas Mann, captures at least some of the book's themes about art, aesthetics and death, by changing the central character, von Aschenbach (played in the film by Dirk Bogarde), from an author in the book to a composer in the film. Visconti claimed that he was simply following Thomas Mann's claim that he had based von Aschenbach on the composer Gustav Mahler. The film's score, predominantly Mahler's Third Symphony, functions as an ironic commentary in a number of different ways. Principally it sets the central character up as a romantic tragedian, obsessed with his own mortality in the decaying cityscape of Venice. That this figure may or may not represent Mahler, tracked by his own music, is a neat commentary on the romantic tradition. Elsewhere, music in the form of a light operetta mocks the guests at the Hôtel des Bains. The androgynous boy, Tadzio, object of von Aschenbach's repressed desire, is represented by the 'innocent' tones of *Für Elise* as he sits at a piano. We later hear the same tune in a flashback sequence as von Aschenbach recalls a childhood encounter with a prostitute. Music, through the repetition of a simple tune, allows us to compare Tadzio's apparent innocence with that felt by von Aschenbach as a young man.

[17] Leonard Rosenman, quoted in *Soundtrack: The Music of the Movies* by Mark Evans (New York 1975), p. 266

[18] Amin Bhatia, interview, February 1996

In general the more interesting interactions of music with narrative lie outside the Hollywood tradition. Film music is inevitably subject to a wider social and cultural context for its 'meaning', as Leonard Meyer notes in *Emotion and Meaning in Music*:

> Particular musical devices – melodic figures, harmonic progressions, or rhythmic relationships – become formulas which indicate a culturally codified mood or sentiment. For those who are familiar with them, such signs may be powerful factors in conditioning responses.[19]

In ancient Greek drama, music and texts were more closely linked, not least because they were usually composed by the same person. Music enveloped words in a phonic alphabet, serving the physical drama:

> Here the musical rhythm was contained within the language itself. The musical rhythmic structure was completely determined by the language. There was no room for an independent musical setting; nothing could be added or changed.[20]

The twentieth century has seen a similar kind of complementarity in the opera form of Bertolt Brecht:

> Music must not, like a narcotic intoxicating opiate, prevent the listener from thinking, but much rather, it must demand [thought]. This had been furthered by the independence which [music] had once again achieved as a result of the separation of the arts which had been welded together in the 'total artwork' [*Gesamtkunstwerk*]. The word–tone relationship was altered so that the musical tone did not duplicate the word, but rather critically interpreted it. Music should not 'serve' but 'mediate'; it should not 'intensify' or 'assert' the text but 'interpret' it, and 'take the text's message for granted'; it should not 'illustrate' but 'comment upon' the text; it should not paint the 'psychological situation' but 'present behaviour'.[21]

Music in the Brechtian theatre serves as a form of dramatic punctuation. It distances the spectator from the subjective meanings of words and correctly positions him 'objectively' as the play rolls on before him. But this does of course depend upon a fixed idea of what music actually 'means'. If music is simply a formalized series of tones which plays without any meaning then one of the central aesthetics of Brecht's theatre becomes

19 Leonard Meyer, *Emotions and Meaning in Music* (Chicago: 1957), p. 267

20 Thraysybulos Georgiades, *Music and Language* (Cambridge: 1982), p. 6

21 Kenneth Fowler, *Received Truths: Bertolt Brecht and the Problem of Gestus and Musical Meaning* (New York: 1991), p. 16

somewhat unstable. Brecht places great emphasis on the attitude of the musician towards the text that constitutes the song, as well, of course, as on the listener who 'receives' the sung text. The text, taken together with the music (gestus), is a rhetorical device which represents political ideas or, perhaps better put, political emotions within a social context.

Film music does not have simply to follow or imitate visual movements. Nor does it have to be unobtrusive. In Hanns Eisler's view music can be equally important an element as the image itself, structurally equivalent but not reliant on its own internal limitations (such as the need to resolve a melodic pattern) for its impact. The need to complete a broad musical pattern is one of the most limiting aspects of music and the one that most threatens its functionality. Eisler is particularly critical of the leitmotif which he believes needs a large-scale musical work to be able to work properly. He therefore recommends a movement away from melody towards shorter, more flexible musical phrasing:

> Since the motion picture is not a [unified] work of art, and since music neither can nor should be part of such an organic unity, the attempt to impose a stylistic ideal on cinema music is absurd . . . What is needed is musical planning, the free and conscious utilization of all musical resources on the basis of accurate insight into the dramatic function of music, which is different in each concrete case.[22]

Bernard Herrmann's preference for writing music that relied on small cellular musical units demonstrates the wisdom of Eisler's claim. In the broader sense, Eisler and other experimenters (certainly not confined to film-music composers) were calling for artworks to be considered as open works, subject to a wide variety of interpretations, much as Burch had called for in his critical writing. Music needed to be as flexible as possible, never extending its effect into the film for purely musical reasons, but solely for structural purposes.

One of the most personal and at the same time most 'open' of film makers, Federico Fellini, was constantly experimenting with the processes of reception and evaluation that his films went through. Despite his well-known dislike and distrust of music in general, Fellini forged a long-term partnership with one of Europe's most adroit composers and arrangers of music designed to interplay with the image, Nino Rota. In Fellini's *La Dolce Vita* (1959) Rota's omnipresent score might just as well be the background music of the people in the story, Rome soundtracked by contemporary

---

[22] Hanns Eisler, *Composing for the Films* (New York: 1947), p. 80

Italian pop music as Marcello Mastroianni turns the radio dial. It's a kind of musical 'mirroring'. Rota's score was clearly inspired by what he heard on the radio, yet he also allows the radio to displace his non-diegetic score in places, making the soundtrack of this world more apparently real. In Fellini's later *Toby Dammit* (1967), music is used in a similar way to unify the experiments Fellini was making in exposing the apparatus of the film studio as just another part of the narrative. This Brechtian strategy – the alienation effect – is far harder to make a success of in film than it is in the theatre. Fellini exposes the medium in which he works by showing its behind-the-scenes workings, and even extends this to the editing process itself, where sounds and images are constantly juxtaposed to create a confusing but nevertheless realistic exposition of the film-making process. This odd harmony is the totality of the film, which Fellini goes on to explore further in his later films. In *Toby Dammit* music synthesizes the confusion of represented reality by unifying and setting a tempo to the film. The most striking example of this in *Toby Dammit* is a sequence set in a television studio, where Ray Charles is heard on a record player singing 'Ruby'. As the song begins, a wide-angle shot shows the emptiness of the studio. The camera focuses on Terence Stamp's character as a girl slowly approaches him, Fellini occasionally cutting back to the wider studio shot. The song accompanies an apparently insignificant event whose mood it entirely controls. Fellini uses the song in its entirety, thus stretching out the scene far longer than it might otherwise be until we realize we are experiencing the scene through the consciousness of Stamp's character, an alcoholic for whom the external world is becoming a more and more difficult space in which to survive. Fellini's use of music dominates the diegetic existence of Stamp, who becomes a robot unable to respond to the approaches of the girl, who appears to be acting out the lyrics of 'Ruby', a caricature of the seductress in the song.

RESISTANCE TO SOUND

Throughout the late 1920s and early 1930s the pioneers of the sound film strove for naturalism or else at the other end of the scale an almost abstract use of sound as a montage element. Naturalism was in many ways a direct by-product of the sound-recording equipment at their disposal. Chasm-like sound fields were an automatic result of not having directional microphones; therefore scenes involving numbers of actors or a variety of sound sources tended to reproduce the cacophonies of everyday life with some accuracy. Differentiating sound elements with anything more than rudimentary contrasts was much more difficult. Stories abound of the difficulties and limitations attached to the recording of even comparably straightforward dialogue scenes. Much of the problem stems from the fact that microphones were not yet capable of directional pick-up, therefore every sound on the studio floor became a potential bit player in the scene under construction. Coupled with this, film cameras were noisy, gargantuan monsters that needed to be housed in sound-proofed kiosks rather similar to sentry boxes which removed any possibility of camera movement beyond the most elementary tilts and pans.[1]

The composer Max Steiner[2] recounts an incident in 1930 in which it took two days correctly to rig the studio floor for a double bass player to avoid sound overlaps and distortions, at an extra cost of $75,000 as the entire cast and crew had to be kept on the floor in order to test playback. Without the luxury of re-recording, a director could not of course make changes to the soundtrack in post-production. The resulting picture tended to reduce action to a rather stage-like accumulation of dialogues.

[1] 'Compared to its silent counterpart, the talking cinema was considered an "inflexible institution", above all because certain latitudes in spatial and temporal construction available to late silent narratives were not permitted in the early sound film', from Nancy Wood, 'Text and Spectator in the Period of the Transition to Sound', Ph.D. thesis, University of Kent, 1983

[2] Max Steiner, *Music Comes of Age* (New York: 1935)

David Barrist, writing in 1927 for the Philadelphia trade paper *The Exhibitor*, was unequivocal:

> The complete flop of the Vocafilm in New York, the rapid downslide that Vitaphone is taking and the utter lack of interest in Movietone and the other 'talkies' simply prove what shrewd observers have long contended – that the talking movie is merely a novelty to be used sparingly and that any attempt to offer it as regular fare is doomed to failure. It is absurd to talk of supplanting in public favour the magnificent orchestras and really fine organs in the average first-class theatre with the cold, rasping Noisytone inventions.[3]

In addition to resistance from exhibitors and film makers, the dawning of the sound era also brought a number of critical objections, the response of distinguished British documentary maker Paul Rotha being typical:

> The addition of sound and dialogue to the visual image on the screen will tend to emphasize its isolated significance . . . as the sound and dialogue take longer to apprehend than the visual image. Dialogue, by its very realism, represents real time and not the filmic time of the visual image. Dialogue imposes such restrictions on the director that all forms of cutting and cross cutting become impossible.[4]

Rotha believed that sound or, more accurately, the dialogue film should be restricted to the social documentary and newsreel, since neither of these forms made any claim towards dramatic content. He is at the same time, however, quick to defend the use of music and natural sound sources since he believed that music and sound effects were an essential element of film montage, the key aesthetic in cinematic art:

> In the same way as an effect is built out of the pieces of film by the act of montage, so will little portions of sound be built up into new and strange noises. The process of short-cutting in visual images will be paralleled in the mixing of sounds. Even as visual images mix and dissolve one into another so will sound images mix and dissolve, according to the nature of the scene and as indicated by the scenario montage . . . Contrast of sound will be used in the form of the relationship of sound volumes. It will not be possible, except in rare cases, to cut direct from one sound to another as with the visual image, unless there is a background of music to soften the contrast.[5]

3 Quoted in *Harrison's Reports*, 9:1, 24 September 1927
4 Paul Rotha, *The Film Till Now* (London: 1931), p. 307
5 Ibid., p. 310

Rotha's pessimism about the future and usefulness of the dialogue film is taken up by another contemporary theorist, Rudolf Arnheim, in his comprehensive commentary on film aesthetics, *Film as Art*:

> It is obvious that speech cannot be attached to the immobile image (painting, photography); but it is equally ill-suited for the silent film, whose means of expression resemble those of painting. It was precisely the absence of speech that made the silent film develop a style of its own, capable of condensing the dramatic situation.[6]

Arnheim separates the function of music from film and situates it squarely as an aspect of stagecraft, the musical expression of man in action. In opera music and dialogue can be integrated because the dialogue exists as a secondary element to the music. In film, dialogue hampers physical action:

> The average talking film today endeavours to combine visually poor scenes full of dialogue with the completely different style of rich, silent action.[7]

At the root of the early criticisms of the emerging sound technology is a fallacious approach to the aesthetics of cinema which rests unduly upon the historical circumstances of the birth of film. Rather than valuing image and sound equally, the image, largely it seems because it occurred first, is venerated to a level where it becomes seen as virtually an orthodoxy. The fact that the silent image remained silent for the first twenty-five years of the history of cinema because of a technological lack is circumvented.

Arnheim's critical strategy is more subtle than to fall headlong into a historical fallacy. He simply claims that it is within the given nature of film that it is primarily a visual medium. This basic ontological claim is not opened up by him to further analysis. His perspective on the essential predominant nature of the film image has proved enduring. As late as the early 1970s, supposedly serious writers on film were still offering up remarks like:

> The essence of the cinema is basically visual, and every sonic intervention ought to limit itself to a justified and necessary act of expressive integration.[8]

Cinema is a composite art form and therefore some sort of alchemical quest for its pure essence is likely to be fruitless. Arnheim's analysis of the sound cinema as being in some way a 'contradiction of principle' is based on

[6] Rudolf Arnheim, *Film as Art* (London: 1958), p. 186

[7] Ibid., p. 188

[8] Gianfranco Bettetini, *The Language and Technique of the Film* (The Hague: 1973)

his views that artistic media should not be combined in the first place. That cinema, even denuded of sound, was already a composite art form seemed to escape his attention.

Other critics were more optimistic, however. Alexander Bakshy of *The Nation*:

> When the talking picture mechanism is made perfect the really important development . . . will definitely direct the talking picture away from the stage and toward a new, authentic motion picture drama. This evolution is inevitable. It is dictated by the inner logic of the medium.[9]

Rouben Mamoulian's 1929 *Applause* has undergone something of a revaluation in recent years. An example of a popular 1930s genre, the backstage musical, *Applause* is notable for the way in which it deploys sound to render movement and setting more plastic, more palpable. With a plot that is at best conventional, *Applause* derives its story from the atmospheres backstage in a burlesque house. Sound is used to marshal concepts of visual space in a way that no other film had done before. Much of this effect is articulated through Mamoulian's precisely choreographed camera movements, but there is more than that:

> For a certain scene, I insisted on using two separate channels for recording two sounds – one, soft whispering; the other, loud singing – which later would be mixed, so that the audience could hear both simultaneously. It seems funny today that this was a revolutionary breakthrough.[10]

In a way, Mamoulian anticipated Bela Belazs' much later comments on the subjectivity of optical space:

> A completely soundless space . . . never appears quite concrete, and quite real to our perception; we feel it to be weightless and insubstantial, for what we merely see is only a vision. We accept seen space as real only when it contains sounds as well, for these give it a dimension of depth.[11]

City Streets of 1931 explores sound as an impressionistic element. Flashback sequences feature overlays of sound treated as a montage element. In one sequence, Sylvia Sydney is in jail and we hear an audio flashback of an earlier conversation she had with her lover:

[9] *The Nation*, 20 February 1929

[10] Rouben Mamoulian, *Hollywood Voices* (New York: 1967), p. 64

[11] Bela Belazs *Theory of Film* (New York: 1970), p. 206

> I conceived the idea of running an audible soundtrack over a silent close-up of Sylvia Sydney which would express her thoughts and memories. No one thought audiences would be able to accept this kind of audible inner monologue and reminiscence combined with a silent face. The audiences understood and accepted it quite easily.[12]

In *Dr Jekyll and Mr Hyde*, made the following year, the astoundingly effective transformation from benign doctor to the bestial Mr Hyde is mirrored on the soundtrack by the sounds of a human heartbeat speeded up and mixed with the decaying vibrations from a struck bell producing a highly effective correlate to the images of supernatural mutation. More than any of his contemporaries, with the possible exception of René Clair, Mamoulian's sound-space becomes a narrative element in itself. It is constantly cluttered, revealing depth and a lifelike quality of imminent chaos. In some senses Mamoulian uses the soundtrack pointillistically. In the way a painting can be built up as a series of coloured dots to be decoded by the spectator, so it is with his soundtracks. Their effectiveness works largely on a subconscious level. In interviews he displayed an uncanny ease regarding the possibilities of sound recording:

> I was convinced that sound on the screen should not be constantly shackled by naturalism. The magic of sound recording enabled one to achieve effects that would be impossible and unnatural on the stage or in real life, yet meaningful and eloquent on the screen.[13]

In *Love Me Tonight* (1932) Mamoulian tried his hand at the full-blown musical. He had, before his immersion in cinema, been a highly successful director of opera and theatre and was therefore already familiar with notions of musically enhanced performance. This film shows the extensive influence of René Clair in its light, witty juxtapositions using music as a counterpoint, but in certain montage sequences Mamoulian appears to overtake his inspiration. A magnificent opening montage sequence shows us a city awakening in the early light of a new day. The montage bears a strong conceptual resemblance to the most famous scene in Mamoulian's earlier Broadway smash-hit *Porgy*.

Another of the high points of the early sound musical was the 1929 *Broadway Melody*, with an original score by Arthur Freed and Nacio Herb Brown, as well as a number of hit songs ('You Were Meant for Me', 'The Wedding of the Painted Doll'). Like *Applause* it is a backstage musical that

---

12 Rouben Mamoulian, *Hollywood Voices* (New York: 1967), p. 65

13 Andrew Sarris, *Interviews with Film Directors* (New York: 1967), p. 346

explores the trials and tribulations of a cast of hoofers as they struggle to put on a show. Interestingly there are a number of moments within this film where one begins to see clear signs of stylistic departure between the soundtrack and the picture; for example, one scene shows a girl in close-up whilst on the soundtrack one hears the car that has just delivered her driving off. Space and time begin to move towards one another just as soundtrack and picture begin to depart.

playback and the early sound musical

Given sound's obvious concomitant – music – the ambition of many of the prominent film studios was to produce musicals or at least films with music in them. This was in many ways the easiest form of project to handle, given the recording technology available. Certainly it was easier to synchronize musical performance to musical playback than it was to record and synchronize speech. The early revues were a mix of musical numbers with some token dramatic sketches thrown in. Amongst the plethora of early film musicals, *The Vagabond Lover*, *Rio Rita* and *The Street Singer* were typical. Certainly they were expensive to produce and their impact dwindled in the marketplace after just a couple of short years. Those that have survived and remain reasonably well known were the brighter exceptions in an otherwise fairly murky catalogue.

The playback system quite literally separated the soundtrack from the image.[14] The cast and crew on the studio floor laboured to achieve, in the case of performed songs, a satisfactory lip-sync effect. Yet sound was a persuasive addition to cinema and many of the technological innovations during the 1930s are a result of the accelerated desire to synchronize satisfactorily words or performed music to the on-screen image. In the clear siting of the image as the 'source' of sounds rather than for example the other way around – an illustrated radio theatre? – the factually separate recordings of both elements become somewhat buried in the refinements of sound editing that marked the years 1930 to 1935. The ambition by virtually all mainstream film makers was to disguise the separation of the soundtrack and image, in the interests of constructing something akin to a filmic reality. This was done partly by a succession of ingenious editing solutions, for

---

[14] The writer Rick Altman has suggested that this factor has done much to shape our notions about the ideologies of sound and image on a theoretical level. *Introduction to Cinema Sound*, Yale French Studies, 60, 1980, p. 6

example, cutting to sound, carrying a sound over the edit point into the next scene or manipulating the levels of foreground sources, and latterly by the swift adoption of sound-on-film recording stock.

Congress Dances (1931) was a musical produced by the German studio UFA using the playback method, but it is notable for its relative fluidity in staging compared to other films produced at the same time and using similar recording methods. The sequence shot for the song 'Just Once for All Time' sung by Lilian Harvey lasts for two and a half minutes and breaks down into some twenty linked shots. To compare this method of recording with the British film *Sunshine Susie* (1931), which recorded its music score at the same time as shooting its scenes, is illuminating. Louis Levy, the musical director of the British production, recalls the intricate patience needed to record even the most simple staging of a song:

> We never enjoyed the luxury of running the whole thing through. Instead we did it in the old silent manner of cutting after a few seconds of recording, to get a new camera position. After the first few bars the director would shout 'Cut!' Then a new set-up with new positions would be given and then we would shoot and record a few more bars. Even the incidental music was made in this bar-by-bar fashion. When we had decided on a piece of music to accompany any one scene, the band would play off-set while the actor went through his actions or lines in time with the music.[15]

The sheer complexity involved in making cuts in post-production to the delicate constellation of film and its separated soundtrack had an interesting side effect on the work of the film censor. In Britain, and one suspects that this must also have been the case in other countries, the implementation of the censor's decisions led to severe technical difficulties. A cut in one place led to lapses in continuity and synchronization elsewhere in the film. At the British Board of Film Censorship, the Warner Bros. Vitaphone system was not installed until 1931, some four years after its invention and widespread adoption. The problems with maintaining continuity meant that in more than a few cases films were passed without cuts; if they did require extensive cuts then they were banned altogether.

What is significant about the crossover period between the silent era and the early sound era is the speed with which many film makers adapted to the intricacies of recording and scripting sound elements. Richard Watts Jr., an early critic of sound technology, relented as early as 1929:

[15] Quoted in *The Technique of Film Music* by Roger Manvell and John Huntley (London: 1957), p. 37

As one who fought despairingly in the barricades against the coming of audibility, I must keep on admitting – as I have for several months – that it would be absurd, even if it were possible, to do away, at this period in the photo-plays progress, with the new invention.[16]

Ernst Lubitsch and René Clair

Film makers such as Ernst Lubitsch and René Clair championed sound from its earliest introduction and explored the potential of music as both an enhancer of and a replacement for dialogue. Clair had already explored musical accompaniment as a mimetic companion to on-screen action during his silent films of the 1920s. The almost cartoon-like musical buffoonery of films like *Paris qui dort* was further explored in his early sound works. Lubitsch offered up a way of taking what was best in silent film – movement – and combining it with the advantages of sound effects and dialogue. *The Love Parade* in 1930 demonstrates Lubitsch's fondness for shots without synchronized sound that permitted him full camera movements. In other sequences sound is excluded altogether in favour of a camera movement. *The Love Parade* features a running gag where Maurice Chevalier tells a number of courtiers the same *risqué* joke. Each time he nears the punch-line his voice goes into a whisper and the camera pulls back (thus making Chevalier inaudible) to look at the scene from another angle.

Lubitsch produced two other musical comedies in quick succession, again deftly integrating music, dialogue and sound effects within the fast-moving narratives of *Monte Carlo* (1930) and *The Smiling Lieutenant* (1931). *Monte Carlo* particularly features some spectacular settings for song renditions, one in particular being the 'Beyond the Blue Horizon' song sung by Jeanette MacDonald on board the Blue Coast Express as it thunders along the Côte d'Azur. The rhythm of the train journey in the song merges with the sound of the locomotive wheels on the railway tracks. The following year Lubitsch moved on from musical numbers to experiment with dialogue as a device for aural counterpoint against background music in *One Hour with You* in which dialogue is rendered as rhyming couplets to create a frenetic pacing for otherwise rather stagily shot compositions.

René Clair's *Sous les toits de Paris* (1930) was the first sound film produced in France and features music in a central role. Its subject is the street life of

16 *Film Mercury*, 1 August 1929

the city and in particular the life of an itinerant, Albert, and his friends and their attempts to win the hearts of the beautiful Pola. The opening shot of the film introduces the title song which recurs several times in differing arrangements throughout the film. The song is introduced to accompany an impressive crane shot which begins at street level and finishes up among the chimneypots of the Paris skyline. Music predominates, both over dialogue and over sound effects. Sometimes music functions as a sound effect – a man is punched out to the sound of a violently stabbed piano chord, or a conversation is mimicked by a musical interchange. Claudia Gorbman[17] points towards a 'masking tendency' in *Sous les toits de Paris* which she claims works to displace, rather than to diffuse, key moments of excessive dramatic tension. The example cited is the climactic fight between Albert and his rival Fred in which music is surprisingly absent but in which natural sounds become strangely disenfranchised from their on-screen sources, resulting in an impressionistic audio blur of a crowd watching a fight. As the fight reaches its climax Clair seems deliberately to block our vision by the juggling of obtuse angles and the interpolation of obstacles into our visual field. This visual rupture is signified on the soundtrack by the singular approach of a passing train whose deafening presence eventually dominates the visual field as well. Clair manipulates his soundtrack enormously to yield up the information he wants to supply to his audience, regardless of whether the method of doing so is realistic or not.

Many of the best surviving feature-length films from the early sound era were really silent films with synchronized musical accompaniment and selective sound effects. Beyond musicals there were pure 'talkies' in which any music included provided an explanation of its presence within the picture; an orchestral flourish would be revealed as an orchestra playing in the background of a small café, for example. Taking realism to almost absurd lengths this new rationale proved fairly pervasive. One might compare these early sound films with the early 3-D films of the 1950s where obedience to the new technological marvel tended to override any other artistic consideration.

What of the film makers whose reputation had been established before the birth of sound? Frederick Murnau, the acclaimed German director of amongst other things *Nosferatu*, continued to work without sound even as late as 1930, refusing to recognize the potential of the new technology:

> The only point on which I would assert myself is that the ordinary picture, without Movietone accompaniment, without colour, without prismatic effects and without three dimensions [all these were being spoken of at once as new additions to moving

[17] Claudia Gorbman, *Unheard Melodies* (Bloomington, Indiana:1987), p. 143

> picture art], but with as few subtitles as possible, will continue as a permanent form
> of the Art. Future developments may give birth to other forms but the original form
> will continue with an identity of its own.[18]

Murnau's response was to retreat away from the studio environment and to seek new subjects in a kind of crossover form somewhere between a naturalistic style and an early form of documentary. *Our Daily Bread*, Murnau's final studio film, was shot virtually entirely on location in the Dakota wheatfields and was resolutely silent. One might also mention the renowned director of silent epics Cecil B. DeMille, whose lacklustre sound career was launched by the rather forgettable *Godless Girl* in 1930. Despite DeMille's apparent inability to direct naturalistic dialogue, a trade paper, *Film Mercury*, did remark that the film's sound effects were among the best it had heard that year.

Many studios gave dialogue film projects to new and relatively unknown directors, the intention being that they could gain experience in the new techniques and pass on that experience to the studios better-known directors who had already built a reputation during the silent era. John Ford's first film, *The Black Watch*, in 1929 is an example of this practice. It uses basically silent film techniques to integrate music and song into its story of a military regiment. There are several dialogue passages, however, that were inserted at the insistence of the studio and were not even filmed by Ford himself. These are static constructions and consist of love scenes between two of the main characters.

Raoul Walsh's *In Old Arizona* from the same year limits itself to largely synchronous sound recording and a flatly realistic style. Performances throughout are mannered, dialogue is over-enunciated in order to ensure it is picked up by the microphone, which is always anchored to a point somewhere around the centre of the frame. One scene shows the hero, played by Walter Baxter, hovering around a clump of sagebrush in the middle of an otherwise sparse backdrop – naturally the sagebrush contained the hidden microphone. Solutions to this embarrassing stasis came relatively swiftly:

> If it was fraught with danger to move the amplifier with its supersensitive vacuum
> tube, someone said, why not move the condenser microphone attached to the
> amplifier? Thus the actor was able to walk about slightly. The increased radius of
> action was only 3 to 5 feet – the length of the flexible gooseneck which ran from the
> amplifier to the microphone. In this way the periodically paralysed actor began to
> amble once more, and the director heaved a (small) sigh of relief.[19]

18 *Theatre Magazine*, January 1928

19 Meuller and Rettinger, *SMPE Journal*, July 1945, p. 50

Interestingly, one of the most often praised characteristics of these early experiments in sound is the illusion of sound 'depth'. Sound becomes softened as characters move away from the camera, music from an orchestra in a night-club scene decays naturally as the camera moves across the dancefloor. This naturalism does not appear to have been deliberate in many instances but is chiefly the result of working with a single omni-directional microphone placed near to the camera's point of view. The chief practical innovation was the introduction of the boom microphone, a pole-mounted device that allowed the microphone to track scenes suspended just a few inches above the actors' heads.

All Quiet on the Western Front (1930) by Lewis Milestone represents a departure from strict synchronization in its use of background atmosphere tracks re-creating the sounds of the battlefield. Alongside sync dialogue the atmospheric effects achieve an almost poetic realism. Milestone was an experienced director during the silent era and here uses his virtuosity to harness the new possibilities of sound. It's easy to see *All Quiet on the Western Front* as a silent film with a soundtrack that functions as an abstract, heightened element. Milestone conceived the film visually, subordinating dialogue to visual images and using sound effects realistically, though not necessarily in sync with picture action. A memorable sequence illustrates Milestone's flair for editing. Moving shots from a crane showing soldiers running towards an enemy position are alternated rhythmically with static shots of the enemy's machine-gunners. This sense of visual rhythm acquires a chilling intensity when the sound effect of machine-gunfire is overlaid and we see its effects graphically illustrated. The score by David Broekman is sparsely melancholic, acting as a dramatic foil to Milestone's clever juxtaposition of sound effects.

In *The Front Page* (1931) Milestone takes the separation of speech and action to new extremes, actually cutting scenes during speeches and forming an abridgement into the next shot. This naturally had the effect of speeding up dialogue but at the same time went some way towards reintroducing the kind of lyrical, fluid editing that characterized some of the best silent films.

Another good example of the use of off-screen sound came with Fritz Lang's 1932 *The Testament of Dr Mabuse*, where a whole range of industrial sounds and techniques are used forcefully to generate an atmosphere of metropolitan dread. In this stylized late example of German expressionist cinema the ghostly presence of the arch super-criminal Dr Mabuse continues to haunt the city he wreaked havoc upon in the earlier (silent) *Dr Mabuse the Gambler* (1922). Sound brings to Lang's visionary sense of composition and cutting a third dimension, expressed even in the opening shots set in a factory as the camera tracks through tables laden with bottles vibrating to the sounds of some sort of giant industrial press. The relentless thud of the motor sound tracks a fugitive as he attempts to evade capture. As doors are opened and closed the sound grows louder or softer, even distorting. As the fugitive escapes from the factory, he emerges on to a totally silent and deserted street disrupted suddenly by the crash of a large piece of masonry which narrowly misses him. Similarly there is the clatter of an oil drum as it rolls down a gangplank towards the fugitive, again to miss him and burst into flames. Only the sound effect of the oil drum is present, and no attempt is made to represent the flames. The sound effect, whilst highly artificial in its clarity and its isolation (since there are no other sounds of any kind), is nevertheless highly effective, apparently predicating man-made objects over natural sounds and thus heightening our impressions of a totally industrial landscape which terrorizes man. In a later scene, the character Baum reads the notebooks of Dr Mabuse alone in his study. A single sustained high note on a violin creates a mood of tension, as we hear Baum 'reading' and then we see the ghostly apparition of Dr Mabuse materialize opposite Baum at the table and whisper a coda to the will, with a warning about man's deepest fears. The whispered dialogue is disconcerting in its softness, and underlines the ambiguities in this scene, where we are unsure whether Mabuse is simply a figure of Baum's imagination or ours.

Alibi (1929), a film directed by Roland West but written by ex-Ince scenario writer C. Gardner Sullivan, made much use of near silence as a direct counterpoint to sound. It received highly positive reviews, most of which picked up on the way in which the film foregrounded sound atmospheres. King Vidor's otherwise scrappy 1930 film *Hallelujah!* also made much of natural sounds present during recording. In a chase sequence through a swamp all that can be heard is the breathing of the two protagonists combined with the wind in the trees, the rustle of swamp grass and the cawing of bird life.

Another film which received positive reviews for its rendering of atmospheres was *The Right to Love* (1930), which achieved an unusually high level of sound quality:

> The excluding of bothersome noises is highly successful for, because of the background of silence, the player's voice is more life-like than ever. The quiet may seem at times too noticeable, but this is only because one has become accustomed to hearing the intrusive mechanical undertones.[20]

20 *New York Times*, 2 January 1931

W. S. Van Dyke's *The Thin Man* (1934), a combination of detective story and comedy of manners, is a surprisingly modern-looking and -sounding film as conversations take place with an ease of movement and dialogue delivery that belies the technical apparatus behind it. Certainly Otis Ferguson reviewing the film for *The New Republic* was not short of praise:

> All in all it was a miracle of co-ordinated talents – writing, casting, acting, W. S. Van Dyke's direction and the staff men under him, on cameras and in the recording and cutting rooms, who assisted in catching the spirit of every scene, from cocktails and jazz pianos to gunfire.

Japanese cinema during the early sound era

Whilst not gaining the same retrospective accord as the fluid lyrical French sound cinema of the 1930s, the films of major production studios in Japan such as the Shochiku company bear certain similarities in style, if not subject matter. This was a period of militaristic expansion in Japan and there's little doubt that an agenda of censorship and control was operating to some degree. Yet even a film so apparently celebratory of the sporting and military life as Hiroshi Shimizu's *A Star Athlete* (1937) is ablaze with visual and aural experimentation. Ostensibly a documentary-style record of a march by a group of military cadets, the film features extensive experiments with travelling dolly shots, subjective camera angles and extended single tracking shots. The soundtrack is a complex mesh of naturalistic sound mixes, with many jokes involving the fact that the camera is travelling nearly all the time.

The most interesting Japanese film of the period, however, is definitely Heinosuke Gosho's *The Neighbour's Wife and Mine* (1931), a nearly feature-length sound-on-film comedy using a technology developed by Tsuchihashi Takeo, an ex-accompanist musician to the silents. The film is a charming comedy about a henpecked would-be playwright under pressure from his wife to finish a commissioned play for the local theatre. Easily distracted by all manner of passing sounds he is eventually distracted enough to go to see his new neighbour, ostensibly to complain about the hot jazz blaring from their living room. He is lured inside by his neighbour's attractive wife, who also happens to be the singer with the band, and a session duly commences with the playwright getting drunker and drunker as the music gets more and more vigorous.

Even via subtitles one can see that the dialogue is casually naturalistic, a marked departure from the earlier stagey style of screen acting. This aspect attracted the interest of a critic, Tamura Yukihiko, who in his review of the film remarked that:

> None of the cast had experience on the stage, but this actually worked in their favour, as lines are spoken in an extremely natural manner. Ensuring that dialogue is delivered in the same tone as everyday conversation should be a matter of the utmost concern to the producers of Japanese talkies.[21]

Music, almost entirely diegetic, plays an important part in *The Neighbour's Wife and Mine*. Even the opening sequence introduces a wide panning shot of a village and we see a travelling musician walking along a path banging a percussion instrument. The camera sweeps past, however, and gradually the music fades away, an interesting take on the idea of aural perspective. A landscape painter casually whistles the theme from René Clair's *Sous les toits de Paris* – an important reference to a breakthrough film in terms of its soundtrack.

At his neighbours', the playwright listens to a variety of contemporary jazz tunes, all of which are boisterously performed by the band with a lot of quick cutting between players. The walls of the room are covered with references to European and even Soviet films. This film is in some ways unusually self-conscious in the modernist style that it is trying to appropriate.

the early soundtracks of Alfred Hitchcock

European film makers seemed to adapt to the possibilities of sound faster than their American counterparts. Hitchcock, in particular, seized on the possibilities of binding music, dialogue and sound effects into a highly effective *Gestalt* with which the spectator could be manipulated. His first sound film was *Blackmail* (1929), large sections of which were re-recorded dialogue since the producers' (but not Hitchcock's) intentions had originally been to release the film as wholly silent. Hitchcock had recorded his scenes as if they were dialogue which allowed, in post-production, for the layering of dialogue in a decidedly non-naturalistic style:

[21] *Kinema Jumpo*, 21 August 1931, quoted by Iwamoto Kenji in *Reframing Japanese Cinema*, eds Arthur Nolletti Jr. and David Desser (Bloomington, Indiana: 1992), p. 320

After the girl has killed the painter, there is a scene showing a breakfast, with her family seated around the table. One of the neighbours is discussing the murder. She says, 'What a terrible way to kill a man, with a knife in his back. If I had killed him I might have struck him over the head with a brick, but I wouldn't use a knife.' And the talk goes on and on, becoming a confusion of vague noises to which the girl no longer listens. Except for the one word 'knife, knife', which is said over and over again and becomes fainter and fainter. Then suddenly she hears her father's normal, loud voice: 'Alice, please pass me the bread knife', and Alice has to pick up a knife similar to the one she's used for the killing, whilst the others go on chatting about the crime.[22]

In *The Thirty-Nine Steps* (1935) Hitchcock utilized sound as an ironic counterpoint to convey an emotional reaction. A woman finds a corpse on a train and at the point at which she screams we hear the shrill whistle of the train as it enters a tunnel. Effortlessly, we have been transferred into the next scene. At another point, the rhythmic noise of the train's wheels on the track becomes synthesized into a vocal chant of 'He musn't, he musn't, he musn't'. With techniques like this Hitchcock was proving that, far from inhibiting film technique, sound was capable of adding an entirely new form of narrative to the story.

Sound for Hitchcock very often reveals the subconscious meaning of an image. The opening of *Murder!* (1930), for example, focuses at a low angle upon a black cat – a traditionally bad omen – prowling a deserted alleyway, while the soundtrack itself resonates with the screams of a murder victim and her attacker's footsteps clicking on the pavement. Music on the other hand fulfils a rather different function, often being deployed diegetically in shot to suggest types of social order. It's interesting to note how centrally Hitchcock locates music in his early and later sound films. Several of his protagonists are in fact musicians: a composer in *Waltzes from Vienna* (1934), a drummer in *Young and Innocent* (1937), a music teacher in *The Lady Vanishes* (1938), a pianist in *Rope* (1948), female singers in *Stage Fright* (1950) and the remake of *The Man Who Knew Too Much* (1956), and a bass player in *The Wrong Man* (1957). Elisabeth Weis[23] has speculated that Hitchcock adopts music so centrally in his strongly stylistic films because of its pre-existing structure, metaphorically referring to a pre-ordained order against the constraints of which the destinies of his characters are tossed.

In the original version of *The Man Who Knew Too Much* (1934), classical music forms the setting for two pivotal murders in the film: the murder at the

22 François Truffaut, *Hitchcock* (Paris: 1960), p. 72

23 Elisabeth Weis 'Music and Order in Hitchcock', in *Ideas of Order in Literature and Film*, ed. E. Weis (New York: 1977)

concert house, where the victim is the dancing partner of the heroine Mrs Lawrence, and the climax, which takes place during a concert at the Albert Hall. Both murders are concealed by music and at the same time orchestrated by music. Gunshots occur on the beat of a piece of music, a warning is transmitted from the hero to his friend in the form of wrong words sung to a hymn whilst they are hiding out during a church service, and windows shatter musically to illustrate a bullet's ricochet. Music becomes a continuum of background order through which heroes chase villains and are endangered in doing so. The fact that Hitchcock so often chooses to illustrate murders with diegetic music may be a way for him to claim that evil and danger are constantly present in life. Music, however, is not necessarily to be seen as something representing an abstract property of good, since it is chosen not with any specific cultural affiliation. Hitchcock's choices of music remain resolutely populist and very often he used songs to exploit their familiarity to the audience and also their easy emotional appeal to trigger feelings quickly.

Songs can also of course be used to pin or establish guilt through association. Guilt is pinned directly on the heroine in *Sabotage* (1936) by the chorus of the song 'Who, who, who killed Cock Robin?'. Whilst in *Blackmail* the device is used more associatively as the girl murderer is haunted by the song her victim sang to her shortly before she stabbed him to death. Songs can also be used to show moral influence by a stronger character upon a weaker one as in *Shadow of a Doubt* (1943), where an uncle's often hummed waltz theme gradually is taken up by his niece. The repetition of the waltz throughout the film as a key transition device gives the musical theme a powerful symbolic quality that becomes redoubled each time we hear it and note the progressive moral decline of the central character.

the voice in the early sound film

In any recording in which the human voice is present, an inevitable anthropomorphism leads us to focus our attention upon that part of the recording and to relate other elements on the soundtrack back to the voice as primary co-ordinate. Roland Barthes locates this point of interest as the point at which language and the pure vocal sound intersect. This point in the experience of a recording he terms the 'grain of the voice',[24] the point at which the voice is a sound with emotional significance because some sort of

24 Roland Barthes, 'The Grain of the Voice', in *Image, Music, Text*, ed. Stephen Heath (London: 1977)

meaning not quite at the level of linguistic comprehension has been found. Barthes' definition of the grain is 'the body in the voice as it sings', which sites value in some sort of inner commitment to the physical activity.

By analogy we could say that in listening to the soundtrack of an early sound film we too are listening for some sort of authenticity amongst the trebly drone of a decaying tape. This ideal authenticity can be translated equally into a desire for realistic spatial positioning within each shot as well as a vocal 'grain' in the sense that Barthes seems to desire. But this spatial positioning is open to inconsistencies, both technical and semiotic.

One might consider firstly the voice in its role as a voice-over narrator, carrying us forwards or backwards through the film's story. Spatially this voice is foregrounded on the soundtrack, it dominates, it directs, it informs us. One might think of the narrator of *The Power and the Glory* (1933), in which Henry (Ralph Morgan) serves as our narrative guide back through the life of the recently deceased Thomas Gardner (Spencer Tracy).

The voice has the capacity to offer us information over and above what the image shows us in a way that neither sound effects nor music can. Its authority exists because it is rarely challenged by other voices given the same primacy. Think of the documentary, and the almost universal acceptance given to the single voice-over commentator. Double those commentators and halve the perceived authority of each. The voice has a far greater flexibility through space than does the visual; a voice can hear around corners, through walls, through a blindfold and so on. The voice as voice-over is taken largely on trust, as if it somehow guarantees cohesion. The ambiguity here is that it has authority simply because it remains isolated from the rest of the soundtrack.

In the recording of conventional dialogue scenes during the early sound era certain codes that had evolved during the silent era needed to be re-examined. Much of the weight of narrative progression had traditionally fallen on to the intertitle, which was largely used to summarize what had gone before, and to transport the audience into the next narrative scene. This seems to have been accepted without complaint, but dialogue intertitles pointed up only too clearly the limits of silent film. Dialogue as intertitle was cumbersome and time-consuming to use in all but the most elementary cases, where its effectiveness was redundant anyway. With sound, film time now became regulated by the speed of the human voice, which was considerably slower than the speed of cutting that silent-film directors had become used to. Dialogue overlap between scenes or travelling shots that followed the speaker as they moved across the scene seemed to offer at least something of a solution but neither of these devices appears to have been attempted until around 1931.[25]

Christian Metz has pointed to the focus in our everyday descriptive language that assigns primacy to the visual over the aural. Descriptions of aural objects become reduced to predicates in sentences where the visual is given the status of a subject. We describe sounds in clusters of adjectives whereas we can simply point to visual objects. In analysing cinema this can constitute a problem in describing narration as simply 'voices off'. Voices off screen is a clearly inadequate descriptive term since in reality the voice predominates over the image.

realism: sound effects and source music in *Scarface*

Scarface, Howard Hawks' explosive 1932 gangster movie, is a film unusually anchored in the real world of sounds and sound sources. The microphone reveals little trickery and is used primarily to confirm visual action. Non-diegetic music is strikingly absent from the film as a whole although music does play a significant role in the narrative. The central character, Tony Camonte (Paul Muni), is a psychopathic hoodlum who kills without emotion and often without provocation. We first see him in silhouette in a night-club as he is about to execute his former boss and before we see even his shadow we hear the aria that he whistles each time he is about to commit murder. This trademark character device is doubled by his sidekick's habit of tossing a coin before he too kills someone. The aria is used at several key points in the film to underline impending violence, both for the characters within the story and for the audience. Although the intention is that we should 'hear' the aria as if it were coming from the lips of Tony Camonte each time, the visual compositions and cutting sequences tend to undermine this sense of realistic anchorage to the whistle's source. The whistled aria tends to creep into scenes as almost a piece of mood music, its significance amplified each time we hear it because of our growing familiarity with what it portends. Probably the most effective scene is where Tony's sister Cesca is playing a light ragtime piece at the piano to Tony's sidekick, whom she has just secretly married. Her performance is trivial and her glance is constantly off screen to her seated lover, yet it is interpolated by the ominous whistle of Tony's aria as he ascends the staircase to the apartment. We already know

[25] Erno Metzner, 'The Travelling Camera', *Close Up*, June 1933

that Tony has warned off his sidekick from becoming involved with his sister so as an audience we realize the significance of what is about to happen. Interestingly, neither of the two lovers appears to 'hear' the whistle: it is reserved as a signifier for the audience alone. Tony's on-screen announcement is a knock at the door which when answered results in the fatal shooting of his sidekick.

Elsewhere in the film, background noise is realistically and impressively rendered. The constant background presence of Chicago's street traffic is a dull roar at the back of every scene. The other most frequently recurring sounds are gunfire, screaming, screeching tyres and breaking glass. Particularly in the case of gunfire, there is little attempt to correctly mix it into each scene. It has been dubbed on during editing and consequently is amplified out of all proportion to the other sounds in scenes where it occurs. This seems to be a self-conscious piece of style, however, since there are two transition sequences where gunfire is used almost as a leitmotif. One superimposes a blazing machine-gun over the familiar device of pages flying from a calendar and the other shows the abstracted clatter of a ticker-tape machine as it prints out a message.

Sound is also used to convey a rather dark brand of humour. Tony's 'secretary', an incompetent and illiterate hitman, consistently fails to answer the telephone correctly, and his increasingly hopeless conversations with the unheard caller become a running gag. Finally, sprayed with bullets, the hitman hears the telephone ring and automatically staggers over to answer it, for the first and last time in his life remembering to get the caller's name before he collapses and dies.

surrealism: Jean Vigo, Maurice Jaubert and L'Atalante

L'Atalante was made in 1933 and was the last film by the young French director Jean Vigo. Its soundtrack is worth examining for the ways in which it incorporates a number of different layers together with a sophistication and lyricism which no American film had achieved at the time. Maurice Jaubert wrote the score, which combines conventional dramatic themes with diegetic performances of popular songs. Amongst the many visual treasures of *L'Atalante*, which might be described as gently surrealist, it is the way in which music and sounds are constantly fragmented often to the point of abstraction which creates the lasting impression. Ostensibly a low-key moral fable about a young girl who marries the skipper of a barge that navigates the canals of northern France, *L'Atalante* is also about the relationship between the simple rhythms and harmonies of life afloat versus the morally lax society that intrudes upon the couple from a rich gallery of characters and situations on the land that surrounds them. In a film that constantly points up the contrasts between two different ways of life, and the young bride's ambiguous loyalties to her husband and to the temptations of urban life, music is used at every opportunity to reflect the conflict. The boat becomes a bridge between the jaded pleasures of the city and the pure realms of the imagination as represented by an elderly sailor named Père Jules, whose cabin full of mementoes and souvenirs from a lifetime's sailing include a number of mechanical musical devices: strange and exotic automata, musical boxes, a magnificent phonograph and various musical instruments.

These musical devices provide many of the film's most arresting moments; Père Jules at one point manages to make a phonograph record he is holding in his hands play by absent-mindedly running his finger across the grooves in its surface, and we are presented with accordion music, which we understandably assume to be the record. Amazed at his discovery, Père Jules stops and then tries again but this time nothing happens. We hear the laughter of the cabin boy and the next shot reveals that he has been sitting in the cabin all the time with an accordion on his knees. Angered by this trick, Père Jules then winds up the phonograph, puts the record on and, as the needle makes contact, the soundtrack swells with a waltz which clearly does not emanate from the record itself but from the film's composer. Jaubert's waltz continues and the skipper Jean is seen swimming under water searching for the image of his absent wife, who once told him that if he loved her he would see her image under water. We see her projected form hovering like a ghost under the water, animated by the waltz and superimposed on the face of her distraught husband. The introduction of Jaubert's waltz theme triggers the start of an extended series of scenes, all illustrated with the same continuing musical theme, which catalyses the films denouement, the return of the bride to her husband. What is remarkable about this continuous musical illustration is the ingenuity with which Vigo presents us with possible diegetic sources, most notably a sequence in which the skipper, now hauled from the water, is led by Père Jules and the cabin boy on to the deck of the boat. The cabin boy leads this small procession carrying the phonograph in his arms whilst it appears to be playing. As they reach a bench on the deck they all sit down, and Père Jules takes the phonograph from the boy, sets it down and simply places the needle back to the start of the record, perfectly matching a natural rest in the waltz time. The waltz continues, we cut to the skipper preparing for bed, contrasted with parallel shots of his wife undressing in a dingy hotel room somewhere on land. As they both try to sleep, the waltz appears to carry each of them off into erotic fantasies only finally to shake the skipper from his bed with the realization that he is sleeping alone. His reverie is brought to a full halt by the klaxon sound that tells us that a new day has started and provides a convenient bridge into the next scene, which is much more documentary-like and unpunctuated by music.

Other key points in *L'Atalante* are illustrated or triggered by music or mechanical sound sources: the couple's first argument near the beginning is due to the bride, Juliette, attempting to tune the radio to a Parisian station much to her husband's annoyance. Elsewhere, popular songs dominate (apparently this had been a request passed on to Vigo by the film's distributors, Gaumont, before shooting began). One of these, 'The Pedlar's Complaint' composed by Jaubert but with lyrics by Charles Goldblatt, seems to have been delivered with some mock-epic irony reinforced by the occasionally overdramatic flourish from Jaubert. In another scene the composer also provides us with an Indonesian theme during which Juliette is led astray on the dance floor by a pedlar who lasciviously describes the extremities of experience to be had in Paris to her as they move across the floor. Of the main score to *L'Atalante* there isn't a lot to be said in terms of its musical uniqueness; its power lies in its structural daring. Jaubert's music seems constantly to try to capture the discontinuity of film time and filmic events. Often presented in very short phrases, it serves as an index of changing visual elements, and particularly as an index of cuts between different scenes in the body of the film itself. Jaubert was a composer with a great degree of self-awareness both of his own style and of the craft of film music in general. He sharply distinguishes between the proper function of music in the silent cinema, and the way it should be utilized in the early sound period. Freed from the necessity to substitute music for dialogue, Jaubert believed that film music should never attempt merely to follow events on screen but should prepare the audience for changes in dramatic mood or visual style:

> Music is by nature continuous, organized rhythmically in time. If you compel it to follow slavishly events or gestures which are themselves discontinuous, not rhythmically ordered but the outcome simply of physiological or psychological reactions, you destroy in it the very quality by virtue of which it is music, reducing it to its primary condition of crude sound . . . If I reject entirely all musical

annotation or synchronization, it is because I believe in the essentially realistic character of the screen.[26]

Jaubert concentrates upon the inherent instability of film narrative: its constant pulling away from any real semblance of photographic truth; its ability effortlessly to cross time and space between the cement of an editing cut; its ability to portray memories through flashbacks and dreams, and even to picture the thoughts of characters, making the on-screen subconscious literal and explicit. Jaubert sees it as the function of the film composer to:

Feel the exact moment when the image escapes from strict realism and calls for the poetic extension of music . . . We do not go to the cinema to hear music. We require it to deepen and prolong in us the screen's visual impressions. Its task is not to explain these impressions, but to add to them an overtone specifically different – or else film music must be content to remain perpetually redundant. Its task is not to be expressive by adding its sentiments to those of the characters or the director, but to be decorative by uniting its own rhythmical pattern with the visual pattern woven by us on the screen.[27]

Jaubert was a communicator in music, a *mélodiste* (sometimes attributed to his Mediterranean origins – he was born in Nice in 1900), but before pursuing a musical career, he was first a lawyer, qualifying at the precocious age of nineteen. His entry into music was first as a part-time critic and he became friendly with the composers Honegger and Ravel. He began to compose some time in the early 1920s, but in 1926 was asked by Jean Renoir to make the musical selections for *Nana*. This was followed by a second film for Renoir, *Le petit chaperon rouge*. While continuing to write his own symphonic pieces Jaubert worked as a musical arranger at Joinville Studios. In 1932 he met and worked with the Prévert brothers during their post-production sessions on *L'Affaire est dans le sac* and it was this association that took him into the mainstream of French cinema in the 1930s. Jaubert composed incidental pieces for directors such as Jean Painlevé (*Le Bernard-l'hermite*), René Clair (*Quatorze Juillet*) and Henri Storck, but it was in 1933 that he met and began collaborations with Jean Vigo.

Before *L'Atalante* there was *Zéro de conduite*, a lyrical and often anarchic story of life in a provincial boarding school. Claudia Gorbman makes an excellent analysis of this score in her book *Unheard Melodies*,[28] pointing out

26 Maurice Jaubert, 'Music on the Screen', in *Footnotes to the Film* (New York: 1937), p. 108

27 Ibid., p. 111

28 Claudia Gorbman, *Unheard Melodies* (Bloomington, Indiana: 1987)

that Vigo took the unusual step of recording certain of his orchestral passages in reverse only to play them back on the finished soundtrack the 'right way round', producing an eerie effect where attack is preceded by its decay. This fits in perfectly with Jaubert's intention to mirror the visual lyricism of Vigo's film and to liberate the creative rather than reproductive powers invested in the humble phonograph.

In terms of Vigo's concert music, his first piece, *Le Jour*, was written in perhaps 1932 or 1933 but was not widely reviewed until 1936. Reviews were, in the main, highly positive:

> Maurice Jaubert is not embarrassed by the frames of the past.[29]

> We are in the presence of sane, vigorous and authentically popular art.[30]

Jaubert's film music, however, garnered him the most attention, since between 1929 and 1939 he wrote scores to thirty-eight films. His symphonic piece *La Suite Française* was written to accompany a documentary film which conjured images of the Seine river through different seasons of the year. It was given to the director of that film, Jean Lods, in advance of editing, so that montage scenes could be co-ordinated to the score.

In one of the most interesting experiments in film music history, the French director François Truffaut chose to exhume certain pieces from Jaubert's film-score repertoire for his film *L'Histoire d'Adèle H.* (1975). Jaubert, dead for some thirty-five years when Truffaut took this decision, was certainly in no position to object. *L'Histoire d'Adèle H.* is based on a short story about a daughter of Victor Hugo who falls in love with an English lieutenant and, in an act of mad love, decides to follow him around the world in the face of his indifference. It's a genuinely disturbing film about a fractured love affair seen from the obsessive viewpoint of the hapless Adèle Hugo. Truffaut utilizes Jaubert's main themes from two documentaries, *La Suite Française* and also a series of short compositions Jaubert wrote for Henri Storck's *Ile de Pacques*. He also utilized in a rearranged form music from *L'Atalante*. Significantly all three of Jaubert's scores here recycled concern water as a central narrative element in the films he was scoring. In *L'Atalante* water becomes a symbol for the rebirth of a jaded relationship whilst in *Adèle H.* it is used to symbolize the suffering of a spurned and self-deluded individual. Images of water or of waterborne transportation are central to *Adèle H.* In a series of three nightmares suffered by the central

29 Paul Le Flem, *Comoedia*, 4 May 1936

30 Robert Bernard, *Les Nouveaux Temps*, 11 July 1936

character water prefigures death or a loss of identity. Selecting from Jaubert's earlier scores some of the most melancholic elements, Truffaut creates something rather close to a conscious form of seance, an evocation of the kind of poetic realism that Vigo conjured up so effectively. In *La Chambre Verte*, made two years later, Truffaut again 'quotes' from Jaubert, this time using a concert piece, the nostalgic *Concert Flamand*. This film is about a man who builds an altar in his home to his dead wife as well as to his comrades who were killed beside him in the terrible slaughter of the First World War. At one point near the end of the film, the central character, played by Truffaut, explains to a friend why he has decided to choose a certain composer to accompany a memorial service, and the camera moves in to a photograph on a table of Maurice Jaubert conducting an orchestra shortly before his death on the battlefields of France at the start of the Second World War:

> I realized that his music, full of clarity and sunshine, would be the best to accompany the memory of all those dead.

L'Atalante is very far from being a smoothly contoured film. It's difficult even to assess whether it represents Vigo's original artistic conception, since he was after all seriously ill during much of the filming. Dramatically the film is unevenly proportioned – whilst the beginning and end are strongly structured, the middle section of the film is disjointedly weak, with little of the brisk economy with which Vigo begins and ends his story. Vigo has completely reworked an original script and story idea by a novice writer called Jean Guinée and the impression is sometimes of a script that has been pulled in two opposite directions. Its power resides in individual sequences but this was not enough to save the film from almost universally bad notices from the French critics at the time of its initial release. The distributors in France, Gaumont, panicked and decided to try to inject some commercial substance quite literally into the body of the film.

Capitalizing upon the commercial success of a song released the same year, 1934, as *L'Atalante*, 'Le Chaland qui passe' by Lys Gauty and Cesare Andrea Bixio, the film was retitled with the song's title and most of Jaubert's score was lopped out to be replaced with a successive repetition of Bixio's song. To compound this, the film was also re-edited with many of the most distinctive sequences excised. The ability of Gaumont's publicity machine to remodel recent history for its own ends was startlingly brazen. In a press release to mark the opening of the film in Marseilles:

> Thanks to C. A. Bixio's celebrated melody, so admirably sung by Lys Gauty, *Le Chaland qui passe* . . . will certainly not pass unnoticed! Already that evocative melody can be heard in every street. An equal success is assured for *Le Chaland qui passe* as a film.[31]

and, worse still, further afield than Paris, an Algiers paper:

> *Le Chaland qui passe* is a film inspired by the celebrated song so admirably sung by Lys Gauty.[32]

Le Chaland qui passe was as much a commercial failure as *L'Atalante*. Vigo died in October 1934 at the age of thirty. There followed in the decade after his death a steady reassessment of his earlier work as well as *L'Atalante*, thanks to the influence of a number of critics. As often happens after a war, a noticeable loosening of the moral climate in France took place and Vigo's work became reinterpreted as a symbol of youthful liberty. *L'Atalante* and its original fifteen minutes of music by Jaubert have been through a series of restorations and the version currently in existence and premièred at the 1990 Cannes Film Festival[33] is generally thought to be more or less as Vigo intended.

avante-garde early sound films

Away from the organized and salaried world of the studio productions, and the massive communications programmes of Soviet Russia, independent film makers in Europe and America during the 1930s were beginning to develop the material possibilities of sound film in a completely new direction. Why, for example, bother to record an orchestra in a studio when the process of composition could now be made as simple as the addition of physical scratch marks to the soundtrack of the film strip itself? Given this possibility the parameters of the soundtrack opened up to encompass a language in itself – the language of shocking preciseness. There is after all not much ambiguity in a precision scar, merely degrees of millimetre to the left of a picture frame. Whilst there was undoubtedly an impulse towards experimentation and the freedoms therein, the various experiments that began in the 1930s were also a result of a burgeoning independent

[31] Quoted by P. E. Salles Games in *Jean Vigo* (Paris: 1957), p. 189

[32] Ibid., p. 189

[33] *L'Atalante*, 86 min PAL VHS, Artificial Eye 004

community of independent film makers in both Europe and the United States. Lacking the centralized and systematic research funding of their contemporaries in the Soviet Union, these Western film makers nevertheless absorbed the published manifestos and articles of the great Russian directors such as Eisenstein, Pudovkin and Vertov which appeared in translation outside the Soviet Union very often contemporaneously with their domestic publication. To an extent the Western avant-garde in film making in the 1930s was a rather fragmented and even disenfranchised pool of activity; nevertheless a substantial body of work emerged, the influences of which percolated through to inform much of the more commercial new wave of film makers who broke through after the end of the Second World War.

By genre, the so-called 'city symphony' had the greatest potential to interest a wide audience. Walter Ruttmann's outstanding 1927 *Berlin, Symphony of a Great City* was a heightened form of impressionistic documentary incorporating abstract photography and a full orchestral score. The soundtrack was a montage of fragmentary noises recorded on location. Ruttmann's film was one of a number about cities made in most of the major film-producing countries in the late 1920s. His next project was *Weekend* (1928), a film with no pictures, simply a montage of sounds. Hans Richter described it:

> It was a symphony of sound, speech fragments and silence woven into a poem. If I had to choose between all of Ruttmann's works, I would give this one the prize as the most inspired. It re-created with perfect ease in sound the principles of picture poetry which was the characteristic of the absolute film.[34]

In terms of an aesthetic manifesto on film sound, the most influential source of ideas was 'Statement on Sound', written jointly by Eisenstein, Pudovkin and Alexandrov and published in 1928. This work attempts to set forth certain principles about the sound film, despite the fact that sound-film production was some way off in the Soviet Union due to its still-primitive technological infrastructure. The principle of montage is cited as the central determining element in film assembly and language. Sound was viewed as the next most fundamental determinant of the future film style, and was, through what the authors saw as the inevitable commercial triumph of the dialogue film, a direct threat to montage since it undermined the rhythmic principles of construction that had marked out some of the greatest Soviet films:

34 Hans Richter, quoted in *Experimental Cinema* by David Curtis (London: 1972), p. 39

> To use sound in this way will destroy the culture of montage, for every adhesion of
> sound to a visual montage piece increases its inertia . . . only a contrapuntal use of
> sound in relation to the visual montage piece will afford a new potentiality of
> montage development and perfection.[35]

Interestingly, the authors draw a parallel with the use of intertitles as well as the explanatory close-up as elements similarly threatening the effectiveness of montage. It was thought that sound should act non-synchronously with the image to arrive at a new international language of sound that would not confine each country's cinema to language-bound borders.

This sense of sound not serving the image but acting as a separate, equally important component of the cinema experience is the basis for most of the sound film experimentation of the 1930s. To see how such a principle might work in action one might consider Pudovkin's 1933 film *Deserter*, in which he asked his composer Shaporin for:

> . . . the creation of a music the dominating theme of which should throughout be
> courage and the certainty of ultimate victory. From beginning to end the music must
> develop in a gradual growth of power. This direct unbroken theme I connected with
> the complex curves of the image.[36]

Pudovkin then attempted to define the sound elements themselves in a spatial mosaic that worked in harmony with Shaporin's score:

> I took sound strips and cut . . . and the images associated are sometimes much
> shorter than the associated sound piece. Sometimes I have cut the general crowd
> noise into phrases with scissors, and I have found that it is possible to create a clear
> and definite, almost musical rhythm.

For many who saw *Deserter*, the overall impact was confusing. In a film about the triumph of a workers' revolution some American critics misread the rising exultant tone of the music as the triumph of the repressive bosses rather than the workers' victory it was supposed to celebrate.

The following year, 1934, saw the emergence of a small film featuring music by the French composer Arthur Hoérée called *Rapt*. Hoérée contributed a striking piece of music to accompany a storm scene in which he instructed the studio orchestra to improvise an imitation of the physical sounds of a storm – wind, rain, thunder and so forth. Having recorded this,

[35] Sergei Eisenstein, 'A Statement', in *Film Form* (New York: 1949)

[36] V. I. Pudovkin, 'Film Technique and Film Acting', in *Film Sound: Theory and Practice*, eds Elisabeth Weis and John Belton (New York: 1985), p. 90

Hoérée then, by judicious cutting and splicing, created a storm collage of some hundred metres of sound stock. The original sounds made by the orchestra had been tampered with to the point where they were virtually unrecognizable, elements were reversed, segmented, stripped of their attack and decay and reconstituted into something far more expressive than any ordinary musical rendering of a storm. Hoérée himself believed that:

> The total psychological content of the scene had been treated musically with fragments spliced together.[37]

As with Maurice Jaubert working as a contemporary to Hoérée it can be seen that this kind of manipulation of recorded sound was in fact quite popular amongst the more adventurous French film composers. *Rapt* may well have been inspired by Jaubert's work on *Zéro de conduite*.

Allied to experiments made with film montage, the recombination of already recorded sound elements, there was another development that appears to have emanated from experiments conducted by the Russian mathematician Arseni Avraamov at the Experimental Film Institute in Leningrad in 1930. Avraamov worked with drawings of basic geometric shapes which he then photographed on to a film strip. He found that any repeated pattern produced a distinctive sound. Pitch was controlled by the frequency with which the shape appeared on the film and volume was controlled by the length of exposure; for example, the tendencies towards white photographic surfaces produced louder sounds. Using double exposures even a primitive kind of polyphony was possible. Avraamov's particular interest was in exploring musical microtonalities and his experiments with photographing sound were a means to this end rather than an attempt to create a new way of utilizing the film soundtrack for artistic purposes. A colleague of Avraamov, N. V. Voinov, progressed these studies somewhat further. An animator with the institute, Voinov experimented with more complex patterns of shapes with more deliberate relationships between them to produce more advanced sounds, eventually arriving at a chromatic scale of more than seven octaves! Voinov actually succeeded in synthesizing photographically Rachmaninov's C minor Prelude and Schubert's *Moments Musicaux*.

In France and Europe, sound-on-film experimentation seems to have been more confined to drawing or painting directly on to the film surface itself. Hoérée claims to have invented sounds with the paintbrush, yet there

37 Interview with Arthur Hoérée, Paris, 25 April 1979, quoted in 'Avant-Garde Sound on Film Techniques' by R. S. James, *Musical Quarterly*, vol. 22,1986

seems to have been similar activity in England, for example with the films of Jack Ellit, who simply bypassed the camera altogether, painting his films directly on to each frame of the film strip.

The progressive Bauhaus painter László Moholy-Nagy was also working on the integration through montage of sound into the fields of painting. By 1930 he had begun work on several sound-on-film projects and, as Kostelanetz claims in his biography,[38] had published an article in which he suggested that sounds be traced directly on to the soundtrack. In practice he animated increasingly bizarre alphabets of fingerprints, letters, even facial expressions with sounds drawn directly on to the soundtrack, producing something like a shorthand for visual expression. Moholy-Nagy saw the revolutionary possibilities in these new methods of scoring, asserting that film composers adopting his techniques would:

> be able to create music from a counterpoint of unheard of or even non-existent sound values.

Oskar Fischinger elaborated the process a stage further, attempting to codify a musical language system that could then be used fully to explore the relationship between sounds and pictures. Fischinger was especially interested in the relationship between distinct abstract sounds, the essence of an object and its sound; for instance, a billiard ball hitting a roof tile is highly characteristic. Fischinger's aim was nothing less than a codification of a complete library of different types of non-musical sounds. In creating a library and a language, his work as an animator could be vastly extended, or so he believed. At a meeting in 1931 of the Haus der Ingenieur, Fischinger provoked no small degree of attention when he revealed the results of an experiment to record the literal sound of an Egyptian pictograph (representing a snake). Once threaded through the projector, Fischinger's precise scratch marks were converted rather alarmingly into a strangely lifelike synthesized hiss–s–s–s–s. His attempts to develop his experiments into a fully fledged theory on the relationship between written language and sound floundered through lack of funds, and Fischinger did not manage to capitalize upon the success of his earlier experiments.

Kurt London, a remarkably prescient composer and early commentator upon developments in film music, remarked in 1936 that these experiments might lead to a time when:

---

38 Richard Kostelanetz, *Moholy-Nagy* (New York: 1970), p. 136

> One might do without an orchestra and instruct a composer to put his music
> together in patterns upon paper, which would then be photographed and then
> produce a very strange and quite unusual sound.[39]

The Russian film scholar Leonid Sabaneev claimed further that sound-on-film techniques actually extended the sonic universe,[40] leading us away from the 'confinements' of the orchestra with its mere twenty or thirty different timbres. He further predicted the demise of scores, parts, engravers and copyists, as well as all other forms of intermediary between the composer and his audience.

Whilst sound-on-film techniques have done little to change the way in which film composers and soundtracks in general are constructed today, they did nevertheless mark an important watershed of maturity in conceptual thinking about the artistic possibilities of the soundtrack. As time could effectively be frozen into a still photograph of a musical moment, this pause for thought did plant some seeds which broke new musical ground and for the first time really put the manipulation of individual sounds at the centre of an agenda. Sound-on-film techniques did much to pave the way for the electro-acoustic music and the *musique concrète* of the 1950s.

The other strands of avant-garde film making in the 1930s were those films that used a resynchronized music track added after recording but which nevertheless foregrounded music as a central element. These 'abstract' films can be compared with the experiments of the Futurists and Dadaists of a decade earlier. Jo Gercon and Hershell Louis's *The Story of a Nobody* (1930) was a far more accessible work than, for example, anything by Hans Richter. Its subject was still the basic materialism of cinema but its explorations were wittier than the largely technical, machine-fetishized studies seen earlier. *The Story of a Nobody* takes the subjective point of view of a boy and a girl and their developing relationship over a thirty-minute period but seeks to describe their communication with each other in terms of the objects both of them see from their own subjective viewpoint. The film had a sonata structure and was divided into three sections, each assigned a different tempo: moderately quick, slow, very quick. Split screens allowed the relay of often fairly complex streams of conversation to the audience without them ever needing to hear or see the couple, since everything they are talking about is illustrated by objects.

[39] Kurt London, *Film Music* (London: 1936), p. 197

[40] Quoted in 'Music and the Sound Film', *Music and Letters*, vol. 15, 1934, p.149

Lewis Jacob's *Commercial Medley* (1933) took trailer reels from mainstream cinema attractions and reworked them to satirical effect, again using music as an important linchpin in the process. Music normalized a set of absurd and impossible trailers, both providing the context in which the audience could enjoy this parody but at the same time also serving to illustrate how far in terms of irony *Commercial Medley* was removed from its innocuous sources.

In terms of a full-sound film, however, *Lot in Sodom*, made in 1933, was probably the first American avant-garde sound feature. Ostensibly a queer sub-Freudian retelling of certain Old Testament incidents, *Lot in Sodom* used a specially composed score by Louis Siegal and even a cast of extras. Shot predominantly in slow motion, the film boasted plenty of controversial scenes of nudity but its overall tone was lyrical. Designer Mary Ellen Bute and her partner cameraman Ted Nemeth made several impressive abstract sound films during the 1930s. Each used synchronized sound matched to an image and then developed it as an animation along a given chromatic scale. Similar in many ways to Oskar Fischinger's experiments, Bute and Nemeth's work tended to give music a more fundamental role, complementing rather than strictly corresponding to the visuals. *Anitra's Dance* (1936), *Evening Star* (1937), *Parabola* (1938) and the colour films *Toccata and Fugue* (1940), *Tarantella* (1941) and *Sport Spools* (1941) are typical of their work. Mostly their subjects were small, three-dimensional found objects – a pingpong ball, cut-out models, buttons, etc. – which were then imbued with 'dramatic' qualities and transformed into bit players on a small tabletop stage.

It's also worth mentioning Joseph Cornell's free-wheeling *Rose Hobart* (1936–9), a film that may just have prefigured the MTV-style music video clip. Cornell reconfigured portions of a long-forgotten support feature called *East of Borneo* to fashion a bizarre ersatz love poem to the fictional Hollywood starlet Rose Hobart. Backed by a jukebox full of trashy 1930s pop songs, *Rose Hobart* is a glorious disassemblage of the Hollywood star system and also of a particular brand of adventure yarn.

This remarkably innovative chapter in animation and music, tracing sounds directly on to the film material, finally achieved a kind of breakthrough with the films of New Zealander Len Lye and Canadian animator Norman McLaren. In his 1955 short *Blinkity Blank*, McLaren uses an aural backdrop of improvised jazz selectively to 'sample' visually to produce a dazzlingly kaleidoscopic freeze, as literal an animation (if not quite as sensational) as Yves Klein's 'paint-wrestling' experiments with naked débutantes in Paris at around the same time. McLaren took sound animation to an astonishing level of sophistication. He was able by minute visual refinements to produce variations as slight as one-tenth of a tone and sound durations of as little as one-fiftieth of a second with over one hundred different dynamic shadings.

THE FORMATION OF FILM MUSIC CONVENTION

film theory in the 1930s and 1940s

By the mid-1930s the sound film had cemented itself as the predominant mode of cinematic exhibition and experience. In the light of this a number of critical studies and what might even be viewed now as manifestos began to emerge from academics and others in both Europe and the United States. In many cases these studies attempted to provide a taxonomy of the sound film, and within a number lengthy consideration was given to film music. The commentators range from the strictly theoretical to critics who were also practitioners of film music. Much of the discussion on film music *per se* and its role in the cinema originated in England, where there was an unusually high concentration of jobbing film composers originally from a concert-hall milieu. This lent an air of sophistication to the film-music profession.

Opinion might be viewed as split between two camps: those composers who felt, by the mid-1930s, that film music had achieved a kind of maturity or stability and was therefore worthy of recognition as a musical form in its own right; and those on the other side who saw film music as a corrupted, toothless offspring of theatre music (which was of course itself an inferior art form).

Usefully in 1935 Raymond Spottiswoode, a working composer and theorist, attempted to try and delineate some of the functions of film music in the early sound film. He selected five characteristics, which he listed as follows:[1]

1   *imitation*   where a score imitates natural sounds or the tonal qualities of speech

[1] Raymond Spottiswoode, *A Grammar of the Film: An Analysis of Film Technique* (Berkeley: 1962), pp. 192–3

2 *commentary* in which the score takes the part of a spectator giving an often ironic commentary on events on screen

3 *evocation* music that works to reveal something about the characters, a leitmotif might be an example

4 *contrast* where the score appears to contrast dramatically with the image and creates a definite effect

5 *dynamism* music working together with the composition of successive shots to accentuate the impact of cutting or editing points

Of these, numbers two, three and four are predominantly Western techniques, whilst five seems very like the Soviet principle of montage. The demands that montage appeared to make of the music that tracked it were considerably more advanced technically and aesthetically than the standard practices thus far in Western film-music circles. It was not until the 1950s that Western composers were regularly using asynchronism or counterpoint as a basis for their compositions for film scores. The convention was still at this point towards a kind of musical illustration through underscoring, despite the fact that all underscoring really does is to confirm the dramatic content of what can already be seen.

Certainly some of the better film-music composers of the 1930s and 1940s were already aware of the limitations of style. Kurt London warned that:

> If music is employed to strain after effects which the film itself cannot induce, then it degrades the film and itself.[2]

In many cases slavish Mickey-Mousing music was employed to mask technical and, worse still, dramatic flaws in the film itself. However, one should not get too carried away with arguments about counterpoint vs. parallelism. At this time it was a fairly central argument amongst composers reaching its fullest statement in the essays of composer Hanns Eisler and critic Theodor Adorno, who attacked the soporific effects upon an audience of most mainstream film music being produced by the Hollywood studios. Later commentators, writing in the 1950s and 1960s, chief amongst them Siegfried Kracauer,[3] have tended to play down the argument, citing both types of composition as examples of commentating music which serve equally as opinion-forming aids to the deciphering of the underlying themes of the story.

London, like many of the more successful film composers who had not

2 Kurt London, *Film Music* (London: 1936), p. 125

3 Siegfried Kracauer, *Theory of Film* (New York: 1965), pp. 133–56

previously enjoyed a virtuoso career in the concert hall, laments the lack of seriousness with which film music was treated at the time:

> The music which accompanies the film is still struggling for its place in the sun; the film people themselves almost invariably treat it very casually and are not quite clear in their own minds about its importance; musicians take it up more for the sake of fees than for art's sake, and he is a rare exception among them who shows any sympathy for its novel forms; the public finally does not trouble overmuch about music because it always fails to understand the cause and effect of film musical ideas.[4]

Hubert Clifford, a composer and journalist writing in the early 1940s, questioned whether the material riches on offer to successful film composers might eventually make film a more attractive medium than opera since it offered greater dramatic possibilities. Benjamin Britten, the composer, seemed to agree:

> There are great possibilities in music for the films, but it must be taken seriously by the director and composer, and used as an integral part of the whole thing – not just as a sound effect, or to fill up gaps during the talking. The nearest approach I've seen to this has been in the Disney cartoons and a few French films.[5]

Another highly successful British composer of both film and concert music, Arthur Bliss, took a similar line:

> When you see a well-dressed man, you are not conscious of his clothes; you are just pleasantly aware that here is somebody well turned out. The total impression is satisfying, though you can't exactly say why. Film music should have this effect on the cinemagoer; he should not be conscious of it as something distinct from the film itself. The twin principles of vision and sound should merge and achieve a unity – as they do in ballet, or in the music-drama of Wagner; the composer has to be a kind of musical epigrammist, compressing the sense of an idea into the shortest possible time and conveying it with the greatest economy and effectiveness.[6]

Bliss was also very honest about his motivation to work in the cinema, it was primarily the money. This is certainly borne out by Bliss's way of turning every one of his film scores into free-standing concert works. However, within the films themselves, the impact of his music was highly effective.

Probably the most important theoretical contributions to the consideration of film music in the 1930s and 1940s were those made by Eisler and Adorno.

[4] Kurt London, *Film Music*, p. 126

[5] Quoted in *British Film Music*, ed. John Huntley (London: 1947), p. 158

[6] Ibid.

Their thesis on the function and dysfunction of film music was an ongoing project spread across a number of works but centrally stated in Eisler's book *Composing for the Films* (1948), and in a number of joint essays with Adorno. Central to their work was an appreciation of the strangeness of cinema. Film offered its earliest spectators something completely new. A moving world flattened and stripped of colour and sound, a world populated by spectres. What were the actors up there on the screen – were they living or dead?

Eisler felt that the very nature of this shocking encounter with non-living projections served to alienate the audience from the spectacle they had paid to see. A direct encounter with machines supplying 'recorded' entertainment was too much for an audience already aware of their own mechanization (and marginalization) within the workplace.

> Music was introduced as a kind of antidote against the picture. The need was felt to spare the spectator the unpleasantness involved in seeing effigies of living, acting and even speaking persons, who were at the same time silent.[7]

and . . .

> Its social function is that of a cement, which holds together elements that otherwise would oppose each other unrelated – the mechanical product and the spectators.[8]

Eisler points to the cinema as a totally mechanical space in which any intrinsic entertainment or information content is modified and ultimately censored by those that control the means of film production, i.e. industry and capital. Film music for Eisler is simply a representation of music, stripped of its emotional sincerity. It becomes 'music for pleasure' placed within the picture-space largely for its soothing effect, lulling onwards the spectators' dreams of consumption. By neutralizing the projector's noise with music, the illusion of live entertainment is preserved. Instead the audiences have been duped into paying for a mass-produced, endlessly reproducible, homogeneous spectacle that cannot speak for them or for their position in society:

> The origin of motion-picture music is inseparably connected with the decay of spoken language. It is hardly accidental that the early motion pictures did not resort to the seemingly most natural device of accompanying the pictures by dialogues of concealed actors.[9]

[7] Hanns Eisler, *Composing for the Films* (London: 1947), pp. 75–6

[8] Ibid., p. 59

[9] Ibid., p. 76

Presumably, for Eisler, live dialogue would have gone some way towards providing a solution to the alienating effects of the silent screen. Possibly Eisler was not well acquainted with an earlier series of experimentation with live speech as an accompaniment. But this was an expensive method of creating a live soundtrack and the practice, although toyed with in most countries, did not really take off. For this very reason, Eisler is presumably arguing, film music serves as a perfectly bland and reproducible substitute for the spoken voice. However, since sound dialogue became the norm some years prior to Eisler taking up his pen, one might think that he would have viewed the early sound cinema with enthusiasm. Yet it is the advent of music, the saccharine rhythms of the mainstream, that Eisler is really objecting to. Eisler's basis of attack on the classical model of film scoring, that it serves only to disguise in the spectator their alienated situation from the culture industry, would seem to hold also for dialogue. And the same went for music considered in any sort of social context. The selling of concert tickets, the mass pilgrimage to a concert hall, the purchase of a record – all these activities seem equally compliant.

Eisler's critique that film music conceals alienation does not seem to be a charge that can solely be levelled at film music, but rather at the finished film. Film music cannot be proved to be quantifiably any more responsible for lulling an audience into passivity than sensuous lighting, or 'realistic' acting. The alternative is a Brechtian cinema, with all the materials of construction exposed. Eisler does not succeed in making it clear why film music should be considered as especially guilty of stultifying an audience when it seems obvious that any other element within the finished (studio) film could be working towards the same end.

Films themselves become, in Eisler's view, veiled exhortations to conform, to consume, to be content. Techniques of 'surprise' – fast cutting, close-ups – are clever attempts to provide an audience with an impression of immediacy, of spontaneity – in fact, the entire picture is a false mesh of subjectivity into which the witless spectator is co-opted.

Eisler's antidote to the tyranny of 'classical' (American) film music remains unclear. His call for greater progressiveness in the creation of music seems to side-step the issue of the functionality of film music. A film music that dwarfs the other narrative elements, progressive or not (whatever that might be), serves only to impose its own 'tyranny' upon the spectator. By the early 1950s Eisler seems to have realized just how hard it actually is to create popular music that also has artistic validity.

As a kind of footnote to the better-known views put forward in *Composing for the Films* one might look at the later version of Eisler's views which appears in a curious document now known to Eisler researchers as the *Letter to West Germany*.[10] In the letter, which Eisler wrote from self-imposed exile in Los Angeles to a musician in West Germany (Eisler was from the East), he makes a number of important remarks which do much to suggest a subsequent fascination with the 'applied music' of which film music is a branch. The problem for serious music is that in its lust for experimentation, often for the sake of experimentation alone, it has marginalized its audience and has itself fallen into something like a twelve-tone cliché:

> As serious music increasingly isolates itself, light music – which has long since become a product of a monopolized industry – takes hold among ever larger masses of people. And while light music does not require either an ability to listen to or understand music, serious music grows increasingly complicated.[11]

Eisler remarks that those asking the leading questions in music now are the musically illiterate, are musical laymen. In functional or applied music (amongst others Muzak, film, radio and TV music), he sees an all-encompassing wave threatening to change concert music altogether:

> One could maintain, with some caution, that applied music will gain hegemony in the future, at least during a transitional period. This will not lead to the demise or even the end of concert music; rather it will change it – the concert style will be 'applied'. Moreover, by means of applied music a new musical style will be the quickest to take hold of the masses because it gives music the backbone so necessary for the present and enables it to rise from the private to the general and the social.[12]

The fault or the problem of cultural receptivity seems to lie in the channels of communication that govern the relationship between composer and audience. One might imagine that Eisler's view of precisely how these channels are mediated would enter into his account of why applied music became so popular (even outside the realms of film music). Applied music disguises the alienation that all workers feel, but what does concert or serious music offer?

> The listener should know that listening is subject to historical change. If he demands intelligibility, he will be asked, which kind? Is Bach or Beethoven easily

[10] Hans Myer, 'An Aesthetic Debate of 1951: Comment on a Text by Hanns Eisler', *New German Critique*, no. 2, 1977

[11] Hanns Eisler, *Letter to a Musician*, reprinted in *New German Critique*, no. 2, 1977

[12] Ibid., p. 69

understandable? Yet, the art of these masters reached the highest level of perfection, and is the goal of popular culture . . . The listener should know that not every piece of music can be understood immediately. This is certainly true of all genres of music. Listeners and composers must learn to distinguish between genres which can be easily understood and genres which make it difficult for the listener – even demand a certain preparation. We composers should demand the same realism of listeners that they justly demand of us.[13]

Eisler does not make it clear exactly what 'serious' music is offering aside from the experimentation for experimentation's sake which he professes to be against. Since serious music had by 1950 been more or less removed from mainstream popular culture, Eisler seems unable to say from a purely compositional point of view how the bridge between serious or concert and applied music can be bridged. He remarks that it can only really be represented by musical notes on paper. The real work lies in educating the listener to train up their critical faculties. Socialist popular art is to be achieved through cultural planning, which was attempted to a large extent in the German Democratic Republic throughout the 1950s and 1960s but without any real lasting cultural impact.

The *Letter to West Germany* is really a plea for the rehabilitation of a genuine *volkstümlich* popular culture within socialist principles and a call to abandon the hollowness and superficiality of the kind of cultural sponsorship taking place in Russia under Stalin. Eisler surely had in mind the kind of work he had produced in collaboration with Brecht back in the 1930s, which was genuinely popular and musically challenging.

Even in Eisler's lifelong defence of *volkstümlich*, there is still a tendency to view critically his appropriation of many of the aesthetic ideals of so-called high art, as if popular and aesthetic were mutually exclusive terms. Eisler's attack in *Composing for the Films* seems to be more on the listless, passive acceptance of the music of cinema by the audience and of their apparent faith in the emotions or associations that the whole opiated stew is supposed to trigger. Yet why is intellectual exertion or mental effort associated so closely in classical aesthetics with value?

If one were to take the supposedly sheep-like activity of a member of the audience rocking her head to and fro and softly singing along to a typical Jessie Matthews song from a typical 1930s British film musical, is this solely a passive and undemanding activity? A philosopher such as John Dewey[14]

13 Ibid., p. 71

14 John Dewey, *Art as Experience* (Illinois: 1987), p. 162

would say that it isn't, that in fact at the very least feelings of embarrassment and a fear of social sanction have been deliberately overcome in order to commit to singing along to a simple popular song.

That popular forms of music tend to appeal on a sensual level is not in itself anti-intellectual (from the point of view of either the music's audience or the music's creators). If music can be made accessible to a wide audience easily then any study or appreciation of that music is likely to be enhanced by intellectual study, not diminished. Because popular music seems to be so much more 'in the world' than high cultural musical forms, it tends to get relegated to its own area of the academic curriculum. At the time when Eisler was writing, 'cultural studies' hadn't yet been invented. Eisler and Adorno's criticisms remained steeped in the language and segregational practice of high cultural aesthetics whilst not making any attempt to understand the appeal of the popular music forms so often adopted by the film studios in the 1940s.

On a very different theme the doyen of cartoon music composition, Chuck Jones, issued his own manifesto of a sort in 1946 in an article in the film journal *Hollywood Quarterly*.[15] Jones complained that the cartoon had been inhibited from real stylistic growth by being used primarily as an entertainment tool. Its music had been overly concerned with correct 'Mickey Mouse-style' synchronization and less with musical innovation and development. The work of the Walt Disney studios was singled out for particular praise, particularly a few sequences in *Fantasia*. Jones singled out six areas where he believed that the cartoon was uniquely suited to provide a creative solution. Much of what he said turned out to predict accurately the face of American television in the 1950s. The combination of imaginative animation and well-chosen or composed music, Jones believed, could revolutionize areas as diverse as educational products, television signature or 'ident' sequences, documentaries on folklore and satirical sketches. Jones went on to champion the abstract or 'absolute' animations being made already and called for more experimentation into the creation and use of a kind of graphic alphabet in which different symbols bore a direct relationship to specific sounds:

> The field of graphic symbols is a great but highly unexplored field. It will, I believe, prove an important one to the musician, and to any audience that is interested in satisfying the visual appetite, side by side with the auditory appetite.[16]

[15] Chuck Jones, 'Music and the Animated Cartoon', *Hollywood Quarterly*, vol. 1, July 1946, p. 364

[16] Ibid., p. 370

British film music 1935-50

One of the high points of British film music was Arthur Bliss's score to the science fiction film *Things to Come* (1936). H. G. Wells, author of the book on which the film was based, praised Bliss's efforts but maintained that the march which Bliss chose as the main musical motif was not entirely satisfactory. However, the music went on to become one of the best-known film scores at the time. The conductor present at the recording sessions for the soundtrack was Muir Mathieson:

> The opening of the film includes scenes of Christmas. A group of children are playing with their new toys and the music is gay, being scored for woodwind, strings and harp. Gradually the camera closes in to reveal that the toys are toys of war – model guns, tanks and bombers. The music of the children is slowly swamped as a deepening menace creeps in, depicted in the music on the brass, which becomes progressively more dissonant. The famous march theme is heard first as the World War commences and troops are mobilized. It is very heavily scored, with a large percussion section. Further strong musical sounds are used for the scenes of the enemy's first attack. After war on a vast scale, the world is in ruins and pestilence breaks out, spread by a desperate foe; music underlines the emotional nature of the scenes. There follows a period of reconstruction and a sequence in which new machines build the cities of the future. Bliss produced some remarkable orchestral sounds to suggest the great, hidden power of the equipment, using the humming effects of large masses of strings in unison, with alternate sections bowing or playing pizzicato. The final scenes in the picture show the departure of a space cylinder to the moon. The space gun fires and the rocket, with two young people inside, starts on its journey into the sky. In a large observatory, their parents see the cylinder as a very small speck against a starry background. Cabal speaks: 'For man no rest and no ending. He must go on, conquest beyond conquest . . . all the universe or nothing . . . which shall it be?' A flowing string melody plays under the scene, until the two men stand looking at the great mirror of the telescope. As the last lines are spoken, a full choir, singing wordlessly, gives out the final statement of the epilogue scene, and the film ends with this expression of human triumph amongst the stars.[17]

The situation in Britain in the late 1930s was simply that there weren't enough good home-grown composers to go round. Those that excelled at the craft were booked up for months or even years ahead. John Croydon, a film producer, said:

[17] Muir Mathieson, quoted in *The Technique of Film Music*, eds John Huntley and Roger Manvell (London: 1957), p. 55

> Most really good British composers are difficult to get for film work. Even when they are able to spare the time to score a good British picture, they write their music with one eye on concert hall receipts which may later accrue from the score, and as a result the unity of the film suffers.[18]

Almost alone of all European countries in the 1930s, Britain imported a number of prominent continental film composers to work on its domestic product. This was against a harsh background of a national quota of domestic film production introduced in 1927 by a government anxious to prevent a complete overrun by the growing power of the American producer-distributors. This climate of protectionism threw up a number of bizarre maverick figures who came to dominate the British film industry in the 1930s. Pukka characters such as Captain the Hon. Richard Norton, a flamboyantly mustachioed and monocled would-be movie mogul (British and Dominion Films), the teetotal big-game hunter Lady Yule (British National Films) and J. Arthur Rank, a flour magnate and Methodist teacher from Yorkshire, who saw film making as a way of promoting Christian values. Unfortunately much of the expansion in film making was funded by loans rather than by a more natural increase in capital value. Like a bubble economy in miniature the expansion in the British film industry in the 1930s was a boom heading for a bust. This did not, however, curtail the invigorating influence on the industry of a new generation of studio production heads like Alexander Korda, Michael Balcon, Herbert Wilcox and Basil Dean. Many of the most successful producers and directors making British films were recently arrived European *émigrés* fleeing an increasingly right-wing atmosphere in many countries. This cosmopolitan community undoubtedly enriched rather than impoverished the industry, although contemporary opinion was rather more xenophobic:

> To a large extent therefore, our British cinema, at the outset of its second decade of protected life, will be dependent for its prestige and profit upon Messrs . . . [followed by a long list of producers, directors, technicians and musicians with distinctly foreign names] . . . On these gentlemen and their creative attitude to our English industries, our countryside, our people (and our banking system), we depend for the projection of our national life. On their deep, inborn sense of our history, our heritage and our customs we depend for the dramatization of our English traditions as well as for the more mundane business of fulfilling our British quota.[19]

18 John Croydon, quoted in *British Film Music*, ed. John Huntley (London: 1947), p. 158

19 'The Flora and Fauna of the British Film Industry', *World Film News*, September 1937, quoted in *The Age of the Dream Palace* by Jeffrey Richards (London: 1984), p. 44

Amongst the European composers who worked with varying frequency in Britain during the 1930s and 1940s were Anton Karas (*The Third Man*, 1949), Hanns Eisler (*Abdul the Damned*, 1934), Ernst Toch (*Catherine the Great*, 1933; *The Private Life of Don Juan*, 1934), Kurt Schroeder (*That Night in London*, 1932; *Wedding Rehearsal*, 1932; *The Private Life of Henry VIII*, 1933), Nino Rota (*The Glass Mountain*, 1948) and, perhaps the best known, Miklós Rózsa, introduced by Muir Mathieson in 1936 and immediately making his distinctive mark with *Knight without Armour*, *The Squeaker*, *The Divorce of Lady X*, *The Four Feathers*, *South Riding* and *The Thief of Baghdad*. The respected French composer Arthur Honegger supplied the score to the 1938 version of *Pygmalion*, and the *émigré* Russian composer Mischa Spoliansky supplied the scores to the highly successful *King Solomon's Mines* (1936) and *Sanders of the River* (1935).

This esoteric collection of composers established British films as some of the most interesting of the period, at least in terms of their soundtracks. The overall tendency was towards twentieth-century compositional styles, considerably more demanding on an audience than the simpler nineteenth-century stylings of Hollywood during the same period. Perhaps this accounts for the extreme disfavour which British films found among the predominantly working-class audiences that supported the bulk of domestic box-office turnover. These audiences, very aware that much of what they were invited to pay money for and see was the result of the quota system (with its 'quota quickies' – studio films shot with minimal skill and care simply to fulfil the quota), were often vocal in their preferences for the American product, which favoured movement over speech and melody over dissonance:

> British films have never in all my life made the slightest impression on me. They are dull, ugly and uninspired . . . There are very few real British film stars, and those stars of the stage who grace the screen at intervals are too old to photograph well, poor dears.[20]

British films, as well as being technically inferior to American films, were class-ridden products where seemingly the whole country spoke with the same carefully modulated Oxford tones which alienated the bulk of its audiences.

An interesting case in point is the 1938 film *Moonlight Sonata*, a lightweight romance distinguished by the presence on screen of the

20 Interview with a thirty-year-old female clerk, quoted in *British Cinemas and Their Audiences* by J. P. Meyer (London: 1948), p. 98

distinctly heavyweight concert pianist Ignace Jan Paderewski. In a faintly ridiculous plot involving Paderewski falling in love with a Swedish aristocrat in a castle replete with moonlight, painted backdrop mountains and the maestro himself in performance, the problems of British film making in the 1930s can be seen. Naturally the film garnered fairly good critical notices – this was after all a vehicle for Paderewski, who at the end of his career (he was seventy-five when the film was made) had retired into something like a reclusive hermitage. However, the story, the acting, the design and the overall conception of *Moonlight Sonata* were definitely third rate. To the bulk of the audiences who saw the film, the thrill of watching Paderewski perform was limited and the film did not do well in commercial terms.

Many of the music soundtracks in Britain which can be considered to have been artistic successes during the 1930s and 1940s were not strictly speaking-drama projects but rather a hybrid species of documentary; for example, *Night Mail* (1936), scored by Benjamin Britten to poems by W. H. Auden, or *Coal Face* (1935), also by Britten, in which the labours of miners are soundtracked by a solo piano and choir to great effect, or the wartime quartet of films scored by William Alwyn: *Desert Victory* (1943), *Tunisian Victory* (1944), *The Way Ahead* (1944) and *Our Country* (1944). Many of these films received public screenings and so would have reached a wide audience. Scores by Richard Addinsell (*Special Dispatch*, 1941; *ATS*, 1942; *The Siege of Tobruk*, 1942; and *Troopship*, 1942), Christian Darnton (*You Can't Kill a City*, 1945; and *The Antwerp Story*, 1945) and Alan Rawsthorne (*Street Fighting*, 1942; and *Burma Victory*, 1945) all contributed to the growing reputation of British documentary film making.

One might also consider the wartime newsreel film – with record cinema audiences and a propaganda remit to fulfil. Two particular hits from the war years were newsreel films of Hitler which had been recut and looped so that in one Hitler appeared to be doing the 'Lambeth Walk' (a popular musical comedy song), whilst in another he was shown meeting Mussolini and in thrall to the rhythms of 'I Can't Give You Anything But Love, Baby'. These highly effective recuts of what was originally Nazi propaganda film reached huge audiences in the Allied countries and had an impact far more immediate than any commentary.

Other prominent British feature films of the period included *Dangerous Moonlight* (1941), which even contained an original 'concerto'. In fact it was more like a miniature symphony. Scored by Richard Addinsell, the story revolves around a Polish fighter pilot who, having fought against the Germans for his own country, flees to Britain to join the RAF and continue the fight when

Poland is overrun. Rather than use an existing symphony, Addinsell wanted to create an original piece which would for ever be associated in audiences minds with the theme of the film, Poland at war. The central piece, known as 'The Warsaw Concerto', had the desired effect and sold as sheet music in the thousands. Some nine minutes long, the piece is vaguely reminiscent of a concert pianist pastiching Rachmaninov, a sort of tabloid concerto instantly accessible and memorable and laden with an ersatz late-nineteenth-century pomp.

In 1941 appeared *49th Parallel*, a highly skilful action film about the attempted escape from Canada of a small group of submariners from a bombed German U-Boat. It marked the first time that the British composer Ralph Vaughan Williams had ever written music for a film. *First of the Few* (1942) stands as one of composer William Walton's finest film scores, containing the stirring 'Prelude and Fugue to the Spitfire' whilst the score to Powell and Pressburger's *The Life and Death of Colonel Blimp* (1943) is, although in a much lighter idiom than Walton's, an excellent example of the ways in which nineteenth-century source music (ranging in this case from Mendelssohn to Wagner) could be matched by a talented composer (Allan Grey) to original compositions much more in a swing style, like the theme 'Commando Patrol', which, although used purely as background music in the film, sold in volume as sheet music.

The year 1945 was outstanding for both British films and their soundtracks: *Henry V* (William Walton), *Blithe Spirit* (Richard Addinsell), *I Know Where I'm Going* (Allan Grey), *The Way to the Stars* (Nicholas Brodszky) and numerous others appeal, but it is Walton's score for *Henry V* that seems to answer a particularly complex challenge, since it simultaneously addresses the need to create a satisfactory musical rendering of a specific historical period as well as being a soundtrack particularly associated with musical notions of 'Englishness'.

The film presents a view of Shakespeare's play set in 1415, filtered through its 'performance' to a crowd contemporary with Shakespeare in Elizabethan London, and in passing includes some approximations of theatre music from that period. Rather than attempting to create a fake historical milieu, Walton opts for a much more personalized score which encompasses a tremendous dramatic range. A composer contemporary with Walton, Hubert Clifford, expresses his view of the score's impact:

> For me, the musical high spot was the Passacaglia which accompanies the interpolated scene of the death-bed of Falstaff. This music moves with simple dignity and a

restrained pathos, and adds to the scene something which will make it remain long in the memory. For sheer excitement – which provoked the sophisticated audience at the press preview to an ovation – the crescendo of the French cavalry charge which commenced the Battle of Agincourt would be hard to surpass. The gathering momentum of the charge was enhanced by the cunningly mixed soundtrack. A long cross-fade brought the music to the foreground, interchanging in prominence with the harness and armour clanking sound effects as the charge gathered its impetus.[21]

Christmas carols, Te Deums and 'The Agincourt Song' all play their part in the score to *Henry V*, but it is the dramatic subtlety of Walton's score that imprints the film. The sheer number of musical ideas jostling for prominence is astonishing when compared to the more introverted score for Kenneth Branagh's 1989 remake of the film scored by Pat Doyle: Walton's gift for the odd small inventive melody as the fleet sets sail for France, or the French theme scored with French horns – the English are scored with a trumpet, and the silent rests in the night-time camp scenes before the Battle of Agincourt. The music critic Hubert J. Foss once described Walton as being Keatsian in his sense of beauty, as possessing some 'sense of old unhappy far-off things and battles long ago',[22] and in the score for *Henry V* it's easy to see some truth in that. Walton repeated his Shakespearean scoring with *Hamlet* in 1948, working closely with Laurence Olivier. Muir Mathieson, the musical director on the film, recalls the recording process:

The arrival of the Court is heralded by trumpet calls. Then come the players, introduced and accompanied during their performance by a small group of musicians. We hear first the music makers; for this the composer provided a delightful period work for violins, cello, oboe, cor anglais, bassoon and harpsichord. After a section of this realistic music, a full symphony orchestra of some fifty players takes up the theme as the camera moves around to show the reactions of the King. The camera, taking in a full orbit in its movements, re-focuses on the actors and the music reverts to the small group of instrumentalists. The actor-king has been poisoned; the King can stand it no longer. The full power of the big orchestra rises up, underlining the dramatic content of the sequence, swamping the small group, and ending in a tremendous crash chord as the king roars, 'Give me some light.' In this example the music becomes an integral part of the film. The core goes beyond the realism of the small band shown on screen and extends into the emotional texture of the sequence showing the Court and its badly shaken sovereign.[23]

[21] Quoted in *British Film Music* by John Huntley (London: 1947), p. 75

[22] Ibid., p. 172

[23] Muir Mathieson, 'A Note on *Hamlet*', *Film Music*, 13, January–February 1954

With very experienced composers like Ralph Vaughan Williams and even mavericks like Noël Coward in the wings, British film producers were to some extent spoilt for choice in the years immediately after the war as production picked up again. However, with a still-restrictive choke on materials for production, British films continued to be dogged by visual poverty.

Ever since the runaway success of *The Private Life of Henry VIII* in America in 1935 there were numerous attempts to get all-singing all-dancing authentic British musicals off the ground and exported to the US, where huge audiences for musicals were already waiting. There were brave attempts (often staffed largely by American designers and technicians – but unfortunately funded in Britain) such as *Champagne Charlie* (produced by Ealing Studios) in 1944. *Champagne Charlie* was a period piece with songs by some of Britain's best songwriters of the time, a lot of mid-nineteenth-century light romantic pastiche and a lot of songs about drinking and carousing: 'Rum, Rum, Rum, I Do Like a Drop of Gin' and 'Ale Old Ale'. It was not very good, but achieved a modest box-office profit on its home territory before recouping a larger profit overseas. Another period piece with songs was *I'll Be Your Sweetheart*, an interesting film about the early Tin Pan Alley songwriters of London at the turn of the century. Great songs (by, amongst others, Val Guest, Harry Dacre and Manning Sherwin) and well-staged dance scenes attracted good critical notices for 1945.

American film music 1935–50

The music department of a major American film studio was, by 1935, a highly developed system of intricately divided labour. Functional divisions between Research, Production and Post-production sectors ensured that studio music departments worked at optimum capacity across a whole series of films at the same time. Within the music departments there were 'chase' specialists, main title specialists and umpteen other categories of specialist but potentially the most troublesome division was between composer and orchestrator or arranger, both of whom were expected to co-operate and present the results of their collaboration to the head of whichever music department they were assigned to.

A further erosion of the composer's status and authority in the 1930s was the creation of long-term contracts between composers, musicians, orchestrators and their studios which effectively bound all parties together across a number of projects and ensured that in the vast majority of cases copyrights resided with the commissioning studio and not with the composer. Composers therefore were considered as craftspeople in much the same way as set designers and any associated notion of authorship or of artistic control over their work on a soundtrack was subject to the complete final authority of the studio's administrative functionaries, specifically the musical director and the project producer.

Typically the composer would first 'spot' the film (often accompanied by the music editor) – in other words, identify the places on the soundtrack where music would be used. The composer then sketched out ideas on between two and eight staves of music per cue. These notes were then passed on to a studio orchestrator or arranger who selected which instruments would follow which lines. Most composers were quite capable of doing their own orchestration but in many cases were prevented from doing so by the rigidity (and strong union control) of the organizational structure within most studios.

There were composers who insisted on doing their own orchestrations. Bernard Herrmann was one. Others such as Max Steiner and Erich Korngold established fruitful working relationships with skilled studio orchestrators such as Hugo Friedhofer. Often the orchestrator wielded considerable influence over the composer and even helped to define certain composer's trademarks. Edward B. Powell's influence on the final shape of Alfred Newman's scores or indeed the entire Twentieth Century Fox violin heavy 'sound' cannot be underestimated.

New categories of specialization were created overnight. One of the most difficult areas of film music preparation had been the slow, inaccurate and laborious business of 'spotting' the finished film. There were no footage counters and Moviolas (a kind of desktop projector which allowed a scene to be viewed frame by frame if necessary) were primitive at best. Timings therefore were done by the composer in a projection room with a stop watch. This was the basis on which cue sheets evolved.

Innovators with studio clout like Max Steiner and Alfred Newman (musical director with Twentieth Century Fox) did more to change the way that film music actually takes shape than anyone before them. Steiner's music closely follows the rhythmic development of a scene, mirroring not so much the emotional cadences as the technical progression of shots, cuts, pans and dissolves. Probably Steiner's most lasting contribution to film music and the film music industry was the development of the 'click track' method of scoring, previously used primarily in animation.

The click track refers to the number of perforated holes at the edge of a strip of celluloid. As each perforation passes over the head of the sound projector it produces a characteristic 'click'. In creating a click sheet, a composer could precisely record the duration of a shot, or the length of a piece of dialogue, or the point at which a cue begins and ends. Every second twenty-four frames of picture hit a cinema screen, producing the impression of movement, and this yields 1,440 pictures or frames each minute. The composer needs to create an audible series of cues on screen which will provide an extremely precise guide to the duration of any given sequence, and for this the 'click track' is essential. Given a chase scene in which a composer is looking to use music with say 140 beats per minute, he divides the number of frames per minute (1,440) by the beats per minute (140) which gives a figure of 10.28.

The music cutter can now punch a hole into every tenth frame, providing a fully synchronized series of cue points throughout the scene to be scored. Steiner's technique remains the normal mode of practice for many composers today. Naturally Steiner himself was a past master, his two Oscar-winning scores for *Now Voyager* and *Since You Went Away* being remarkable pieces of fluid but highly controlled composition, fully developed suites in miniature, changing mood and tempo with impressive ease.

Another popular studio composer was Erich Korngold from Vienna, who had had a long apprenticeship in the theatre. His earliest successes were operatic, and indeed his subsequent transplantation to Hollywood did little to quell the more extravagant aspects of his work. For Korngold, film was like an opera unimpeded by the theatrical limitation of performances taking place in real time. His intensely passionate music seeks out the emotional patterns of leading characters, imprinting each with a precise musical signature. In the composition studio, underneath the playback screen, Korngold seemed effortlessly to match music to picture cues, composing music perfectly centred on the emotional peak of a scene, almost to the second.

Hugo Friedhofer, the orchestrator and composer, described Korngold thus:

> Naturally there was tremendous respect for Korngold, who really had *carte blanche*, and Korngold was one of the only men that I know that had the power plus the *chutzpah* to go to Hal Wallis or his associate Henry Blanke, who were producing all these wonderful epics, and say, 'Look, would you give me a little more footage here?' or he would say, 'I would think this scene would be better transposed to this spot.' And they listened to him and he was almost invariably right. This of course was

based on his long experience in the theatre in Vienna. A successful film composer has got to be primarily a man of the theatre. And I think that a great many of us [composers] know a hell of a lot more about what is effective theatre than a great many men who are sitting in seats of power and 'pass down the tablets from Sinai'.[24]

One obvious point arises from the way in which most studios operated. Scores were almost always not composed until after the film had been shot. The composer was therefore presented with a finished film in rough cut, which often had been produced with no clear idea of musical direction or, even worse, had been cut together to the strains of a spectacularly inappropriate temp track.

The conflation of the executive function with the labour function in a studio system led in more than one case to prominent composers eventually landing the jobs of musical directors – Max Steiner at RKO and Alfred Newman at United Artists and then Twentieth Century Fox. Despite, therefore, the assumption held by many film music composers at the time that the best film music is the score that the audiences don't notice, it seems likely that within such a collective organization as the studio the desire to stand out as an individual creative talent must have been considerable. Therefore, within a system that encouraged a model of classical symphonic composition as the norm to be expected, a composer had only a limited range of expressive tools at his disposal with which to stand out from the hundreds of other jobbing film composers working in the American film industry during the 1940s. These tools of differentiation might be characterized as:

1 *Arrangements* By adopting an unusual style of musical arrangement a composer could achieve and develop a distinctive 'voice'. A good example here would be the work of Bernard Herrmann, who throughout his long career as a film composer consistently opted for small group arrangements or gave prominence to unusual combinations of instruments.

2 *Ethnicity* By drawing on a unique (mainly European) tradition of musical composition steeped in the native folk melodies of the composer's homeland. Such an example would be Miklós Rózsa's or Erich Korngold's work which, when blended with the techniques of Wagnerian operetta, the creation of leitmotifs and

24 Interview with Hugo Friedhofer, *Film Music Notebook*, vol. 1, Fall 1974, p. 19

tightly parcelled chunks of instant musical emotion, can be very effective.

The classic American studio score of the period between around 1935 and 1950 tended towards a lush, full symphonic scoring and orchestration, the use of melodies as leitmotifs and the underscoring of dramatic action at every opportunity. Dialogue or other forms of narrative exposition was the dominant element fostered on the soundtrack and on the studio floor. It was this that kept audiences engaged and aware of the progress of the story, at least so conventional wisdom went.

Despite the rigid structures of the studio system, there were a number of personalities whose musical abilities and characteristic styles of working allowed them to stand outside that system, although to some extent these iconoclasts have paid a price in limited commercial success. Bernard Herrmann is an obvious example, as is perhaps reflected in his own definition of himself as less a film composer and more a composer who occasionally wrote film music.

Herrmann was born in New York City in 1911, graduating from the Juilliard school of music in the mid-1920s. Whilst still a student he had exhibited an unusually strong interest in the latest styles of musical composition to come out of the European scene, which at this time had only a very limited audience in the United States. He formed the New Chamber Orchestra at the age of twenty, devoted to performing avant-garde music of both American and European composers. From 1933 onwards, Herrmann was employed by CBS as an in-house composer (initially for radio) and subsequently as a conductor, rising to become chief conductor of the CBS Symphony Orchestra in 1940. Through a series of network radio programmes (*Exploring Music* and *Invitation to Music*) he continued to publicize the lesser-known aspects of the American contemporary musical canon as well as the outer reaches of European music.

It was in 1936, however, that he met and began working with Orson Welles on Welles' radio productions for CBS featuring his own theatre company, the Mercury Theatre of the Air. In 1940 Herrmann was offered the scoring job on Welles' auspicious first feature, *Citizen Kane*, by many standards a watershed in film-making history. As Herrmann freely admitted, he knew nothing about film composition, which, as Welles was also a first-time director for RKO, led to a certain freedom of association on the set that more established composers were usually denied under the usual pressures of working for one of the large studios. Herrmann was present on set for most of the filming of *Citizen Kane* and the resulting score clearly reflects a closer psychological reading of the central character in musical terms than was normally heard in a score.

Rather than score for a full orchestra in *Citizen Kane*, Herrmann incorporated smaller musical groupings and unusual combinations of instruments. Herrmann had in mind the hymn 'Dies Irae', a piece of music which he associated with 'vanity', surely the central and consuming theme of *Citizen Kane*. In fact the only sequences in the film that are scored fully for orchestra are the pastiche opera sequence, *Salammbô*, and the final score. Herrmann does certainly use leitmotifs but with a far simpler form, a matter of a few notes rather than an extended melody sequence. In dialogue scenes, Herrmann retains this virtue of understatement. Susan's suicide attempt, for example, produces a dissonant rendition of her aria leitmotif on the soundtrack. In general one might say that this capacity for understatement, set against the musical *trompe-l'oeil* of the majority of studio composers, could have been a natural continuance of the techniques he evolved during his radio work, where underscoring could actually prove quite distracting from dialogue. Other aspects of Herrmann's technique was the use of upbeat short musical signatures to convey the passing of time, the progressively building circulation figures of the newspaper Kane controls and the magnificent conceit of a decaying waltz pattern foreshadowing an impressionistic montage of Kane and his first wife at the breakfast table over a number of years. Interestingly these short sequences were composed by Herrmann from reading the script and in advance of filming, so Welles shot and edited his material in order to fit Herrmann's musical sketches.

The main musical motif, that of Charles Foster Kane, came from an idea by Welles. Kane is honoured at a party at the newspaper and the feelings of his employees about their barnstorming boss are summed up in the song 'There is a man . . .', which we see Kane performing in a kind of impromptu vaudeville sequence for the amusement of his employees. The song is based on a Mexican standard ('A Poco No' by Pepe Guizar) with new lyrics by Herman Ruby. Herrmann uses this song, or the first four notes, throughout the film as Kane's main motif, 'Power', which gathers melodic complexity and dissonance as we move towards the moral morass of Kane's later life in the loneliness of Xanadu. For the parody of a typically turgid nineteenth-century opera, *Salammbô*, Herrmann came up with a nice rendition of something Richard Strauss might have written, although arranged in a key above what a singer would be able to achieve. This was, of course, necessary for Welles' intention to portray the character of Susan as somebody completely inadequate for the operatic part that Kane has forced her to take.

One might also comment on the arrangement of the soundtrack and the sound recording effects generally in *Citizen Kane*. We become acutely aware of the spatial quality (perhaps one should say quantity) of scenes through the intelligent and adroit use of microphones. Certain aural transitional devices (other than music) are noticeable, such as the neat and witty transition between the crowd applauding Kane the canvassing politician to the sound of one pair of hands clapping as Kane sarcastically applauds Leland's campaign speech. Leland's reply then bleeds into Kane's voice again back on the campaign bandstand.

Although nominated for an Academy Award, Herrmann didn't win with *Citizen Kane* in 1940, although his second score did win the Oscar that year for the film *The Devil and Daniel Webster*. His only other collaboration with Welles was on *The Magnificent Ambersons*, from which he withdrew his composer's credit after a violent disagreement with a studio recut of the film (which was also enforced against Welles' wishes).

The Devil and Daniel Webster saw Herrmann conjuring traditional American folk melodies to diabolic effect. The film itself, by Stephen Vincent Benet, is a modern restaging of the Faust legend, now set in New Hampshire. In one highly effective sequence the distinctly demonic Mr Scratch turns a barnyard dance into a devilish hoedown to the tune of 'Pop Goes the Weasel', played at an impossibly fast speed on the fiddle. To capture this extraordinary effect Herrmann re-recorded the same violin part over and over again, finally playing them back together to simulate a fiddle held in the grip of a supernatural player.

In *Hangover Square* (1944) Herrmann provided a superbly abrasive score to a story about a composer prone to periodic bouts of murderous psychosis (triggered by hearing discordant sounds) as he tries to complete a concerto to impress his nice upper-middle-class girlfriend and at the same time to write popular throwaway music-hall tunes for his bitchy mistress. As Claudia Gorbman writes,[25] music in *Hangover Square* indeed structures the narrative but at the same time Herrmann's score is also a reflection of a damaged psyche trapped within a world of intolerable social claustrophobia. One of the central symbols in *Hangover Square* is a street barrel-organ and its owner, who seems to stand at the intersect of many of the narrative's key events. Gorbman and Michel Chion point towards this barrel-organ as harbinger and signifier of music's indifference to temporal events that are

---

[25] Claudia Gorbman, *Unheard Melodies* (Bloomington, Indiana: 1987), p. 153

not part of the score itself. One scene involves a grisly murder taking place soundtracked by the relentless and heedless hurdy-gurdy of the barrel-organ. Chion offers the following analysis:

> Emotion arises not from identifying through music with the character's feelings (which are normally treated as the most important thing in the world); on the contrary, emotion is born from seeing the individual's drama as it unfolds to the world's indifference. We call this music anempathetic since it doesn't care, and for this very reason takes on, in a massive transference often due to mere coincidence, the weight of a human destiny which it at once sums up and disdains.[26]

One could compare the above murder scene and its musical accompaniment with Herrmann's later work on Alfred Hitchcock's *Strangers on a Train*, where a woman is strangled to the sound of a fairground merry-go-round which later churns away to the climactic struggle between the hero and the villain. More recent incorporations of the same technique would include the deadpan playing of Roy Orbison's 'In Dreams' in *Blue Velvet* (1987) to accompany a graphic sequence of the character Jeffrey being beaten to a pulp by the deranged Frank Booth, or the infamous torture sequence in *Reservoir Dogs* (1992), soundtracked and abstracted by the early 1970s pop song 'Stuck in the Middle with You' by Stealers Wheel, with its dumbly vacant, rasping rhythms foreshadowing various unspeakable acts to be performed on a cop held hostage.

If Chion is right in stating that *anempathetic* music actually does have the effect of making us feel more for the characters because of the indifference of music (which we then interpret as the indifference of the world at large), then this would seem to work directly against the normal practice of film scoring, where underscoring nearly always bears a reasonably close relationship to the character's current fortunes or emotional state within the narrative.

Herrmann was a composer sufficiently at ease with the art form of film music to endow it with a genuine affective depth but also with a rare economy of means. In his long relationship with Alfred Hitchcock, Bernard Herrmann perhaps found his ideal creative partner. Hitchcock's cool, rational persona combined with Herrmann's well-known irascibility first in *The Trouble with Harry* (1955), a thriller riddled with black humour which Hitchcock seemed afterwards to regard as the most personal of all his films. With a jocular main theme replayed in various ways throughout the film, *The Trouble with Harry* also flashes darker, unexpectedly violent moments, represented by

26 Michel Chion, quoted ibid., p. 160

Herrmann as scherzos. These passages are not simply arranged in diatonic harmonies but break with them – passages end on unexpected notes, unstable chords motivate further passages – it's the sense of a musical texture that dominates rather than any easily remembered melody.

It is melody that could perhaps be most closely identified with rationality. It creates patterns that lodge easily in the listener's mind. With Herrmann what melodies there are owe more to the unusual instrumentation involved or their musical colouring:

> I think a short phrase has certain advantages. Because I don't like the leitmotif system. The short phrase is easier to follow for audiences, who listen with only half an ear. Don't forget that the best that they do is half an ear . . . The reason I don't like this tune business is that a tune has to have 8 or 16 bars, which limits a composer. Once you start you've got to finish – 8 or 16 bars. Otherwise the audience doesn't know what the hell it's all about.[27]

Herrmann's chordal language seems simultaneously to harbour major and minor chordal implications which operate *across* the events offered up by Hitchcock in his usual highly planned (down to the level of a storyboard) shot structures.

It's with *Psycho* (1960) that Herrmann and Hitchcock's singular talents coincided to the greatest effect. *Psycho* was Hitchcock's only real outing into the 'horror' genre but also provided ample doses of a humour so black it was lost on most of the contemporary audiences who saw the film when it first came out. The first reviews all but ignored Herrmann's mesmerizing score, even the specialist journal *Film Quarterly*[28] displaying almost total ignorance of the thirty-odd film scores Herrmann had written before *Psycho*, calling him 'an old radio man', acknowledging that the score was 'immensely effective' but conventional.

Conventional it was not. For a start Herrmann used only strings, which put immense restrictions upon him as a composer as well as depriving him of some of the traditional musical means of generating shock effects. Herrmann deliberately subverted the normal associations that an audience has with a string-based score. In a later interview[29] he claimed that he was trying to create a 'black and white' sound to complement Hitchcock's starkly monochromatic visuals. Despite his choice of instrumentation, Herrmann

27 Royal S. Brown, 'An Interview with Bernard Herrman', *High Fidelity*, 26 September 1976, p. 66

28 *Film Quarterly*, vol. xiv, 1960, p. 49

29 Leslie Zador, 'Movie Music's Man of the Moment', *Coast FM & Fine Arts*, June 1971, p. 31

was nevertheless choosing to foreground that part of the orchestra with the greatest dynamic range. At the same time, with strings forming the largest part of a conventional orchestra, their sheer number allowed Herrmann still to create antiphonal effects. Herrmann would no doubt have agreed with Rimsky-Korsakov's statement:

> Stringed instruments possess more ways of producing sound than any other orchestral group. They can pass, better than other instruments, from one shade of expression to another, the varieties being of an infinite number.[30]

There are no tunes or recognizable melodies in *Psycho*. Herrmann's motifs remain short but constantly imitative of forward movement. The most famous of the forty music sequences in *Psycho* is the murder in the shower scene, which in the director's original cut was included without a score. It was only as an afterthought, when Hitchcock realized he was unhappy with the shower scene montage, that he asked Herrmann to score the scene. This sequence consists musically simply of sharp downward bow strokes and piercing glissandos which almost seem to mimic directly the sound of screams. Elsewhere on the *Psycho* soundtrack can be found canonical themes that seem to echo the abandoned splendour of the Bates house, tonal meditations on watery ends as the body is dumped into the swamp and the extended three-minute sequence, 'The Peephole', a dazzling piece of psychological speculation building in Bates' fevered mind as he watches Janet Leigh undress in her motel room.

Alongside Bernard Herrmann a small handful of other composers came to represent (at least in retrospect) the golden age of the studio symphony-based score. Alfred Newman was certainly one of these figures. He composed in a far sunnier and more tonal landscape than Herrmann, and he was also less flagrantly experimental in his choice of orchestral arrangements. It would be hard to say, however, that he was less talented than Herrmann. As indicated above, Newman combined the abilities of composer with those of a studio executive – general music director at Twentieth Century Fox – a rare feat. A one-time supper club piano player, Newman made his name during the late 1920s and early 1930s as a talented arranger for theatre and film. He arranged Charlie Chaplin's score for *City Lights* (1931) amongst others. Amid a notable field of contemporaries such as Franz Waxman, Bronislau Kaper, Dimitri Tiomkin and Miklós Rózsa, only Alfred Newman was not actually a composer transplanted from another musical

[30] Nikolay Rimsky-Korsakov, *Principles of Orchestration* (New York: 1970), p. 8

idiom. Although Newman was undoubtedly capable of orchestrating his own compositions, he was actually employed within the studio framework primarily for his compositional skills. Other highlights from Newman's long and distinguished musical career include *The Razor's Edge* (1946), *Captain from Castille* (1947) and *Prince of Foxes* (1949).

Newman understood screen emotion and how to create it immediately and with an economy of means. He wrote an astonishing 255 scores[31] and received nine Academy Awards. He was overtly fond of leitmotifs, the simpler the better so that they could be transposed for a variety of instrumental settings. In his manipulative grasp of the harmonic palette, his instantaneous ability to shift from major to minor keys, perhaps Newman could be compared to Johann Strauss.

A Tree Grows in Brooklyn (1944) is an interesting example of Newman's work, since it shows him in collaboration with another strong creative force, Elia Kazan. Given the unashamedly sentimental story, based on a best-selling book, of a Irish-American family struggling to survive in a turn-of-the-century slum, Newman might well have chosen to go completely over the top, matching melodramatic music to every wistful lingering look across the Barrio. However, paired with director Elia Kazan's emphasis on performance rather than effect, Newman's score is confined to conjuring up a sense of ramshackle community. At the outset, music is almost omnipresent. The opening titles feature three strongly contrasted pieces of music: a hurdy-gurdy organ, a majestic though fractured brass waltz, and some ragtime piano. These collide into each other as the camera takes us down into the cacophony of Brooklyn's streets. During the early part of the film, the hurdy-gurdy organ animates street scenes, a kind of all-purpose signifier of motion, display and again something of Chion's notion of music as a disinterested presence in an urban setting where people are marginalized. The interior of a shop vibrates to a ragtime piano roll which by the next scene has collapsed into the hesitant stabs of a novice piano player as we move from the shop into the claustrophobic stairwells of the boarding house where the Nolan family live (and where the piano novice is obviously a neighbour). These musical transitions are almost continuous until we get into the story proper. By the end of Act 1 the music has retreated almost completely and dramatic conversations are dealt with by adroit camerawork rather than by melodramatic musical techniques. Newman adopts the sentimentality of the popular melody and places it

---

[31] *Film Music Notebook*, no. 2, 1976, p. 8

firmly in a realistic urban setting.

Comparing the above score with his earlier *Wuthering Heights* (1939) is revealing since it shows Newman operating with considerably less restraint, not overly successfully using leitmotifs to ally each individual cue with a character within the film. The tragic heroine Cathy, therefore, becomes a waif fêted by strings wherever she wanders. The themes Newman has written bear perhaps one or two hearings but as they have been employed as leitmotifs we are obliged to hear them over and over again, leaving a strong sensation of mere melodrama. Small wonder then that the scene featuring Heathcliff and Cathy running towards each other on a clifftop has become the stuff of parody, if not latterly farce.

Miklós Rósza

Rózsa has throughout his career offered a peculiar kind of high-velocity drama and emotionalism in his film scores, particularly those from the 1940s and early 1950s. Originally from Hungary, and born in 1907, like his fellow countrymen Béla Bartók and Kodály, Rózsa was from an early age fascinated by the rich expressive musical textures of Hungarian folk music. Rózsa's compositional career got off to a flying start when his 'Hungarian Serenade', written in 1932, was greatly praised by Richard Strauss when it premièred in Paris. Theme, Variations and Finale Op. 13, composed the following year, was an even greater success. In 1934, Rózsa met Arthur Honegger for a concert presentation of both their works. It was Honegger who introduced Rózsa to the cinema. Whilst resident in London, Rózsa wrote some ballet music which brought him to the attention of Jacques Feyder, who commissioned him to write *Knight without Armour* (the producer, Alexander Korda, was a compatriot of Rózsa), which was a success, as were his two next scores, *The Four Feathers* and *The Thief of Baghdad*. The advent of the Second World War saw Rózsa transplanted by Alexander Korda to Hollywood and his first Stateside success was *Jungle Book* (1943) for Disney. Rózsa wrote the suite. He clearly felt himself to be more than able to handle the vicissitudes of Hollywood:

> One of the things I quickly came to realize about Hollywood music was that there simply was no style as such, and what I managed to do in 1944 in [*Double Indemnity*] I count as something of a breakthrough. Many of the early musicians working in Hollywood sound films were former Broadway and silent film conductors, song-

writers and vaudeville artists . . . the general idiom was conservative and meretricious in the extreme. I introduced certain asperities of rhythm and harmony which wouldn't have caused anyone familiar with the serious music scene to bat an eyelid. The musical director of Paramount couldn't stand the score from the beginning, and told me so. Did I really have to have a G sharp in the second fiddles clashing with a G natural in the violas an octave below? Couldn't I change it, just for his sake? In his opinion the place for such eccentricities was Carnegie Hall not a movie studio. I refused to change a note, and thanked him for the compliment; he assured me it wasn't meant as such and prophesied that the score would be thrown out lock, stock and barrel after the sneak preview. In fact everybody liked what I'd done and the score remained intact, but the story gives one some idea of how difficult it was to maintain any decent level of musical integrity in the Hollywood of those days.[32]

Rózsa's score for Hitchcock's 1946 *Spellbound* is probably his best-known and best-loved soundtrack. The film remains one of Hitchcock's worst. In the bizarre overheated atmosphere of a country-club clinic, psychoanalyst Ingrid Bergman falls for amnesia-prone Gregory Peck, currently masquerading as the new director of the clinic. Rózsa's score is out and out melodrama, billowing rushes of violins providing emotion where Peck and Bergman play on auto-pilot. What Rózsa does add, however, is one of the first partly electronic scores, using the Theremin to provide an interesting musical approximation of schizophrenia. The love theme bears a strong rhythmic resemblance to a theme which is used elsewhere in the film to signify murder. Gregory Peck's slow movements towards Ingrid Bergman's lips to take a lingering kiss are doubled in musical sequence structure with his later moves towards her sleeping body with a razor blade.

Whatever the problems with Hitchcock's scenario, the score to *Spellbound* is an effective piece of musical psycho-drama in its own right. Rózsa always concerned himself with reaching to the heart of whatever psychological states his characters seemed to embody at any particular point in time.

His chief innovation was to utilize the Theremin, an early example of an electronic instrument. Sounding like a sci-fi relative of the slide guitar, the Theremin was played by wavering a hand over a sounding board which directly controlled the sound oscillations. The instrument's tremulous otherworldly sound suggested all sorts of psychological fractures which of course explained its success in *Spellbound*. Rózsa then went on to use it again in *The Lost Weekend*, which in its story of an alcoholic's catharsis called for similar musical representations of a mind at the end of its tether.

[32] Christopher Palmer, *Rózsa: A Biography*, extract reprinted in *Film Music Notebook*, vol. 2, no. I, 1976, p. 8

Hollywood had never been noted for its great leaps of imagination and Rózsa was typecast to some extent during the 1940s as the musical master of the inner psyche. He scored several *films noirs*, beginning with *Double Indemnity* in 1944 and encompassing such classics as *The Killers* (1946), *A Double Life* (1948), *Kiss the Blood off My Hands* (1948) and *The Naked City* (1948). In the 1950s, having successfully scored *Ben-Hur*, Rózsa went on to work on other historical epics including *Quo Vadis* and *El Cid*.

Of all the scores recorded during what we now think of as the classic studio period of American films, probably the one that attracted the most attention (in fact over four hundred recordings exist of the title song) is the score by David Raksin to *Laura*, a film directed by Otto Preminger.

On a plot level the film itself is classic *film noir* – a detective story which revolves around the investigation of the murdered Laura. What is striking is the way in which music is used so thoroughly to allow the murdered Laura to coexist preternaturally alongside her investigators. One tune predominates – David Raksin's theme, which is used non-diegetically (in the titles) and then diegetically in a number of ways (the radio in Laura's apartment, an orchestra in a restaurant, a record that spins on a record player) to point up the different forms of dependency on the absent protagonist that others in the story have. That Raksin chose to use a popular style of music in *Laura* is perhaps largely the result of the directions he was given by director Otto Preminger and producer Daryl F. Zanuck. Raksin describes the initial meeting:

> When I first saw the picture I realized that it was really a story about love within a detective story context. I was unaware at the time that Preminger had tried to get 'Summertime', from *Porgy and Bess*, to use as the theme of the picture, but Ira Gershwin had refused permission. At our first conference Preminger announced that he was going to use [Duke Ellington's] 'Sophisticated Lady'. I suggested right away that it was wrong for the picture, whereupon Preminger said, 'What do you mean, dear boy, the wrong piece? Don't you like it?' I assured him that I liked the piece and its composer, but that did not make it the right theme for his film. He wanted to know why not, so I said, 'Because it already has so many associations in the minds of people that it will arouse feelings that are outside the frame of this picture. I also think that you have made some kind of connection between the title, Sophisticated Lady, and your conception of this girl.' At this Preminger blew a fuse and almost shouted, 'The girl is a whore – she's a whore!' . . . Isn't it odd: the idea that she slept around a little was considered to be very jazzy in those days.[33]

33 David Raksin, interviewed by Elmer Bernstein, *Film Music Notebook*, vol. 2, no. 3, 1976, p. 13

Royal S. Brown[34] has speculated that the 'Laura' theme is used repeatedly and primarily in the film to present others' idealized conceptions of her, music as fetishism. 'Laura' is a pop song which signifies those good-time-girl aspects of Laura that would have had to have been skirted around gingerly by Preminger and his writer.

Kathryn Kalinak[35] has seized upon the theme of Laura as evidence of a leitmotif system in action. What she does not comment upon, however, is that the type or genre of music, pop in *Laura*'s case, doesn't often lend itself to deployment as a leitmotif. Certainly if a single theme's repeated appearance is linked to a single character (almost regardless of how that character is signified) then there are at least similarities to a leitmotif system of musical designation.

Subsequent to the film's release there was an unprecedented demand for the music to the film. Fox, the producing studio, commissioned lyricist Johnny Mercer to write lyrics to Raksin's music and when the song was published it almost immediately became adopted as a standard by the popular singers of the period.

modern theory and the studio system

If one looks at the situation in the US from the mid-1930s to the mid-1940s one finds firstly a booming box office with a huge domestic marketplace where American movies were, as now, able to recoup relatively easily their production costs without having to rely on overseas sales. Coupled with this one finds a sophisticated studio production and distribution system where musical directors, composers, arrangers and musicians were simply kept on staff ready to reproduce whatever musical sketches were asked of them at a moment's notice. Recent studies by film researchers of a psychoanalytic disposition, amongst others Kathryn Kalinak (*Settling the Score*, Madison: 1993) and Caryl Flinn (*Strains of Utopia*, New Jersey: 1993), have focused on Hollywood studios in this period as highly patriarchal institutions purveying an extremely formulaic product in which film music serves to reinforce sexual inequalities and historical idealism through a range of practices.

Caryl Flinn points to the 'backward-looking tendency' of much American studio music of the 1930s and 1940s. One might also, of course, level a similar

---

34 Royal S. Brown, *Overtones and Undertones* (Berkeley: 1994), p. 89

35 Kathryn Kalinok, *Settling the Score* (Madison: 1993)

charge against symphonic film music in general, not specifically the product of American studios. Music in the Hollywood studio becomes a symbol of a utopian ambition, a world-making desire to refashion the everyday in the cloak of an illusory harmony, created by the music on the soundtrack. Flinn singles out *Meet Me in St Louis* (1944) for its emphasis on accessible popular tunes as befitting a film whose theme is a celebration of small-town America in the late nineteenth century and at the same time an endorsement of the onslaught of technological progress. A song such as 'The Trolley Song', with its bright cheerful melodies and folksy advertisements for young love, is also about automation in the workplace although wholly free of any comment about the implications upon labour of increased automation.

In *film noir*, Flinn finds the 'lost Utopias' of memory, pools of tranquillity in an everyday world of violent exchange. These are often rendered as flashbacks to happier times in the central character's life. *Film noir*, with its emphasis on the protagonist-as-narrator, offers up an interesting site upon which to explore some of psychoanalytic theory's basic positions on the role of the auditory realm in the formation of the subject.

Flinn interprets the flashbacks (a staple element of many *films noirs*) as sites for the reclamation of 'lost' female objects, lost musical moments. Her position, in accord with other practitioners of psychoanalytic theory, gives music and other auditory objects a central role in the subject's sense of self. Sound is registered by a child before even simple visual patterns and much of that sound can be attributed directly or indirectly to the maternal presence, the mother's voice.

Guy Rosolato[36] presents music as the means by which the maternal object is restored and the subject regains some of the 'plenitude' experienced as an infant:

> One might suggest that it [the maternal voice] is the first model of auditory pleasure and that music finds its roots and its nostalgia in an originary atmosphere, what might be called a sonorous womb, a murmuring house – or music of the spheres.

Roland Barthes presents a notion of the voice in music as possessing some sort of authentic 'grain' which has a uniquely salutary effect upon the listener. The song sung by a female voice is the way in which *film noir* transports its central characters back to a utopian space in which harmony existed before their journey into the everyday world. For Barthes[37] the vocal grain is some sort of stamp of authenticity, proof that the performer's whole

36 Guy Rosolato, 'Repetitions', *Musique-en-jeu*, no. 9, November 1972

37 Roland Barthes, 'The Grain of the Voice', in *Image, Music, Text*, ed. Stephen Heath (London: 1977), pp. 179–89

body is engaged in the act of making sound. Julia Kristeva[38] presents the concept of the maternal chora, the non-verbal language between mother and child which sustains the child and is awakened once again in certain forms of vocal music.

Flinn incorporates the above theorists to claim that film music is intrinsically appealing because it reawakens memories of childhood plenitude; however, at the same time she also points up the strong bias against female subjectivity held by many psychoanalytic theorists. The idea of music as a lost maternal object claims a strong connection between the female body and regression which in psychoanalytic terms implies a flight from reality towards some infantile state – not an appealing platform from which to try to construct a feminist theory of film music. Flinn concludes that for the Hollywood studio composers working in the 1930s and 1940s the conscious reworking of many works from the light romantic canon of the nineteenth century was a conscious attempt to evoke plenitude in their audiences and perhaps also to replenish their role as jobbing composers within a highly institutionalized system.

cracks in Utopia: experimental film in America in the 1940s

Much of the experimentation done during the 1930s and 1940s tended to be live action and grounded in character studies. Possibly one might see many of them as a reaction to the studios' styles of story-telling which were still based very much in the realm of melodrama.

Maya Deren's *Meshes of the Afternoon* (1943) and *At Land* (1944) were both to a greater or lesser degree independently produced. They are disquieting sketches in atmosphere, association and character, sometimes heavy-handed in their adoption of the then fashionable symbolic language of Jungian psychology. In *Meshes of the Afternoon* objectivity and subjectivity blur in the central female character (played by Deren herself), who sees herself in a dream return to her empty home and then commit suicide. Both films were illustrated by brief passages of baroque classical music. Two other notable films by Deren are *A Study in Choreography for Camera* (1945) and *Ritual in Transfigured Time* (1946), both of which explore a specially choreographed dance which carries across various editing cuts to produce a

[38] Julia Kristeva, *Desire in Language* (New York: 1980), p. 286

kinetic sheet of continuously rhythmic movement. The second film used professional dancers to play the parts of two characters who meet at a party and begin a romance, marked substantially by various forms of ritualized movement. Both films use music continuously as a governing principle, whereby the films turn from being merely illustrative to embodying a plastic event.

The Whitney brothers, John and James, both experimented with various forms of animation using an optical soundtrack. Their non-representational films are primarily about the movements of geometric forms in relationship to their drawing work on the sound strip. Influenced by Moholy-Nagy and Oskar Fischinger's work before the Second World War, their work held some brief interest for contemporary critics.

Another film maker as interested in the possibilities of representing dance was Thomas Bouchard. He chose unusual themes, ideally looking to produce patterns of movement that portrayed the dancers in split seconds when they lose awareness of the routine they are dancing; exploring themes such as religious ecstasy and precise isolations of movements from ethnic dance forms. Later work saw him turn towards the documentation of painting, including a collaboration with the composer Edgar Varèse to produce *The New Realism of Fernand Legér*, which in addition to Varèse's music, included a commentary by the film maker himself.

The biggest experimental splash of the 1940s in America was Hans Richter's delirious, episodic, camp film *Dreams That Money Can Buy*, based on five scenarios written by Fernand Legér, Max Ernst, Marcel Duchamp, Man Ray and Alexander Calder – a modernists' star vehicle if ever there was one. Seven characters visit a psychiatrist in heaven because they wish to shuck off the mortal coil. The psychiatrist reveals to them the images of their dreams and sends them back down to earth, happy in a kind of waking dream. Marcel Duchamp contributed a live-action version of his famous painting *Nude Descending a Staircase* to which John Cage supplied music. Darius Milhaud supplied music to a story by Man Ray, and Calder's famous mobiles are complemented by music from Varèse.

new life in Europe

In the years that followed the Second World War something quite drastic happened to the cinematic imagination. In fact cinema, the art child of the twentieth century, passed through an accelerated adolescence taking into its archives a number of key films that helped to bring it at least some way up to date with advances made fifty years earlier by literature. The addition of sound and the technical problems incurred in the second half of the 1920s did much to slow down the 'art of movement' that some of the greatest of the silent-era directors had created. By the mid-1940s American cinema was knee deep in a quagmire of formulaic melodramas produced by the main studios at an astonishing rate. Of course given such volume of production there were also a number of great films that entered the pantheon each year but, at the risk of generalizing, these films were great not as examples of kinetic cinema but because they contained fine performances or scripts or told a simple and affecting story well. Due to the industrialization that now dominated the film industry, the vast majority of releases were made for commercial gain. The studios did not create an environment in which experimentation with the basic aesthetics and politics of cinema was welcomed. The French critic Alexandre Astruc summed up this period of rupture in a famous essay in 1948:

> I call this new age of the cinema that of the Camera Stylo. This image has a very precise sense. It means that the cinema will break away little by little from the tyranny of the visual, of the image for its own sake, of the immediate anecdote, of the concrete, to become a means for writing as supple and as subtle as that of written language. No area must be barred to it. The most austere meditation, attitudes to all human works, psychology, metaphysics, ideas, passions are very precisely its province. Indeed these ideas and visions of the world are such that today the cinema alone is capable of giving them full realization.[39]

In essence what happened to the cinematic image is what had already happened within most other art fields some decades earlier. The creative impulse was to present a general shift away from the directly representational – an attempt to 'copy' something out there in the world – to an interiorized attempt to portray the psychological processes that for each of us is the world 'out there'. The antecedents were there in the modernist literature that was even by the 1940s a critical orthodoxy and in much of the quantum leap forward painting took in the first half of this century. The new cinema in Europe (particularly in Italy) was creating stories that looked more like documentaries than movies. Theatricality was out, and characters no longer drifted through scenes constructed solely to move the story on. The dramatic story became secondary to a dramatics of

[39] Alexandre Astruc, L'Ecran Français (Paris: 1948)

character and environment and the striving for a kind of psychological truth. Cinema could now be used realistically, to address an audience made up not of psychological agreement but of radical disunity. Audience and image encountered each other directly, in the uncompromising and challenging work of new directors such as Roberto Rossellini, Michelangelo Antonioni, Luchino Visconti and Federico Fellini.

The emergence of new categories of cinema was inevitable. The all-American genre of action movies – *film noir*, the Western, the screwball comedy and the social melodrama – had become to some extent parodies of themselves. The managerial virtuosity that had organized the typical Hollywood film studio as if it were turning out Fords instead of films had also been responsible for slavishly imitating its past successes. Innovation, particularly when it involved the setting aside of genres, was not normally welcomed by the studio bosses.

Italy was probably the first country to establish a distinctively original style of film in the years immediately following the war. Italy's large film industry had been left relatively intact during the war years. Furthermore, unlike Germany, Italy had maintained a resistance movement throughout the war years which itself pointed towards a national consciousness in need of popular, liberating entertainment. This entertainment is postulated by Gilles Deleuze as encompassing 'a new kind of tale, capable of including the elliptical and the unorganized'.[40] In luminous black and white photography, stories, fragmented, show apparently realistic scenes from everyday life within a wider concept of narrative and closure than the American action film. The cinematic events that reinvigorated the burnt-out shell of Italian cultural life were certainly one of the direct influences on the French New Wave which flourished a decade later.

Even a conventional story about an illicit affair, *Ossessione* (1942), became something highly original in the hands of Visconti, who manages to make his two pursued lovers both realistic and mythic at the same time. The other two breakthrough films were Rossellini's grim *Rome, Open City* (1946) and *Paisan* (1946). Neo-realism was a formal artistic rejection of the principles of Fascism, basically indistinguishable from social realism founded on broadly Marxist principles, and contained the same paradoxes – that facts remain in the service of a greater truth.

Giovanni Fusco and Alessandro Cicognini were two of the more prolific composers involved with directors such as Roberto Rossellini and Vittorio de

[40] Gilles Deleuze, *Cinema 1: Movement–Image* (London: 1989), p.211

Sica. Both composers had been active in film in Italy since the early 1930s and brought with them a sophistication and understanding of screen emotion and timing that supported rather than subverted the narrative experimentation that was taking place. Their scores, by appearing so obviously as just that, a piece of film music, helped to win audiences over to what were often stories very short on incident. One might think of Rossellini's *Voyage to Italy*, where very little actually happens on a plot level (or even in some scenes on a dialogue level) yet one is drawn into the lives and concerns of two people caught up in the ritualized behaviour of a disintegrating marriage. A failure to communicate, to act in any way, to escape from boredom, imprisons a young wife and her older husband on a country estate near Naples. The frigidity felt by the wife is everywhere contrasted with images of simple earthiness – peasants, sensuous Roman statues in a museum, cohesions with a collective past that is so elusive to modern man raised in urbanity. According to Parker Tyler:

> We look at her, we look at what she sees, we look at her looking at what she sees. Suddenly she changes before our eyes, and the continuity of reality persists as if we had not reached a dramatic climax that would normally transfigure the screen. This is what makes Rossellini seem dull to many people, and he *is* dull in the way that Bach is dull when he does not supply the dramatic emphases we would like to hear.[41]

In his first film that captured international attention, Fellini's *I Vitelloni* (1953) captures the tragi-comic lyricism of small town idling as a group of five young men in their mid- to late-twenties hold on to a kind of adolescent camaraderie in a perpetually out-of-season Rimini, playing pool, hanging around boardwalks, chasing girls and working in dead-end jobs. All of them are to a greater or lesser degree sympathetic characters yet all are spoiled, naïve and desperately provincial. The music, by Nino Rota, pitches them into this world where time is running away from them and their dreams increasingly jar with the banal realities of their everyday lives. Music is present in many social events – the beauty contest, the cinema, a carnival or two – and in these sequences displays the kind of up-tempo fairground quality often associated with the composer. The specifically local characters seem to swell into universal figures; their loneliness, their disappointments and their confusions become ours.

Rota's arrangements render the keyboard a touchstone whereby the simplest flourish makes whole worlds come into view. The keyboard

---

41 Parker Tyler, New York Film Bulletin, 27 March 1961

interpolates past times into present, possible worlds into actual. Its archetypal familiarity manages to be nostalgic and dynamic at the same time. Rota's music sometimes appears unsophisticated, fluffed out with nostalgia and too concerned with evoking powerful feelings of community. In the same way as Fellini mixes fictional and actual universes so does Rota – his key compositional device is the *ritornello*, a kind of 'gallop'. In this form, a style where the cumulative rhythms swallow up any idea of a musically present moment, is to be found Rota's acute sense of film time. Even his most apparently sentimental pieces have a relentlessly cheery efficiency to them. One is reminded again of Michel Chion's notion of a 'disinterested' music that almost mocks the characters caught in its temporal strands.

In *I Vitelloni*, and in most of the other early Fellini films with Rota scores, where the carnival-of-life metaphor is not called into operation, Rota paints spare affecting melancholy melodies which capture brilliantly the simple dreams and disappointments of the five young men. In the dark alleyways, the empty market squares and the windswept waterfront their lives are played out. The music is almost mocking, the sound of a festival drowning out these young men's struggles to gain some sort of a consciousness of their situation. The 'intellectual' of the group, Leopoldo, is lured by a visiting famous actor down to a secluded part of the beach at night. Leopoldo believes it is because the actor wishes to hear Leopoldo read extracts from his play but the actor's purposes are revealed to be sexual. During a windswept walk down to the beach together, Leopoldo's incriminatingly banal chatter as he tells of his frustrations at living in Rimini are backed only by the howl of the wind. At the moment where Leopoldo realizes why the actor has brought him to the beach, the score kicks in, gently mocking Leopoldo as he runs away. This sense of the music somehow providing or representing the conditions of psychological imprisonment that root the characters in their mundane lives is carried through to the end. Even when one of the characters finally manages to leave the town to begin a new life in Rome the music, like a curtain, sweeps into hearing as the train pulls away from the station. The final image of a young boy running along the platform waving goodbye and then turning, walking back along the tracks carefully balancing on a rail as Rota's score increases in confidence, is extremely powerful.

The sense of a character's whole world being controlled and defined by music seems to be one of the elements that served to delineate neo-realism from what had gone before. To some extent neo-realism is about the packaging of clichés – the clichés of the commonplace – and representing them as paradigms of a new way of seeing. Rota's music is itself a cliché. The

FILM MUSIC AND COPYRIGHTS

Film brought with it new categories of industrial relations – new industrial archetypes, the producer, the distributor and the exhibitor. Producers contracted with financiers and also with distributors. For much of film's history these relationships were fairly hierarchical. The major American studios controlled, from the 1920s until the late 1940s, the majority of production personnel, including composers. Everybody was fully employed and the studio owned the products of their labours, and enjoyed a mono-polistic grip on distribution. This system was not economically efficient, particularly as the studios functioned as financial intermediaries not only for their own in-house products, but for independent producers as well, borrowing money from banks to invest in specific projects. The studios sold creative products which relied on at least some degree of innovation for their success. As the American studio organizations grew larger, more aggregated and more difficult to manage, innovation was replaced by formula.

The swift rise of the film industry in many countries during the first quarter-century was directly linked to film's basic commodity form. Film was synthesized performance, but one that could be endlessly replicated. A distributor was free to order as many prints as he liked, guided only by his experience in a particular market with a particular type of film product. Costs to both him and his buyers, the theatre managers, were amortized over a succession of showings, especially as the earliest film exhibitors simply moved from place to place to maintain an audience hungry for novelty.[1]

The most radical economic aspect of film was its reproducibility. The idea of an artwork being reproducible was not in itself new. The issue of reproducibility had been troubling cultural critics since the birth of photography. Walter Benjamin[2] points towards a future museum filled not

[1] Peter Bachlin, *Histoire economique du cinéma* (Paris: 1947), p. 15

[2] Walter Benjamin, 'The Work of Art in the Age of Mechanical Reproduction', *Illuminations*, 1978

with unique art objects but with copies. Replication in traditional aesthetics is often held to devalue the original (in Benjamin's sense to deprive it of its *aura*). Film broached a number of entirely new aesthetic and economic issues, but the issue of reproducibility remained central to both fields of investigation.

Film also raised new questions about ownership and copyright. Until the rise of videotape and videodiscs, audiences could not 'own' a film. Their experience of it was controlled by the professional exhibitor. Compare this with the gramophone industry, whose rise is roughly contemporaneous. Recorded music represents an altogether different kind of commodity. The contract between manufacturer-producer and consumer is relatively straightforward. The consumer buys, for perpetuity, a copy of the master recording, and pays a price for the privilege. The record remains a stable commodity which can be bought and sold. Even if the published piece of music ('the type') is out of copyright, the recording ('the token') remains commercially valuable. The exchange value of film is realized at the point of exhibition, the ticket price alone. The consumer does not 'buy' the film in any sense, but merely 'rents' the experience by each performance. With most other forms of commodity, the process of disseminated ownership passes from manufacturer to wholesaler to retailer and finally to the consumer. Most commodities can be sold once, and this sale in effect removes the commodity from the market, but a film remains on the market for the life of each individual print. It does not require the presence of its performers and can therefore be endlessly replayed.

In the silent era, where live accompaniment was the norm, the erratic quality of those musical performances only served to emphasize the mechanical indifference of the film image to its locale as, unimpeded by a fudged cue or an out-of-tune piano, it played on, the dull mechanical whir of the projector making everything else contingent. Instability of early film oxides apart, a finished film is durable. It cannot be 'used up' and its commercial value may therefore be exploited theoretically for ever, creating revenue for the original owner who is perhaps long dead. By appreciating this characteristic of film, one can understand how it was that the film industry evolved with such momentum, and how it was that certain production, distribution and exhibition chains culminated in the major studio groups of the 1930s and 1940s, which integrated all functions.

The huge changes in economic conditions in the immediate post-war period, improvements in transportation, the baby boom and the tremendous success of television in the United States ate into cinema as a leisure category. Audiences also became more selective and box-office receipts declined sharply in the 1950s and 1960s. Many studios slipped in and out of insolvency; others responded by spinning off many of their in-house functions. The key in-house activity, the selection of scripts, was also under threat from independent producers, who developed their own and packaged them with the actors they wanted before approaching the studios for financing and distribution. This policy of contracting with independent producers did not necessarily result in cheaper films; in fact in many cases quite the opposite happened. But it did result in more marketable films that were seen by more people.[3]

The success enjoyed by a small group of film composers (typified by Henry Mancini) in the late 1950s and early 1960s did much to rearrange the basic power relations between freelance composers and what was left of the American film studio system. During the peak years of the studios, composers owned virtually nothing of the rights to their scores written under contract. Each deal approached the condition of a complete 'buy out' and all rights were handed over by the composer upon receipt of their fee. As David Raksin emotively put it in a 1974 article:

> We have put up with the most consistently inhumane work schedules within the frame of film employment and accepted the appropriation of our right to legal 'authorship' of our own music (would you believe that Twentieth Century-Fox Film Corp. is the '*author in fact*' of *Laura*?). We have only ourselves to blame. And we ought, among other things, to have been more persistent about reminding the studio barons that we are the only group among those who contribute to films who defray the costs of their own employment – by that portion of the royalties from the performance and sale of our music which goes into the studio treasuries.[4]

In the majority of countries where copyright laws exist, music rights are divided fifty-fifty between recording rights and publishing rights. Since most of the studios owned music publishing divisions they automatically retained full control of the publishing half, leaving the composer with the revenue income from airplay and record sales (mechanical royalties and performance royalties). Revenues to both the composer and the publisher are then administered through a collection society such as ASCAP in the USA and MCPS in the UK.

Since many of the newer alliances between composers and film makers

---

[3] James Robins, 'Organization as Strategy: Restructuring Production in the Film Industry', *Strategic Management Journal*, vol. 14, 1993, p. 115

[4] David Raksin, 'Whatever Happened to Film Music', *Film Music Notebook*, Fall 1974, p. 24

were forged through independent production companies the studios became relegated to the position of distributor rather than creator of a finished product. Mancini's early relationship with Blake Edwards' independent production outfit enabled him to retain music publishing rights and to set up his own publishing company since an independent producer in most cases did not have the infrastructure to handle collection and administration of music rights.

In the eyes of the law (and also in that of philosophical treatises on individuals and copyrights), there persists the idea that composers own the rights to something they create. Over the past hundred years there has been an expansion of intellectual property laws to encompass almost every product of intellectual labour. Indeed, as the US constitution illustrates, one might argue that these property rights were invented to encourage investment in intellectual labour. Article 1, Section 8, clause 8:

> To promote the Progress of Science and useful Arts, by securing for limited Times
> to Authors and Inventors the exclusive Right to their Writings and Discoveries.

Many studios, however, having invested in composers' endeavours, denied to them the right to use their music in any other context. In extreme cases this could lead to ridiculous situations where composers were denied the right to perform in public a score they had written because they no longer controlled the rights. The more high-profile and powerful composers in the US film industry, Burt Bacharach, Henry Mancini, Elmer Bernstein and Leonard Rosenman, have consistently lobbied for some kind of limitation on the rights that studios acquire when contracting a composer. Bernstein has argued that a studio should be able to acquire solely the rights to use a particular piece of music in the film, and no further rights.

From the composer's perspective the inability to access old scores for the purposes of re-recording for a modern commercial release has led to, in certain cases, real impoverishment of the composer, and to the continuing lowly status of much film music that is not pop-derived. Since copyright laws allow for the employer to construe themselves as authors of creative works in cases where an employer-employee relationship exists, Bernstein questions the very status of these labour relations:

> At some point we must question whether a creative artist can ever be construed to
> be an individual who works under direction and supervision, and whose creativity
> falls within fixed hours and working conditions. The artist in our society is in fact a
> person producing an art product which another individual can either rent or buy.[5]

[5] Elmer Bernstein, *Film Music Notebook*, vol. 2, no. 1, 1976, p. 33

In the early 1950s a group of film composers attempted to represent themselves collectively through a trade guild. The action was filed with the US Labor Relations Board, who held that the composers were not technically employees of the film studios:

> Where the person for whom the services are performed retains the right to control the manner and means by which the result is to be accomplished, the relationship is one of employment. While on the other hand, where control is reserved only as to the result sought, the relationship is that of an independent contractor.[6]

This ambiguity surrounding the employment status of a film composer is compounded by the impracticality of specifying working hours in any employment contract, although the schedules and deadlines given to composers became increasingly tight in the 1950s and 1960s, as studios tried desperately to reduce production budgets.

[6] 117 NLRB 13 (1957), quoted ibid., p. 34

SOUND EVOLUTION: THE IMPACT OF RECORDING TECHNOLOGY

By 1950, magnetic tape had been in use as the main mastering system for over a decade. Its ease of use as a medium had produced a new generation of recording producers who were able to personalize the recording technology to such a degree that whole new categories of recording artists emerged. In commercial terms, the impact of vocal pop music was the revolution that turned the recorded disc from a reference tool into a mass leisure product. Record producers were able to 'manufacture' performers as well as just make records. In much the same way, by 1970 the category of 'sound designer' began to make an appearance on the list of film credits. Photography as an activity and more significantly as an industry had become irrevocably associated with music. As it quickly became a commodity, music made fortunes and with an expanding new teenage market, music became the main preoccupation of the audio industry. Radio, hand in hand with the mass availability of records, boosted the stature of the DJ to cultural harbinger and arbiter of the dissemination of music to the masses. Music ruled the roost and although radio drama had flourished since the 1930s and in some cases had become a highly creative medium (one might think of the Mercury Theatre's *War of the Worlds*) it was the cinema that led phonography into new fields of experimentation.

The 1950s was a dynamic period in terms of the soundtrack. Not since the 1920s had there been such an intense, industry-wide search for innovative ways to bolster cinema's sagging audiences. Stereo sound of an inferior sort finally emerged from the sound laboratories of Westrex in 1954, when John Frayne demonstrated a photographic (optical) stereo process. The experiment was not a success, however, since many within the industry were already showing more interest in the developing technologies that used magnetic sound. Projection systems were almost as numerous as the studios, and each was fully proprietary.

Film sound technology had been steadily advancing since the 1940s but new developments were not necessarily taken up by the movie theatres. The switch to wide-screen presentation in many of the best cinemas in the West throughout the 1950s also brought a new generation of films recorded with magnetic stereo sound, a superior recording method designed to displace the rule of the optical soundtrack. In terms of film sound, stereo recording has generally meant sound distributed between four channels, three across the width of the screen and a fourth (surround) channel which delivers a sound field from the rear of the auditorium. It is the surround channel that allows certain kinds of atmospheres to be created 'around' the audience, since it is not concerned with supplying specifically directional information (although it can of course supply this if necessary). In the early stages of stereo recording these four channels appeared on the film strip itself as four magnetic stripes, two on each side of the 35mm film. This proved an expensive mastering process since the magnetic coating had to be applied after the film itself was printed and then allowed literally to hang up and dry before being applied along the whole length of the film. Sound then had to be re-recorded end to end.

Despite its cost and delicate nature, magnetic sound was a vastly superior recording process, bringing with it greatly expanded frequency ranges, better signal-to-noise ratios and better dynamics to cope with amplification. The two main magnetic systems adopted were Twentieth Century-Fox's four-track 35mm CinemaScope system, introduced for *The Robe*, and the six track Todd-AO system used for 70mm films such as *Around the World in 80 Days* and *Oklahoma!*

Whilst a number of films were recorded using the magnetic soundtrack during the late 1950s the majority of actual release prints which were shipped out to the all-important regional movie theatres were still printed with optical soundtracks. The true impact of this innovative recording technology was curtailed by the reluctance of theatre owners to upgrade their projection equipment to cope with yet another change of exhibition standards hoisted upon them by a Hollywood forever trying to innovate itself away from the threat of television. There is some dispute over which system, magnetic or optical, was the cheaper system to use. William Lafferty[1] reports that the magnetic process was cheaper and that the savings could be anything up to eighty-five per cent of the costs of processing and printing optically soundtracked film material, yet this seems to be strongly

[1] William Lafferty, 'The Early Development of Magnetic Sound Recording in Broadcasting and Motion Pictures 1928–1950', Ph.D. thesis, Northwestern University, 1981

contested by other sources, for example Tony Spath and Dave Harries of Dolby Labs.[2] Certainly the optical process was a simpler and more robust process, and later innovations such as the Dolby systems from the late 1960s onwards did much to improve sound quality, but the sheer expense of installing the necessary sound projection equipment in the average movie house resulted in the early demise of stereo magnetic sound by about 1960. John Belton comments:

> Fox insisted on a stereo-only policy and rented CinemaScope films only to those theatres equipped to show them in stereo. But when other studios using the CinemaScope process began to make prints available in an ersatz optical stereo format known as Perspecta Sound and in monaural optical versions, Fox relented and released films with dual, magnetic and optical, soundtracks. As a result of this concession to exhibitor complaints about cost, only one quarter of all movie theatres around the world ever installed stereo magnetic equipment.[3]

Failing to price their innovation in step with the market sealed the fate of magnetic stereo sound systems. Whilst this may have been a historical injustice as John Belton claims, it was nevertheless a fatal mistake. At the time, cinemas were in a period of consolidation trying to remain open in the face of falling audiences worldwide. It is not surprising that many theatre owners resisted the building of new sound installations, when they received little in the way of financial support for these systems from the main film producers. Because of the failure of small theatre owners to adapt to stereo sound, filmgoers were obliged in most locations to watch a mono version of what was very often a stereo film. Something of a two-tier exhibition circuit existed for a while, particularly in urban areas where audiences could choose whether to see the mono or stereo version of a film – and ticket prices naturally reflected the perceived difference in quality. A film such as *The Robe* (1954) managed to pull in some impressive figures from both the prestige circuit in its magnetic stereo sound version and the smaller mono-equipped theatres. But the bulk of the $24.6 million box-office gross that it earned was from the stereo-equipped theatres. This would have been due to a carefully planned release programme targeted at first-run, premier-quality cinemas, precisely those that would have made the jump to fitting magnetic stereo sound systems.

Stereo sound, and its variant 'surround sound', had more or less vanished

[2] Tony Spath and Dave Harries, 'Music Mixing for Dolby Stereo', *Studio Sound*, Ocotober 1989

[3] John Belton, '1950s Magnetic Sound: The Frozen Revolution', in *Sound Theory, Sound Practice*, ed. Rick Altman (New York: 1992)

from the exhibition circuits of America and Europe by 1960, but both phenomena did much to extend the notion of 'off-screen' space. With speakers placed at the extreme right and left in a theatre, voices (heavenly voices in the case of *The Robe*) really could come from wherever the sound engineer wished them to come from. Whilst stereo sound failed on the exhibition circuit, the magnetic system of recording sound, backed by the muscle of America's electrical giants, lasted. A two-tier system of sound recording had emerged; during production, magnetic tape was favoured because of its many advantages (instant playback being one of the main ones), whilst the optical soundtrack remained the standard method of combining pictures and sound on the finished print which was distributed to the cinema circuits.

More and more directors were investigating the smaller production crews made possible by the new technologies available in cameras and particularly in sound recording. The advent of the Nagra III recorder in 1958 brought a new freedom to portable sound recordings. Sound also became multi-channelled, making possible a greater dimension of screen realism, which in turn dictated the aesthetic demands of many film makers who strove for greater and greater sonic fidelity. Multi-channel recordings made possible the depiction of a precisely choreographed audio 'depth', minutely obeying the strictures of time and space. With more and more time being spent on sound co-ordination during post-production, best practice in sound dubbing became a matter of filling out the ambiguities of the picture with the hard 'facts' of sound recordings.

MUSIC EVOLUTION: NEW DIRECTIONS IN ORCHESTRAL MUSIC IN THE 1950s

By the 1950s there were perhaps three new directions in which concert music was being steered by its more forward-thinking exponents. First, there was the continuing story of musical serialism, an experiment begun some three decades earlier and exemplified in the work of American composer Milton Babbitt and his attempts to combine a highly rigorous approach to composition with the benefits of new emerging computer technologies. Second, there was a growing interest in the role of chance in musical composition – as expressed in works by John Cage such as *Music of Changes* or *Imaginary Landscape No. 4*, both being performed for the first time in 1951. This method of composition was to influence many European composers, principally Pierre Boulez and Karlheinz Stockhausen. Third, and just as important since it really began to influence everything else in music, was the invention and legitimization of electronic music. There had been serious musical works before that had hinted at the power of electronics. Messiaen's *Turangalila* Symphony from 1946 had used the Ondes Martenot organ in certain passages; Edgar Varèse had incorporated pre-recorded discs into the 1925 *Intégrales*. But the technology had not been easily available for others to follow up on these promising starts.

Another development was the experiments of the French composer and scholar Pierre Schaeffer into an approach to music he labelled *musique concrète*. The experiments began with the simple incorporation of musical or natural sounds from gramophone records into larger compositions. These sound sources might be played backwards, speeded up, slowed down or whatever the composer desired. With the introduction of magnetic tape around 1950, Schaeffer's experiments could become more advanced, since it was now easier to record new sounds and to distort or alter old ones. Composition for Schaeffer becomes more like an art of selection, with each sound chosen and distorted and then rearranged to form the finished piece. A composition such as *A Man Alone* is typical of Schaeffer. The piece is divided up into a number of self-contained soundscapes, called 'movements' (out of deference perhaps to musical tradition), lasting in total around twenty minutes and containing sections with descriptive titles such as 'Partita', 'Scherzo', 'Erotica' and so on.

Against a musical background that was steadfastly moving away from large-scale compositions for symphony orchestras, the shedding by the American studios of their music departments (or at least large parts of them) did much to influence the style of film music internationally. With the rise of the independent producer, arrangements were written for smaller and smaller units of musicians. In the case of jazz this was obviously a happy convenience but for more traditional forms of musical scoring the results were mixed.

The innovators, such as the key directors of the French New Wave, profited from greater control over the musical solutions to their own works. Films such as *Hiroshima, mon amour* (1959) achieved an astonishing fusion of musical styles, avoiding any kind of musical-dramatic determinism. Indeed, this freedom from many of the conventions surrounding music cues has done much to plant the notion that these films somehow possess more liberty than others. It was more that certain French films of the 1950s integrated music to such a degree as a basic and essential constituent of the soundtrack that, combined with the new fluid picture-language, even the neo-romantic themes seemed new.

Hiroshima, mon amour, *Alphaville* (1960) and *Last Year at Marienbad* (1961) all make extensive use of architecture as an element of picture composition and by analogy in a self-consciously 'structural' deployment of music. Music is very often used referentially in the films of New Wave directors such as Alain Robbe-Grillet, Alain Resnais, Jean-Luc Godard and François Truffaut. Music prefigures action, and introduces irony, thus becoming an element of style. Robbe-Grillet recently claimed[1] that the very odd baroque-tinged organ music in *Last Year at Marienbad* by Francis Seyrig (brother of the film's star, Delphine Seyrig) was put on to the film at a late stage in post-production as a crowd pleaser. Robbe-Grillet, who wrote the film for Alain Resnais to direct, had originally wanted to populate the film with bizarre noises recorded on location and distorted during the film's sound-mixing, but this was thought likely to confuse the audience. The

[1] Alain Robbe-Grillet interview, Norwegian Film Institute, Oslo, 6 May 1996

effect would have been a dramatically divided sonic world, split between the soft, deep carpeted interiors of the baroque hotel where the story is set and the exterior world of fountains, gravel drives and wind. Instead, Seyrig's score alternates in the opening sequences between an outrageous, mass-like baroque fugue for organ and a romantically charged series of string-led orchestral progressions which foreground the narrator's voice, guiding us through the empty splendour of a magnificent hotel. Whilst the music remains always tonal there are hints of an inner discord which is never fully incorporated. Neither of the musical forms seems really to inhabit the film but rather floats on the surface like a glaze. As the camera enters the populated chambers and ballrooms of the hotel, the harmonic language changes and the music becomes much less overtly romantic. The tempo noticeably decreases as strings give way to a sonorous organ as the camera carries us through room after room. The effect is entirely seductive in combination with the images, but also disorientating in a film where characters seem imprisoned not only spatially but also temporally within the vast hotel.

The music used in many of the New Wave films embodies a particularly European take on musical romanticism. François Truffaut's whimsical, autobiographical take on childhood, *Les 400 coups* (1958), uses music by Jean Constantin, who had composed or performed hundreds of successful songs and who embodies French post-war musical life through interpretations by Yves Montand and Edith Piaf. Truffaut probably saw Constantin's music as symbolizing much of his own childhood. The small amount of music which Constantin provided for the film effortlessly evoked nostalgia whilst becoming immediately popular with the pop and jazz orchestrations that were the composer's trademark. Constantin even turned the main theme of the film into a song, 'Comment voulez-vouz?', which was released in advance of the film.

Antoine Duhamel was another New Wave collaborator, with certain compositional similarities to Bernard Herrmann. Duhamel worked with Truffaut, Godard, Alexandre Astruc and Claude Chabrol. For Truffaut's 1968 *Baisers volés*, Duhamel was obliged to construct a score around part of the film's main title theme, a popular song, 'Que reste-t-il de nos amours?', by the singer Charles Trenet, which, in varying forms, is heard some twelve times during the film and serves to comment upon Truffaut's *alter ego*, the long-running character Antoine Doinel.

The music supplied by Georges Delerue to many of Truffaut's later films is as sparing (as little as eight minutes in *L'Amour en fuite*), but evokes the spirit of intense longing so often associated with Truffaut's gallery of male protagonists. Interestingly, before *L'Amour en fuite* (1978), Truffaut had chosen to work with Duhamel for several films before returning to Delerue. *L'Amour en fuite* continues the biography of the character who started life in *Les 400 coups* and contains a small number of flashback scenes to earlier films scored by Duhamel, but on this occasion the original music in the earlier films is excluded.

The most notable difference from the Hollywood tradition of romanticism is that orchestral flourishes are not generally used to track movement but rather to set a scene; in this sense, certain cues by composers such as Delerue or Duhamel are almost a pastiche of Hollywood film music, whilst at the same time subscribing totally to the emotional pull of such music. In Jean-Luc Godard's *Alphaville* (1960), the musical allusions (mainly melodramatic orchestral cues) are like a musical comment on the kind of *film noir* scores that Miklós Rózsa was turning out in the 1940s and at the same time serve to locate us back in the film's narrative at points where Godard's dramatic experimentation seems to be getting out of hand. Purporting to reveal what is 'hidden' by society, the musical cues in *Alphaville* are a form of invocation, a calling down of the spirits of the American B-movie of the 1940s, and at the same time an exposure of some of the deeper political values of the industry in America that produced those films.

Other notable French soundtracks of the period were Georges Auric's neo-romantic flourish to Cocteau's dazzling *Orphée* (1950), and various soundtracks by Georges van Parys, a real veteran of the French cinema (whose first work was *Le Million* for René Clair in 1930), specifically *French Can-Can* (1954), *Les Grandes manœuvres* (1955) and *L'Homme à l'imperméable* (1956).

Other strains of musical modernism emerged from countries such as Sweden and Denmark. Ingmar Bergman's *The Seventh Seal* (1958) was scored by Erik Nordgren and marks a change in the way in which the director incorporated music into his films, taking a less seductive path and allowing the music to undertake a more complex relationship with the on-screen action. The film is set in medieval Sweden and concerns a chess game which a knight plays with Death, and the people whose lives he briefly passes through. The structure is highly plastic and owes something to the graphic narrative style of Kurosawa. Music is used sparingly. In the opening sequences, a passage from the Bible is narrated over pictures of a stark coastline in high contrast. The music opens as a discordant choral scream as the text (from Revelations) is read. Black and white tonalities (aesthetic and moral) figure throughout the film and the music reflects this. At one moment it offers a sweetly caressing chorale, sung with only vague allusions to any kind of medieval song structure, whilst at other times the instrumental passages, almost always used as very short ten-to-twenty-second cues, are violently uncompromising.

Chiefly, Nordgren's work for Bergman on *The Seventh Seal* avoids any real kind of allusion to historical realism and concentrates instead on rhythmic experimentation producing a language of phrases which is highly energetic, reminiscent of Stravinsky or Scriabin. Nordgren's slowly evolving luminous passages full of surprising triadic references offset by angular non-tonal undertones also mark indelibly some of Bergman's most famous mid-period films: *Wild Strawberries* (1958), *The Virgin Spring* (1959) and *The Magician* (1960).

It was during the 1950s that Japanese films, led chiefly by the output of master directors such as Mizoguchi, Kurosawa and Ozu, broke through to an international audience. Composers such as Taknashi Matsuyama (*Rashomon*, 1951) and Masuru Sato (*Throne of Blood*, *The Lower Depths*, 1957; *Yojimbo*, 1961) fused Eastern concepts of percussion with Western concepts of harmonics to great effect.

Mizoguchi's *The Crucified Lovers* (1954) boasted a superb score by Fumio Hayasaka and remains one of the decade's most successful integrations of music, dialogue and sound effects. The traditional Japanese style of percussion is abrupt and often borders on pure sound effect, which surely gives the composers a greater flexibility divorced from the more traditional Western forms of melody and harmony. Coupled with the spectacular graphic style that was so emergent in Japanese cinema during the 1950s, Mizoguchi and Hayasaka create an immersive flow of music that resembles sound effect. In a scene where the two lovers are betrayed, we follow the informer running away (from the camera) into the middle distance at which point a musical motif softly played on a stringed zither-like instrument appears in auditory 'close-up'. It functions as a commentary on the betrayal itself, an intrusion by an invisible narrator. Music also imitates sound effects. In the scene in which two characters fight in a thicket of bamboo, Hayasaka provides sharp percussive clusters also made on bamboo instruments. Noël Burch has claimed that it is the very construction of not only Japanese music but also the language itself that sets up a strange mutuality that allows each to integrate with the other so successfully.

The Japanese tradition of theatre music, Noh, and the folk music instrumentation of the *koto*, *shamisen* and the *shakuhachi* combined exotically with influences clearly derived from Western avant-garde traditions. One might think of the *Sprechgesang* of Schoenberg, for example. In Noh drama the concept of *parlando* (an imitation of the spoken tone of a voice) is important and in Japanese concert music of the 1950s this convention became open to new interpretations which percolated through to techniques adopted by film music composers. Toshiru Mayuzumi's 1958 symphonic work *Nirvana* juxtaposes texts performed in a *parlando* style with dazzling, almost aleatory explosions of percussive energy.

Perhaps the most original and distinctive of all Japanese film music composers is Toru Takemitsu, whose work began in the early 1960s and is exemplified in *Woman in the Dunes* (1964). Here real instruments are used but are radically altered during the recording process to achieve a psychological pitch of dream-like intensity, music imitating the slow relentless drift of the ever present sand that imprisons the two main characters. Takemitsu's work begins often from the sustained exploration of a single sound – the dampened chord of a piano, for instance – and is then expanded towards a kind of vertically integrated score that seems to weave across the fabric of the film's narrative rather than to track action in a more traditional linear form. His work has been described as 'slashing the monotony' of film music, which it does by its minimalist approach. It seems probable that Takemitsu was a formative influence on Ennio Morricone in the way that highly unusual instrumental textures are placed together in a very sparing way. Takemitsu's approach to film scoring often seems to proceed from a non-dramatic initial premise:

> Film music is like a passport . . . a visa offering the composer complete freedom. Whenever I go abroad, even though I don't understand a word of the language, I often head straight for a movie theatre because in seeing a film I sense something about the people there. In movies I can see their real lives and sense their inner lives as I watch the images unfold on the screen. Even without language I feel that I can understand them – a musical way of understanding.[2]

Takemitsu's central preoccupation was the timing and placement of music. He himself drew parallels between the aesthetics of Japanese gardening and landscape painting and the way in which he approached the 'spotting' of his films. Throughout the 1960s Takemitsu sought to integrate more traditional Japanese instruments into his film scores; *Kwaidan* (1964) features an extended river battle scene in which rival armies of troops

2 Toru Takemitsu, quoted in *Music for the Movies: Toru Takemitsu*, a documentary by NHK and La Sept/Arte, 1994

attempt to win control of a river while perched uneasily in small wooden barges gridlocked together in watery combat. The sequence which cuts away frequently to panning shots over an ancient landscape tapestry showing much the same kind of scene is marked by the use of a plucked bow set against discordant percussive clusters.

From India the films of Satyajit Ray, particularly the superb 'Apu' trilogy, brought the exotic sounds of Ravi Shankar (*The World of Apu*, 1959) to a Western audience. A distinctive style of Indian film music has evolved since the 1930s and is derived from a number of sources, both Western and Indian. Whilst Shankar is not a film music specialist but a major Indian composer, in his film work can be found elements of classical, folk and devotional music. One can also detect the influence of Western popular music, particularly in the vocal technique of the singers. This contrasts with the typically Indian feel for ornate melodies which are not based upon harmonic progressions, but where harmonies are incidental. As the genre has developed, attempts have been made to work in harmony and counterpoint, but in a fairly unsophisticated way. As time went on Ray, like his contemporary Ingmar Bergman, integrated Western classical music into his films, principally Bach and Mozart.

In the former Soviet Union and in the Eastern Bloc countries the emphasis was on social realism. The Russian economy was directed towards priorities other than film and by 1952 annual production had dropped to as few as five films a year. In this least inspiring period of Russian cinema the subjects were predictable and in the main hagiographic. Patriotic themes included the positive impact of technology, war heroism or politically reworked stagings of traditional Russian folk tales or operettas. As Stalin's (he was known in his 'cultural' mode as 'The Spectator') public paranoia grew, he dared less and less to venture out to Moscow theatres and filmed records were made of many new plays to be screened for him in private. This, of course, ate into the state budgets for film making. In 1953 alone, some twenty of these filmed performances were made.

In East Germany the DEFA organization promoted pretty much the party line but isolated moments of interest emerged, such as *Our Daily Bread* (1947), scored by Hanns Eisler, a *Trümmerfilm* or 'film from the rubble', about a working-class family engaged in the struggle to rebuild their country. In Czechoslovakia animation began to flourish under state support and Jiri Trnka's feature-length puppet film *The Czech Year* (1947) with a soundtrack by Josef Trojan was released to a generally positive international reaction.

A small number of British films attempted to create, in their use of music, some kind of representation of other cultures: Elizabeth Lutyens score for *World without End*, William Alwyn's score for *Three Dawns to Sydney* and, most famously, the zither music featured in *The Third Man*, which summoned up a feeling of romantic nostalgia for the city of Vienna, personifying the city through the sound of the instrument. One of the most distinctive and unusual British soundtrack recordings of the period was based on the bizarre machine processes conjured up by director Alexander Mackendrick for his Ealing comedy *The Man in the White Suit* (1950). Beginning with a jazz record by Red Nichols and the Five Pennies, Mackendrick describes the process:

> I got the sound department to mark on a huge piece of graph paper every drum beat, every note of the clarinet and bass. So then they knew I was mad. But we replaced the notes with sound effects – such as blowing a trumpet under water, which sounds very vulgar and very funny. Then we reconstituted the whole thing on five tracks and mixed them – with the results that you know. I think there are too few directors who really love the soundtrack and the imaginative use of sound.[3]

In the USA, aside from the tremendous inroads made by jazz into the world of film soundtracks, there were two other tendencies which were apparent by the 1950s. One was the willingness of American composers to try out some of the more difficult aspects of European concert music as inspirations for their film work; the other, the rise in the number of serious composers who were now interested in picking up at least the occasional piece of work in the film industry.

One might think of Leonard Rosenman's serially inspired score to the 1955 thriller *The Cobweb*, which broke new ground when it emerged, in contrast to his music for *East of Eden*, a Cain and Abel update set in the Midwest farmland the year before, with its sinewy melodies reminiscent of the aching romanticism and innocence of Samuel Barber. In *The Cobweb*, Rosenman seems to have been aiming at a kind of expressionism, on the basis that certain events in the film are set in an insane asylum and that using serial music to control the pitch of the notes seemed to provide a suitable representation of neurosis. Most of the score is written for a small chamber-style orchestra, although the title music was written for piano and orchestra, each miked separately according to Roy Prendergast's[4] analysis of the score, so that it was possible to exercise control over the relative levels during the recording process (as the piano was to vary in pitch so much).

3 'Alexander Mackendrick at Quimper', *Sight & Sound*, Summer 1990, p. 149

4 Roy M. Prendergast, *Film Music: A Neglected Art*, (New York: 1975), p. 120

Leonard Bernstein's score to *On the Waterfront* seemed to break many precedents of film-scoring technique. It's an immensely powerful score which almost seems to ride parallel along the length of the film as a separate dramatic element in its own right, which is unfortunately its biggest problem. Bernstein's iconoclastic approach to film scoring is evident throughout, so much so that in places it seems to work against the dramatic intent of the story. The opening sequence is marked by a crescendo of percussive effects, yet all we actually see are some panning shots around the dock area with men loading and unloading crates. Other sequences segue the woodwind textures of the main theme into bizarre skits, such as a speeded-up version of 'Here Comes the Bride' as the main characters enter a drunken wedding party. Bernstein's music virtually ignores the prerogatives of dialogue and consequently is simply turned up and down in volume in the final sound mix each time a character speaks. There are occasional moments, however, where Bernstein's inexperience as a film composer produces some unexpected innovation. At a point where the main characters kiss, the swelling strings cease and the kiss itself occurs without music, lending the scene some poignancy.

On the Beach (1959), a popular anti-nuclear thriller, has a score by Ernest Gold, a veteran of numerous B-movies What is fascinating about the score is that it consists almost entirely of variations on the popular song 'Waltzing Matilda'. As the film opens we see a shot of the submarine surfacing as a single trumpet introduces the Matilda theme, which then broadens out into an orchestral version of the same song. The theme is used in a number of different ways throughout the film: as a 'Mickey-Mousing' device in a beach scene, where Peter and Mary Holmes playfully romp in the sand; in a lively bouncing rendition as another character walks along a railway platform; and even as a signal to foreboding when supplemented by a chromatic bass. Stanley Kramer, the director, seems to have picked 'Waltzing Matilda' because the story is set in Australia and the song is more or less regarded as their second national anthem. Its simple but dignified melody is easily associated with the kind of die-hard survivalism one might imagine the survivors of a nuclear war to possess. In the remaining musical themes, Gold experiments with 'shock chords' to pronounced effect as we survey the empty city centre of San Francisco which had once teemed with people.

SCORING HISTORY

As cinema audiences declined throughout the 1950s a number of attempts were made by different studios to deliver the kind of epic historical drama pioneered by D. W. Griffith. On a sprawling cinematic canvas key events from the history of Western civilization were conflated and re-imagined in the formulaic codings of the conventional Hollywood romance. *The Robe* took the story of the Passion and reworked its themes through the tale of a Roman soldier present at the crucifixion, who subsequently converts to Christianity and leads a guerrilla-like band of fellow worshippers who have assumed a subterranean existence to avoid further persecution by the Romans. With a soundtrack by Alfred Newman, *The Robe* is heavily populated by heavenly choirs and symphonic flourishes in the usual overbearing Newman style. Introducing a wordless chorus (in the manner of Debussy's *Les Sirènes*) Newman does manage to produce some memorable accompaniments, although his technique is primarily that of mood setting, since he rarely makes any attempts to develop any kind of leitmotif approach.

Part of the problem with scoring historical films is the difficulty of being in any way authentic with the music. A basic stylistic choice must be made by the composer at the start of the assignment. Often an odd kind of musical language emerges that isn't historically accurate but retains a musical logic and discipline of parts, allowing for a variety of treatments of the main themes in the score. This dilemma was obviously felt more keenly by some composers than others. Miklós Rózsa, for example, expended considerable energy in tracking down first-century-BC Roman (actually purloined Greek and Hebrew music) sources as the basis for his score to *Quo Vadis?*, even at the cost of sacrificing some of his traditional style:

> The dramatic music of *Quo Vadis?* is much less polyphonic than my previous film
> scores for the only reason that extended polyphony would have clashed
> anachronistically with monodic music performed on-scene throughout the picture.[1]

Since then more value has been placed upon historically authentic recordings of pre-twentieth-century music, which has affected approaches to film music. One might argue that this tendency has been nurtured by the theory and practice of musicology, whose archaeological approach has tended to be driven by a search for authenticity. Whether or not film music should attempt to reproduce music from a historical period is a difficult question to answer in absolute terms. In many cases it is tempting to say that it depends upon the artistic intent of the film maker, but at the same time there seem to be some basic principles that demarcate successful renderings of historical music from unsuccessful ones.

In the case of a real historical musical work, authenticity seems closely linked to reproducing the intentions of the composer. Alain Corneau's *Tous les Matins du Monde* (1992) takes this very tension as the subject of its story, which is set in seventeenth-century France and tells the story of the relationship across a lifetime of two musicians, a master, Sainte Colombe, and his pupil, Marin Marais. The film's theme is the devotional nature of musical performance and the perfection of technique. Marais, a successful court musician at the Palace of Versailles, mourns the memory of his teacher, who chose a life of ascetic isolation, and scorned the success of his pupil. Since both personalities were real rather than fictional entities, much of the music heard in the film consists of improvisations for bass viol on pieces composed by Marais, but there are also pieces heard through performance by composers contemporary to Marais such as Couperin and Lully. Corneau and his musical consultant Jean-Louis Charbonnier scrupulously preserve the sparse feel of authentic performances of the period and at the same time mythologize the central characters. Corneau also includes a non-diegetic score by the contemporary Spanish composer Jordi Savall, which imitates the style of Marais and Couperin. The original score interweaves well with the original pieces, although the self-consciously low-key solo performances and painterly *mise-en-scène* create a sense of aesthetic self-absorption that contrasts with what is basically a melodrama.

To reconstruct a historical piece of music also involves selecting the optimal version of that work for the contemporary audience. Clearly it is impossible to hear a piece of historical music in quite the way that it was heard

---

[1] Miklós Rózsa, 'Quo Vadis?', *Film and TV Music*, 11, 4 November 1951

by audiences at the time it was composed. Modern audiences have different musical ears and different autobiographies as listeners. We filter cultural history constantly; what we now consider to be a masterpiece of its time (as well as our own) would not always have been popular with its contemporary audiences. It is the performance of historical music that is possible to reconstruct, not our own identities as late-twentieth-century listeners.

The musical performances that make up the greater part of *The Chronicle of Anna Magdalena Bach* (1968) by Jean-Marie Straub illustrate the tedium to modern ears of historically accurate performances. Leaving aside Straub's highly systematized aesthetic ideas for his film, the music itself of a biographized Bach performing various pieces of his own music in undifferentiated concert settings is dull and pedantic.

In the case of music which attempts to approximate to a sense of musical period, although being an entirely new piece, film composers tend to trade on popular ideas of authenticity plundered from musicology. Certain instrumental sounds become synonymous with certain cultures and certain eras. This becomes a kind of stylistic shorthand which cinema audiences absorb and accept without even realizing it.

Miklós Rózsa's later work on *Ben-Hur* (1959) reuses some of the source materials uncovered for *Quo Vadis?*. The opening prelude celebrates the might of the Roman Empire as we open on a panoramic view of a triumphal march by Roman legions through the capital. As we move closer into the procession and pick out the character of Ben-Hur, the Christian slave, a more tender theme opens up and engulfs the main march. Woodwinds with chimes flourish momentarily and then we hear Esther's passionate theme (she is Ben-Hur's romantic interest) before returning to the main theme.

This personification device, a differentiation between the pomposity of the surrounding environment and the spiritual nature of Ben-Hur's inner strength, is restated throughout the film, a relationship of dual orbits, each theme pregnant with its opposition.

Personal opposition between protagonist and antagonist expressed in musical leitmotifs is common in the Hollywood epic film scores of the 1950s. In their good-natured reinterpretations of history as a pageant of phenomenal events, the American historical epics of the 1950s (and also the historical epics of the silent era) reduce vast arenas of endeavour and conflict to simple dramatic oppositions between duelling individuals.

Alex North side-stepped the question of authenticity by moving away from the traditional approaches when he scored *Spartacus*. North was perhaps an unusual choice since much of his previous film work had been jazz-inspired. His approach was strikingly modern, with little attempt to conjure up any direct musical allusions to the ancient world. He opted for a musical portrayal of the cruelty of the Roman world in which Spartacus the slave lived. North even used an ondoline, a French electronic instrument, to suggest a totalitarian authority:

> I wanted to write music that would interpret the past in terms of the present . . . I prefer not to quote authentic material as such but to sop up everything relevant I can find. In *Spartacus* I tried for a deliberately cold and barbaric quality, avoiding strings until the thirteenth reel, when the love story begins to blossom between Kirk Douglas and Jean Simmons. I relied on combinations of brass, woodwinds, and some quite unusual and exotic percussion – for instance I underscored a party scene with novachord, vibes, marimba, boobams, crotales, fixed piano, harp, lute, guitar, sleigh bells (various pitches) and Chinese tree bell.[2]

As for the biblical epics, films such as *King of Kings* (1961) and *The Greatest Story Ever Told* (1965), where the figure and life of Christ were not merely adjuncts (as in *Ben-Hur* and *The Robe*) but the centrepiece, the music soothed the demonstrators protesting against a celluloid depiction of Christ. Both films present an orthodox Christian picture of Christ, despite the fact that *The Greatest Story Ever Told* was shot in Utah in the winter with a crowd of Navajo Native Americans as extras. Alfred Newman's score for the film is a remarkably restrained piece of work, opting to portray the passion of Christ the individual rather than the world in which he lived. Newman makes expert use of strings, often allowing them to carry the orchestra. Brass is used as a counter: for example, on the journey as Christ and his disciples begin their travelling ministry. Some stirring choral sequences are also used, most notably in the march up the hill towards the inevitable crucifixion. For the resurrection, interestingly Newman opts to use a sequence from Handel's *Messiah*: the contrast is not jarring, a tribute to Newman's skills as an arranger and composer. *King of Kings*, with its score by Miklós Rózsa, called for the composer to write music to his third crucifixion scene! The Virgin Mary is portrayed with soothing oboes and the nativity with lullabies for chorus and orchestra. The temptation of Christ in the desert is marked by a sinister twelve-tone motif; clearly the Devil in Rózsa's universe didn't get all the best tunes. The most interesting sequence by far is Rózsa's working out of the theme for Salome's dance, a dynamic piece full of attacking, shifting rhythmic patterns, careering arabesques and spectral

---

[2] Alex North, interviewed in *Film Music Notebook*, vol. 3, no. 1, 1977

percussion. It remains flawed on the re-recording,[3] however, because of the jarring presence of a flute trilling away far too prominently in the mix.

In an article on the scoring for *Julius Caesar*[4] Rózsa ponders on the problems surrounding the scoring for Shakespearean films and comments on Mendelssohn's romantic musical setting of *A Midsummer Night's Dream* being anachronistic by modern-day standards. Rózsa opted for capturing in music the universality of Shakespeare's drama and gave each of the four main protagonists a leitmotif or theme. He chose not to score the assassination scene itself but put his emphasis on the resulting impacts of the crime on the population of Rome, with the funereal speeches delivered to the lament of a women's chorus.

In the 1990s a new kind of history film has emerged in Britain – a radical reworking of literary sources – two notable examples being Derek Jarman's *Edward II* (1991), based on a sixteenth-century play by Christopher Marlowe, and Sally Potter's *Orlando* (1993), based on a novel by Virginia Woolf. Both use their literary sources as frameworks to explore historical tropes and the representation of history by cinema. Each adopts an unequivocally modern approach to the music soundtrack.

In Simon Fisher Turner's case for the score of *Edward II* he recorded many of the sound textures used on the set's location during filming. He then used these sounds as the raw materials from which to build up tracks. For example, a rhythm track is created from the (sampled) sound of a police truncheon recorded during the film's riot scenes, a bell is made from the sound of a poker and dialogue is wound into a repeating pattern of strange percussion. The soundtrack to *Edward II* makes a few concessionary nods in the direction of using authentic instruments, such as its inclusion of psaltery and mandola and the reliance on a peculiarly medieval-sounding percussion motif, but these are combined with hamstrung guitars, bassoons, synthesizers and other electronica in such a way that the whole is contemporary but also timeless. Turner deals with the creation of atmospheres rather than melodies and sees himself as a close collaborator with the director's own ideas, hence his desire to be on set as much as possible during the recording of a film:

> I supply music for the director's images, to try to capture a sense of his ideas of the music he would like to hear if only he could compose himself. As a composer I am continuing a tradition [of film music] but hopefully also changing it. Music supports

[3] CD recording of score to *King of Kings*, MGM25

[4] Miklós Rózsa, 'Julius Caesar', *Film and TV Music* 13, 7, September–October 1953

the image a great deal, and it can manipulate your emotions a great deal. It should be used very subtly, music both loves and hates the image. Most directors have no idea, and are unwilling to see what can be done these days with a little imagination, and a lot of trust, time and patience. Because I try to cross over into a sound collage space, I tend to get misinterpreted, not only by the director but by the sound editors as well. I have often been wrong in trying out my ideas for the mixture of collaging found sounds and music, but for me the difference is that as I prefer to be on the set or location when the film is being shot, my found sounds come from the actual process of the making of that particular film. They are certainly not sound effects, but it is a fine line between what the sound editor, or FX person does, and what I do.[5]

With many of the sounds themselves forming during the post-production process, the notion of historical research into a period's instrumentation and musical flavour is losing favour to a more freewheeling modern interpretational approach. Sally Potter's working method on *Orlando* was similar to Simon Fisher Turner's in that music was generated during the post-production process almost archaeologically through digital sampling technology. The main difference being that Sally Potter thought of herself as a director, rather than a composer:

I co-wrote the score with David Motion. I had been searching for a musical identity for the film for months, and had been listening to certain pieces of music over and over again while writing and shooting. I finally engaged a music supervisor as a kind of sounding board. The weeks of the edit flew past, and there was still no score; the upshot was that the music supervisor put me together with David Motion, an engineer/producer who hadn't written a film score before. We went into a studio and I recorded on an eight-track all the tunes I could hear in my head. Then he arranged some of the songs for instruments, or wrote instrumental parts around them, reinvented some of the cues and brought in other instruments. Then he put all the material into a sampler, and we sat and worked together on the score at night, while the film was being mixed during the day; but I had no intention originally of composing the score.[6]

In re-creating the musical sound, but more importantly the feel of earlier parts of this century, the musical palette for many composers remains relatively open. Mark Isham's scores for two recent films set in the 1920s, *The Moderns* (1988) and *Dorothy Parker and the Vicious Circle* (1993), play upon and ultimately subvert our associations with café music from the period:

5 Simon Fisher Turner, letter to the author, February 1996

6 Interview with Sally Potter, *Artforum*, Summer 1993, p. 91

For *The Moderns*, |the director| Alan Rudolph was quite specific, he wanted the romance of Paris. The whole film deals with the concept of what it was like to be modern, at any point in history. So we had some fun with having the score start off somewhat traditional, in the sense that it was all acoustic music that might have been heard at that point in time, and mutate it over the course of the film. The music of that period is quite well known to me, certainly the jazz music of that time and the classical music that was being influenced by jazz, Stravinsky and Erik Satie. The intention was to start off with some of those associations, the violins, the tango feel to the band, but then as the scene goes on we start to add more electronic elements and the picture itself starts to get stranger and stranger in an effort to discuss the more general concept of being modern, as opposed to modernity, at a single point in history.[7]

Film music addresses history by the manipulation of basic musical symbols, which are derived from certain kinds of instrumental sound. This has become codified over the history of film music into a highly efficient musical shorthand which most audiences seem to understand on an unconscious level due to their biographical histories as listeners. Our appreciation of the aptness or otherwise of such a score will be dependent upon our pre-existing knowledge of the musical symbols invoked. On aggregate our increasing exposure to music made not just in our own time but to that exhumed from pre-twentieth-century idioms should make our musical understanding richer when it comes to the manipulation of musical history in historical films. However, so little is understood about the ways in which we as listeners form hypotheses about the musical surfaces we listen to (and believe we understand) that this cannot be claimed with confidence.

[7] Interview with Mark Isham, April 1996

FILM MUSIC AS A KIND OF LANGUAGE

From the earliest days of music being used in film, the idea of creating a specific 'mood' to order was of interest to film makers. The specially tailored mood music collections, or the wholesale plundering from nineteenth-century sources during the silent era, establishing a durable mode of operation. The process which started there continued with originally written scores for film which were more readily able to exploit the tacit musical associations of the audience. Film music is a highly coded form of emotional message; its tones and cadences seem to appeal to something 'wired in' to us, triggering the appropriate emotional response at the appropriate moment. The film music conventions established in the first quarter-century of cinema have proved remarkably durable. George Antheil, a successful composer of both film and concert music, acknowledged the strange power of music to manipulate the emotions:

> Hollywood music is very nearly a public communication, like radio. If you are a movie fan (and who isn't?) you may sit in a movie theatre three times a week listening to the symphonic background scores which Hollywood composers concoct. What happens? Your musical tastes become moulded by these scores, heard without knowing it. You see love, and you hear it. Simultaneously. It makes sense. Music suddenly becomes a language for you, without your knowing it.[1]

Trying to understand how music achieves its effect is steeped in problems. Trying to use language to build up a genealogy of film music's variety of effects tends to mystify rather than demystify the music itself. Understanding in music, according to the philosopher Roger Scruton, consists of recognizing the gesture which the music enacts. Yet this assumes that the same gesture can be discerned by all listeners to the piece, and that there is therefore a 'correct' and an 'incorrect' understanding of a piece. All

[1] Tony Thomas, Music for the Movies (New York: 1973), p. 171

of which requires further underpinning and a regress into some kind of close parallel between music and language, which takes us back to square one.

One of the more unsuccessful attempts to link music's inscrutability more definitively to language was Albert Schweitzer's[2] much-discussed study of J. S. Bach. Schweitzer attempted to show how Bach's instrumental music followed a similar patterning to music used in the composer's musical settings of poetry. By taking the poetic text as a blueprint and applying it back into Bach's instrumental pieces, Schweitzer hoped to show that Bach's musical illustration of particular types of poetic language were part of a wider musical coding he used, which could be 'read' textually.

The musician Deryck Cooke in *The Language of Music*[3] adopts Schweitzer's method, using as a starting point an analysis of several musical settings of verbal texts by various composers. From these Cooke then attempts to transpose specific emotional meanings from various specific musical phrases accompanying the verbal texts. Using these as a kind of 'code breaker' Cooke then attempts to apply these principles to larger instrumental works by the same or different composers. Like Schweitzer, Cooke's abiding belief seems to be that certain musical phrases are inextricably 'a language of the emotions, akin to speech'. These theories depend on all possible descriptions of music somehow boiling down to finite verbal descriptions.

Pace Scruton, Ludvig Wittgenstein claimed that to understand a verbal sentence was to be able to replace the sentence with another that says the same thing. Clearly this method could not be applied to Cooke's system.

The philosopher Suzanne Langer attempted to steer observations about music away from any kind of syntactic or verbal definition. Musical objects do not designate something in the world in the same way that language supposedly does:

> For the elements of music are not tones of such and such pitch, duration and loudness, nor chords and measured beats; they are like all artistic elements something virtual, created only for perception . . . sounding forms in motion.[4]

Cognitive accounts of musical intuition embrace very different concepts from conventional linguistics, yet the developmental structures of language

2 Albert Schweitzer, *J. S. Bach* (New York: 1945)

3 Deryck Cooke, *The Language of Music* (London: 1959)

4 Suzanne Langer, *Feeling and Form* (New York: 1952), p. 107

acquisition and development do parallel those that allow us to comprehend and generate musical structure. The most striking parallel between words and music is that both depend radically upon experience in order to be intelligible.

As 'art' music since the eighteenth century has tended to become more instrumental (as opposed to vocal) in form, this has created a special aesthetic category for music which has resisted comparison with other categories. It isn't so much that music is incomprehensible to us as that it flutters on the edge of something as comprehensible and as 'readable' as ordinary language itself. This incommensurability has haunted Western music criticism for much of the last two hundred years, as it has tended to regard individual musical works as pieces to be deciphered to reach a finite and singular meaning, as if they were a piece of literature or a scientific paper.

Both music and language are based upon an articulation of sound into discernible units and a kind of grammar, although in the case of music this grammar may be metaphorical. Even a musical form as functional as film music is largely understood from this perspectival bias, hence the conventions that have arisen with different kinds of musical cues being invoked slavishly, as if they were elements in a lexicon. Music is a part of the world. It is not a detached realm and it is highly communicative, even if not in the normal terms of a song or a ritual. T. W. Adorno[5] claimed that music's ability to communicate depended upon its 'language character', that music is socially mediated and that it is most itself when it emulates certain principles found in language.

The father of semiology, Ferdinand de Saussure (a contemporary of Freud), claimed that to understand a language it was necessary to see each element of that language under study (e.g. an individual word) against the backdrop of society's whole linguistic system. This insight later became one of the founding principles of structuralism:

> Language is a system of signs that express ideas, and is therefore comparable to a system of writing, the alphabet of deaf mutes, symbolic rites, polite formulas, military signals, etc., but it is the most important of all these systems. A science that studies the life of signs within society is conceivable; it would be a part of social psychology and consequently of general psychology; I shall call it semiology. Semiology would show what constitutes signs, what laws govern them. Since the science does not yet exist, no one can say what it would be; but it has a right to

[5] T. W. Adorno, 'Music Language & Composition', reprinted in *Musical Quarterly*, vol. 77, 1993

existence, a place staked out in advance. Linguistics is only a part of the general science of semiology; the laws discovered by semiology will be applicable to linguistics, and the latter will circumscribe a well-defined area within the mass of anthropological facts.[6]

Between written language and its pronounced sound lies a world of discontinuity. This is one of the most essential features of language and one of the ways in which language most differs from music. Saussure differentiated two orders of relationship that are indispensable to language: the syntagmatic and the paradigmatic. The syntagmatic element of language has to do with the positioning of a sign in any particular sentence. In any given sentence, the meaning of a single word is determined partly by its position in the sentence and its relationship with the other grammatical units of that sentence. Paradigmatic elements are the relationship of a single word to other words, which might have filled its place but have been displaced by it. These displaced words form paradigmatic 'sets' of similarities: other words with the same grammatical function, other words with related meanings (synonyms and acronyms) and other words with similar sound patterns are three examples of paradigmatic sets. In selecting a word to use in a sentence we perform something like a rapid scanning process of paradigmatic possibilities until we find one that will play the appropriate role in the sentence we are constructing.

David Clarke[7] finds a similar axial relationship in music, claiming that a symbiosis between paradigmatic and syntagmatic attributes holds for much of the music produced in the West over the past twenty years. Tonal works follow a broadly syntagmatic axis whilst atonal works, through a reliance on thematicism, exploit paradigmatic principles.

Lerdahl and Jackendoff[8] in *A Generative Theory of Tonal Music* analysed the relationships between musical idioms and a pre-existing deep structure in music that resembles a musical grammar based on certain 'preference rules' which determine how musical sequences are likely to be constructed. Their intention is to try to construct an explanation of musical cognitive capacity utilizing concepts borrowed from linguistic theory (most notably the work of Noam Chomsky). They claim to have identified the basis of a 'generative grammar' that by implication acknowledges the fact of musical universals. The notion of a 'generative grammar' implies that music might

[6] Ferdinand de Saussure, *Course in General Linguistics* (New York: 1966), p. 16

[7] David Clarke, 'Is Music Like Language?' *Musical Times*, January 1996, p. 10

[8] Fred Lerdahl and Ray Jackendoff, *A Generative Theory of Tonal Music* (Cambridge, Mass: 1983), p. 8

be compared with mathematics, where infinite sets of numbers can nevertheless be operated upon by finite formal number and symbol systems. The analogy is that, from the limited tonal range available to human perception, an infinity of possible musical works can be created.

They supply other concepts which they believe characterize musical intelligibility for the listener, rules which function rather like linguistic grammar, determining how phrases can be put together. Other rules are 'preference rules', which describe how it is that we recognize musical conventions in different genres of music, including film music. The authors see the intuitive experience of music as an activation of certain preferences (based on knowledge and experience of musical idioms) from a wider range of presented Well-Formed (i.e. grammatical or sensible) musical structures. Musical understanding then involves a process of retrieval and comparison with similar instances from past experience within the overall condition of Well-Formed grammar. They claim that grammar as a rule giver is not as important in music as it is in language. The concept of 'preference rules' does much of the work in Lerdahl and Jackendoff's theory that grammar is supposed to do in linguistics, although the two should not be directly compared since the clearest parallel to linguistic grammar is the concept of Well-Formedness, the basic condition of intelligibility within a predefined notational system.

What emerges from their study are strong parallels between the deepest structures of language and the organizing principles that determine our musical intuitions: both are cognitive processes. We structurally process music according to some sense of temporal patterning, based upon relationships between 'key' musical events and subsequent 'lesser' events. It's the perception and, in a familiar musical idiom, the anticipation of those events that permit enjoyment or loathing as the case may be.

The whole fabric of continuity in the Western music system has been torn apart in the past two or three decades. The process of universal amplification has rendered musical performance indistinguishable from its electronic reproduction. Any aspect of recorded music can now be edited down to the microsecond at any stage in the life of the recording to be redeployed in a completely new musical context. Radio and TV continually split extracts and segment musical beginnings and endings. Whereas once timbre was demoted in favour of written notes, music now privileges the recording or the live performance. Amplification produces musical experiences that do not correspond to how the music may be notated (if indeed the music is notated at all). Brian Eno recalls such an experience:

One of the most interesting musical experiences I ever had was hearing a Philip Glass piece performed at the Royal College of Art in 1970 or something. This was when he was using real rock'n'roll instruments and they were very loud; he had four electric organs, two electric saxes and a couple of other things . . . It was loud and completely repetitive, but the most interesting thing was that you were constantly hearing melodies. Now, I know those melodies weren't being played, but I was finding them there. What's happening is that the job of finding narrative, finding melody, and finding sense in the music is being passed over to the audience. They are being given a mix, and then being told, 'OK, go and find your way around', and the difference between the middle-of-the-road and the other stuff is how much you're being led through the music. Everything we call MOR is music that very specifically takes you on a particular narrative and melodic journey and puts all of its focus of attention there. This doesn't seem to me very interesting at the moment.[9]

As each musical work, at least each progressive piece, tends to work against the general principles of the musical genre in which it is born, there is a basic principle of conflict underlying modern music. Adorno saw this tension between the universal and the particular as an essential characteristic of the language character of music. Absolute musical autonomy is highly contentious as a concept since it strips music of any characteristics to which meaning can be attached. Musical meaning, not least for film music, lies outside the piece of music itself and resides in the set of paradigmatic conventions that marks out genres and sub-genres.

critical language and music

Critical language that describes music operates in a continuum where it is expected that the reader has no great difficulty in imagining a piece of music that is 'florid' or 'neo-romantic'. Particularly in the case of a description of, say, a tenor saxophone phrase as 'florid', there is an implicit notion of music offering up immutable aspects of itself as if language were adequate to capture it.

For example, what does it mean to describe a piece of music as 'profound'? We all believe that we have some idea of what is meant by profundity when applied to both music and to a text (or a film sequence), but the concept is very difficult to weigh out in any helpful analytical way. The term profundity seems to hover in the area of indeterminacy between language and music,

[9] *The Wire*, May 1996, p. 37

both linking the two worlds and at the same time holding them apart. The philosopher Peter Kivy's book *Music Alone* ends with a chapter entitled 'The Profundity of Music'. Kivy attempts to build up a basis for argument where he can safely judge a piece of music to be profound in terms of its being able to satisfy certain criteria which he puts forward.

Kivy suggests that a piece of music can be profound if it is able to satisfy three basic conditions. First, the musical work must have a subject – it must be about something. Second, the subject of the musical work must itself be profound. And third, the music must treat the subject matter in an 'adequate' way to address the subject (of profundity). One might level the same prerequisites at film. Kivy's definition is supplemented by an admission:

> The problem is that we – at least I – have no clear idea at all why serious, well-educated, adult human beings should find pure musical sound of such abiding interest that we are moved to call the subject profound.[10]

Even given this, Kivy observes that there are a number of musical works that are quite routinely called 'profound' by a number of critics and admirers. Ascriptions of this kind imply that the experience of listening and recognizing profundity is a cumulative one, a judgement made of the piece as a whole. This kind of cumulative judging process also applies to a consideration of films. Can the constituent parts of a film, particularly its music, be called profound because of their contribution to the (profound) whole? Can the short and often repetitive cues which are the stuff of film music ever be called profound?

The last films of Polish film maker Krzysztof Kieslowski are regularly described as profound, dealing as they do with some rather weighty metaphysical questions. His fertile partnership with the composer Zbigniew Preisner produced films and music of a highly distinctive sort. The special atmospheres unique to Kieslowski's cinema and Preisner's music have done much to open up the often difficult themes of these films to a wider audience.

Preisner's music is immediately recognizable: sparse, elegiac yet colourfully dynamic. His music to *The Double Life of Véronique* (1991) might well be referred to as music which is profound, at least in passages. Yet to say that the score to *The Double Life of Véronique* is profound in this kind of holistic way is to try to present an experience of the music that transcends the amount of emotion triggered by each cue or movement within the score.

---

[10] Peter Kivy, *Music Alone: Philosophical Reflections on the Purely Musical Experience* (New York City: 1990), p. 216

Perhaps some parts of the score might be considered 'less profound' whilst others move us beyond expression. Yet those less moving parts must contribute something of value to the overall piece.

In *The Double Life of Véronique* a promising young singer, Veronika, collapses onstage during a concert in a town in Poland. In France, apparently at the same moment, her double, Véronique, awakes with the sudden desire and ability to sing, as if guided by the swan-song of her dead double. The idea of a transference between souls is the theme of the film. The vocal elements that Preisner uses are extracts from the poetry of Dante phrased in Old Italian, although Kieslowski claims[11] that they have nothing to do with the subject of the story, although they may have inspired Preisner to write the music in the style that he did.

On one level the music aspires to high culture in its adoption of the baroque style, but in its short phrases it is also very modern. The digestibility of Preisner's music has obviously helped it sell in large numbers all over the world. Deconstructing Preisner's music in search of the kernel of profundity is perhaps an unfair exercise, since to describe the experience of profound music is to explain what profundity actually is, but it may provide some clue towards specifying at least some of the elements that must be present for a piece of music to be considered profound.

The repetition of key musical phrases in the soundtrack seems to offer the listener a key with which to unlock the whole mystery, both of the fragmented music and of the apparent passage of souls between Veronika and Véronique. The tremendous emotional impact of the music might partly consist of this feeling of being on the edge of understanding it.

Musically, repetition itself can convince us that a piece is profound. On successive hearings we focus in more on the structure of the piece, the greater understanding of which merely increases our belief in the profundity of the music. *The Double Life of Véronique* redoubles musical theme with dramatic theme, underlining the profundity of the story's theme: that perhaps the soul does exist, and that perhaps music is its carrier. In a film that is very much about emotion, this highly emotional score is calculated to produce feelings in us very like those that we experience in other moments of profound insight. Part and parcel of a continued immersion in Preisner's music is the feeling of anticipation, which seems to propel us, the listener, into a position of musical omnipotence, being able even to predict what will happen next. This is another aspect of the apparent profundity of the score.

11 *Kieslowski on Kieslowski*, ed. Donusia Stok (London: 1994), p. 179

Whatever musical profundity actually is, and whether or not it applies to the music of Zbigniew Preisner, it must be taken to apply to the music as a whole, not to any one of the individual cues within a given score. Since each unitary cue will trigger one predominating emotional response, only to be displaced by the next, then any ascriptions of profundity must refer to elements transcending individual cues. Each part of the music in Preisner's score structurally informs the whole and this is really the appeal of his music. He creates sharply defined but relatively complex (largely through their instrumentation rather than through any structural complexity) musical cues which are then knitted together into an intricate yet discernible framework.

Much the same might be said of many other composers, and certainly composers working with film, yet with Preisner these elegant constructions have been consciously deployed as analogues to the metaphysical probing of Kieslowski's films.

Despite the fact that descriptive adjectives can be levelled at music and even appear to be full of insight and coherence, there remains a wall between our descriptions of musical passages and those passages themselves. Language can apparently become a simulacrum of music but music can never be collapsed into language. It is not so much that music resists being parcelled up into discrete syntactic clusters like nouns, verbs or adjectives; it is more that it lacks the basic ontological status from which to dissemble itself in the first place. Music has no synonymy, or what philosophers of language term entailment.

In describing music, traditionally, the choice has been between mystification through adjectival overuse and through the technical language of musicology. Both forms remain separate from the listening experience. Music's inherent sensuality arrives as a *Gestalt*. It evaporates when broken down into discrete analysis, therefore any writing needs to try not only to capture the feeling of the music under examination but also to point up something about the unique strategy of resistance or affirmation that is inherent in every piece of music.

musical archetypes

Film music in its tightly coded frames of reference seems to offer itself up to certain kinds of archetypal interpretations. This is, however, illusory since music itself has no absolute content. But there are parallels between notions of the archetype and the ways in which we tend to talk about certain kinds of artistic conventions, in this case, musical conventions.

It was Jung who first proposed the idea of archetypes to explain the origin of certain kinds of mental processes. He believed that the concept of the archetype within the collective unconscious of society explained many of the subliminal workings of the individual psyche. He characterized archetypes in the following general way:

> They exist pre-consciously, and presumably they form the structural dominants of the psyche in general . . . As *a priori* conditioning factors they represent a special psychological instance of the 'pattern of behaviour' which gives all things their specific qualities. Just as the manifestations of this biological ground plan may change in the course of development, so also can those of the archetype.[12]

Jung denied that archetypes were ever available to conscious perception. He conceived of archetypes as patterning conventions that inhabit the collective unconscious, an unknowable nucleus that 'never was conscious and never will be . . . it was, and still is, only interpreted'.[13] Jung's theory of archetypes was introduced in 1919 in order to help explain why psychotic imagery in several patients he was treating fell into distinct patterns. Jung felt that these patterns were oddly reminiscent of fairy tales, myths and legends, and that such stories exhibited a certain commonality across cultures. The common threads lay mainly in the areas of imagery, which Jung termed primordial images. Such images he saw as fundamental, since all subsequent images were to be derived from them. They are also independent of consciousness and arise without warning in dreams, fantasies and artistic creation. Jung's writings embraced the concept of the archetypal, progressively moving him away from explanations of behaviour centred in experience towards a consideration of deep or innate mental structures as explanations for abnormal psychology. The most important concept to grasp from Jung's writing is that he is not claiming that the content of mental imagery is innate but that the form and patterning of it are, and it is these facilities that are passed on from generation to generation:

> The archetypal representations (images and ideas) mediated to us by the unconscious should not be confused with the archetype as such. They are very varied . . . and point back to one essential irrepresentable basic form.[14]

12 C. G. Jung, *The Visions Seminars* (Zurich: 1976), p. 4

13 C. G. Jung, *Collected Works* (London: 1970), vol. 9, para 266

14 Ibid., vol. 8, para 417

A musical archetype might be characterized as a soundless, rhythmless impulse of sonic images or impressions, what Yolande Jacobi[15] described as a living system of reactions and aptitudes that ultimately help to shape new musical ideas. A musical archetype might also be similar to the philosopher Henri Bergson's notion of '*éternal incrées*'; a tonal map of prefigurations activated by exposure to music in which mental energy fields constantly form and re-form musical *Gestalten* – modulations, leitmotifs, repetitions and other associating structures that underscore the listening experience. This process of 'capturing' musical imagery from the wider set 'offered' to the conscious mind may also help to explain some of the processes involved in compositional choices as well as the process of musical interpretation or understanding.

Archetypal forms of musical intuition have occasionally cropped up as a literary subject. In *Swann's Way,* Proust's connoisseur character Swann is profoundly affected by music, which invokes sequences of recollection involuntarily. He repeatedly is exposed to the same phrases of music in different locations and at different times, the recall of the earlier experience being described in terms that bring out the powerful archetypal nature of musical recall:

> What had happened was that the violin had risen to a series of high notes, on which it rested as though expecting something, an expectancy which it prolonged without ceasing to hold on to the notes, in the exaltation with which it already saw the expected object approaching, and with a desperate effort to continue until its arrival, to welcome it before itself expired, to keep the way open for a moment longer, with all its remaining strength, that the stranger might enter in, as one holds a door open that would otherwise automatically close. And before Swann had time to understand, to think: 'It is the little phrase from Vinteuil's sonata. I musn't listen!' all his memories of the days when Odette had been in love with him, which he had succeeded, up till that evening, in keeping invisible in the depths of his being, deceived by this sudden reflection of a season of love, whose sun, they supposed, had dawned again, had awakened from their slumber, had taken wing and risen to sing maddeningly in his ears, without pity for his present desolation, the forgotten strains of happiness.

Music for Proust's character seems to offer a passage into the numinous, an almost religious state of connection with the transcendent nature of time and individual experience. Music organizes and dredges memory, invoking

15 Yolande Jacobi, *Complex Archetype Symbol in the Pschology of C. G. Jung* (New Jersey: 1959)

something akin to a feedback system. The repetition of musical experience creates a residual psychic structure which becomes archetypal.

In the German writer E. T. A. Hoffmann's early-nineteenth-century *The Kreisleriana*, a mix of fiction, music criticism and quasi-philosophical musings, the author contemplates the synaesthetic experience (where the aural and visual senses become fused and the synaesthete hallucinates images at the same time as hearing sounds) of his pseudonym and *alter ego*, the music teacher Johannes Kreisler. As sounds appeared to him as colours, Kreisler was constantly processing a mental gallery of colourfully modulating patterns into imagistic collections with a range of emotional associations. To a modern film audience, dark or minor piano chords in a deep register provoke images ranging from terror to mild discomfort and melancholy, whilst the higher notes transport them into happier states. Hoffmann's writing posits the idea of certain musical tonalities producing fixed associations, an idea which captures something of the archetypal possibilities of music.

Attempts have even been made to suggest a site in the human body where archetypal prefigurations might reside. Anthony Stevens, a biologist with Jungian sympathies, suggests that it is in the DNA structure itself that we should look for the location and transmission of archetypes. Stevens suggests that DNA itself is the 'replicable archetype of the species'.[16] In a similarly biological frame of mind, Stein suggests that biological survival itself depends upon the activation of archetypal mechanisms of self-preservation. An organism, to survive, must recognize that-which-is-not-itself. Stein claims that living organisms activate pre-existing perceptual patterns which recognize that-which-is-not-itself. Accordingly the organism interprets this 'other' and determines what sort of action needs to be taken, if any. Stein argues that the information processing that goes on involves the relaying of messages at the basic cell level. Stein considers the concept of message-bearing as an archetypal activity and compares the work of templates, genes, enzymes, hormones, pheromones *et al.* with directly archetypal messenger-figures such as Hermes, Prometheus or even Christ.[17]

A possible archetypology of film music might begin at the physical level and focus on the familiarity of certain sonic effects. Music can act upon the body in a variety of different ways, through its rhythm, its pitch logic, its dynamics, its sound colour and texture and its performance context. Of these, rhythm is probably the most galvanizing, but even by putting forward

[16] A. Stevens, *Archetype: A Natural History of the Self* (London: 1982), p. 73

[17] L. Stein, 'Introducing Not-Self', *Journal of Analytical Psychology*, 1967, pp. 97–114

a case that, say, most members of any given viewing audience will find William Walton's score for *Henry V* (1944) progressively more exciting in the battle scenes and the climactic charge by the French cavalry, only permits some very broad generalizations to be made about the impact of music. Since film music is deployed in a highly coded way to provoke reaction or arousal, one might think that some sort of all-inclusive taxonomy might be produced that can render the precise effects of film music decipherable in the same way as the generative structures of language can be revealed. This, I think, is illusory and is perhaps best proved by reference to the failure of semiotics[18] to produce a complete sign system to explain other aspects of cinematic 'language'.

Lerdahl and Jackendoff's work specifies in some detail musical preference rules which could certainly be compared with 'archetypal' rule structures. These deep-seated rules for construction may explain why as listeners we do not have to learn a musical grammar 'from scratch'. A great many musical concepts seem to be already 'wired' in. Like Noam Chomsky's notion of a universal grammar, musical cognition may also be generative. Lerdahl and Jackendoff's musical grammar is an attempt to specify how our mental abilities 'organize' the perception of a musical signal. We regularly make musical intuitions from even tiny fragments of a piece of music; Lerdahl and Jackendoff suggest that this is because of our genetic inheritance. They use the limited differences between musical idioms to point towards the limitations in human musical cognition. They link the 'deep structures' of musical intuitions by analogy to the idea of a musical archetype, where archetypal patterns emerge as a consequence of four basic components of musical grammar:

> We propose that archetypal patterns emerge as a consequence of the preference rules for the four components of the musical grammar. A passage in which the preference rules maximally reinforce each other, within each component and across components, will be heard as 'archetypal'. As more conflict appears among preference rules, the passage deviates more from archetypal form and is heard as musically more complex.[19]

Whilst they make no claim that musical archetypes are empirically 'discoverable', they assert that archetypes are useful as stable structural descriptions produced by the concepts of grammar they outline. An

[18] Christian Metz, 'The Cinema: Language or Language System?', *Film Language* (New York: 1974), pp. 31–91
[19] Ibid., p. 289

archetypology of film music would in theory consist of an exhaustive history of individual distortions of a deeper archetypal form. By analogy, one might think of jazz vocalists and the ways in which a written song manuscript might be interpreted as a series of distortions by the interpretations of different singers. The archetypal form of the song itself is unreachable and equally there can be no 'neutral' reading of the manuscript, since the reading itself would necessitate interpretation. Many songs that subsequently became eulogized as jazz classics may be blues structures only incidentally. One might think of Billie Holiday's reading of 'What a Little Moonlight Can Do'. The instance of Holiday's performance served to transport the reputation of the song from one musical idiom (pop) into another (blues) solely by virtue of Holiday's singular interpretation.

The archetypal patternings alluded to by Lerdahl and Jackendoff's preference rules define musical cognition. They are not themselves perceptually derived. How these 'engrams' actually work in invoking strong emotional reactions is still largely unexplored, but the highly associative melodies of film music offer a reasonable starting point for psychological and musicological research to begin.

THE REMAKING OF GENRES

A new and more sophisticated English-language film journalism emerged from the early 1960s and was to reach its zenith of theoretical sophistication in the 1970s with the re-evaluation and re-incorporation of the so-called genre film into the body of respectable cinema. This evolutionary process was influenced primarily by European journals such as *Cahiers du cinéma* and by theorists such as Roland Barthes and Peter Wollen. It trickled down into mainstream journalism represented by critics such as Andrew Sarris (*The Village Voice*, New York), Parker Tyler (*Film Culture*, *Film Quarterly*, New York) and even the late 1960s writing (and experimental film making) of Norman Mailer. This overhauling of the way in which films were analysed and reviewed did much to change the way in which the public perceived film stories. The sum result was that a new kind of self-consciousness entered film making with respect to the internal history of cinema as an art form.

Perhaps the clearest signs of a new consciousness about stories could be seen in the new critical readings of older films, particularly American studio films of the 1940s and early 1950s: films by directors such as John Ford, Douglas Sirk and Vincente Minnelli, films such as *Young Mr Lincoln*, semi-rehabilitated by *Cahiers du cinéma*, which reversed the old critical conception of genre films as the artistic inferior to auteur film making in which the director is perceived as the sole creative voice. The considerable value of many of these so-called genre films was seen in their occasional ability to challenge the limits of the institutional cinema, and even to find a way of speaking distinctively through it. Genre was recognized and finally celebrated as the industrial prototype every director is given by the producer. Those films or directors that manage to emerge from the studio machine with their distinctive style intact are great indeed.

Film music that manages to pull something unexpected out of the hat within what is ostensibly a genre film is therefore also of interest. Yet here there arises a problem of interpretation; since music is finally only reducible materially to its sonic effects it is difficult to isolate music that flexes against the boundaries of genre without also being aware that what one may be dealing with is not a genre film at all, but something much more flagrantly individualistic, auteurist. One can point to maverick composers such as Bernard Herrmann (or even Miklós Rózsa during his *film noir* scoring days) as possessing a distinctive musical voice, although most of his work was with directors who were auteurs such as Alfred Hitchcock, even if he was working with variations on the thriller genre. In his avoidance of extended melody Herrmann does much to disrupt one of the most basic film music conventions used by the studios between the 1930s and the 1950s and epitomized in Max Steiner's scores to *King Kong* (1933), *Gone With the Wind* (1939) and *The Big Sleep* (1946).

The massive organization of the Hollywood studio system created a rigid hierarchy within the music departments of each company. This very organization and the high turnover of projects often dictated the musical sounds that were produced, as Miklós Rózsa observed:

> When I did my second picture, *Lady Hamilton*, the union said I would not be allowed to orchestrate. I had to look for an orchestrator, something I had never done in my life. I was accustomed to writing the score, first in very loose sketches, then in full score. Now I had to start out writing exact sketches. The Italians call this process *spartita* – condensed score. You can learn it, and I did. I tried many orchestrators, and my scores sounded as if they had been written by someone else. I told the orchestrators, 'Don't write in anything I haven't written down,' but they said, 'We will make it sound lush.' I said, 'Don't make it lush, leave it as it is.' I finally found a man who did what I wanted with the score. With the Hollywod tempo, it is not possible to write out the full score.[1]

Thanks to the impact of structuralist-derived theories of communication there was a renewed interest in myths and archetypal story forms reinterpreted as symbolic 'workings-out' of core values and problems within this or that society. Within American film, the most potent myth of them all, the 'Western' was most keenly studied. Jim Kitses' book *Horizons West*[2] presented Westerns in terms of a number of constituent antinomies – the individual versus the community, nature versus culture, wilderness versus civilization – and charted the various phases of theoretical adjustment and incorporation these antinomies had passed through since the 1940s.

[1] Miklós Rósza, quoted in *Soundtrack* by Mark Evans (New York: 1975), p. 252

[2] Jim Kitses, *Horizons West* (Bloomington, Indiana: 1969)

The relationship between Westerns of the kind made by Sergio Leone and the more mythological ones by John Ford which now have the status almost of cinematic archetype has been one of progressive deconstruction. The Western writers and popularizers of the 1930s – characters such as Owen Wister – developed the Western as a racist genre, 'manifest destiny' heading West at the gallop. Fellow writer William S. Hart even entitled one of his tales *The Aryan*. Since the late 1940s the Western has mutated into the anti-Western, where the spirit of the West is invoked allegorically to denounce the traits of cowardice, prejudice, pugnacity or mob hysteria to be found in the East. The archetypal simple values of the Western's pioneering hero have been replaced by the modernist sentiments of doubt, self-reflexivity and moral relativism. On a literal level, the spectacular use of the American landscape on location had been progressively replaced in the 1950s and 1960s by largely studio-bound Westerns such as the remake of *Stagecoach* (1966) starring Bing Crosby and Ann-Margret. Pauline Kael observed in a perceptive 1967 review:

> The new Western is a joke and the stars play it for laughs, and the young film enthusiasts react to the heroes not because they represent the mythological heroes of the Old West but because they are mythological movie stars. The world has changed since audiences first responded to John Wayne as a simple cowboy; now when he does the same things and represents the same simple values, he's so archaic its funny. We used to be frightened of a reactionary becoming 'a man on horseback'; now that seems the best place for him.[3]

Yet despite the inconsistencies in tone and technique, the Western survived throughout the turbulent re-evaluations and reworkings of the decade. Its music suffered relatively little of the revisionism that overtook the myth, at least not in the American-made Westerns. The basic orchestral style of the genre, perhaps coloured with banjo, guitar or harmonica, signified values associated with the wild and limitless expanse of the American landscape. The classic scores of the 1950s, Dimitri Tiomkin's Oscar-winning *High Noon* (1952), André Previn's *Bad Day at Black Rock* (1954), *The Big Country* (1958) by Jerome Moross and Elmer Bernstein's *The Magnificent Seven* (1960), are all in one way or another tinged with the influence of American folk music, Bernstein's *The Magnificent Seven* particularly so.

The most radical paradigm change in the musical treatment of the Western genre stemmed from the fertile creative partnership between Italian

---

3 Pauline Kael, *Kiss Kiss Bang Bang* (London: 1968), p. 42

director Sergio Leone and Ennio Morricone. Morricone came from a journalist background, but had also studied music at the University of Saint Cecilia, becoming involved with an orchestra that specialized in performing old film scores in a concert-hall setting. Out of this grew his own critical musing on the role, function and aesthetics of film music. His early scores and title songs for Italian-Spanish B-Westerns such as *Gringo* and *Gunfight at Red Sands* in 1963 were not particularly distinctive. It was with his first score for Sergio Leone, *A Fistful of Dollars* (1964), that Morricone announced himself as a formidable presence. Leone's films were visually startling, highly graphic in an almost comic-book style, parcelling up figures' progressions through empty landscapes in what approximated to real time. The characters were amoral rewritings of the conventional American Western hero, although the notion of any kind of deliberate quest had been replaced with simple response functions to a hostile environment. Certainly Leone's reputation as a musical director, carefully planning the function of music within each scene, and his generosity with space on the soundtrack set Morricone's music in an ideal frame, foregrounding the music's sonic impact as opposed to the emotional. This was an appropriate treatment for a cycle of films that deconstructed the basic make-up of the traditional Western hero.

Morricone's music is directly inspired by the instrumentation if not the rhythms of rock and his minimalist reverberating sounds perfectly matched Leone's parched visuals. His unusual choice of instrumentation – cheap electric organs, ocarinas, out-of-tune brass instruments, the electric guitar, bits of scrap metal, and strangely arranged vocal passages (used as instruments rather than carriers of lyrics) – works brilliantly with his erratic shifts from full junkyard orchestration to the arching sustain of a single instrument. For *A Fistful of Dollars* Morricone collaborated with Alessandro Alessandroni, who provided the distinctive guitar and whistle effects, and his choir I Cantori Moderni performed the vocals.

The popularity of the Spaghetti Westerns (and of the record sales that accompanied the more successful titles) underlined the changing audience, who now rejected the more traditional forms of Western. Leone's blackly comic and fatalistic vision reduced the West to a killing ground marked off by extended visual longueurs in which figures are simply choreographed through empty landscapes accompanied by sparse almost atonal noises rather than the booming Appalachian lyricism of a decade before. It is the Western soundtracks that Morricone remains the best known for, despite the fact that they only make up about ten per cent of his total output.

As well as reinventing the musical conventions of the Western, Morricone had by the end of the decade done much to refresh another long-standing genre, the horror film, largely thanks to collaboration with another musically sophisticated director, Dario Argento. In two films for Argento, Morricone constructs a basic mesh of fragmented and hamstrung rock-guitar effects which are then augmented with other contrasting elements: free jazz in *The Cat o' Nine Tails* (1969) and simulated human heartbeats and breathing in *The Bird with the Crystal Plumage* (1970).

Although Morricone wrote literally hundreds of scores during the 1970s and 1980s and won Oscars for *Days of Heaven* (1978), nominations for *The Mission* (1986), *The Untouchables* (1987) and *Bugsy* (1991), as well as scooping Italy's prestigious David di Donatello award for his work on Giuseppe Tornatore's *Everybody's Fine* (1990), his music continues to evade easy categorization. One could perhaps isolate his tendency to avoid traditional symphonic development, concentrating instead on creating overlays which get at the thematic heart of the film rather than the incidentals demanded by a particular action sequence. Praise for Morricone's contribution to cinema has been universal; Italian musicologist Sergio Micelli calls him 'the father of the modern arrangement', whilst Laurence Staig goes even further:

> Morricone is without a doubt one of the greatest composers of all time, whose imaginative arrangements and sometimes surreal use of instruments are quite unique. He is a perfect example of an avant-garde composer who is capable of reinterpreting the danger and excitement into mainstream melodic orchestration.[4]

In his focus on the impact of pure sound, in the Westerns directed by Leone (and to a lesser extent his later Westerns for other directors), Morricone confounds the expectations of genre and goes some way towards reclaiming the subjectivity of the musical experience within an objectified field of musical idioms deemed appropriate to previous definitions of genre music. In avoiding the use of leitmotif, Morricone exposes the structural disunity of cinema in a way that was far more concealed within a John Ford film, even one as great as *The Searchers*, scored by Max Steiner.

[4] Laurence Staig and Tony Williams, *Italian Westerns: The Opera of Violence* (London: 1975)

THE FRENCH NEW WAVE AND JAZZ

In its reworkings of genres from the American cinema (specifically the gangster and police thriller formats), the French New Wave was a successful response to the post-war domination by the American film industry. In its heady incorporation of cliché, pop culture, sex and violence the New Wave films introduced a new and oddly self-conscious style of cinema to an international audience.

The New Wave is presented by Gilles Deleuze as an aesthetic response to a crisis or redundancy in the American film image that was apparent by the mid-1940s and certainly by the early 1950s, when many of the main Hollywood studios began to dismantle themselves because of the cripplingly high overheads their operations necessitated. Deleuze refers to the classic Hollywood studio film as being primarily an 'action image' and links its crisis to a number of factors both social and cultural. What is interesting is that at the point at which American cinema became a victim of its own vast economic integration, other less industrialized forms of American culture were blooming: literature, painting and music.

> The soul of the cinema demands increasing thought, even if thought begins by undoing the system of actions, perceptions and affections on which the cinema had fed up to that point.[1]

An alternative agenda to purely commercial ends became more possible after the Second World War, partly due to the availability of cheaper 8mm and 16mm film gauges. These new stocks were more adaptable to light conditions, allowing film makers to move away from the studio-bound settings of the 1930s and 1940s. The notion of filming with economy and movement in a natural setting wasn't new. Alberto Cavalcanti's *Rien que les heures* (1926) or René Clair's *14th July* (1932) were both highly naturalistic, but these were

[1] Gilles Deleuze, Cinema 1: Movement–Image (London: 1989), p. 206

193

largely shot as exteriors. The films of the Italian neo-realist movement, the French New Wave and the American independent cinema sought out locations in the everyday interiors of homes, offices and even cinemas.

The various new streams of film-making activity in Europe were reactions to the dominance of the mainstream American entertainment industry of the studio era, the 1940s. However, in America times were changing and the studio system was losing its hold on the in-house talent it had been depending upon. Weakened by television the studios began to experience competition from a new kind of independent film producer. In this new return to a smaller form of industry, the American independent cinema was more able to absorb influences from other areas of the American arts and to approach film with the same confidence with which American painters were now beginning to dominate the art world. In painting, the so-called New York School (de Kooning, Rothko, Kline and Motherwell and, of course, Jackson Pollock) pioneered a vivid style of highly personal art known as Abstract Expressionism. The concentration of painters in one city allowed New York to displace Paris as the world's art capital. Abstract Expressionism intensified the ongoing debate about Modernism with its tendencies towards fragmentation, introversion and discontinuity. In the field of art a break with 'mimesis' or any attempt to imitate or approximate to reality became the orthodoxy.

Correspondingly, in music, jazz had moved centre stage in the American critical imagination.

The growing acceptance of jazz as a serious music in America from the 1940s on probably did more than anything else to break up the dominance of the symphonic orchestra as the mainstay of the film soundtrack. Its acceptance in the circles of high culture was ambiguous, however, as playwright and screenwriter Ben Hecht lamented in 1954:

> A lowbrow renaissance is being drummed up by the lads who do the heavy aesthetic thinking in New York. The pages of the art-enfevered periodicals are full of hallelujah's for Ring Lardner, Joe Cook, Rube Goldberg, Ann Pennington, jazz ballads, Jack Dempsey, Charles Chaplin, etc. I find in these eastern essays small enthusiasm for the subject under discussion, but a large boast of the writer's ability to enjoy things you might think out of his line – he being so fancy-minded and high-falutin' a fellow. I am annoyed at these falsetto cheers set up by our eastern cognos-centi for rough-and-tumble entertainment. They are certain to hurt the robust talents by identifying them as art.[2]

[2] Ben Hecht, *A Child of the Century* (New York:1954), p. 333

Jazz revolutionized the pairing of music to image in so many ways that the subsequent rise of the pop song and the pop score became inevitable. Chiefly, for film music, jazz broke up the Wagnerian reliance on leitmotifs and themes and replaced them with an impressionistic musical commentary that functioned much more like an omnipotent narrator within the film than a film score. The nature of expression itself was more aphoristic, and in this post-Romantic age, many critics such as André Hodeir found that this type of musical expression was a truer sign of the times than the systematized hierarchies of a symphony orchestra. Jazz was very often intentionally complex, a strategy by many of its best exponents such as Charles Mingus and Thelonious Monk to preserve its exclusivity. As it evolved further from the Swing of the 1930s into the Bebop of the 1940s and early 1950s, jazz was often misunderstood or not understood at all; but as a vehicle for a highly personalized form it changed the paradigms of American music and of musical expressivity.

The use of jazz as a soundtrack element moved film music away from any semblance of thematicism or, much less, mimesis. Jazz delivered a form of inner musical game to the screen image, a way of deepening the cinema of image into the extraordinary dimension of complex (musical) time. This tendency towards a kind of psychic automatism was certainly influential on other art forms both within America and internationally. Certainly Deleuze's idea of an imperilled 'action image' would correspond in certain fundamental respects to a general movement away from mimesis in the cinema. The same currents were felt in literature as well: Samuel Beckett's *Waiting for Godot*, Eugene O'Neill's *The Iceman Cometh* and Tennessee Williams' *The Glass Menagerie* all explored themes of mental fragmentation, of lost illusions and of the loss of compassion.

With the economic crisis that affected the big Hollywood studios in the late 1940s came the ascent of the independent film maker, who worked on a single film project at a time, assembling his company and artists for the duration of the production. These films were generally low-budget formulaic pictures, often riding on the back of popular concern over a particular social issue.

In film, the acted story now unfolded on a living documentary-style background, as exemplified in the work of American independent film maker/TV actor John Cassavetes, whose *Shadows* (1960) is a largely improvised film that makes the most of its New York City locations and amateur cast. That Cassavetes should have chosen jazz reveals much about his wider attitudes to scoring and to the film industry itself:

> I've always been able to work with anybody that doesn't want success. Jazz musicians don't want success . . . They have these little tin weapons – they don't shoot, they don't go anywhere. The jazz musician doesn't deal with structured life – he just wants that night, like a kid.[3]

The score to *Shadows* nearly didn't come off, since financing problems for the film as a whole (much of the film was paid for by Cassavetes himself) also impacted upon the music, which was due to be recorded by Charles Mingus. According to Brian Priestley[4] the money came through from donations to a late-night talk show called *Night People* presented by Jean Shepherd. *Shadows* features a marvellously incandescent score by Charles Mingus and his tenor saxophonist Shafi Hadi that perfectly counterpoints the hand-held camerawork, naturalistic performances and locations Cassavetes favoured. *Shadows* is a film about characters on the periphery of urban life. They play jazz music professionally with limited success, and the score weaves around the music they themselves create. Particularly in facial close-ups, the improvisational quality of Mingus' double-bass plucking serves as a kind of interior monologue, an analogue to the pitch if not the content of a character. Basswork also serves to catch the low bubble of the streets, set against the dampened roar of traffic. Hadi's tenor tends to paint characters in movement or in some kind of emotional conflict. The score is above all affectionate, and subtle in the rarest way. Music and image each allow the other space in which fully to reveal itself. Cassavetes clearly knew the value of silence and saw similarities between his approach to film and the musical style of the great jazz bassist Charles Mingus:

> He was always torn between the two – the mathematical beauty of the composition and the freedom of improvisation. We had the same kind of artistic fury that hits you. You're all loose – well, we pretend we're loose and in the end we're dictators.[5]

Another notable American independent production of the same year was Robert Franks' boho–absurdist one-acter *Pull My Daisy* (based on a play by Jack Kerouac), a brilliant free-wheeling film that was largely ad-libbed, chaotic, and consisted mainly of an extended and wholly inconsequential conversation between assembled beat celebrities on life, the universe and everything else. David Amram provided the soundtrack as well as appearing in the film himself.

[3] Interview with John Cassavetes, *The Wire*, July 1984

[4] Brian Priestley, 'Beating Time', *Sight & Sound*, April 1992, p. 27

[5] *The Wire*, July 1984

Film, like music, unfolds in time, and this is its most basic ontological aspect – change. The subjective perception of these changing events, on both a plot level and the material levels of the film passing through the projector, is predicated on an awareness of rhythm. The rhythm of change, the internal circles, repetitions, deviations and changes that for each of us is the experience of watching a film or listening to music. Jazz answered at least some of the stylistic demands being made by this renewed, more plastic style of story-telling. As narratives became at the same time simpler but also more fragmented, as multiple-time frames within a story juggled for prominence, jazz – with its aesthetic of imperfection – captured musically some of the sense of spontaneous authenticity that many film makers were looking for. Like the documentary form of film making, jazz and improvised music in general take our own perceptions of coherence as their subject.

On a musical level it tended to be the blues aspects of jazz rather than the dynamic rhythmic pulse that were used. It was very often then more of a 'jazz style' that was being played with rather than anything one was likely to stumble across in a club. The styles of jazz that did make it on to the film soundtracks were derived from the sounds of the big touring bands of the 1940s – Stan Kenton, Woody Herman – brash themes that perfectly caught the personality of the modern man likely to be a character in the new, European-influenced cinema. Ironically jazz, certainly more an American art form than European, came to represent a new spirit in cinema, one that might be characterized as existential and open-ended. The 'events' these new characters went through in the course of a film were as much psychological as temporal.

Jazz as a subject of any kind first appeared in the late 1920s in the form of musical shorts, precursors of today's MTV clip. These were primarily simple registrations of performers literally recorded in front of a microphone. Examples from the 1930s include shorts by Woody Herman, Jimmy Dorsey and Artie Shaw, Benny Carter, Duke Ellington, Jimmy Lunceford and Cab Calloway. The record companies apparently saw these shorts as excellent cross-promotional devices and usually crammed three to four numbers into each short, which was then exhibited as a support to the main feature. The brightest, most photogenic stars of the emerging urban jazz circuit in America were whisked off to Hollywood to appear either as themselves or as some composite jazz-living character in the many backstage musicals and dramas that were then so popular. Benny Goodman and Tommy Dorsey, both popular leaders of swing bands, went this way – Tommy Dorsey ending up in the dreadful 1941 *Las Vegas Night*, in which his own modest band (five reeds, seven brass and a rhythm section) were then overwhelmed by musical backing in the form of a huge string orchestra. Interestingly the co-opting of performers into bit parts in musicals or dramas was mainly limited to white performers. The black musicians seem to have survived the transition to film slightly better with the benefit of posterity – the appearances of Cab Calloway (*International House*, 1934) and Duke Ellington (*Belle of the Nineties*, 1934) are mainly presented as self-contained numbers with the musicians playing themselves.

Jazz as lifestyle had long been a source of lurid fascination to American producers. For example, think of Kirk Douglas playing someone obviously supposed to be Bix Beiderbecke in the splendidly trashy *Young Man with a Horn* (1949). Leslie Kardos' 1950 *The Strip* had Mickey Rooney as a jazz-drumming protagonist caught up in murder in LA and featured strong inputs from Jack Teagarden, Louis Armstrong and Earl Hines, but jazz here forms a backdrop rather than a reflection of psychological processes.

Before this there were odd but interesting experiments in joining live-action musical celebrities with well-known cartoon franchises, like Betty Boop's adventures with Louis Armstrong in the 1932 *I'll Be Glad When You're Dead, You Rascal You* or with Cab Calloway in *Minnie the Moocher*. Both films use Roto-scope techniques to place live-action heads on to cartoon bodies to moderately comic effect.

Other departures included continuing breakthroughs in the avant-garde animation field by Oskar Fischinger, whose amazing adaptation of Ralph Rainger's symphonic jazz work *Radio Dynamics* ended up as *Allegretto* (after Fischinger negotiated its release from the cutting-room floor of *The Big Broadcast of 1936*, a more mainstream revue film by Paramount Studios). Animations by pioneers like Norman McLaren and Len Lye used jazz pianists, Oscar Peterson, for example, as sources of musical departure.

As an atmospheric resource, jazz proved ideally suited to the emerging short film. Its uses were many and bizarre. Jean Painlevé's 1945 short film *Vampire* is a nine-minute meditation on the parasitic charm of the vampire bat, using Ellington's *Black and Tan Fantasy* to accompany the last moments of a distressingly fluffy rabbit. In 1963's *Le Paris des mannequins* the ultra-prolific Jacques Loussier provides a pleasing soundtrack to a documentary fast-track through the fashion world of Paris, which he also soundtracked in another documentary of the same year, *Le Paris des scandanavies*. Loussier came almost to define the soundtrack to the short film during the early 1960s, scoring well over sixty films in France and the UK in something like four years. His music was ideally suited to the needs of a twelve- or fifteen-minute snapshot of a particular subject – fast-moving, textually loaded pieces of apparent spontaneity that must have been an editor's joy to cut pictures to. Martial Solal, whilst nowhere near as active, was similarly employed in a number of short-film projects and even composed the score for a 1966 documentary on nuclear power (imaginatively titled *Le Réacteur nucléaire*). He also managed to provide the highly effective score to *Voyage vers la lumière*, a sixteen-minute hallucinogen-inspired science fiction film by Pierre Unia made in 1968. In the main, however, short films tended to utilize existing recordings rather than specially commissioned pieces. A good example of this is the 1962 *Die Schleuse*, a short film made by the Cologne-based sculptor Harry Kramer, which uses Art Blakey to striking effect, or Rens Groot's 1959 animation to Bix Beiderbecke's *In a Mist*. *Gyromorphosis* by Ny Hirsh similarly matched the Modern Jazz Quartet's recording of *Django* to an impressionistic study of three-dimensional form. The short films made during the 1950s and 1960s by a number of European artists showed the enervating effects of using improvised music alongside a rigidly predetermined sequence of images. John Hubley's free-wheeling *Harlem Wednesday* blended a quasi-documentary view of Harlem streetlife with the paintings of Gregorio Prestopino to a soundtrack by Benny Carter. Shirley Clarke's collaboration with saxophonist Ted Macero for the 1958 *Bridges Go Round* pursues a similar kind of abstracted impressionistic technique. Jazz music helped to take what was left of the impressionistic cinema out of the galleries and into the streets.

Quite why jazz rose so successfully during the early and mid-1950s to become the sound of choice for many of the most creative film makers of the era may have something to do with the fact that producing jazz as a soundtrack was certainly a lot cheaper for an American or any other studio than retaining its own in-house studio orchestra and associated music departments. The Paramount move in 1948 following an anti-monopoly ruling by the US Supreme Court saw the studio trying to divest itself of many of the more costly elements of its infrastructure. For medium- and lower-budget productions an orchestra was a luxury not many could afford and within a few short years the symphonic orchestral sound that had been *de rigueur* during the golden age of the 1930s and 1940s was relegated to just the blockbusters, historical epics like *El Cid*, *Ben-Hur* and so forth, that came to define the more extravagant end of the studios' output.

Jazz as a soundtrack mirrored and embodied the literary aspirations of many of the key creative forces in the artistic underground in most countries that had any kind of real counter-culture. In 1951, Alex North wrote the score to Elia Kazan's very successful film version of *A Streetcar Named Desire*. The play is set in New Orleans and North, an experienced theatre composer, utilized jazz and blues currents in bringing it to the screen. The way in which he deployed the music is as innovative as the arrangements he chose to use. With small group arrangements, he attempted to link as much as possible the narrative underscore with the omnipresent jazz that filters from the Four Deuces Café, giving the main score of the film opportunities to develop from the musical cues given on screen. In addition to this, music very often works against the action on screen. Having given each character within the film their own 'theme', North often allows the characters own subjective themes to overshadow whatever outward action they become embroiled in. In this sense, many passages of the score to *A Streetcar Named Desire* are duels between quite separate themes and in these cacophonous overlaps are rooted the conflicts between the three central characters, Blanche, Stanley and Stella.

Jazz was a highly emotive form of music, supposedly embodying freedom. When combined by sharp-eyed independent producers with the counter-culture, the mix was incendiary. *The Wild One* (1953) was probably the first film to use jazz in such an explicit way to define a (youth-orientated) stance against society at large. The film's style is naturalistic, the staging of scenes and the use of interior and exterior locations are realistic:

> The characters of the play are present-day young people, full of tensions, for the most part inarticulate about their problems and, though exhibitionists, still confused and wondering. These characteristics suggested the use of contemporary jazz as an important segment of the score. This music, with its complicated, nervous, searching quality, seemed best suited to complement these characters.[6]

The jukebox is king of all it pervades in *The Wild One*. Blasting out the sounds of Shorty Rogers and the Giants, the source of the sound (a café jukebox) is more often than not acknowledged visually. There are also more traditional forms of illustrative music, even extending so far as specific leitmotifs for certain characters. Frequently a conventional string-led music sequence arises out of a rhythmic pulse first begun as a defiantly jazz motif.

In effect the speedy legitimizing of jazz in the cinema created an ersatz counter-culture, a non-culture, the sort of weird amalgamation that could only have been born in a producer's cash-addled brain; para-beatniks, para-

<hr>

[6] Fred Steiner, quoting Milton 'Shorty' Rogers, *Film Music Notebook*, no. 2, 1976, p. 26

bikers, para-poets, para-speed-freaks, para-existentialists. With the continuing influence of the Actors' Studio and its new gallery of anti-heroes, both America and Europe became briefly lost in an exploitational ransacking of teenage culture, barely a couple of years after its birth.

Elmer Bernstein's 1955 score to *The Man with the Golden Arm* and his 1957 *Sweet Smell of Success* both utilize high-profile jazz elements. *The Man with the Golden Arm* (again utilizing Shorty Rogers arrangements) features a highly memorable opening title sequence, which went on to become an instrumental hit in its own right. Bernstein's swanky, confident score liberates the film from becoming another *Lost Weekend*-style homily on the evils of addiction. Music in the film becomes a commentary on the progress of Frankie, the central character, in his efforts to secure regular gigs as a drummer. When we see Frankie playing along with the band, his music also serves to drive along his own story.

> The script had a Chicago slum street, heroin, hysteria, longing, frustration, despair and finally death . . . There is something very American and contemporary about all the characters and their problems. I wanted an element that could speak readily of hysteria and despair, an element that would localize these emotions to our country, to a large city if possible. Ergo – jazz.[7]

In Frankie's tormented, narcotics-addicted mind, the searing screeching tones of a wailing jazz sax become an acute index of his own desperation and psychological isolation. In the elements of the score that are not provided by the band playing live, Bernstein utilizes the rhythms rather than the elements or instrumentation of jazz.

Frank Sinatra's role as Frankie Machine in *The Man with the Golden Arm*, hopelessly addicted, but photogenically luminous, painted up a link between jazz and drug abuse which was then reproduced with wildly varying results in other 'social concern' films such as *Stakeout on Dope Street* (1957), *Les Tricheurs* (1958), *Cry Tough* (1959), *The Young Savages* (1961), *Synanon* (1963) and even in the emerging European sexploitation industry in the shape of *Swedish Girls in Paris* (1960).

When jazz has worked well in cinema it's because it has got as close as possible to being a correlate of personal expression. Gone was the idea of an omniscient narrative instructing us to read the film in a certain way. What was left was something far more challenging. What closer form of personal expression can there be than everyday speech with all its stuttering

7 Elmer Bernstein, quoted in *Film Music: The Neglected Art*, by Roy Prendergast (New York: 1975)

imperfections and what closer form of musical equivalent can there be to everyday speech than jazz with all its uncertainties, semantic 'mistakes' and creative individuality? Jazz in film works in a similar way to speech within a film. Both are apparently spontaneous expositions where the main goal is self-expression and communication rather than any kind of 'genre fulfilment'. Both are 'generative' in that they apply rules to a set of deep syntactic structures, to produce potentially endless chains of communicable 'sentences' (or phrases). When combined with a premeditated art form like the cinema, jazz's similarity to language becomes explicit – spontaneous improvisation within a definable parameter (e.g. a 'scene' or 'shot'), yielding a completely unique fragment of self-expression. One might think of Jack Kerouac's typing of *On the Road* on a single sheet of paper – a kind of automated writer's babble where composition takes place a split second before performance (the writing or playing):

> Time being of the essence in the purity of speech, sketching language is undisturbed flow from the mind of personal secret idea-words, blowing (as per jazz musician) on subject of image. Begin not from preconceived idea of what to say about image but from jewel centre of interest in subject of image at moment of writing.[8]

Jazz, and particularly the hard-driving musically complex form known as bop, itself supplied the post-war generation of largely white American writers with a powerful model through which to achieve their literary ambitions. Bop was, however, an élite practice – élite because of the sheer difficulty of playing it and élite because as a live phenomenon it was sufficiently abrasive to alienate many casual listeners. A writer like Jack Kerouac's identification with bop geniuses like Charlie Parker, Fats Navarro or Bud Powell underlines the intention in his writing to try to mirror aspects of spontaneous composition. Beat writing like bop music's assimilation by white and black communities alike retained many associations and filters with the kind of 'high culture' associated with other apparently revolutionary movements from the European avant-garde such as the Futurists or more latterly Fluxus. This bracketing of the jazz soundtrack and beatnik-style movies in general (*Pull My Daisy* being perhaps the most arch incarnation) with high-art associations ultimately spelt the death of what might be called the 'classic' underground film (exemplified as vehicles through which the counter-culture is glimpsed voyeuristically 'at home' being themselves, being weird and ending in the predictability of Warhol's

[8] Jack Kerouac, 'Essentials of Spontaneous Prose', *Evergreen Review*, Summer 1958, pp. 72–3

Chelsea Girls in 1966) since most of its trademarks and trappings had become clichéd.

Jazz as soundtrack came to signify personal expression – a character's secret and internal voice. Jean-Luc Godard integrated jazz with his own unique style of cinema rapidly, one possible reason being Godard's penchant for the short musical phrase, the cue that, endlessly repeated, becomes something less than a leitmotif but something more than simply a signifier. In addition to Godard, other noted New Wave directors such as Truffaut, Jacques Rivette and Chabrol were also willing to experiment with the fluidity and freedom that improvised music was able to offer.

In the space of a few short years a number of domestically successful French films were produced that used jazz both as a style and as a soundtrack. Some of the better examples were: *Sait on jamais?* (1957), directed by Roger Vadim with a score by John Lewis of the MJQ, *Breathless* (1959), directed by Jean-Luc Godard, score by Martial Solal; *Lift to the Scaffold* (1957), directed by Louis Malle with a score by Miles Davis; *Les Liaisons dangereuses* (1960), again by Roger Vadim and with a score by Thelonius Monk and Art Blakey; and *Deux hommes dans Manhattan* (1958), a film by Jean Pierre Melville scored by Martial Solal.

Jean-Luc Godard's *Breathless* is the story of a cop-killer's last few days on the run in Paris. As much as anything *Breathless* helped to define most instinctively the game-playing with cinematic clichés that was the *nouvelle vague*. Its core subject is freedom – compounded with the glamour of criminality. Refracted through Cécile Decugis' highly fluid editing style, this is a narrative that has been pared right back to the bone. Nothing is superfluous, everything is rhythmically incorporated into Martial Solal's superbly urbane score, which sets up a momentum that entirely governs the flow of events. Time becomes completely elastic, yet strangely realistic (because time for all of us is highly elastic), slowing down and speeding up as we jump frenetically from scene to scene, from the 'real' time frame of the street scenes, to the uncertain time frames of Patricia's apartment. All is regulated by (or perhaps conforms to) the score itself – in this instance, the soundtrack was assembled after the film, but in some passages it would not be hard to believe the pictures were assembled around the soundtrack. *Breathless* is fantasy in motion – to which Solal's score provides the interior, insuperable rhythms of make-believe, as the central character, driven to his end by the demands of genre rather than local situation, struggles to assert his own identity as the rhythm – and the net – of law and order closes in. Even in a film as technically adventurous as *Breathless*, it would be possible to argue that jazz was actually deployed fairly conservatively, once again fulfilling its signified function as the transport of fermenting revolt, of counter-cultural style.

Dialogue in *Breathless* acquires a strange arbitrary quality and Godard simply invites us to observe. The story itself is simple pulp and the characters are merely represented; there is no real attempt to 'psychologize' them. What we see is precisely what they are. Jazz music becomes a unifying device. It seems spatially to determine many aspects of the characters' movements, choreographing their interplay in an apparently meaningless universe.

Louis Malle's *Lift to the Scaffold* with a score by Miles Davis tells two parallel stories whose characters (a murderous adulterer and two delinquent teenagers on the run) are combined near the end of the film as the adulterer's car is stolen by the teenagers as he remains trapped in the elevator of an office building. Davis provided two scores: one softly muted but with dark undertones generated by piano and bass which tracks the adulterer and his mistress as she waits for him to return to her after killing his wife, and one much 'hotter' theme, a series of racing scale improvisations. Royal S. Brown[9] perceptively characterizes this tendency to treat music almost as a separate aesthetic element as typical of French films of this period.

Jazz, then, in much of the more intelligent cinema of the late 1950s, is used primarily in a gestural way, to point to other cultural pools, in much the same way as *Breathless* is an affectionate parody of an American gangster film. In *Breathless*, his first feature, Godard presented a soundtrack that was highly sympathetic to his subject. So sympathetic in many scenes that Jean-Paul Belmondo is seen driving his car and reacting to the music. (This scene was reprised years later in the American remake with Richard Gere driving in synchronized sympathy to a Jerry Lee Lewis track, against an obviously artificial sunset backdrop.) In some of his later films, such as *Bande à part* (1964), Godard would deliberately deploy music that was 'unsuited' to the scene, for example a brass band play a waltz as two burglars attempt a break-in, confounding an audience and at the same time providing Godard's own unique commentary on the alarming ease with which genres become conventions (finally calcifying into expectations). In Godard's 1963 film *Contempt*, producer Carlo Ponti actually went as far as to remove Godard's originally commissioned score (a series of romantic ballads by Georges

[9] Royal S. Brown, *Overtones and Undertones* (Berkeley: 1994), p. 186

Delerue) and replace them with a 'jazz' score by Piero Piccioni, presumably hoping to recapture the unique charm (and commercial success) of *Breathless*. Godard withdrew his name from the credits, and the original score was duly reinstated.

The use of jazz as a gestural form of expression in film, a kind of correlate to a character's internal speech, has now become cemented as standard film music practice. Jazz proved so adept at providing a mood or signifying a free-wheeling approach to its subject that it became used by everyone from government information-film makers to the most wilfully avant-garde. If anything film score jazz worked its way through sheer over-exposure in the 1950s and early 1960s down the cultural register until as a form it seemed to reach the point where it has remained ever since. Jazz when incorporated now into the moving image has a kind of air of resignation, a kind of fenced-off boho-cool, not totally incorporated but yet no longer so defiantly individualistic. One might think of Robert Altman's 1993 *Short Cuts* with its Hal Wilner score of new down-at-heel songs written by pop musicians as diverse as Bono, Elvis Costello, Iggy Pop and Gavin Friday and sung in melancholic fashion by the great Annie Ross (an ex-member of 1950s jazz vocal group Hendricks, Lambert and Ross). Ross's character within the film is a melancholic jazz singer doomed to wander for ever the twilight world of LA's supper clubs and piano bars. Her songs do not emerge as statements of individuality but rather serve to signify her defeated resignation and absorption into the clichés of showbusiness. They also comment obliquely and ironically upon aspects of the fragmented narratives of *Short Cuts*. That the irony eventually includes Ross's own character, who sings blankly on stage following her daughter's suicide, functions, if one wishes to let it, as a metaphor for the way in which the essence of the song, the singer's individuality, has been sucked out of jazz by the cinema so that all we are left with is a representation of the blues. Altman of course realized this and turned the paradox against itself which is what makes his use of the musical soundtrack so effective in the film.

The way in which jazz came to be used in American and European cinema in the late 1950s and early 1960s exercised an immeasurable influence on the way in which pop music came to be used in film during the following decades. A key part of the revolution in film music that stems from this period is the deliberate decision to return music as far as possible to diegetic or on-screen sources. In a way what this did was to reintroduce music to the lives of the characters; suddenly they appeared to have concerns, memories and associations far wider than the arc of their story within the film. When

Godard chose to have his characters dance to a big beat pop number on a jukebox in *Bande à part*, he is acknowledging the parallel life in collective memory that the jukebox triggers. Music becomes alive through the jukebox in a way that no off-screen music could ever engineer. His characters celebrate the joy of immersion in a common culture, and when they dance they dance not as professionals but as passionate amateurs – fans. Records and even the radio are predominantly solitary experiences, and only the jukebox is expressly designed to be used in public. This moment has since been refracted even further by Quentin Tarantino as a reference point for the John Travolta–Uma Thurman jive sequence in *Pulp Fiction* (1994). In an interview with the BBC[10] he recounts showing the Godard sequence to his actors before filming his own scene. As Tarantino points out, why these scenes are enjoyable is that we are caught up in the pleasure felt consciously by the characters on screen. Pulp fiction caricatures dancing to retro jive music in a retro 1950s diner – as explicit an example as any of the infinitely mirror-like world of pop culture.

10 BBC TV *Omnibus*, September 1994

THE RISE OF THE POP SONG

Elmer Bernstein has claimed that the death of the classical film-music score began in 1952 with an innocuous pop song that was used in the title sequence of the classic Gary Cooper Western *High Noon*. The song itself, 'Do Not Forsake Me, O My Darlin'', sung by Tex Ritter, went on to become a substantial hit in its own right, and it was this initial instance of commercial success, Bernstein claims, that sent every producer scurrying in search of songs for their next picture.

High Noon brought with it, as well as its song, an unusual emphasis on the psychological processes of the protagonist. As Gilles Deleuze claimed, slowly but surely the American dependence on the action film was being eroded. The most famous sequence in the film musically is the climactic countdown to the big gunfight, where Gary Cooper is left alone in his office watching the clock tick towards doomsday. As he proceeds to draw up his last will and testament, the slowly swinging pendulum of a clock controls the tempo of a progressive and particularly stark theme from composer Dimitri Tiomkin, as we sense palpably the rising tension.

In a film full of adroit musical touches, Tiomkin chose in certain scenes to treat some aspects of dialogue operatically. The quoting of an oath of vengeance by a departing town judge to the marshal is fully underscored by the orchestra, a device which had been used the year before in similar fashion in a less well-known British film *The Rocking Horse Winner* (1949), with music by William Alwyn, where individual lines of dialogue are actually anticipated by the music.

High Noon wasn't of course the first film to be released with a catchy song on its soundtrack. Walt Disney had been building up its jukebox for years, but had not aggressively exploited the songs it owned as commercially available soundtrack albums. Soundtracks to films such as *Spellbound* (score by Miklós Rózsa), *The Song of Bernadette* (score by Alfred Newman) and *The Third Man* (score by Anton Karas) were all released in the 1940s but proved to be isolated examples.

Perhaps the biggest influence on the behaviour of film producers was the phenomenal success of television. By 1950 most American cities had at least one television station, whilst New York and Los Angeles had seven each. In 1951 it was reported that on average movie attendances in those American cities with a television station had fallen by between twenty and forty per cent. Restaurateurs, night-club owners and even public libraries (the New York Public Library reported a fall in book circulation that year) were affected by the new home-entertainment medium.

The Hollywood studio system crumbled under a combination of falling revenues and hostile judgements in the Supreme Court. Probably the most hostile was the judgement *United States* vs. *Paramount et al.* in 1948, where the eight controlling companies in the American motion-picture industry at that time (Paramount, Loews/MGM, RKO, Twentieth Century Fox, Warner Brothers, Columbia Pictures, Universal, United Artists) were effectively stopped from controlling the product that was exhibited in their own theatres. They had been charged with deliberately keeping out foreign products and discouraging domestic competition in an effort to ensure that their theatres played their own movies. This speeded up a process of decline and divestment which resulted in substantial job losses in every division of the motion picture industry. Some of that talent headed for the bright new world of television.

The first wave of television programmes comprised predominantly variety shows, often sponsored: *Texaco Star Theater* with Milton Berle, Ed Sullivan's *Toast of the Town*, Sid Caesar's *Show of Shows* and, the most successful of them all, *I Love Lucy*, with Lucille Ball and Desi Arnaz Jr. These were predominantly live shows (although *I Love Lucy* was taped), as was a stuttering range of very cheaply produced dramas (such as *Man against Crime* which, because it was produced live, contained a 'search scene' at the start of each episode which the lead actor could vary in length depending on how the network schedule was running!).

The real breakthrough in television production and the development that allowed the medium to compete on nearly every level with motion pictures was the rise of the recorded TV serial. Shows like *Dragnet*, *Gunsmoke* or *Alfred Hitchcock Presents* utilized many of the audience-hooking tricks that cinema had first tried out. Of these, music was a key ingredient in the armoury. Yet relations between the newly wealthy TV networks and the older feature film producer/distributors remained distant.[1] Much of the

---

[1] As late as 1954, Jack Warner at Warner Bros. apparently attempted to veto any domestic scenes in a Warners' movie where a television set was visible.

more successful television was being produced by ex-movie personalities and industry players who had been released from their contracts by hard-up studios: for example, Lucille Ball, Hal Roach and the mighty Revue Productions, a subsidiary of the talent agency MCA.

Paramount had acquired an interest in ABC in the 1940s at the instigation of the then Paramount boss, cigar heir William Paley. Most of the studios had leased their back-catalogue titles to the networks of regional American stations that couldn't afford to run more than a few hours of original programming each day. However, one of the first proper deals whereby a movie studio would produce programming for first-run release on a TV network was the deal that ABC made with Walt Disney in 1954 to produce the Disneyland series. Warner Brothers made a similar deal, spinning series out of three of their back-catalogue movie properties (including *Casablanca* – the TV series!).

A succession of deals between 1953 and 1956 saw a number of the bigger movie distributors off-load their back catalogue to third-party buyers. Typical was a deal where RKO sold their entire back catalogue of some 740 titles dating back to the 1920s together with an operative studio to General Teleradio, an offshoot of the General Tire and Rubber Company, for $25 million. The ready availability of films to the TV networks and regional affiliates by a host of new distributors led to a discounting frenzy and the rise of packaging as stations were coerced into buying larger and larger quantities of films at apparently knock-down prices. Films became a vital cornerstone in every stations schedule and this in turn directly influenced the quality and style of the made-for-television material that was being produced by the mid-1950s (especially as most of the more expensive drama was now being produced for the networks by the studios themselves). By the end of 1957 over one hundred US-produced episodic series were either on the air or in production.

The demand for music was considerable. In formats that were either twenty-four or forty-eight minutes in duration, cue music performed a vital task in preparing the audience for the frequent commercial breaks, each break being preceded by a cliff-hanger. The dramas normally played out in these classic television series tended to be pretty simplistic. There was not much room for detailed psychological portraits of any of the characters and music tended to be required mainly to track climactic action sequences. The exception to this was the theme music to the main title which was a vitally important part of the station's on-going battle to identify itself against its rival stations throughout the evening. Main-title sequences needed to be immediately recognizable, dynamic and appeal to the key demographics that the stations and their enthusiastic advertisers were seeking. In American terms in the mid-1950s this would have been primarily the young family audience (the real-life Brady Bunches) with a father in work, a mother in the home and two or more teenage children just at the beginning of a lifetime's consumption.

One of the biggest film composers of the 1950s and 1960s, Henry Mancini, learnt his craft in a series of Big Bands during the 1940s. Joining Universal Studios in 1952 as a staff composer, he spent many years working as instructed on short cues from a never-ending supply of scoreless B-movies. Often one film would contain the work of two or three different composers;

> I would compose the little transitional bars of music between my own stuff and the cues out of the studio library that went into a film. It was called 'stocking' and it gave the illusion, but illusion only, of being a whole score. If I had something that I did all by myself, then I would approach it as trying to get some sort of cohesive style. But at Universal in those days we had several staff composers . . . what we would do is, we'd look at a picture, usually they were ten-reelers and we'd take the library music and we'd each score five reels apiece or so . . . you'd take out what you needed from the library and write it into your score when you needed just that much tension music or chase or love music. Then the orchestra would come in and record the whole thing for the final version of the film.[2]

Having used his Big Band experience to good effect in arranging the scores for *The Glenn Miller Story* (1954) and *The Benny Goodman Story* (1955), one of Mancini's first film assignments was Orson Welles' *Touch of Evil*; he went for an abrasive Latin rock feel, countering the darker themes of the story. Welles had his own detailed ideas for the music to his film and one of the elements which he was particularly interested in bringing out was the source music to be heard from radios and bars in the Mexican border town where the story is set. Mancini might have been one more talented but largely unsung composer had it not been for the phenomenally successful TV theme for *Peter Gunn* (1958), which went on to become a hit in its own right. It's a flashy driving theme that draws heavily on the West Coast 'cool' style typified by Shelly Manne in its use of a walking bass and drums, but it combines this with a definite feeling for rock'n'roll with the synchronization of piano and guitar lines playing in unison. The theme was subsequently re-recorded and

[2] John Caps, 'The Lyricism of Mancini', *Film Music Notebook*, 1976

released under Mancini's own name (a move reluctantly agreed to by RCA after Shorty Rogers turned it down) certainly one of the first times a TV theme had been released on record (the theme to *Dragnet* had been successfully re-recorded for commercial release by bandleader Ray Anthony a few months before). The album was also recorded in stereo (still not yet a mass-market phenomenon) and each cue had been carefully re-recorded by Mancini to render each track complete in the album rather than simply tailing off as the original cues on the soundtrack did. This attention equally to the film soundtrack itself and to the careful re-recording of the soundtrack album marks Mancini out as one of the first composers to think in terms of two functions for the soundtrack recording. Significantly, from *Peter Gunn* onwards, Mancini retained a substantial slice of the publishing rights which netted him considerable wealth. The album for *Peter Gunn* occupied *Billboard*'s no. 1 slot for weeks and stayed in the Top 100 for nearly two years. The producer of *Peter Gunn* was Blake Edwards, whose eyes were squarely on the movie business. He induced Mancini, who, thanks to *Peter Gunn*, had suddenly become a successful recording artist (as opposed to simply a composer), to compose and perform the music for *Breakfast at Tiffany's*, a film based upon one of Truman Capote's whimsical novellas.

Breakfast at Tiffany's (1961) boasted a seductively lilting and melodic title song, 'Moon River', scored by Mancini and with lyrics by Johnny Mercer. Audrey Hepburn's beautifully tender voice sings the song on the original soundtrack whilst the released soundtrack album features a decidedly MOR strings-with-chorus version. The song appears about only four times throughout the film and stands in contrast to the other cues which are either straight source music or more conventionally 'dramatic' pieces. Part of the success of 'Moon River', with its highly engaging melody and dreamy lyrics, is because it is used sparingly; Mancini trusts the dramatic qualities of the melody line itself to narrate the on-screen emotion. It appears to capture Holly Golightly's thought processes perfectly and conjures up a fairy-tale feel that is so much a part of the book's appeal. One critic praised the score as embodying 'the very taste of caviare'. The Oscar-winning success of this score cemented Mancini's reputation as a film composer with the golden touch. It also did much to ensure the future importance in the film industry of the hit song as an essential part of the film's content and marketing mix.

Mancini did more than anyone else to alter the landscape of film music composition. In a post-jazz-scoring climate, he reinstated melody and proved that emotion can be wrung from more than simple string

POP CULTURE AND FILM MUSIC

In a marvellously upbeat account written in 1959, Francis Newton described the inexorable rise of pop music as:

> One of the last frontiers of private enterprise. On these rhythmic waves buccaneers of the old type can still sail their ships as gentlemen of fortune: out-smarting one another and anyone else, greasing palms, steering nimbly through the whirlpools of promoting, record-making, publishing, managing, booking, plugging and the rest. This is still the world in which smart young men can make it. The organization man, the tame psychologist, the economic adviser are still far away. And so long as the cost of production of the hit tune or song, on which the industry rests, remains as low as it does (and that is a great deal lower than a film, a TV show or a stage show), the jungle will continue to flourish in it, and the panthers will continue to prowl it, as they do the rather similar garment trade, enjoying the kill as much as, and perhaps more than, the actual meal.[1]

The inroads made by pop composers at the end of the 1950s influenced to a greater degree than anything else the character of all subsequent film music. Where pop influences had guided the successes of trained composers and arrangers such as Henry Mancini, pop music in its simplest and brashest forms now partnered films from almost every country. Of course pop had always existed – it was simply shorthand for saying that something was popular – but from the mid-1950s onwards a new kind of confusion crept into the definitions, compounded by the urgency of its newest form, rock and roll.

The early youth-fixated movies of the 1950s were rock movies lacking rock stars, although the seeds of youthful rebellion finally achieved a kind of soundtrack when Bill Haley's 'Rock Around the Clock' ignited the carefully packaged *Blackboard Jungle* (1955). International youth culture had now

[1] Francis Newton, *The Jazz Scene* (London: 1959), p. 183

become a subject encompassing teenage rebellion, fun, fashion and small-town life. On the success of this, Bill Haley and his band of ageing boppers were hastily repackaged into a throwaway story about a band from the sticks trying to break into the New York music scene. *Rock Around the Clock* (1956) was an immediate hit and launched an era of cinema seat-slashing and other highly participatory practices at screenings of a whole host of cash-in movies: *Don't Knock the Rock* (1957), *Shake, Rattle and Rock* (1957), *Rock, Pretty Baby* (1957) and, perhaps the best of all, *The Girl Can't Help It*, also from 1957.

Naturally the pace subsided after a couple of years and the new genre, youth movies, settled into a consummate pattern of banal mediocrity, particularly in Britain, where a dreadful crop of films celebrated the parochial appeal of Tommy Steel (*The Duke Wore Jeans*, 1958), Cliff Richard (*Expresso Bongo*, 1960) and Billy Fury (*Play It Cool*, 1962).

The force that saved the youth movie was also the force that probably saved pop music from a premature implosion: an injection of new talent from outside the USA. The Beatles were authentically British (specifically Liverpudlian) and were, as Nik Cohn observed:

> Always perfectly self-contained, independent, as if the world was split cleanly into two races, the Beatles and everybody else, and they seemed to live off nobody but themselves.[2]

This enclosed quality was brilliantly exploited in Richard Lester's inventive portrait of the Beatles, *A Hard Day's Night* (1964), which in terms of its sophisticated style and speed rewrote the language of filmed pop culture. Here was a film that in its subject, visual language and music was irrefutably about pop and very much of pop. Lester's film fashions a kind of diary covering thirty-six hours in the life of the Beatles, glimpsed at the height of their powers as entertainers and all-round icons. Showcasing some of the band's biggest hits to date in a surreal setting, Lester's film displays an eclectic range of influences ranging from Keaton to Fellini to the French *nouvelle vague* with more than a hint of the Marx Brothers thrown in.

Teenage magazines went to great lengths to try to explain the myriad worlds of pop to their readers, the British *Mademoiselle* magazine in 1968 attempting a virtual (and rather complicated) taxonomy of pop for its young readers. Included were such categories as Guts (Bessie Smith, Leadbelly, Woody Guthrie), Rockabilly (Johnny Cash, the Everlys), White Roll (Bill

2 Nik Cohn, *WopBopalooBoplopBamBoom* (London: 1969), p. 126

Haley), Art Rock (Procol Harum), Hate Rock (Frank Zappa and the Mothers of Invention), Classical (the Beatles *circa Sergeant Pepper*), Cocktail Soul (The Supremes) and Middle Class Folk Revival (Joan Baez and Bob Dylan). Perhaps the only thing that all these disparate strands of music and sub-culture had in common was that they had been commercialized very effectively by the international record and entertainment corporations.

Pop culture was carried into the hearts and minds of a relatively wealthy America and Europe on a wave of vastly more powerful media forces. Aside from the ferocious and all-encompassing march of television, newspapers and advertising grew considerably more sophisticated in their manipulation and targeting of the public. New categories of service industry, such as public relations, grew up on the back of this surge and eagerly stoked the fires of mass-market desire. Teenage life was becoming increasingly organized by people who were not teenagers. Albert Hunt, in his contribution to a 1964 study of the mass media, observed:

> This tendency to reduce experience to a formula which fits our most commonplace assumptions can only contribute in the end to the fixing of sharply defined limits of taste and awareness. Anything which questions the commonplace or challenges the imagination is likely to be discouraged. It is this processing of experience that we need to be aware of in confronting the typical products of the film industry . . . a medium that has shown itself to be capable of extending awareness is being used to reflect the most obvious assumptions shared by the greatest number of people, assumptions which tend, in their turn, to be fixed by their own constant reflexion.[3]

The pop album increasingly resembled a film in the sense that it was becoming a much more collaborative process than ever before. As the film industry struggled to legitimize itself as an art form to be taken seriously, so pop pursued a similar ambition resulting in the turgid pomposity of Progressive or, to coin *Mademoiselle*'s category, Art Rock, by the end of the decade. As cinemas inherited to a certain extent a disaffected theatre crowd during the 1960s, so pop (or rock as it really was) inherited audiences from the jazz and folk scenes. As the LP or album became the standard form of musical experience for many people, so more people became aware gradually of a greater range of musical styles than ever before, historically, ethnically and geographically. More and more musicians and composers in the film and pop fields began to experiment with the recording environment itself, controlling the very processes of musical attentiveness, rendering the old

3 Albert Hunter, 'The Film', in *Discrimination and Popular Culture*, ed. Denys Thompson (London: 1964), pp. 113–14

musical language of harmony, counterpoint or meter inadequate.

By the end of the 1960s the pop and rock axis was beginning to take itself very seriously. Kit Lambert, manager of the Who, in 1968 claimed that the Who's '*Magic Bus*' is a 'better' piece of music than Stravinsky's Symphony in Three Movements. At the same time most of the people involved in pop music had very little idea of what was happening in any other musical field but their own, remaining blissfully unaware of the progressive (but admittedly not mass-market) advances that modern composers such as Cornelius Cardew and Harrison Birtwhistle were making in the shadow of pop.

Rock and pop were direct descendants of the pulp novel or the B-movie in their appeal to the culturally disenfranchised. As Nik Cohn perceptively wrote in 1969:

> Superpop? It hasn't been much, it's been simple always, silly and vulgar and fake, and it has been a noise, that's all. In the end, specific records and singers have hardly mattered. Instead it's just been pop itself, just the existence of it, the drone of it running through everything. It has surrounded me always, cut me off, and it has given me my heroes, it has made my myths. Almost it has done my living for me. Six hours of trash every day, and it's meant more to me than anything else.[4]

In terms of instrumental, pop-influenced film music, John Barry was undoubtedly the most successful British recording artist to make the transition to film scoring. In the late 1950s in England he had already had a couple of instrumental chart hits with his own group, the John Barry Seven, as well as having scored an impecunious British teen-riot movie called *Beat Girl* (1962). It was the James Bond film franchises that catapulted him into the upper reaches of success as a composer. His two-minute 'James Bond theme' written for the first Bond movie, *Dr No* (1962), is a compulsive and compact piece of rock-jazz writing, combining distinctly ska-influenced electric guitar and brass and percussion into a tightly structured orchestration. Barry created with this one theme (as much as with his subsequent Bond scores) a highly influential style that permeated the whole industry to at least as great a degree as Henry Mancini's work had. The Bond films are erotic acquisition/destruction sprees as we see each of Bond's fabulous new toys blown to pieces in a suitably spectacular fashion. Bond was a capitalist icon and Barry's music perfectly conveys the wound up, tensile strength of the main character, at the same time as, in its pop stylings, signifying a disposability. Barry's music became not so much a cue

4 Nic Cohn, *WopBopalooBoplopBamBoom*, p. 230

to anticipate on-screen events as a reinforcing mechanism (not really any different from an advertising jingle), constantly keeping the central concept/product (Bond) at the front of our minds. The Bond films were one of the first globally successful franchises. Once the character had been established so successfully with *Dr No* there seemed no limit to the number of subsequent adventures that could be filmed.

As pop grew up, its musical eclecticism broadened slightly, unusual instrumentation appearing at the edges of the aura whilst retaining the archetypal simplicity of the basic blues form. Luciano Berio, the composer, wrote about the Beatles in 1967:

> Every epic form is based upon the revaluation and the respectful transference into another context of the *déjà vu*. When instruments like the trumpet, the harpsichord, the string quartet and the recorder, etc. are used they seem to assume the estranged character of quotations of themselves. The extra instruments are adopted like polished objects from a far-off world reminiscent of the utopia of the return to our origins.[5]

Amplification was a major part of rock's appeal and also, in its degree and deployment, its gradual enfranchisement from pop. It also changed many of the most fundamental aspects of film music in terms of modifying whatever archetypal generative structures had governed the symphonic film score. The loudspeaker was anything but neutral and intruded quite radically upon the musical world. Electric instruments added a strange kind of continuity to group playing, since all instruments were capable of being heard at the same levels if required. New types of what Cornelius Cardew called the 'acoustic aura' became possible, since all instruments tended to blend together, reducing the individual contributions of each player. Feedback itself produced a particular kind of sonic linearity which acted as a counterpoint to the premeditated structures being played by the musicians. This development, progressive throughout the 1960s, reaches its peak in a song like 'Sister Ray' by the Velvet Underground[6] (significantly, linked with Andy Warhol and contributors to some of his antivariational films).

The rock-derived soundtrack often posed unique problems of method since the songwriters frequently had little or no idea of how to arrange their songs for orchestra or how to place their music in the film, and in most cases the songs were composed without the musicians having seen the film, the producer merely being content to promote the band's name in his picture,

[5] Luciano Berio, 'Commenti al Rock', *Rivista Musicale Italiana*, vol. 1, May–June 1967

[6] 'Sister Ray', the Velvet Underground, from *White Light/White Heat* CD

whatever their precise contribution. For the greater part, however, the pop/rock vehicles of the mid- to late-1960s were simply compilation soundtracks of already existing records, paving the way for further exploitation throughout the 1970s and 1980s. Amongst the soundtracks that were specially composed, some of the better examples included Brian Jones' contribution to *A Degree of Murder* (1966), Mike Curb's *Riot on Sunset Strip* (1967), Gorge Martin and the Beatles' *Yellow Submarine* (1968), the Seed's involvement with *Psych-Out* (1968), the Strawberry Alarm Clock's *Beyond the Valley of the Dolls* (1970), Dave Grusin's *Candy* (1969), and *Quiet Days in Clichy* (1970) with songs from Country Joe McDonald.

The motorcycle, with all its connotations of speed and rugged individualism, became a key icon of the 1960s counter-cultural movie. Combined with the heavily amplified guitar distortions of either Jimi Hendrix (*Easy Rider*, 1969) or garage punk bands like the Electric Flag or the Seeds, it redefined and revived some of the key images of iconoclasm first thrown up by the wave of jazz-inspired movies a decade earlier. Rebellion now was a group rather than individual activity, and the plaintive solos of West Coast jazz were displaced by the collaborative din of rock.

Rather different from the rock scene was the emerging iconography of the blaxploitation movie genre. Blaxploitation is the only genre that has become defined by its musical soundtracks. Rooted in the white B-movies of the 1940s and 1950s, blaxploitation movies simply dressed up their black casts and had them run through all the familiar features of the detective B-movie. Whilst most of these films are now lost to obscurity, many of the soundtracks remain popular. In many cases the stars on the soundtracks were bigger names within the black communities than those in the movie. James Brown, Marvin Gaye, Isaac Hayes and Curtis Mayfield were all artists whose careers had begun in the pop industries of Motown, Atlantic and Stax records. Tired perhaps of the easy adulation that had marked their careers since the early 1960s many of these artists began to spend more time in the studio experimenting on new kinds of arrangements. Black popular music by 1970 had moved from being primarily a performance-driven art form to a studio-based one. Issac Hayes' *Hot Buttered Soul* from 1969 contains twenty-minute-long ballads, orchestral backing and even some Burt Bacharach covers.

During this period of transition and experimentation Hollywood unexpectedly emerged as a major player in the commissioning and licensing of this new studio-based black music. No doubt recognizing the powerful pull of artists such as Curtis Mayfield and Isaac Hayes, the record companies commissioned soundtracks which allowed in the non-lyrical sections the instrumental work-outs that artists searched for but could not find in the single and album formats, both of which were dependent on radio play. Expanding the parameters of soul music with lush strings, horns, percussion and complex vocal lines, Isaac Hayes' soundtrack to *Shaft* (1971) won an Oscar with a primarily instrumental score which nevertheless spawned a hit title song. Marvin Gaye's soundtrack to *Trouble Man* (1972) is a low-key, heavily jazz-influenced work-out with Gaye's songwriting and vocals in great form. The album was composed in between his recordings of 'What's Going On?' and 'Let's Get It On', arguably the artistic peak of his career. Curtis Mayfield's soundtrack to *Superfly* (1972) stands up to the best soul music ever produced, and perfectly sums up what the blaxploitation genre was all about: drug dealing, whores, guns and a mythological male protagonist. Mayfield's songs are not simply background wash but are social criticism; the character in the song 'Freddie's Dead' dies whilst 'Pushin' dope for the man!' The very violent *Across 110th Street* (1972) had a superb soundtrack by Bobby Womack and took the blaxploitation movie clichés as far as they could go, finally exploding them and, in doing so, killing off a genre that had run its course.

Diegetically there was very little difference between the way in which instrumental cues were used in these movies and the way in which jazz-influenced cues were used outside the genre. Funk-influenced cues defined almost exclusively urban settings for the blaxploitation movies and were primarily used to create an affectionate link between the characters and a wider reservoir of black culture of which music was the most pervasive element. The instrumental sounds of the wah-wah pedal, the hyperactive hi-hat and the billowing rhythm-driven strings signify a particular style of black urban folklore in the same way that jazz is celebratory in the French New Wave films.

In recent years the pop soundtrack has become such a necessary adjunct of the marketing of youth movies that its use is now universal and in most cases unexceptional. Its breakthrough moments were between the early 1960s and early 1970s, beyond which point pop was a fully incorporated element into the film apparatus. With a trend towards straight cross-licensing rather than the commissioning of new material the possibilities open to both producers and directors of new movies are often somewhat limited. The soundtrack to the American teen movie *Pretty in Pink* (1986) contains a number of (then) respectably well-known artists: Suzanne Vega, Psychedelic Furs, New Order, INXS, the Smiths and Echo and the

Bunnymen, all of whom were at the time signed to A&M records in the United States. But contrast this with the soundtrack to a similarly teen-orientated movie from the same period, *The Breakfast Club* (1985), which helped create a hit song by Simple Minds, 'Don't You Forget About Me', but contains little else of interest on a soundtrack from MCA that looks distinctly like a case of corporate barrel-scraping. This kind of packaging, with varied results, still characterizes most pop music deals that are tied up with the film and television industries. In many cases the deals done are simply between different divisions of the same entertainment conglomerate.

In Europe the tendency has been to package soundtracks with songs that have already been hits in their own right rather than risk a new song or a less well known artist. This despite the fact that this route is one of the most expensive ways to access music for soundtrack licensing, since both publishing and recording rights are being sold at a premium. The popularity of pop compilation soundtracks over the past two decades has led to a marked increase in label bidding wars for both plum pop soundtrack releases and licensed tracks by top artists. In the worst case, as Ron Fair of RCA Records claims; for a single soundtrack rebase, a label may have to deal with thirteen artists, from thirteen labels, with thirteen lawyers, thirteen managers and thirteen publishers.[7]

European media groups are disadvantaged in accessing existing recordings or in licensing a new recording of an old song since they lack the vertical and horizontal integration of American media companies such as Time Warner, with its highly profitable Warner Chappell subsidiary. A 1995 survey by the National Music Publishers' Association estimated that annual music publishing revenue totalled $5.03bn. Whitney Houston's recording of the Dolly Parton song 'I Will Always Love You' for the platinum-selling soundtrack to *The Bodyguard* (1993) serves as a vivid example of how music publishing companies are supposed to function. Whilst the music publishing business is widely viewed as a low overhead high revenue generating activity, it's dynamics are not well understood, and therefore music publishing divisions are often first on the list of assets to be sold when the corporate parent company seeks to pare down its debt. Yet publishing is where the money is made, a fact appreciated by only a minority of film composers when beginning their careers. Quincy Jones:

> Because I spent so much time in the record business, I had a lot of experience in
> dealing with royalties and publishing rights before I started writing for the movies,

[7] *Daily Variety*, 20 March 1995, p. 12

and I had no idea that the film composer shouldn't expect to get a taste of any of that income. The funny part about it is that on the first picture I did, *The Pawnbroker* (1965), I got half the publishing without any argument, and I thought: no sweat, this isn't going to be a problem. Then when I got to California, asking for the publishing rights was like asking to make it with the director's wife. Publishing? You kidding? Sixty per cent of total profits at Warner in 1969 was from the music side of the company.[8]

Particularly amongst independent film producers, there are signs of a more creative attitude towards the sourcing of music for soundtracks. Another recent tendency has been to explore the archives of pop, going beyond the obvious hits to conjure up a sense of time and place and digging deeper for the more obscure songs where some of the usual licensing difficulties can be overcome (although the copyright owners may be untraceable). By packaging these artists in movies whose post-modern sensibilities defy the ravages of time, a soundtrack can prove spectacularly successful – as in the cases of *Reservoir Dogs* and *Pulp Fiction* – yet cost comparatively little to put together.

Often, the film can be of secondary importance to the music deal. American rap singer Dr Dre's film *Murder Was The Case* (1994) spawned a hit soundtrack of contributions by various artists, including some of the top names in hip-hop. It has sold over one million units in the United States and clocks in at seventy minutes, despite the fact that the film itself was nothing more than an extended eight minute music promo. Interestingly, the release label for the soundtrack Interscope (at the time, twenty-five-per-cent owned by Warner Music) licensed most of the other artists on the soundtrack from rival labels. A similar licensing deal, but this time in Europe, surrounded the popular French youth movie *La Haine* (1995) whose director Mathieu Kassovitz initiated two soundtrack CD releases, the first of which, a more conventional soundtrack, sold some eight thousand units in France as against seventy-five thousand units for a second release, which was promoted as *La Haine: Musiques inspirées du film* and contained an eleven song selection of new songs by top French rap acts such as MC Solaar, Sens Unik and IAM. Label manager for the CD, Laurence Touitou of Delabel, said:

It's interesting to make music and images that interact. It's an original concept. It's another way of talking about the film. The younger directors live on the streets and they're very involved in music. They are definitely creating stronger soundtracks.[9]

8 'Quincy Jones on the Composer', from *Movie People*, ed. Fred Baker (London: 1973), p. 163
9 *Variety*, 22–8 January 1996, p. 84

The biggest threat to the autonomy of the film narrative in the era of large and diversified entertainment companies is what kind of a showcase within the film the positioning of the 'hit song' will demand. Music videos are a completely different kind of communication. Their very excess resists most kinds of narrativisation, as can be seen from the placement of musical moments in the American TV series *Miami Vice* from the late 1980s. The musical interludes do little or nothing to advance the narrative or increase our understanding of the characters or help us drive forward the narrative ourselves. As John Fiske has pointed out these digressionary sequences tend to focus upon:

> Objects that are the bearers of high-style, high-tech, commodified masculinity . . . this fragment within the narrative links with other fragments of the viewer's cultural experience (particularly with the iconography of pop music) rather than with the rest of the narrative.[10]

These types of digressionary longueurs are becoming more common, primarily in action genre films aimed at young audiences (fifteen to twenty-five-year-olds specifically – not surprisingly, given that this audience is the most likely to consume merchandising around a film, as well as being the key market for pop music sales). As films become marketed more and more as events rather than simply as films it seems likely that this process of intra-exploitation by entertainment companies will develop into other areas of the film's narrative. Music based television depends more and more upon the film and television industries for its cultural agenda. A recent MTV survey[11] revealed that eighty-seven per cent of their viewers wanted to see more films, and the global network is moving closer to satisfying this demand with specially themed strands of programming that celebrate film franchises such as *Star Trek*, alternating the programming of films and clips from the TV series with music video clips. In many cases the distribution infrastructures set up by the music industry giants such as Polygram, Sony, Warners and BMG over the past forty years are more sophisticated than specialised film-distribution set-ups. Capitalizing on this advantage, most of these music companies over the past decade have sought to reposition themselves as highly diverse entertainment providers with aggressive footholds in everything from film production to the emerging digital gateways of video-on-demand distribution. Polygram, partly owned by Dutch electrical giant

[10] John Fiske, *Television Culture* (London: 1987), p. 257

[11] *Variety*, 22–8 January 1996, p. 86

Philips, has been typical in its move from basic music software production and distribution into feature film production and distribution. In turn this kind of diversification will fuel the future platforms of filmed entertainment and multimedia on new formats such as Video CD, DVD and DVD-Rom.

POP AND THE MUSIC OF CHANCE

Pop and rock soundtracks blurred the gap between the mainstream film industry and the nominally 'uncommercial' or underground cinema. The films of Andy Warhol are a case in point. Whilst in most of his so-called 'superstar' films of the mid- and late 1960s it is dialogue rather than music that informs the soundtrack, music in the form of fragments of everyday aural detritus presented as 'overheard' does play an important part in the 'branding' activities that are so much a part of a Warhol film. These branding activities encompass a kind of selective eavesdropping on pop culture and a deliberate strategy of lifting pop music from its throwaway radio context into the realm of artistic expression so self-consciously aimed at by films such as *Harlot*, *Kitchen* and *Chelsea Girls* (with its multiple soundtracks and double projections). Pop music and its originary metaphor, the radio, have only really become a global phenomenon since the mid-1970s. Before this point its language and references were overwhelmingly Anglo-American. Perhaps the metaphor is more powerful than the sound itself, as John Cage pondered in 1973:

> I imagine that fifty per cent of the automobiles on the highway have a radio going and are existing in a medium of music, though very third- and fourth-rate music. Now I do not believe that kind of music does anything to enhance what is going on within those cars and automobiles; they'd do better just to listen to the whistling of the wind. There's one station now on the radio, in New York, that reminds me of Satie and that is WINS. It's a continuous news station, and the program, if you listen long enough as you are driving along the highway, more or less repeats itself in the same way that the Vexations of Satie would be repeated, because you come back to the weather at regular intervals and, in fact, to the same headline news.[1]

Whatever Cage might have felt about the objective quality of popular

[1] *Conversing with Cage*, ed. Richard Kostalanetz (New York: 1988)

Chance remains fashionable, and at the same time conveys a very serious compositional intent. The inclusion of chance elements seems to challenge the basic integrities of much of the Western art tradition. The intersection of what appear to be merely contingent events into the space of artworks ruptures the whole process of artistic intention. It seems to connect the artwork to a far wider pattern of regularities than the isolated world of the gallery space, the concert hall or the figurational world of cinema.

Chance has become a standard 'compositional tool' in much of the art music produced during the past four decades. One might think of John Cage and a typically challenging series of concerts given with Lejaren Hiller known as HPSCHD at the University of Illinois in 1969. Taking as a starting point a musical experiment by Mozart entitled *Introduction to the Composition of Waltzes by Means of Dice* (consisting of endless possible permutations on a one-minute waltz divided into a number of eight-measure sections, the playing order of which is determined by the throw of a dice), Cage and Hiller create an entire multimedia experience out of the possibilities generated by Mozart's game. Two main sound sources are used, one consisting of fifty-one computer-generated sound fields, each tuned slightly differently and composed by a computer program partly programmed with numerical values abstracted from a text of the I Ching. HPSCHD is a musical work that explores notions of musical texture, as bank upon bank of computer sounds impinge upon the sounds of seven harpsichords each playing a cycle of pieces unsynchronized with the others. The precise nature of this overwhelming sonic experience depends upon where the listener is sitting, the phasing of the listener's concentration and so on, each moment of clarity or dissonance the result of any chance factors. (The original record release, on the Nonesuch label, even supplied additional keyboard scores for the home harpsichordist to join in!)

The conscious losing of compositional control by Cage and many others of his contemporaries has been approached in many different ways of which HPSCHD is but one example. Cage's aleatory elements are primarily derived from his performance rituals, whilst a more traditionally inclined composer such as Iannis Xenakis has used chance at the compositional level, integrating a computer into his composing. To whatever level the notion of chance has been integrated into music, it has in many cases resulted in work which is unusually lucid. In the visual arts Marcel Duchamp's 'ready-mades' are examples of artworks apparently virtually untouched by the artist himself and certainly not by any conventional compositional idea. Music and to a lesser extent painting seem ideally suited to open-ended forms of expression as much as they are open to open-ended forms of interpretation, yet surely film is a more closed art form due to its industrial complexity, and the formulaic and contrived song structures of pop music even more so?

The road movie, as defined by Wenders, and Warhol's home movies double-projected are both signs of an aleatory instinct in cinema. Wenders himself has described the road movie as an itinerary through which his characters reach a point where they are forced to make a choice. Pop music, in the endless turning of the radio dial in search of a station or a song, is glimpsed as a moment of connection, an instant of clarity in a wider field of cultural static. Cinema itself is always engaged with elements of chance, the difference between seven or eight apparently identical takes of the same scene, between deliberately composed foregrounds and uncontrollable backgrounds, the difference even in quality between prints of a film as it slowly decays through constant handling. The film frame itself, the picture boundary, seems to delineate chance activity by reducing the picture space in which it may occur. Chance elements themselves have become associated (perhaps even relegated) with some notion of 'realism'. The unpredictable documentary footage of the pioneers such as Vertov and Cavalcanti seems predicated on a certain level of unpredictability intruding into what otherwise would amount to cinematic essays. The montage techniques of Eisenstein utilize chance elements caught by the camera during shooting as flexible bridging points in the assembly of a dialectic visual message. The commercial cinema one might say has tended to try to eliminate elements of chance whilst other kinds of cinema have celebrated it, although this delineation becomes less valid in cinema that has incorporated pop music in the post-modern era.

Pop music becomes aleatory in cinema when it is shown in a context in which it naturally occurs. Pop heard diegetically on a radio or a jukebox or from a passing car adds to the sense of time and place realism which most films strive for. It fulfils a similar function to the cutaway shot to an inanimate object, the convincing detail that tricks us into believing we have entered another world as richly cluttered as our own. Norman Spenser, the producer of the film *Vanishing Point* (1970), seized on the random features of pop as the overheard in electing to make the soundtrack of the film an approximation of the playlist of a fictional DJ (Super Soul) on a fictional radio station (KOW) in what is basically a trans-American road movie. Most of the pop music was performed and recorded for the film and is a collection of some eighteen soul-influenced pop tunes which are heard throughout the film, making for a reasonably contemporary feel at a fraction of the cost of clearing the licensing rights on a more stellar collection of recording artists.

The pop song that is overheard is also a powerful signifier. It is one of the more ambiguous signifiers since pop music itself is so culturally loaded. Is the director merely trying to conjure up an authentic environment? Is the song being used because of its lyrical content which is perhaps acting as a kind of Greek chorus? Is the film making some sort of cultural critique of past or present pop formats? In most cases the use of pre-recorded pop music tends to grow out of the action contained in the story, as first impressively demonstrated in Michelangelo Antonioni's *Zabriskie Point*, where even a character's wishes are fulfilled and tracked by apocalyptic rock music, the sonic character of which itself seems to explode a millionaire's house to the strains of Pink Floyd's 'Come in Number 51, Your Time is Up'.

Non-diegetically used pop music, that which is simply 'there' on the soundtrack along with the narrator's voice, dialogue and other elements, is a different case. Aside from its possible function as a kind of stripped-down Greek chorus (such as *Four Weddings and a Funeral*'s use of 'Love is All Around') based on lyrical relevance, this kind of pop presence confirms the slick interplay between the different divisions of global entertainment corporations. The song as tacit commentator is almost a genre of film music in its own right and has reinvented the value of a record company's back catalogue. Quentin Tarantino[4] has claimed that when he is planning a new film, one of his first steps is to pick out the right song to use with the opening credit sequence.

In David Lynch's *Wild at Heart* (1990), which is like a meta-road movie, a conventional set of rock and roll songs are reinterpreted with some irony by modern-day performers. This act of reinterpretation serves primarily to confirm a highly idiosyncratic take on the road-movie genre to which Lynch sets out to pay a warped kind of homage. The interpretative play of the film rests in the image field, rather than the iconographic status of the songs themselves, confirmed in the use of cover versions rather than the original recordings.

Conversely, the early American 'travelogue' films of Wim Wenders, particularly *The American Friend* and *Alice in the Cities*, use the atmospheres of rock and roll songs by the original artists to confirm genre and to confirm geographical location. Wenders as a European film maker fascinated with the mythological terrain of the American landscape uses American music to bridge the cultural gap between his own position as an outsider and the

---

4 Interview with Quentin Tarantino in *Celluloid Jukebox*, eds Jonathan Romney and Adrian Woolton (London: 1995), p. 130

borrowed identity his characters adopt as strangers in a strange land. Pop music becomes utopian and Wenders' characters seem to turn into symbols, lost (European) figures in an American theme park.

The idea that pop music redefined through redeployment can subvert the very idea of authenticity has much in common with the use of aleatory elements in the creation of other kinds of artworks. One might speculate about similar desires, to go beyond the conscious moment of compositional choice, to somehow escape an identity as a creating composer or film maker and to rediscover the power of the original moment of rock music, by re-creating the radio experience through the archetypal journey of the road movie.

Popular culture since the post-punk era has entered into a cycle of reruns of earlier youth movements, each retro fetish being further removed from the original culture than the previous. Now the 1950s and 1960s are held up as the quintessence of pop culture. As Will Straw puts it:

> In the absence of a style which innocently and fully can be said to express the present, the attractiveness of styles which seem to embody the historical fullness of the past increases. At the same time it is the plenitude of this embodiment, rather than specific qualities of the historical moment, which threaten to become the important criteria.[5]

It is this 'aura' that Wim Wenders appropriated, using his own favourite 1960s rock songs in the early 1970s. In more recent years, particularly from *Wings of Desire* (1987) onwards, rock songs have continued to play an important part in Wenders' films but have been mainly drawn from contemporary artists such as David Byrne, R.E.M., Nick Cave and U2. These songs, whilst appearing both diegetically and non-diegetically in the films themselves, have tended to fulfil their material role more as staple elements in an impressive series of showcases of contemporary bands. The aura of the original 1960s rock sources has diminished to be replaced with the highly referential songs of U2, a group singularly aware, if not fully in control, of the signs and semiologies of pop culture. Perhaps this is the logical way to continue to give pop or more specifically rock culture the significance it once had. In choosing those artists most aware of the diminished status of the rock song in the post-modern era and inviting them to provide songs in his films, Wenders is perhaps simply reflecting the present closing chapter in rock's iconography.

---

[5] Will Straw, 'Popular Music and Postmodernism in the 1980s', in *Sound and Vision*, ed. Simon Frith (London: 1993)

The soundtrack in modern cinema has become just one more element in a global media language where all traces of personal or national identity have been reduced to the level of imitation. Frederic Jameson describes the situation as a kind of dilemma for the creative artist:

> With the collapse of the high-modernist ideology of style – what is as unique and unmistakable as your own fingerprints – the producers of culture have nowhere to turn but the imitation of dead styles, speech through all the masks and voices stored up in the imaginary museum of a now global culture.[6]

Rock or pop music in its dotage, wholly appropriated by cinema and television, has undergone a death. The semiological death of the pop author/musician. Cinema and television both offer the kind of free interpretational space predicted by Roland Barthes' notion of the death of the author, making the viewer the most important interpreter of the music, which paradoxically liberates the music, to be reclaimed by the unique perspectives of each listener–viewer. Despite the inevitable conservatism that has characterized the packaging of pop as a staple ingredient of film music from the 1950s onwards, pop as a musical form has done much to invigorate traditional film cue music on a creative level. As rock became more complex in its structure and began to take influences from other more challenging areas of modern music, so new concerns with musical content and concepts such as pitch logic, sound colour, texture and performance itself also entered into the common concerns of rock and pop musicians, and no less into their burgeoning second careers as film composers.

One of the most successful and influential rock musicians to compose film music in recent years is the American guitarist and songwriter Ry Cooder. With soundtracks for directors as diverse as Louis Malle, Tony Richardson and Walter Hill, it is for his work on Wim Wenders' *Paris, Texas* (1984) that he is best known. Using the sparest of resources, Cooder created the soundtrack in just three days, playing a kind of fractured blues guitar to the screened images in the studio. In a 1990 television documentary, Wim Wenders described the revelatory simplicity of Cooder's approach:

> When we finally recorded the music, Ry Cooder was standing with his guitar in front of the screen playing directly to the images. It felt like in a strange way he was reshooting the picture and like his guitar was somehow related to our camera.[7]

[6] Frederic Jameson, 'Postmodernism or the Cultural Logic of Late Capitalism', *New Left Review*, no. 141, 1984, p. 65

[7] *Wim Wenders: Motion & Emotion*, Lucida Films for Channel 4 UK, 1990

The 'subject' of Cooder's highly distinctive score is synonymous with the subject of the film – the plight of the individual imagination in a world of pastiche – modern America. A world of surface appearances, stripped of memory or self-reflection, where even one's own autobiography is subsumed into the background noise. The central character, Travis, emerges from the desert after four years, refusing at first even to talk. As his brother gradually tries to rehabilitate him into society Travis embarks on a search for his wife and child whom he abandoned. The search is as much a deliberate act of remembering, both for Travis and for his wife and son, as each strives to reconstruct the lost time during which Travis disappeared. For Ry Cooder:

> It's a journey in this guy's mind and everything else derives from that. Especially that he doesn't talk much. So for me the basic question was, so if he doesn't talk much, does he hear anything? Converting that silence into sound, into melody, this is what the score is. So you take the basic theme and develop it, and each time it's a little more, a little different, and the slightest little nuance is going to push it this way or that.[8]

The evolution in Wenders' soundtracks from appropriated pop song to sparse instrumental lines played and recorded live against the running picture seems entirely consistent with the aleatory impulse that lies at the heart of the director's vision. The score for *Paris, Texas* was one of the most distinctive of the 1980s and has since been widely imitated in the field of commercials and other films, to the point where Cooder's retelling of the primal blues now seems impossible to retrieve from the void of cliché. Similar musical landscapes have been sketched out by other well-known solo artists: Pat Metheny's interpretation of Jerry Goldsmith's score to *Under Fire*, Mark Knopfler's scores to *The Princess Bride*, *Cal* and *Last Exit to Brooklyn* and Eric Clapton's spare doodlings to *Lethal Weapon*.

8 Ibid.

AGAINST THE GRAIN: EXPERIMENTAL
FILM SOUNDTRACKS

In his *Critique of Pure Reason*, written in the 1780s, the German philosopher Immanuel Kant attempts to turn on its head the way in which we regard perception. As Michel Foucault[1] observes, the theory of vision and indeed of knowledge prior to Kant depended pretty much upon the notion of a world identical in essence with its outward appearance. Kant proposed a theory that put the observing subject at the centre of a new epistemology. This paradigm shift in ways of thinking about seeing bears comparison with the kind of formal quantum shift in film-making aesthetics pioneered by Stan Brakhage.

Whilst it would be difficult to claim that any of his films were exactly representative of a movement, as a key avant-garde film maker of the 1950s Brakhage was at the forefront of the equivalent of a Kantian revolution in the epistemology of film. One might see Brakhage as a kind of latter-day romantic idealist producing intensely personal films. David E. James summarizes Brakhage's contribution to film thus:

> The practice he developed was so totalled that it was virtually seamless. So thoroughly over-determined was each moment in it that primary determination seems locatable simultaneously everywhere and nowhere. Each aspect of his intervention, from the style of his films to their international ramifications, articulates the others. This, the reticulated, autotelic integrity of his aesthetic, is the condition of Brakhage's singular achievement; it also predetermines his limitations.[2]

By the 1950s animation, or the manipulation of non-organic forms, had more or less become orthodoxy amongst film makers interested in pursuing personal experimentation without recourse to anything approaching a

[1] Michel Foucault, *The Order of Things* (New York: 1970), p. 32

[2] David E. James, *Allegories of Cinema* (New Jersey: 1989), p. 32

normal film maker's budget. The sound-on-film techniques pioneered by Moholy-Nagy and others in the 1930s were finding their way through to a new generation of film makers and animators who, if they did not employ the same techniques as these early animators, almost certainly shared similar concerns about the aesthetic challenges film had still to explore that were to some degree old news in the worlds of literature, music and painting. Brakhage's business was to share a vision – not a vision in the normal shamanistic sense of art as replenisher but a vision in the purest physiological sense. Brakhage's films offer up as direct a possible experience of what vision is, what the act of seeing actually consists of. In an interview from 1972 he explains his work in the following way:

> I am the most thorough documentary film maker in the world because I document the act of seeing as well as everything that the light brings me . . . I have added nothing. I've just been trying to see and make a place for my seeing in the world at large.[3]

Amongst Brakhage's early films from the mid-1950s are strange little melodramas or fragments from melodramas. The 1955 *Reflections on Black* details a male protagonist's meetings with four different women, shot progressively from his point of view. In the first encounter, vision (read sexual fulfilment) is not 'achieved' and the sequence consists of black frames punctuated by a dialogue soundtrack. We gradually realize that the sound-track, like the fragmentary visuals, is a fantasy projection of the protagonist because when he finally achieves a kind of visual (and therefore presumably 'authentic') union with the fourth woman, the soundtrack ceases and we are left with his own highly subjective visual impressions, roaming the room as the film concludes in what is possibly a state of liberated sexual intoxication.

Brakhage worked with pre-recorded soundtracks by similarly inclined musicians such as Jim Tenney (*Interim*, 1953) and John Cage (*In Between*, 1955). However, after 1955 most of his films are marked by a soundtrack of silence. An exception to this was *Fire of Waters*, a mesmeric study of lightning flashes over a suburban neighbourhood which bears a soundtrack composed at various points of slowed-down birdsong, the speeded-up sound of a woman giving birth and a curious kind of wind-song, rising and falling in intensity.

The raw state of sound cinema, accompanied by the sound of the projector whirring away in the darkness, achieves the kind of programmatic 'musical' aesthetic imagined by John Cage amongst others:

3 Stan Brakhage, *Brakhage Scrapbook: Collected Writings 1964–1980* (New York: 1982)

> Whether or not I make them there are always sounds to be heard and all of them are excellent.[4]

Suddenly the auditory space itself opens up for our close attention. One can find examples of this radical practice as far back as the earliest days of sound. The 1929 Roland West film *Alibi* was reviewed as follows:

> One of the most important works in the development of cinema audibility. Significant because it first showed the value of sound as opposed to speech and with high conclusiveness demonstrated the importance of silence in the midst of vocal.[5]

One might also mention scenes from the film *Battle of Britain* (1969) where dogfighting British and German planes dance in the air to a predictably bombastic score by William Walton only to be accompanied suddenly by an eerie silence; the effect is startling because it is so unexpected. The scenes double in dramatic intensity whilst at the same time becoming more abstracted.

The French writer Jacques Attali[6] speculates that in a world filled by sounds, music itself imposes a kind of silence. For Attali, the phonographic mass reproduction of music functions practically and emblematically to silence music and to strike dumb any kind of social transformation.

In a perceptive essay[7] Marie Nesthus points up similarities between the compositional techniques of Brakhage and those of the modernist French composer Olivier Messiaen. Brakhage calls his film *Scenes from Under Childhood* a 'tone poem for the eye' and acknowledges the inspiration of Messiaen. Although Brakhage doesn't *per se* use Messiaen's music there are some similar concerns with the depiction of the relationship between aural experience and our experiences of colour. Messiaen was attracted to the musical traditions and cultures of the East, particularly the fixed rhythmic patterns of the Hindu tradition, and this concept of a mathematically predetermined musical structure is echoed in Brakhage's abstracted sequences of colourful images arriving in a highly ordered fashion.

In his later works during the 1960s Brakhage progressively refined and formalized his technique of visual representation whilst still delivering intensely personal statements. Since most of Brakhage's output over three decades placed vision as the primary site of revelation it is difficult to discuss

[4] John Cage, *Silence* (New York: 1961), p. 152

[5] Anonymous newspaper review quoted by Lewis Jacobs in *The Rise of the American Film* (New York: 1951), p. 440

[6] Jacques Attali, *Noise* (Minnesota: 1989), p. 120

[7] Marie Nesthus, 'The Influence of Olivier Messiaen on the Visual Art of Stan Brakhage', *Film Culture*, 63/64, 1977

Brakhage's soundtracks in terms other than those of causal linkage to the visual concern. Yet Brakhage's films offer up a unique experience of a 'watched consciousness' in perambulation through microcosms of perceived worlds. In this sense then the primary object on screen is visual space, the space between the camera and the nearest solid forms to it, the distance between us as spectators and the screen and the analytic distance of the camera's focal plane. In some ways Brakhage's work has resonance in the present-day work of video artists such as the American Bill Viola. The difference seems to be in the material lineage each has chosen to follow rather than the subjects. Viola asserts that the fundamental aspect of television technology is the 'live' transmitted event. Video's equivalent of the cinematic montage is the vision-mixer where instantaneous cuts can be made between different camera views. Brakhage remained concerned with the documentation of private visual spaces although consciously not deviating from using film (as opposed to video) technology. Throughout the 1950s and 1960s the cost of film-recording apparatus on 16mm and then 8mm stock dropped substantially, thus helping still further to entrench the alternative film-making community and to stabilize something like a selection of formal materials with which to work.

Brakhage's films are a testimony to the possibility of free transference between different sensory modalities. Sound is often used by Brakhage as an agent of change, signalling junctures in the visual field. A sonic equivalence might be to take a spoken word in its complete and whole form and then systematically fragment it, exploring the tensions between the constituent phonemes and the whole word with its inherent semantic value, between word meaning and its constituent sounds. Much the sort of thing, in fact, that the German experimental poetry form *Hörspiel* claimed to be exploring in the 1960s.

Another American film maker worth mentioning is Jordan Belson, whose abstract animations bear some resemblance to the 1940s work of James Whitney and Hans Richter. But Belson worked on a much more ambitious and public scale, incorporating his animation into mixed-media theatrical events, such as the Vortex Concerts held in San Francisco between 1957 and 1960. Multiple projectors displayed a kaleidoscopic dance of animated geometries which were then accompanied by music from the likes of Stockhausen, Mayusumi and Cage. These pre-1960s happenings featured sound that could be directed via different speakers placed around the auditorium. Belson's films *Flight* (1958), *Raga* (1959) and *Seance* (1959) all investigate the limits of vision and, like those of his contemporary Kenneth Anger, also embody aspects of the occult.

Whilst the introduction of magnetic audio tape led to a greater ease of experimentation with sound stock, it did not necessarily lead to an immediate improvement in the phonographic work being produced in the 1950s to accompany films. If one were to look for the really interesting work being done it was to be found in the more experimental brands of radio work that many creative artists from other areas were now turning to. Although predating the 1950s, Antonin Artaud's astonishing radio performance piece *To Have Done with the Judgement of God* (1947), which combines extended tracts of glossolalia with primitive musical accompaniments, certainly contributed to a progressive rolling back of barriers between traditionally musical sonorities and something approaching noise. For Pierre Boulez:

> The name Artaud immediately comes to mind when questions of vocal emission or the dissociation of words and their explosion are evoked; an actor and poet, he was naturally provoked by the material problems of interpretation, just like a composer who plays or conducts. He showed us how to achieve a fusion of sound and word, how to splash out the phoneme when the word no longer can, in short how to organize delirium.[8]

Aside from radio (which did much to launch Orson Welles upon the world) there were a number of artists from other fields who experimented with cinema in the 1950s, Genet and Cocteau being two particularly high-profile examples. Genet's dreamlike *Un Chant d'amour* was made in 1950 and became something of a gay classic for its celebratory scenes of homoerotic fantasy in a prison. It was, however, released as a silent film without dialogue or music, although the British composer Gavin Bryars subsequently composed a soundtrack for a UK release of the film. Unusually, the music Bryars composed lasts for the entire duration of the film, some forty minutes:

> I broke down the film into the footage of each shot, relating scenes to one another both in terms of their content, who was involved, where it took place, its duration, pace and so on. This analysis resulted in a notation from which I could effect, firstly a 1:1 relationship with sound and film and from that I constructed larger-scale time relationships by working out each component part.[9]

Bryars also chose to reverse this formal relationship between the film's duration and that of the music in a collaboration with UK film maker Steve

[8] Quoted by Allen S. Weiss in 'Radio Death and the Devil' in *Wireless Imagination: Sound Radio and the Avant Garde*, ed. Douglas Kuhn & Gregory Whitehead (Cambridge, Mass.: 1992), p. 298

[9] Gavin Bryars, quoted in *The Technique of Film Music* by Roger Manville and John Huntley (London: 1975), p. 197

Dwoskin, who produced a film based on Bryars' piece for orchestra and tape, *Jesus' Blood Never Failed Me Yet*, first recorded in the early 1970s. The musical piece consists of tape loops backed by orchestral variations. This structure was adopted by Dwoskin, who used identical takes one after the other to achieve an aleatory effect.

Kenneth Anger's vision of the avant-garde in the 1950s was spectacularly unique – celebrating the fake not to say pagan glamour of Hollywood whilst simultaneously putting a torch under the whole emporium. Beginning (at least publicly) with the ground-breaking *Fireworks* in 1947, Anger has brilliantly trodden a path between kitsch and something approaching pure aesthetic revelation. In *Eaux d'artifice* (1953) a series of shots follow a woman running through an ornamental garden and alternate with an almost abstract meditation on the interplay of water from the many fountains to be found in the garden. Combining hand-tinted film with some exquisite editing, this very simple film introduces an almost conscious sense of alchemy. The multiple colour-print overlays of *Inauguration of the Pleasure Dome* (1954) record the apparent invocation of the god Horus combined with the music of Janáček, lending the film a hallucinatory quality. Anger re-edited the film in the late 1960s, replacing Janáček with a curiously mediocre pop song, thereby removing much of the film's original appeal.

Anger is probably best known for the seminal cult picture *Scorpio Rising* (1963). Like so many of his other films, *Scorpio Rising* focuses on ritualistic behaviour and fetishized appearance. In this case the subjects are leather-clad bikers off to a rumble with a rival gang. Anger dwells at length on their preparations, from the donning of the leather armour to the obsessive polishing of chrome. These lovingly composed sequences are intercut with some footage from a long-forgotten biblical drama, *King of Kings*, which adds an element of comedy if not pathos. The soundtrack is a diet of classic 1950s and early 1960s pop songs, primarily chosen, it would appear, for their lyrical content, for their ability to comment on the psychic events secretly unfolding. *Scorpio Rising* is edited ruthlessly, with strictly adhered-to rhythmic montages ending in the fake glory of self-destruction (with the soundtrack appropriately enough reverberating to the Surfaris' 'Wipeout').

Whilst sounds and music, either in their total absence or in their diegetic complexity, have been addressed as a subject by avant-garde film makers since the 1930s, they have not been explored as thoroughly as the process of vision formation and visual perception. Since most avant-garde films are viewed in less than ideal acoustic conditions it is not surprising that there have been few attempts to explore the more creative aspects of contemporary acoustics. As modern music seems to move further away from a focus on its own internal development as evidence of a piece's merits, to concentrate instead on the present audial moment, this would also appear to be true of the way in which music has been used in experimental films in the last two decades.

Sounds or music are sometimes 'treated', to bring them to our attention, either through colliding them with other audio processes or by creating a new one using electronics. This approach calls for a new kind of attention on the part of the listener or viewer, a way of accepting sounds without any formal kind of patterned articulation or extended development. Maureen Turim cites two recent films as examples of this new approach to the sounding elements:

> *Blazes* [Robert Breer, 1975] serves as an example of how a filmic soundtrack can let noise be heard apart from an effect of signification or representation. The sounds in *Blazes* may have natural sources, but they are heard as auditory pulses devoid of specific references, opening the space of auditory fantasy. The auditor becomes sensitive to the repetition, and the structural shift. The mystery of identification of the sound has its own intrigue, but the 'closer' one listens, the more conscious one becomes of the noises' qualities, their patterns, their energies. These discoveries gradually supplant the desire to know the sound as an icon.[10]

In her examination of Bruce Conner's *Crossroads* (1976), a film composed of static frames of the first American atomic bomb test at Bikini Atoll, Turim sees different questions being raised on the soundtrack:

> *Crossroads* is also concerned with sound abstraction but uses a metamorphosis of noise effects into concrete music accompanying a repetitive series of images to open different questions of the relationships of force and signification within filmic composition. The soundtrack begins with a sync track of the explosion which in this special case means that the explosion in the image and the noise of the explosion do not 'match'. The rumbling noises are heard with a delay in respect to the image of the explosion that one would have experienced had one been at the site where the image was taken (the same delay that occurs between lightning and thunder due to the differing speeds of light and sound). In successive images of the explosion the sound is progressively manipulated. First the sound comes immediately when we see the explosion. This is, scientifically speaking, impossible, placing us as spectators in an impossible spatial and temporal representation . . . After the midpoint of the film the sound becomes abstracted as concrete music. It retains elements of the sound of the sync track, though others are added. The sounds are reorganized so that the

---

[10] Maureen Turim, *Abstraction in Avant Garde Films* (Ann Arbor: 1985), p. 48

238

effect is abstract, increasingly removed from the referent which remains in evidence in the image.

The biggest limitation for experimental film making at the moment is the basic medium on which it is created and stored. Both film and videotape (with some exceptions) resist interactivity by the viewer. As film, television, computing and telecommunications converge further it seems probable that the working method known as hypertext will begin to become the basic experimental language of film construction. Hypertext authoring cannot replace traditional art and design media but can powerfully complement them. Interactive media platforms allow the assembler to create a multimedia document which combines the qualities of a number of different media in one piece of work, and most importantly allow the viewer to navigate their own way through the maze. Components within the piece of work can be repeatedly cross-referenced with data in other works. The social, cultural and even ideological implications of this kind of activity are not at all clear at present, since the emphasis at key interactive conferences such as Siggraph is on the hardware rather than the effects of software.

FILMING MUSICAL PERFORMANCE

the musical

More than any other form of filmed performance, musicals represent the utopianism of Western cinema. They are a form that was perfected by cinema's ability to jump the time that in a theatre would be devoted to scene changes, costume changes or other spell-breaking activities. In the musical, time and motion are co-ordinated to the rhythm of song and dance, with everything subordinated to the principal of spectacle. Oddities such as *Meet Me in St Louis* (1944), *Yolanda and the Thief* (1945), *Ziegfeld Follies* (1946), *Summer Holiday* (1948) and *An American in Paris* (1951) were true originals – Technicolor splashes of pure cinematic invention and surrealism, turning the two-dimensional world of the theatre into the three-dimensional world of the *mise-en-scène*.

As Richard Dyer[1] has said, musicals approximate to a sense of what Utopia might feel like rather than how it would be organized. There are essentially two forms of musical. The 'backstage drama' (e.g. *Ziegfeld Follies*) and the adaptation of the operetta form (e.g. *West Side Story* or *Hair*). In the former music is justified because it naturally belongs in the theatrical environment in which the story is set. In the second category, music is literally borne on the air, and characters burst into song. It is the second category that has proved the more difficult to sell to a modern audience, even when carefully packaged with some of the best recording stars of the day like *Absolute Beginners* (1985), a much heralded UK musical that went on to become a box-office disaster.

Escapism was clearly more welcome in some periods than others during the hundred-year history of the cinema, and the success or failure of musicals seemed to index those tastes perfectly. Salvation and happiness were just

1 Richard Dyer, *Only Entertainment* (London: 1992), p. 18

around the corner in the everyday fantasies of the Depression-era 1930s musicals, where fame and fortune were always attainable if one wished hard enough. The Warner Brothers' musicals of this period (*Footlight Parade*, *42nd Street*) have been placed closer to Franklin D. Roosevelt's New Deal than to heaven.[2] In hard times the grind of daily life was reflected in stories but seen through a veil of optimism. Dyer sees a tendency in these musicals to imply that grinding poverty can be solved or at least salved by musical presentations in which abundance (i.e. the big production number) acts as a palliative in itself. This release through abundance obviously compromises any attempt to situate the musical's narrative in any recognizable reality. Yet within the large-scale all-singing, all-dancing landscape something more ambiguous is going on. Dyer points to these numbers as exemplifying a commodification of women (and no less men, except where they appear as the producer- or Svengali-archetype in these stories) as objects:

> The abundant scale of the numbers is an abundance of piles of women; the sensuous materialism is the texture of femaleness; the energy of the dancing (when it occurs) is the energy of the choreographed imagination, to which the dancers are subservient.[3]

This exposure of organized, obedient, choreographed labour demonstrates the strange inconsistencies at the heart of the classic musical. It is as if the expending of energy itself, through dance and through song, is enough to right all wrongs. Siegfried Kracauer remarked that film musicals exposed the primal tensions at the heart of cinema. On the one hand in rendering outbursts of song as naturalistic phenomena musicals exhibit something pretty close to the pure plasticity of cinema, yet at the same time they are often limited by an unneeded allegiance to some kind of a story or intrigue. Kracauer perceptively sees musicals as fragmented wholes in which a world of two opposites coexists and is acknowledged as such rather than a false unity of realism and the formative:

> The musical playfully affirms cinematic values in the dimension of sheer *divertissement*. It rejects, by implication, the claim to dominance of the songs and ballets in which it indulges; and all its staginess does not prevent it from paying tribute to camera-life.[4]

[2] Mark Roth, 'Some Warners' Musicals and the Spirit of the New Deal', in *Genre: The Musical*, ed. Rick Altman (London: 1981)

[3] Dyer, *Only Entertainment*, p. 26

[4] Siegfried Kracauer, *Theory of Film* (New York: 1969), p. 148

This concept of a musicalized everyday, where characters spontaneously burst into song as if it were the most natural thing in the world, is one of the most surreal conceits ever played by the film industry upon its audience. Both dialogue and lyrics bleed into each other in the musical's diegesis. From the perspective of the present day it seems as outmoded and kitsch a form as a Gilbert and Sullivan opera, yet in its kinetic energy and the sheer audaciousness of its staging and design, the classic musicals represent a high point in film aesthetics.

Some of the first early sound era musicals to be grouped together as a recognizable sub-genre were the Busby Berkeley musicals for Warners. These were smoothly concocted formulaic boy-meets-girl stories, in which abundance was on display for its own sake. Bland leading men such as Dick Powell and flat-voiced but pretty starlets such as Ruby Keeler hoofed their way through plots that were dated even in the 1930s. To place Powell in uniform was a tried and tested device; Keeler was simply his sweetheart, whilst the backstage landscape was peppered with interesting characters played by distinctive types such as Aline MacMahon, Sterling Holloway, Joan Blondell or Guy Kibbee. The songs by Harry Warren and Al Dubin were infectious, driving stompers such as 'We're in the Money' (from *Gold Diggers of 1933*) with a high-kicking Ginger Rogers leading a vast chorus of girls decked out in gold coins and a smile. True to the show-within-a-show idea, Busby Berkeley musicals often began with a curtain rising over some variation of the proscenium arch and ended with a theatre audience applauding. But in between these devices the choreographed routines filmed from every which way were purely cinematic conceptions with chorines arrayed in the most fantastic varieties – opening up as flowers filmed from above, as the American flag, as fleshly Catherine wheels and even as musical instruments. Significantly the most recent attempts to revive the musical or a form of the musical have been variations on the backstage story – *Cabaret* (1972), *A Star is Born* (1976), *New York, New York* (1977) and (to a lesser extent) *Nashville* (1975) – where music is a natural part of the universe these stories inhabit and most of the musical performances are given in the context of a show within a show.

Gradually throughout the 1930s and early 1940s the musical began to approach a state of pure representation. The pretence of a backstage story no longer seemed to be necessary. The Fred Astaire and Ginger Rogers vehicles were very often merely paper-thin plots in which the two simply meet each other and then, after a series of misunderstandings and identity mix-ups in pure *opera-buffa* style, progressively slide into asexual rapture represented in magnificently presented dance routines. Astaire's portfolio of films, amongst them *Top Hat* (1935), *Shall We Dance* (1937) and *Carefree* (1938), boasted music written by Gershwin, Cole Porter and Irving Berlin, and taken as a whole represent some of the greatest examples of filmed musical performance this century.

The cycle of musicals produced by MGM from the mid-1940s to the mid-1950s has become known as the epitome of the golden era of Hollywood musicals. Many of its brightest moments were conceived by Arthur Freed, a brilliant producer who, in partnership with directors such as Vincente Minnelli and Stanley Donen, writers such as Betty Comden and Adolph Green and composers like Lerner and Lowe, created brilliant, happy-go-lucky musical *Gestalten* populated by dynamic personalities such as Frank Sinatra, Gene Kelly and Judy Garland. If one were to generalize one might identify an emphasis more on dance than song in the MGM musicals. Whilst the songs were in every way the equal of an earlier era it was in the precise relationship between camera and choreographed movement that a director like Minnelli excelled. Cole Porter scored *The Pirate* (1948) and *Les Girls* (1957) whilst Gershwin wrote *An American in Paris* (1951) (whose stunning stage sets were inspired by modernist French painters), but the definitive picture of the bunch was Arthur Freed's *Singin' in the Rain* (1951), a conscious throwback to the early sound era in both theme and content (many of the songs used had already been used in earlier Freed musicals). Kelly, who co-directed with Stanley Doren, produced a seamlessly brilliant comedy about the movie business itself. *Singin' in the Rain* rehabilitates its songs as representative of happier more carefree times (despite the fact that America in the early 1950s was an infinitely richer place in material terms than during the Depression), thus fulfilling the conventional practice of many other musicals.

There were also some (mainly unsuccessful) attempts to marry the zany surrealism of cartoons with the *chutzpah* of Broadway. A bizarre mix of live hoofing and animated backdrops was typified in *Dangerous When Wet* (1953), an Esther Williams vehicle in which she appears to share an underwater dream sequence with Tom the cat (from the Tom and Jerry cartoons). On a more justifiable level, *The Girl Next Door* (1953) at least had a main character who was a cartoonist. In watching these odd hybrids there is a feeling of compromise as the performer stares wide-eyed out of a screen seeing nothing, as if the best of both worlds has somehow been lost. The most effective use of this technique was Robert Zemeckis's *Who Framed Roger Rabbit* (1988) where the live action versus animation proposition succeeds because the technology that creates the illusion is so good. Alan Silvestri's songs and Jeffrey Price and Peter Seaman's screenplay apply an ironic knowingness to the whole idea and cinematic history of musicals and particularly of cartoon-live-action hybrids.

Given a gradual shift from authentic musically talented performers towards the further deification of 'in-house' star actors and actresses, the studios resorted increasingly to 'ghosting' from the late 1930s onwards. From the start the deception was obvious. It was quite clear to contemporary audiences that Veronica Lake's songs in *This Gun for Hire* (1942) were dubbed, but the studios only reluctantly began to publicize the 'ghost' singers when the soundtrack albums began to be an essential part of the musical's commercial success. When it was suggested that dubbed actresses should not be eligible for the Oscars the secrecy veil was once again lowered by the film companies. Many of the recordings from the 1940s and 1950s list song titles as sung by the characters in the film, leaving the whole question of exactly who sang what unanswered.

In general the more exotic the location, the more likely the characters in a story were to burst spontaneously into song. Typically this could take the form of a pastoral or historical Utopia, preferably one just outside the scope of living memory. Such movies included turn-of-the-century idylls such as *Meet Me in St Louis* (1944), *Gigi* (1958), *Oliver!* (1968), *Hello Dolly!* (1969), *Song of Norway* (1970), or the exotica of the rarely glimpsed black communities assembled for *Hallelulah* (1929), *Cabin in the Sky* (1943) and *Porgy and Bess* (1959).

In 1933 Hollywood released some thirty-seven musicals; in 1943, there were sixty-five and in 1953 a further thirty-eight, but by 1963 the number had dwindled to just four. Despite attempts to ambassador the feeling of a revival (Dimitri Tiomkin wrote in *Variety* as late as 1964 that Hollywood was currently enjoying a second golden age of film musicals) the essential character of the classic musical had changed. Despite the successes of the early 1960s such as *West Side Story* (1961), *Flower Drum Song* (1961), *The Music Man* (1962) and *Gypsy* (1962), these were adaptations of stage shows, not musicals created solely for the screen. The adaptations were highly popular – *The King and I* (1956) and *South Pacific* (1958) were financially very successful; but gone was a system that created and delivered bona fide stars (unless one was to count the tidal wave of Elvis Presley movies that were made during the 1960s) who could sing. The trend moved towards simply dubbing actresses and actors (Natalie Wood in *Gypsy* and *West Side Story*, Sidney Poitier in *Porgy and Bess*, Deborah Kerr in *The King and I*) and where musical stars were used they generally received a lower billing than the imported actors.

Why did the musical fade from glory so quickly? Part of the blame must lie with the film makers and producers themselves and their reaction to new and threatening influences such as television. From a humble beginning in which countless rows of high-kicking girls were the basic ingredient, a number of modifications were tried out with varying success. The public seemed to interpret many of these experiments as gimmicks. Dialogue was rhymed in order to create a more harmonious tapestry of song, dance and story and dance routines became narratives in their own right. The impact of television cannot be underestimated, since its effect upon the studio system was immediate and far-reaching. Hollywood's reaction was to try to kill television with scale. Bigger screen ratios, bigger epic dramas and, in the case of musicals, bigger properties, which inevitably meant playing it safe and adapting well-known Broadway productions with the biggest stars the studios could afford. Gone was the training ground that volume production in the 1930s and 1940s had allowed, including the smaller productions such as *I Love Melvin* (1953), *Give a Girl a Break* (1954) and *So This is Paris* (1955) which had trained numerous choreographers, art directors, musical arrangers and not least actors and actresses capable of singing and dancing.

In a sense the musicals were sustained by the studio system. The centralized training and unique range of in-house creative resources (music directors, orchestras, set designers, dancers, choreographers), coupled with performers literally owned by the studios for which they worked, created a culture in which lengthy rehearsals and a collaborative approach to the end product were not only possible but inevitable. The breaking up of the studio systems in the face of television and the rise of the independent production company signalled the final decline of a pre-eminently American art form. For a brief time in the 1960s the advantage went to Europe and productions like *The Umbrellas of Cherbourg* (1965) were critically raved over, but to all intents and purposes the musical's history was over by the mid-1970s after a final rally of titles failed to set the box office alight.

In recent years the sensibility of the classic musical has influenced many different styles of contemporary film makers, without actually being revived. Musicals have been satirized and parodied by both film and television in the years since the form was at its popular peak, so much so that it seems unlikely that the musical in the classic Hollywood sense will ever be rejuvenated for modern audiences.

The films of Terence Davies have consciously invoked aspects of the utopias offered by musicals without stepping into the genre. Music plays a vital part of Davies's, diegesis, a collective virtual community of memory. (One could also mention the television series of Dennis Potter such as *Pennies from Heaven* and *The Singing Detective*.) Popular music from the 1930s onwards functions as a touchstone for forgotten communities in films such as *Distant Voices, Still Lives* (1989) and *The Long Day Closes* (1992). In what Armond White calls the Proustian musical, Davies refracts common songs and tunes from his memories of working-class Liverpool and allows these song lyrics tellingly to interact with his characters' class-specific attitudes to, amongst other themes, sex and religion:

> Davies reconceives his fondest film genre, the musical, after relating to its forms and sounds . . . he doesn't need a narrative excuse to enjoy the emotional release of song. His creative freedom comes out of the pop era when music seemed to float through the ether, experienced via the radio or at the whim of any individual with a tune in his soul.[5]

Strictly Ballroom (1992) (whose subtitle might have been 'There are no new steps!') by Australian Baz Luhrmann burst exuberantly out of nowhere to reclaim at least some of the lost audiences for the musical. In reality *Strictly Ballroom* simply locked on to an increasingly mainstream appreciation of camp style. Whilst strictly speaking not a musical but a dance film in which music is heard diegetically, *Strictly Ballroom* has many recognizable elements from musicals, and in its story, situated in the bitchy world of competition ballroom dancing, is a kitsch variation on the backstage musical. There's even the familiar storyline of an apparently hopeless dancer replacing the more experienced one at the last minute and naturally enough going on to win the competition.

filmed operas

There are certain cinematic forms which seem alien to the basic idea of cinema, because they seem to utilize so little of cinema's aesthetic possibilities. One of these areas is filmed musical performance, particularly of opera, which in its stagebound version is often static. Nevertheless, enough attempts have been made to film the opera canon for the form to have carved out a sub-genre all of its own.

Critics of the 1940s and 1950s such as Balász and Kracauer insisted that

[5] Armond White, 'Remembrance of Songs Past', in *Film Comment*, May–June 1993, p. 12

true filmed operas should be completely new creations, a million miles removed from the proscenium settings of their theatrical originals. At least with Balász there seems to be a feeling that filmed operas should in fact approach the design-driven closed-off universe of the musical. Kracauer preferred his filmed operas to be shot in a realistic style, although quite how this was to be achieved he does not say. Both opera and film are what Germans would call *Gesamtkunstwerk*, integrating elements from several art fields, yet opera clings so jealously to the rituals of high culture that in its usual context it seems to compromise any real possibility for visual or performative experimentation.

Of the various formats of lyric drama, opera is surely the most conservative. The biggest problem seems to be the repertoire itself, much of which is at least a hundred years old and is still usually performed in the same styles as when written – the obsession with authenticity often resulting in opera being performed in languages wholly unfamiliar to its audiences. Another problem is the conservatism of opera's patrons and a reluctance to embrace experimental approaches to performance. Far too much of contemporary opera is devoted to preserving rather than extending the canon. Even the merchandising for opera performances very often relates not to the performers on display in the auditorium but to the work itself, thus emphasizing the sensation that performance consists of a studied adherence to a text rather than an interpretation by skilled performers. Everything seems geared to the collector's mentality, the completist who wishes to experience every possible 'reading' of a work. Presumably for the serious opera fan there exists somewhere a virtual and exemplary reading. Opera today lacks a regular supply of the kind of unifying, internationally successful new works which characterized its earlier history, and which appealed to a broad audience. It is more than fifty years since Benjamin Britten premièred *Peter Grimes*, which was perhaps the last truly successfully popular piece. Much of opera's popular audience has now deserted it in favour of the more musically accessible (and spectacular) theatre creations of Andrew Lloyd Webber and Cameron Mackintosh. In addition to the sterility of the basic repertoire, there is the essentially static nature of operatic performance to be dealt with. This is one of the biggest hurdles facing film makers trying to adapt opera.

Many of the most powerful twentieth-century operas have not been performed for years, much less filmed. The repertoire with an explicit political agenda, such as the early work of Kurt Weill, is not performed very often. The performance repertoire of opera, like theatre, is subject to fluctuations in fashion yet the emphasis in most of the major opera houses seems to be on developing a repertoire that is defiantly pre-twentieth century. There are sometimes anomalies of history: an opera by Wagner such as *Siegfried*, for example, has only really re-entered the popular repertoire in the last twenty-five years, but with the work of Kurt Weill it is noticeable that it tends to be his later, American work (e.g. *Street Scene*, *One Touch of Venus*) which is performed by the first division of opera companies. Earlier, more 'angst-ridden' operas, such as *The Rise and Fall of the City of Mahagonny* and even the more commercial (and influential) *Threepenny Opera*, are heard far less often. Weill's earlier works contain spoken parts as well as songs, calling therefore for singers to be able to act in stretches as well. In this sense the underscored passages of dialogue can often be compared with scenes scored by film music. Weill's suitability for revival seems to have been coloured by his earlier association with the German playwright Bertolt Brecht, in whose theatre actor-singers such as Lotte Lenya barked rather than sang the lyrics to often delicate musical settings from Weill. In Weill's later American works, particularly *Street Scene*, there are closer similarities to the great American lyric composers of the 1930s, Irving Berlin and George Gershwin.

Recent major additions to the repertoire have included Philip Glass's *Einstein on the Beach* and John Adams' *Nixon in China*, both written in the last twenty years. In choosing to base an opera around contemporary figures, both employ a kind of pop art aesthetic, building their opera around fragments of a myth rather than any real consideration of the historical personalities. Philip Glass's *Einstein on the Beach* is over five hours long and goes to considerable effort, in its lack of an interval and long repetitive sections, to disquiet an audience away from the traditional reverence to the piece so common in opera. Spectators are encouraged to leave the auditorium whenever and for however long they please during the performance. This conscious act of distancing from the traditional formalities of the opera house is a positive evolution. Whether these operas will stand the 'test of time' remains far from certain, although both would seem to lend themselves well to film or television adaptation in an abbreviated form.

Opera is an art form steeped in ritual and administered largely by reactionary bodies that control the performance context to a detrimental degree. In recent years particularly in Europe and America there has been some signs of improvement in the slow acceptance of a cult of the director, in which playful personalities (often from other art fields) have been able to experiment to a certain degree with the (up)staging of so-called canonical works. One of the problems in attempting to impose an auteurist stamp on an opera work is that in the end there are still dramatic limitations to be overcome; the exposition of storylines in opera is desperately slow and is limited crucially by the physical labours involved in singing. Any attempt to move the actors around inevitably compromises their singing, an inescapable dilemma. Yet perhaps to film opera in such a way that these basic limitations can be transcended may not be as difficult as critics such as Balász seem to believe.

The challenge in filming opera is to reinvent an art form which has very little interiority, beyond what can be sketched out musically. Operas are about emotional cadences written large both musically and physically (opera houses tend to be rather large). Opera as a filmed drama tends to replicate these melodramatic styles often for no other reason than deference to the original. Jeremy Tambling[6] analyses the different ways in which Bizet's opera *Carmen* has been treated over the years by film makers. In most cases, Bizet's original opera tends to remain in the background, with film makers concentrating more on the story of the opera. It is the character of Carmen herself who changes the most between versions, reflecting different national interpretations of the character. By 1914 *Carmen* had been filmed at least seven times, only one version of which was Spanish. The 1915 version by Cecil B. DeMille did not use the Bizet score, as copyright was too expensive, but did cast Geraldine Farrar (from the Metropolitan Opera) in the title role. Other versions cast sex symbols in the main part, inventing the idea of Carmen as 'vamp' figure prior to American censorship clamp-downs in the early 1930s. By the late 1960s Carmen had become *Carmen Baby* (1967), a swinger with attitude and bisexual tendencies, running amok in a pop song vehicle only very loosely based on any other interpretations of the story. The black musical version *Carmen Jones* (1954) has not aged well; its exaggerated caricatures of a black urban community (song titles such as 'Dat's Love', 'Dere's a Café on the Corner') where music is a spontaneous part of everyday expression come across as an opportunist cash-in on the success of Gershwin's *Porgy and Bess*. However, in placing the story of *Carmen* in a more populist musical setting, *Carmen Jones* does implicitly question the predominance of the original Bizet opera as high culture.

When Schoenberg discussed the filming of his opera *Die Glückliche Hand* he stated that it should be as sensuously absolute as music itself. This would certainly seem to indicate that he expected something more than a simple

---

[6] Jeremy Tambling, *Opera, Ideology and Film* (Manchester: 1987)

record of a performance. He seemed to be talking about something more abstract altogether:

> It must never suggest symbols, or meanings, or thoughts, but simply the play of colours and forms. Just as music never drags a meaning around with it . . . so this should simply be like sounds for the eye.[7]

This would seem to have some similarity to Wagner's concept of the future artwork being a grand synthesis of drama and music. At the centre of the spectacle is the drama itself; music should amplify what remains unseen:

> The orchestra's equalizing moments of expression are never to be determined by the caprice of the musician, as a random tricking of sound, but only by the poet's aim. Should these 'moments' utter anything not connected with the situation of the dramatis personae, anything superfluous thereto, then the unity of expression is itself disturbed by this departure from the content.[8]

Wagner's approach is hierarchical; in the hands of Eisenstein, a follower of Wagner's ideas on dramatic form, it becomes dialectical. It was not until 1967 that a film theory emerged which adopted the compositional principles of atonality and serialism. Noël Burch's theory[9] demands an equalization of all elements of film composition such that all visual stimuli assume the same importance; therefore the film's represented content becomes only one of several ordering devices. This kind of open cinema seems ideally suited to the representation of opera. An ideal way to overcome the tyranny of the lyrical text and the necessity of mimetic coverage of musical performance. Surprisingly it has been little explored.

In *The Threepenny Opera* most of the settings are based on dance forms, thus promising a spectacle of kinetic movement. This is why the musical transferred well to screen in G. W. Pabst's 1930 production for UFA in Germany. With most works, however, the musical score is predicated on the vocal line, the physical effort of which results in a static performance. Given this it is surprising that opera remains an attractive and prestigious challenge to film makers as different as Ingmar Bergman and Joseph Losey. Naturally the most successful examples of filmed operas are those performances conceived for the camera, as opposed to simple registrations of concert events. Witness the disappointing film version of Andrei

[7] Quoted in David Bordwell, *The Musical Analogy*, Yale French Studies, 60, 1980, p. 141

[8] *Wagner on Music and Drama*, eds Albert Goodman and Evert Sprinchorn (New York: 1964), p. 228

[9] Noël Burch, *Theory of Film Practice* (New York: 1973)

Tarkovsky's production of Mussorgsky's *Boris Godunov* where, due to the technical difficulties of filming at the Kirov Opera in St Petersburg, much of the dramatic impact of Tarkovsky's stage designs is lost in the mid-distance of a wide shot.

One of the few attempts to utilize the ideas of an open approach to the operatic work was Hans-Jürgen Syberberg's interpretation of *Parsifal* (1982), in which some interesting deviations are made from the tradition of vocal performance, not least being the partial dispensing with lip-synchronization, and the integration of the conductor Armin Jordan into the performance playing the part of Amfortas. Most of the singing parts are played by actors and the music was pre-recorded, in keeping with Syberberg's intention to subvert Wagner's concept of the *Gesamtkunstwerk* and adopt a Brechtian strategy of separating out words, music, scenery, cloaking everything in a theatrical two-dimensionality. The conceptualization itself, whilst stagebound, is startling, with the entire opera taking place inside a hugely inflated mock-up of Wagner's death mask. The decay of the operatic tradition is itself part of Syberberg's subject.

A further problem is the repertoire itself with its often very limited relevance to modern audiences, overly sentimental texts and sheer obscurity of subject. A typical example of this is the generic approach to programming typified in the common pairing of two short operas on ostensibly the same subject – Mascagni's *Cavalleria Rusticana* and Leoncavallo's *I Pagliacci* – both stories about forbidden love amongst peasants in southern Italy. Often in performance these texts are performed back-to-back, usually with the same tenor and baritone appearing after a quick change during the interval.

One of the first operas to be conceived as anything like a cinematic work was Menotti's *The Medium* (1951), a modern tonal work presented on film in the style of a Grand Guignol thriller and directed by the composer himself. The main character is a swindling medium who, in the middle of a seance, suddenly feels a choking hand around her throat, setting off a variety of haunted-house staple elements. Contralto Marie Powers played the main part. Vocal passages are relatively spare in relation to the music and the dramatic setting inside a proverbially old dark house allowed for a smooth transference between staged idea and screened result. One of the advantages *The Medium* had (apart from being filmed by its composer) was that it was a musical work set in an unashamedly popular genre. One of Menotti's other works was initially commissioned for television by NBC, *Amahl and the Night Visitors*, and has become the most performed of all twentieth-century operas.

Joseph Losey's filmed version of *Don Giovanni* (1979) solves part of the traditional limitations of staged performances by taking the cameras out on location to some sumptuous villas in Vicenza. There are similarities here with Kenneth Branagh's very popular Shakespeare film adaptations (*Much Ado about Nothing*, *Hamlet*, etc.), which maximize the movement and impact of their locations. Magnificent costume design and superb performances give the whole production an air of hyper-reality. Similarly one might say the same of iconoclast Peter Sellars' *Don Giovanni* set in a New York tenement building with the principals decked out in black leather. Powell and Pressburger's *Tales of Hoffmann* (1952) dispenses with continuity of time and place altogether and experiments with the sheer artificiality of obviously dubbed sequences (what, after all, are rock videos?) where the singer acts and moves, expending very little of the usual face-contorting agonies that characterize live performance.

British producer Don Boyd's 1987 film *Aria* takes the MTV approach and recruits a stable of top directors to record a four-to-five-minute music video of their favourite arias from the operatic canon. The succession of these pieces is the entirety of the film. As a brief record of the passage of a few international directors through a British studio at a point in time where music and British films were still recovering from the musical disaster that was *Absolute Beginners*, the film is mildly interesting. What is not at all clear is the likely audience for such a film. The visual strategies of virtually all the directors distanced them from the traditional opera audience and the presentation of isolated arias in a ridiculously self-conscious way failed to reach the MTV audience.

In the main, films about opera (rather than being operas) have tended to concentrate upon the egos of performers engaged in some primeval struggle to outdo each other. There are echoes here of the traditional backstage musical. The world of opera has simply been a backdrop to the main psychological event, like the backstage musical a prop on which to hang musical performances. A superior example of this is *The Music Teacher* (1988), by Gerard Corbiau, in which a tenor on stage notices an old rival in the audience from years before and suddenly announces his retirement to teach music instead. Inevitably, years later his pupils end up in a competition mounted by his old rival and we enter a gladiatorial contest of music making in which everybody wears Mozart-inspired mask costumes. Much is made of the sheer physicality of singing but the performances are directed for the camera.

An interesting recent film about the art of singing was the French film *Farinelli* (1995), a study of the famed Italian castrato singer of the same name, who toured the royal courts and opera houses of Europe in the mid-eighteenth century, fostering the kind of adulation now given to modern-day pop stars. The music featured is entirely diegetic, consisting of snatches of on-stage performances from the singer's European tours. So the film is not in itself an opera on film but a film about opera as a lifestyle. In the understandable absence of a real castrato singer, a hybrid voice track was created at the experimental music laboratory IRCAM in Paris which fused the voices of the American countertenor Derek Lee Ragin and the Polish soprano Ewa Mallas-Godlewska into a single unearthly entity. The central subject of the film, Carlo Broschi (aka Farinelli), is presented as a tortured, intense freak whose symbiotic relationship with his brother is presented as a keyhole to character.

Chen Kaige's *Farewell, My Concubine* (1992) is based upon a Chinese opera of the same name and set in 1930s pre-revolutionary China but is taken from a novel by Lillian Lee, who uses the opera's basic storyline of doomed love between a fleeing prince and his self-sacrificing concubine (played by a female impersonator) to create a modern fable of forbidden love. The central part of the female impersonator is played by Chinese pop star Leslie Cheung and the on-stage scenes are filmed like an MTV clip.

Diva (1981) by Jean-Jacques Beineix is based on a novel by the post-modernist French writer Delacorta and is the story of a young Parisian mail carrier's love for a famous American opera singer (played by Wilhelmenia Wiggins Fernandez), whose concert he secretly records, only to have his audio tape mixed up with a tape handed to him by a girl whom he sees murdered on the Paris subway. The film is sumptuously good-looking, and is perhaps one of the first truly post-modern films in its easy integration of high culture with the pulp fiction crime genre. Its vogueish soundtrack mixes arias sung by Wiggins of music from Catalani's 1892 opera *La Wally* with romantic piano pieces and futuristic, metallic, rock-inspired suspense themes written by Vladimir Cosma. The issue of recording is a central theme in *Diva*; the American singer who considers all recordings an act of rape, the psychotic hood whose every move is accompanied by an earphone that plays elevator Muzak, the plotting which involves both protagonist and antagonist chasing after two different tapes, all seem simply a contrivance upon which to hang a chain of musically inspired images. Many of the images in *Diva* are oddly stripped of movement, characters seem to spend a lot of time in various states of contemplation, scenes are set for their aesthetic value. *Diva* comes across as a feature-length commercial for an unnamed product, and indeed its style was quickly adopted by the advertising industry.

A more robust film where opera is a motivational force is Werner Herzog's *Fitzcarraldo* (1982), where a crazed entrepreneur of the late nineteenth century undertakes to build an opera house in the middle of an Amazonian rain forest and amongst other things hauls a river boat overland to reach his intended site. This is a drama where opera is primarily used diegetically. An ancient recording of Enrico Caruso plays permanently on Fitzcarraldo's gramophone and inspires him to further acts of eccentricity. The film itself places Caruso's voice into a tapestry of evocative musics that include ethnic Indian music, an electronically treated monotone backdrop of jungle ambience, composed of rain, bird and insect noises, and the sparing inclusion of music by the German group Popul Vuh. The 'grain' of Caruso's voice acts as the signature of a corroding European civilization invading a virgin forest.

Whereas the film musical nearly always takes place in an environment in which the mounting of a 'show within a show' is the excuse to carry the music (and thus to include an audience in a celebration), there is no such diegetic release for the opera filmed as drama. The opera film presents sound itself as the inclusive sensuous element of attraction. Music becomes the normal mode of the opera film's reality, and for this reason the singing must be taken seriously, a narrative limit not imposed on the more flexible film or stage musical. As recording technology becomes better and better a distance opens up between the quality of performance possible on a stage and the extremely high standards now expected from a studio recording. On one level the opera film, even as a straightforward record of a performance, may appear to offer a solution to the difficulties of reproducing a higher and higher standard of music live. With selective post-production technologies, any filmed performance can be made to approach the conditions of the studio. Whether this destroys the aura of a live operatic performance is of course another matter.

With what remains of the opera as a form, the most interesting new work seems unlikely to lend itself well to film, but could perhaps in a condensed form work well on television. Opera's future as a filmed medium seems very uncertain; however, with the advent of new consumer media such as DVD which promise the convenience of a videotape with the digital advantages in picture and sound of the CD, the future for long-form recordings of musical performances by leading stars could undergo a revival. As if in anticipation of this much of the work being filmed now tends to be a straightforward record of a performance, such as von Karajan's series for Philips of filmed performances of major pieces of music (to appear eventually on the same disc). Therefore the impact for posterity of such works is better assessed as an act of archiving than audio-visual creativity.

music in documentaries

Documentaries are not known for their frequent use of music, but when the subject of the documentary is a performing art then everything changes. The increasingly serious terms in which rock and pop music were analysed and digested by American and European media meant that the elevation of rock music in performance to a status worthy of serious documentation was just a matter of time. In jazz the tendency had happened a decade earlier with amongst others *Jazz on a Summer's Day*, a cinematic record of the 1958 Newport Jazz Festival. By the end of the 1960s, pop culture in all its facets had moved centre stage in the American film industry. Michael Wadleigh's high-profile *Woodstock* (1970) swept all before it in terms of running time, cinematic technique and being quintessentially of the moment. The real subject of the film *Woodstock*, however, was the event itself, and the size of its crowd rather than the music *per se*. Endless panning shots of crowds ambling around ever more quagmired campsites are tracked by the performers on stage as much as the other way around. The editing (by Martin Scorsese) with its preferences for montage and split screens seems predicated on a simple ambition to reveal the sheer size of the spectacle. Much of the music and many of the artists involved have faded into obscurity, the brief late 1960s flirtation between rock and folk music having been eclipsed by the rise of a newer, heavier rock music at the turn of the decade. This emphasis on the equality of performers and audience is echoed in other documentaries about music events released at the same time as Woodstock, principally in *Monterey Pop* (1969) and *Gimme Shelter* (1970).

By the 1970s, the content of the rock documentary had shifted squarely back to the performer on stage. The documentary went long form, aiming to capture an event in its entirety, a movement as it were from impressionism to an often over-indulgent realism. *Pink Floyd Live at Pompeii* (1971) was the first 'breakthrough' in-concert movie to achieve widespread distribution, although exactly why remains a mystery. Martin Scorsese's second music documentary project was the epic *The Last Waltz*, which is a straightforward record of the Band's farewell concert from San Francisco on Thanksgiving Day 1976. Aside from a couple of rather unnecessary and not very illuminating backstage interviews, the bulk of the two-hour film is confined to on-stage performance. The epic length of the film is married to the often lengthy instrumental digressions favoured by the group.

More interesting were the small number of ultra-low-budget films that attempted to chronicle the early days of punk rock in Britain and the United States. Basically little more than edited collections of home movies, many of them didn't even have authentic soundtracks. Wolfgang Buld's shambolic *Punk in London* (1977) contained performances by, amongst others, X Ray Spex, the Jam, Sex Pistols, Electric Chairs and the Boomtown Rats as well as sound-bite interviews with various punk luminaries including Mark Perry and Jean-Jacques Burnel. Lech Kowalski's *DOA* (1981) is a work of bricolage, compiling material from a number of sources to contrast the terminal tour of America by the Sex Pistols with documentary material of various kinds about the distinctly bleak London they left behind. *DOA* edits its material well, contrasting the parodic rock star squalor of Sid Vicious' last days with Nancy Spungen in the Chelsea Hotel in New York with the chaos and danger of the Sex Pistols' tour of the Bible Belt states and the feeble attempts by the various British council authorities to limit the spread of live shows in the UK by punk bands. Whilst the performances are mainly by punk bands, many of the extra-diegetic music on the soundtrack is reggae, pointing up punk's links to a wider musical and socio-political underground.

Julien Temple's *The Great Rock'n'Roll Swindle* (1980) was a revisionist version of the Sex Pistols' route to destruction and infamy containing dramatic reconstruction, animation sequences, documentary footage and much of the Sex Pistols' best music, presented primarily as performance sequences but also recontextualized as a kind of light entertainment variety spectacle; Sid Vicious' lip-sync to Eddie Cochran's 'C'Mon Everybody' and the iconoclastic 'My Way' (which created a new icon arguably more powerful than that it attacked) being a case in point – a kind of a footnote to the documentary as fictionalized biopic started by *A Hard Day's Night*.

The Newport Jazz Festival has been covered in at least two concert films, Bert Stern's obtrusive *Jazz on a Summer's Day* (1960) and the US Government-produced *Jazz USA* (1958), a series of twenty-six half-hour films covering a myriad of jazz names recorded in straight performance sequences. Many of the other leading international jazz festivals have also been filmed, again with a similar mixture of performance and local ambience.

Another popular jazz sub-genre is the studio performance film, a good example of which is Ron Mann's *Imagine the Sound* (1981), which manages to contradict the traditions and clichés of both the performance film and the documentary. It features Cecil Taylor, Archie Shepp, Paul Bley and Bill Dixon. There is no audience in the space in which the musicians perform their sets; there is also no attempt made to hide the cameras which are filming the performances and the interviews. Each musical number lasts less than ten minutes and could therefore be shot on a single roll of film, so that editing of the music could be kept to a minimum. Each musician's studio environment is different from the others': Cecil Taylor plays solo piano in an entirely white space, Paul Bley against a black backdrop, Bill Dixon is interviewed in a room full of mirrors and Archie Shepp is surrounded by plants. In performance, the multiple cameras allow both long shots and also tight cuts on to instrumental solos. Jazz performance films in general fetishize technique, hence the careful emphasis on the solo instrumental runs. In a musical form where the performers do not have the kinetic energy, lyrical focus or sometimes charisma of rock performers, the solo fore-grounds the performer's identity; yet this can often result in rather static films.

music and non-performance-based documentaries

Where the subject of the documentary is not music, music itself seems to threaten the authenticity of documentaries. It was the soundtrack that created the orthodoxy of what we now regard as the classical documentary form. Documentaries are complex entities and occupy a zone of representation in which the arts of observing, responding and listening are sometimes at odds with the art of interpreting the events being filmed.

In such a zone, music is highly ambiguous. The idea that music removes objectivity from images goes right back to the aesthetics of Plato and Aristotle, where the process of 'aesthesis' (the nearest translation being perception, although this term would have had a different meaning for the ancient Greeks) is made up of 'imprints' of the world upon the mind. Both Plato and Aristotle use the metaphor of pressure to describe the process of imprinting. We have five senses, but only one consciousness and it is this consciousness that synthesizes sensory 'reports' into an overall image of the world. Of the many different categories of sense experience described by Plato and Aristotle, music is ranked as an image, an imitation of a (real) thing. When listened to, music has the capacity to change our feelings about the object that it accompanies or even in some cases directly imitates. Where Plato and Aristotle described music's ability to alter 'character' we would substitute 'emotions'. Music imitates emotions and therefore, in a documentary context, forces us to draw particular conclusions about what we are seeing.

Raymond Williams suggests that the emphasis on objectivity and its perceived opposite, subjectivity, has created considerable misunderstanding over the years:

> In judgements and reports we are positively required to be objective: looking only at the facts, setting aside personal preference or interest. In this context a sense of something shameful, or at least weak, attaches to subjective, although everyone will admit that there are subjective factors which have usually to be put in their place. What must be seen, in the end, as deeply controversial uses of what are nevertheless, at least in subject and object, inevitable words are commonly presented with a certainty and at times a glibness that simply spread confusion.[10]

Nowhere was this confusion more astutely exploited than in the commercial newsreels produced in a number of countries from approximately 1928 until the late 1940s. These American, Japanese and European variants of the Soviet newsreel work of Dziga-Vertov, such as the famous American *March of Time* series, used music (of an often militaristic vein) blatantly to reinforce a highly biased commentary. Since this was before the advent of television, for many people the newsreel was an important element in forming their opinion about the often tumultuous events happening around them.

In the early travel documentaries of Robert Flaherty such as *Nanook of the North* (1922), the film maker's own sense of a narrative voice to shape the silent events he films provides a humanist narrative in the documentary. In Flaherty's romantic marshalling of reality, Nanook becomes the first star of the documentary film and his struggle against nature the stuff of traditional Hollywood good-versus-evil narrative. Music was often used at the screenings, thus reinforcing the sense of an articulated and subjective documentary process. Another film maker of the 1920s, Joris Ivens, saw the camera as a way of investigating the natural world. In 1928 he made a film about a railway bridge in Rotterdam:

> For me the bridge was a laboratory of movements, tones, shapes, contrasts, rhythms and the relation between all these. I knew thousands of variations were possible and here was my chance to work out basic elements in these variations . . . What I wanted was to find some general rules, laws of continuity of movement. Music had its rules and its grammar of tones, melody, harmony and counterpoint. Painters knew what

[10] Raymond Williams, *Keywords: A Vocabulary of Culture and Society* (London: 1976), p. 312

they could do with certain colours, values, contrasts. If anyone knew about the relation of motion on the screen he was keeping it to himself and I would have to find out about it for myself.[11]

The sound documentaries of the 1930s adopted the principles of collage so popular with the avant-garde film makers of the 1920s and applied it to the soundtrack. The two British non-fiction films *Song of Ceylon* (1934) and *Night Mail* (1936) manage to develop a contrapuntal relationship between image and music or commentary. John Grierson pushed the use of sound in documentaries towards an anti-naturalism, seeing this approach as an alternative to the Hollywood tradition of story-telling.

In the mainstream, however, by the mid-1930s odd conventions of narrator had become commonplace, where the narrator's voice would yoke speech to a kind of rhetorical assertion. A strange expository logic kicked in that often bordered on didacticism. Images served as simple illustrations for the rhetorical claims of a spoken commentary backed by emotive music. The commentary seemed to attempt to solve problems of the visual through explanation rather than to allow the force of the assembled images to weave their own spell.

By the 1960s the emphasis on objectivity was back in style, with film makers' concerns sometimes reaching the point of paranoia. During the production of D. A. Pennebaker's *Jane* (1962), an argument allegedly developed between the producer Robert Drew and Pennebaker over whether the noise of the camera should be filtered out of an extended sequence with Jane Fonda sitting alone with her dressing-room mirror:

> Pennebaker felt that the noise should remain, making it clear that the audience was not seeing Jane alone in her dressing room, but Jane alone in her dressing room with a camera observing her.[12]

In his various documentaries about American institutions made in the 1960s and 1970s, film maker Fred Wiseman excludes music altogether, presumably for similar reasons to those first suggested by Plato. Wiseman's body of work strives to present a kind of unmediated reality, although this is of course impossible. Wiseman did much to entrench the language of the long-form documentary, so much so that by the 1970s, critics were able formulaically to describe what a non-fiction film consisted of:

11 Joris Ivens, *The Camera and I* (New York: 1969), p. 26

12 Stephen Mamber, *Cinéma Verité in America* (Cambridge, Mass.: 1974), p. 95

> Generally the non-fiction film stems from, and is based on, an immediate social situation: sometimes a problem, sometimes a crisis, sometimes an undramatic and seemingly unimportant person or event. It is usually filmed on the actual scene, with the actual people, without sets, costumes, written dialogue, or created sound effects. It tries to re-create the feelings of 'being there' with as much fidelity to fact as the situation allows. The typical non-fiction film is structured in two or three parts, with an introduction and a conclusion, and tends to follow a pattern from problem to solution. Even more typically it is in black and white, with direct sound recording (or simulated sound), a musical score written expressly for the film and conceived as part of a cinematic whole, and, often as not, a spoken narration.[13]

The personal video–diary approach that began in the 1970s stripped the technological apparatus back to a minimum, emphasizing the naturalistic sounds captured during the camera and microphone's encounter with their subject. Wendy Clarke's remarkable *The Love Tapes*, a continuing project begun in 1977, allots a wide assortment of individuals three minutes in which to discuss their own definitions of love. Individual difference is celebrated within a harshly standardized format.

Documentaries have moved into the field of the intensely personal with the widespread adoption of video technology, music being sometimes offered up as a kind of abstracted Greek chorus, as in Marlon Rigg's *Tongues Untied* (1989), where the film maker narrates in rhyme form an incantation of gay black sexuality against a plain background. Rigg's first-person narrator is disrupted at points by a rapping chorus of other gay men who interact with his poetic outpourings.

Music of a more conventionally non-diegetic kind has always been more widely used in Europe than in the non-fiction films of the United States. Hanns Eisler supplied an emotionally powerful score to Alain Resnais' 1957 *Night and Fog*, which examined the phenomenon of the Auschwitz concentration camp just a few short years after it had been liberated. Music here plays against the narration, heightening the majesty of the human voice, which is one of the saddest pieces of commentary recorded, as the facts and logistical details of the Nazi operations are recounted without trace of anger. The music, mainly for string quartet, is highly melancholic but is deployed in a fairly straightforward way throughout the film. The objectivity of the pictures and the dispassionate commentary ensure that the music does not overwhelm our sense of the film's subject.

[13] Richard M. Barsam, quoted in *Reality Fictions: The Films of Frederick Wiseman* by Thomas Benson & Carolyn Anderson (Chicago: 1989), p. 256

Where music was used in the American documentary, as in the propagandist films of the newsreel era, it was to personify the recorded image of the documentary. Typical of this continuing approach were the Walt Disney natural history films of the 1940s, 1950s and 1960s. Many of them were straightforward nature documentaries edited in such a way that some of the animals took on the function of becoming antagonists or protagonists in a drama of the animal kingdom. This technique of dramatization through anthropomorphizing was encouraged directly by Disney himself, his comments regarding *The Living Desert* being typical:

> In sequences where tortoises are courting . . . they look like knights in armour, old knights in battle. Give the audience a music cue, a tongue-in-cheek fanfare. The winner will claim his lady fair.[14]

The many Disney shorts produced during this period tended to sanitize the tooth and claw of the natural world, particularly through the use of music which tended to co-opt the spectator into a kind of moral ranking of the participants in these quasi-dramas which was very often based on whether the creatures in question were appealing or ugly. This tendency to anthropomorphize was formulaically applied by Disney to almost all of his filmed and animated projects, a technique which lost Disney much of the critical support he had earned during the early days of the sound era with his highly plastic cartoon features. Having said that, they were fantastically lucrative, the first two features costing $300,000 and $400,000 and recouping upwards of five million dollars apiece in their first US domestic releases alone.

The films of Errol Morris are serious documentaries with an investigative intent in which music is integrated more fully into the narratives. Morris's most renowned film, *The Thin Blue Line* (1986), is an investigation into a miscarriage of justice where an innocent man is accused of murdering a policeman in a suburb of Dallas in the late 1970s. Through a carefully structured series of interviews with the various parties involved in the case, recorded in a very stylized and cinematic way, Morris creates interlocking jigsaw pieces that assemble detailed spatial and temporal information around the central fact of the policeman's murder. Reconstructions are used, but these are more like deconstructions than anything else, and are highly fragmentary moments, in many case illustrating the lies told to Morris during the making of the film by some of the main witnesses in the case. As in his later film, *A Brief History of Time* (1992), which spins out a biography

[14] Quoted in Richard Schickel, *The Disney Version* (London: 1986), p. 288

of the famous physicist Stephen Hawking into a complex meditation on the interplay between philosophy and science, Morris commissioned scores from the minimalist American composer Philip Glass, who in each case provided a wonderfully understated yet utterly hypnotic music. The score to *The Thin Blue Line* is elegiac and strongly suggests a general atmosphere of hopelessness as we hear testimony after testimony from witnesses who seem to be incriminating the wrong man. Extremely simple, heraldic statements accompany the opening main titles and a subdued see-sawing motif for trombone, flute and keyboards sets up the melancholic feel of the rest of the piece. Glass focuses on minute musical details, tiny fragments of melody intricately laid across the film's maze-like narrative:

> *The Thin Blue Line* is very much like a detective story, a series of interviews. It doesn't need its structure articulated. It needs something a little bit different. What Errol was looking for was a character mood content to go with each character. He wanted it mostly, and very often, not to be what you were looking at. More than any other film maker I've worked with he was willing and anxious to describe in very concrete terms the things he wanted to hear in the music.[15]

This kind of leitmotif-based musical approach for a documentary film remains relatively uncommon, precisely because of music's way of directing the audience to interpret events or information in a subjective way. Yet other subjective narrative techniques, such as the cut-away shot or the over-dubbing of sound, are absorbed without controversy by audiences.

Morris's use of music parallels the more radical radio sound documentaries made by the pianist Glenn Gould for the Canadian Broadcasting Corporation in the late 1960s. Gould chose as his subject for three documentaries a study of people living in the extreme north of Canada. His approach in these remarkably innovative documentaries is to use the interview format in a musical, almost contrapuntal way. By carefully editing a series of interviews with a number of interviewees for each programme, Gould allows the voices to interplay with each other and with background sound effects to create a tonal documentary where the content of what his subjects are saying is constantly vying for the listener's attention with the interview's other status as a carrier of voices abstracted to the point of collaged impressionism. Glenn Gould explained his technique in the following way:

> Our five guests were, of course, interviewed separately. They did not at any time during the making of *North* have occasion to meet, and whichever drama-like

15 Philip Glass, interviewed in *Soundtrack*, September 1989

juxtapositions came about were achieved through some careful after-the-fact work with the razor blade on tape. [The last movement of Sibelius's 5th Symphony] is the only conventional music employed in the programme; throughout the fifty-two minutes which precede it, there are, in the prologue and in the various scenes of which *North* consists, a number of techniques which I would be inclined to identify as musically derived. The prologue indeed is a sort of trio-sonata (Nurse Schroeder, sociologist Vallée and government official Philips engage in the first several instances of a technique I've grown rather fond of dubbing 'contrapuntal radio'). The point about these scenes, I think, is that they test, in a sense, the degree to which one can listen simultaneously to more than one conversation or vocal impression. Few opera composers have been deterred from utilizing trios, quartets, or quintets by the knowledge that only a portion of the words they set to music will be accessible to the listener – most composers being concerned primarily about the totality of the structure, the play of consonance and dissonance between the voices.[16]

16 Glenn Gould, 'The Idea of *North*', 1967; liner notes to *Glenn Gould's Solitude Trilogy*, CBC Records PSCD 2003

FILM MUSIC AND POLITICS

Of all the arts, music possesses the greatest power for social organization.[1]

Arseni Avraamov's *The Symphony of Sirens* was conceived in 1923 as a multimedia performance celebrating the might and emancipation of the Soviet worker. Its contention was that music was an effective carrier of ideology, a force capable of social change, an idea then running strongly counter to prevailing Western artistic ideas of the same period. The surrealists eventually abandoned music altogether, Giorgio de Chirico's line sowing the seeds of distrust as early as 1913:

> Music cannot express the essence of sensation. One never knows what music is about . . . Auditative images are inferior to visual images not only in clarity but also in strictness, and, with all due respect to a few megalomaniacs, they are not destined to strengthen the idea of human greatness.[2]

In general, however, the notion of music as a carrier of ideology has proved remarkably resilient, although it is a body of theory most actively explored by left-leaning critical theorists. At the core it is a desire to demystify music, to pull it off its romantic pedestal, to deromanticize it and treat it as we would any other cultural artefact. This tendency has been inspired by at least three separate impulses: first, our tendency towards greater and greater cultural pluralism, where difference is celebrated rather than persecuted; second, the contributions of ethnomusicology and cultural studies, which have sought after political coding in popular and higher forms of music; and third, the enormous influence of theory and its tendency towards deconstruction. All three processes have sought to dismantle the claim of Western art (dating back to the Enlightenment) to be

[1] Arseni Avraamov, 'The Symphony of Sirens', 1923, reprinted in *Wireless Imagination*, eds. Douglas Kahn and Gregory Whitehead (Cambridge, Mass.: 1992), p. 245

[2] Giorgio de Chirico, 'No Music', 1913, reprinted ibid., p. 162

objective, moral and disinterested. There is a desire, particularly within music studies, to preserve a meaning in music that amounts to something more than simply social glue.

Many commentators on culture ideologies tend to emphasize the shallowness of popular music, contrasting it with the supposedly more rarefied strains of art music, produced away from the pressures of the marketplace. In a capitalist society, only art music, with its transcendent qualities, can remain free and be by implication nonpoliticized. Reinforced by the twentieth century's valorization of instrumental music and the institution of the concert hall, the best music of our culture supposedly remains quite apart from it, detached, disinterested.

Marxist critics tend to argue that to separate any aspect of the arts from the real world calcifies both the artwork and the world it is a product of. They argue that to declare that art, particularly music, is somehow separate from the world that produced it is itself a deeply ideological position to uphold and not at all truthful. Many leftist critics have criticized the transcendent aspects of much of this century's art music because of its remoteness from popular understanding. All music, in their eyes, should be recontextualized within the everyday and should serve the state. This requirement of popular accessibility has been a difficult aspect of theory for many critics to incorporate since their own tastes tend to be far more developed than their audiences'.

In the 1960s many new forms of music were endowed with honorary revolutionary status. The French critic Pierre Lere wrote a famous essay on *free jazz* ('Evolution ou Révolution') which was popularized through its quotation by Herbert Marcuse in *Counterrevolution and Revolt*:

> The liberty of the musical form is only the aesthetic translation of the will to social liberation. Transcending the tonal framework of the theme, the musician finds himself in a position of freedom. The melodic line becomes the medium of communication between an initial order which is rejected and a final order which is hoped for. The frustrating possession of the one, joined with the liberating attainment of the other, establishes a rupture in between the weft of harmony which gives way to an aesthetic of the cry. This cry, the characteristic resonant element of 'free music' born in an exasperated tension, announces the violent rupture with the established white order and translates the advancing violence of a new black order.[3]

Explicitly political affiliations started showing up as content in mainstream films from the 1950s onwards. Directors such as Lindsay

[3] Quoted in Herbert Marcuse, *Counterrevolution and Revolt* (Boston: 1972), p. 114

Anderson, Bernardo Bertolucci, John Cassavetes, Norman Mailer, Jim McBride, Brian De Palma and Milos Forman were just some of the directors influenced by the style of the French New Wave but who also saw cinema as a way of presenting a politicized viewpoint.

Politics, or rather the representation of politics, was a key ingredient in 1960s Western cinema. The conservatism of the 1950s that ideologically mapped out American values as somehow representative of everybody else's was being replaced by a new global politics focused on the material and political inequities that separated First World from Third World. European cinema was confident and productive and many of the most creative producers and directors sought to fulfil audience niches rather than compete for the mass markets of the mainstream American film industry. New streams of left-leaning global cinema from places like Latin America, East Europe and North Africa were being distributed in Europe and America and this clearly also had an influence on the films being made by European film makers.

The hope that many critics and social theorists placed in aggressively strident forms of music such as *free jazz* proved short-lived. *Free jazz* tried to circumvent the traditional music recording and distribution industries through the establishment of collectives such as the Chicago-based Association for the Advancement of Creative Musicians (AACM) where royalties were pooled and alternative concert circuits were established for musicians playing a particular style of music. As Jacques Attali points out, *free jazz* broke down the repetitive hierarchy of Western music and in doing so quickly ran into direct monetary censorship from the other organizations who perceived the improvisational practices of *free jazz* as threatening to an industry built upon the exploitation of copyrighted sound.

The realm of the personal became steadily more public and more political in key films of the period. Individual stories took on an allegorical significance. Political contextualizing and ideological pillaging of both the wider world and the film industry as a system were on public display as never before.

In Agnès Varda's highly original *Cleo from Five to Seven* (1962), a singer waits through the early evening for the results of a cancer test. During this waiting, which takes place almost in real time, the singer meets a variety of people in simple everyday settings, all of which serve to build up her identity for the audience. As Claudia Gorbman[4] has described, the film is full of

---

[4] Claudia Gorbman, 'Cleo from Five to Seven: Music as Mirror', *Wide Angle*, vol. 4, no. 4, 1981

different kinds of narrative 'mirrors', all of which serve to demarcate different aspects of the singer's relationships with her environment as well as screening those relationships for us. Gorbman focuses on the film-within-a-film, a silent movie playing in the cinema of a friend of the singer whom she visits. As Cleo is watching the film, which is a silent movie, we hear the familiar accompaniments of a silent era pianist. But where is the music coming from, since Cleo is viewing the film from the projection booth? Gorbman claims that the musical soundtrack systematically explores the limits of what we are willing to accept as diegetic music. The film is divided up into thirteen chapters each marking off a small section of the two-hour stretch between five and seven. The main 'non-diegetic' score by Michel Legrand and Varda herself adopts a number of different styles throughout the film. Music is clearly an analogue of Cleo's consciousness, which finds expressive form in the brief fragments of Cleo's songs, heard diegetically on a taxi radio.

The role of music in films with a political agenda is not at all clear. As Lydia Goehr points out in a recent article:

> That theorists generally find it extremely hard to describe the relation of musical form (or the internal logic of music's formed-content) to political ideals and social relations does not undermine their conviction that some such relation exists. Indeed they try hard to describe it correctly. In this endeavour they travel across the entire range of metaphors. Thus we hear of music (its logic or form) standing to society in a relation of expressing, mirroring, crystallizing, encoding, enmeshing, highlighting, enacting, confronting, intervening, transfiguring, signifying, symbolizing, transforming, prophesying, and foretelling – and this is by no means an exhaustive list.[5]

As Jacques Attali and many other philosophers have recognized, the conceptual content of music is obscure. Music is noise restrained by certain form-giving codes; it resembles a language yet is not fully one. Therefore how can it be capable of carrying any kind of ideological message? Music and the soundtrack are basic elements in the language of film. Yet aside from the avant-garde margins, few film makers have attempted to challenge the language of cinema, preferring to situate their politics within the field of dialogue. Music and the other elements on the soundtrack have not experimented with qualities of indeterminacy, as Lindsay Anderson observes in an interview from 1970:

[5] Lydia Goehr, 'Political Music and the Politics of Music', *Journal of Aesthetics and Art Criticism*, vol. 52, no. 1, Winter 1994

> I think film can and should operate with exactly the same kind of freedom that we already grant to literature, painting, theatre, or any other form of art. I think the cinema is still trying to recover from the impact of sound. Oddly enough, the silent cinema, which we're accustomed to patronizing as primitive, was actually freer and drastically more mature than the sound cinema.[6]

The old modernist idea of the aesthetic moment lying in between huge sound fields of fracturing dissonance finds its nearest equivalent in the amplification of rock music, but in many cases once a song had made the transition from record to film soundtrack this amplification itself was carefully modulated within an overall soundmix that gave preference to dialogue or non-diegetic sound effects.

Given pop or rock music's obvious participation in a commercially driven recording industry, it is not surprising that its role in revolutionary cinema has been compromised. The main film music discussion groups on the Internet are almost exclusively devoted to instrumental composition rather than pop compilation soundtracks. That rock music proved to be the eventual signifier of a cinematic counter-culture illustrates the political ambiguities of music itself. The sleeve notes to the original LP release of Michelangelo Antonioni's *Zabriskie Point* (1970) unwittingly point up the inherent instability of rock music as signifier:

> Today's artists, such as Antonioni, deal in the presentation of total concepts. There cannot be any loose ends, for each factor must have the power to provoke and to evoke. Therein lies the importance of the music in *Zabriskie Point*. It is more than just a case of a film of today demanding the music of today. Contemporary music doesn't merely tell a story or set a mood; it is the story and it is the mood.[7]

The equation of dissonance with revolutionary political purpose was an unwritten coda to the dominance of pop or rock on the soundtrack. The rock music aesthetic which preaches revolution is something of an irony. Situated at the cultural borders where high and mass art boundaries tend to dissolve, rock music in its packaging and marketing, in its formulaic sound and in its instinct for a kitsch bricolaging of the wider culture, is anything but inherently revolutionary. Pop music, and rock music only marginally less so, is a central player in what Lawrence Alloway so brilliantly described in 1959 as the 'drama of possessions'.

Yet perhaps this is all that music is able to do. Pop or rock music's double

---

[6] Lindsay Anderson, quoted in Joseph Gelmis, *The Film Director as Superstar* (New York: 1970), p. 157

[7] *Zabriskie Point* soundtrack LP, MGM 2354 040

bind is its representation of counter-cultural elements whilst being economically very well rewarded in many cases. The music seems constantly to assert its independence (bands like Rage against the Machine, for example) by continuing to function against the general background, the music business, from which it declares its difference. Music's freedom then is a form of resistance, a negation of whatever it chooses to declare as 'other'. Perhaps it isn't even relevant if rock music actually achieves this distance. Music articulates its vision in abstract codes, not concrete ones, therefore its 'political' content cannot be judged by comparison with other arts such as literature or painting. Certainly, Adorno and Hanns Eisler maintained that in its abstraction music succeeds in being truly political, whereas in its supposed 'transcendence' much instrumental music remained merely ordinary. In abstracting the familiar, the resulting aesthetic disturbance can motivate social change.

Representative of the idea that self-realization comes through consumption, rock music has become the indispensable element in the marketing strategy of a film. Its primal authenticity, its original power to galvanize and to surprise and just occasionally to articulate social comment, now appears (with some exceptions) to be little more than a memory recycled by cinema and music television. We have entered what the French situationist Guy Debord referred to as the 'society of the spectacle', in which everything is up for recontextualization. Rock music glimpsed through a series of dimly lit symbolic moments: the (literally) orchestrated murders by Charles Manson and his 'family' of followers tracked by the Beatles 'Helter Skelter'; the Rolling Stones playing at Altamont against a background of violence; the articulate mayhem of Punk. From the early 1950s onwards, each fashion change, each political flirtation, each new leader of a youth 'movement' has been fully enabled only with the co-operation of the media. In the glare of the spotlight, subcultures tend to fulfil their own prophecies.

For film music to reflect the counter-cultural intents of film makers of the 1960s, one might suppose that its very function in the body of the film would have undergone some kind of rupture. Yet surprisingly this rarely happened. Authenticity in rock music, as Simon Frith[8] has made clear in his essay on Bruce Springsteen, has got little to do with truth or reality. Authenticity in pop culture is a highly relative term, usually posited in relation to the perceived inauthenticity of others.

The baby-boomer generation, who grew up in a 1960s atmosphere of rock music utopianism, were amply supplied with a music that articulated their

8 Simon Frith and Lawrence Grossberg, *We Gotta Get Outa This Place* (New York: 1992)

Cold War anxieties. Notions of authenticity thus became a central strategy in rock music, a way of incorporating the increasing cynicism felt by a generation weaned on the patently bogus American Dream. Even the rock music of the late 1960s seems optimistic compared with the various subcultural innovations that have taken root since then. The postmodern sensibility of youth subcultures today are infinitely more sophisticated than those of yesteryear. To attempt to posit rock music as a genuinely revolutionary message in today's cinema would miss the point entirely. Rock music can never directly overthrow the *status quo*, all it can do (in the case of lyrics) is to represent certain gestures to be found in the wider society or (in the case of instrumental music) to shake up people's expectations. The music's authenticity survives and even prospers squeezed up against a hyper-sophisticated marketing campaign for the film as a social phenomenon. The promotion of the British film *Trainspotting* (1996), with its carefully compiled soundtrack, is typical.

The impact of music politically is, of course, socially determined. A web of social institutions and cultural practices mediates all our listening experiences, noted theorist Theodor Adorno in his critical writings as long ago as the 1930s. Adorno foresaw the decline of interest in 'serious' music in the face of popular music, the ultimately valuable music of exchange. Adorno[9] claimed that listeners were being 'infantilized' by the music production and distribution industry, that popular music was becoming inseparable from its exchange value, leading to a situation where listeners avoid the innovative in favour of the familiar, thus defending their accumulated 'exchange value'.

Even more complex forms of art music suffer the same fate, caught up in a media–driven trivialized approach which either fragments a piece into easily ingestible parts or fetishizes the Wagnerian motif, thus placing the emphasis on musical details instead of on musical wholes. Paradoxically, as music became more culturally isolated, so greater value was placed on its transcendent qualities, thus safely removing it from the arena of discourse and therefore direct political meaning.

Adorno sees the Wagerian motif as fundamental to the malaise he saw in film music composition. This over-reliance on the easily remembered phrase to be tacked on to a character in a film and revisited whenever the character undergoes a dramatic change Adorno found deeply regressive. His preference for the complex twelve-tone music of Schoenberg, much of which is more intelligible on paper than in performance, exemplifies the defensive position that his criticism adopts in the face of an all-consuming

[9] Theodor Adorno, *In Search of Wagner* (London: 1981), pp. 43–51

mass culture. Integrity, Adorno is saying, lies in the inaccessible, and in the long-form musical work, rather than the extract, the detail which distracts serious contemplation.

A tendency from the 1950s onwards was the movement away from large-scale orchestration. Film music became a kind of chamber music (albeit of many different kinds) in the new era of independent film producers and directors working on a project-by-project basis. The enormous resources available to composers in the Hollywood studios of the 1930s and 1940s (and to arrangers, conductors, musical directors and orchestrators) no longer existed and in this climate of reduced opulence and economic restraint composers survived by being flexible. The stylings of the classical eras of film music seem cluttered and ornate in comparison with the simple sound pictures constructed by a composer such as Jerry Goldsmith, whose themes predetermine much of the orchestration. Goldsmith himself has remarked that the less music there is, the more emphasis it has,[10] and this approach informed many of the more interesting film scores of the 1960s and 1970s.

The new minimalism which typified the main thrust of film music in the 1960s is particularly suited to the realm of the personal, and owes a lot to the advances made in recording technologies. In a cinema where the concept of 'seeing' (descriptive objectivism) has replaced the concept of 'action', as Gilles Deleuze has claimed,[11] the scope for reinvention is considerable. As music ceased to track movement its relationship with the image became more complex. With the advent of electronic music, the soundtrack itself became a seamless web of information, each element riffing off the others.

As a general tendency one could claim that film music has become more dialectical since the innovations of the French New Wave in the late 1950s and early 1960s, instructing how to see, how to feel. In the early films of Jean-Luc Godard, to describe something is to observe something in mutation, hence his attraction towards the fixed shot. Images are assembled, designed to be 'read' in a way that the earlier cinemas of movement (the action film) were not. Thus, to return to Gilles Deleuze, the predominant sensory concern in the image becomes time rather than movement, the length of time that a shot endures, the pressure upon the filmed subject of being 'described', being 'read':

> Even when it is mobile, the camera is no longer content sometimes to follow the
> characters' movement, sometimes itself to undertake movements of which they are

[10] Joseph McBride, Filmmakers on Filmmaking (Los Angeles: 1983), p. 141

[11] Gilles Deleuze, Cinema 2: The Time-Image (London: 1989), p. 9

merely the object, but in every case it subordinates description of a space to the functions of thought. This is not the simple distinction between the subjective and the objective, the real and the imaginary, it is on the contrary their indiscernibility which will endow the camera with a rich array of functions and entail a new conception of the frame and reframings.[12]

The apocalyptic existentialism of Michelangelo Antonioni's *The Eclipse* (1962), scored by Giovanni Fusco, fuses a neo-romantic sensibility brought out by Fusco's music with the detailed depiction of the psychological states of his character Vittoria (Monica Vitti) as she drifts through a dislocated series of encounters with different people in the small town where she lives. The musical accompaniments are handled in a conventional manner by Antonioni. As Vittoria and her lover walk through a park they are tracked aurally by a pianist from out-of-frame who is evidently there in the park with them and whose music continues to track them as they walk on. In Antonioni's objectified universe, people become objects to be 'redeemed' as humans by Fusco's romantic score, which functions as an allusive device. In a world filled with spectacular examples of technological progress which dominate every visual aspect of the landscape (the eternal present), only people have a past, a past of disappointments, painful memories and uncertainties. Fusco's music seems to be tracking a very human 'tiredness' and directly offers up a key to deciphering the objectified characters.

Jean-Luc Godard's astonishing (but commercially unsuccessful) *Les Carabiniers* (1963) is a parable couched in Brechtian style, set in an undefined country in which two peasants are enlisted to fight in an unspecified but clearly European war and gleefully participate in all sorts of atrocities. They move from capital city to capital city, collecting picture postcards of the places they have ransacked, before finally returning to their dilapidated farm and their mother and sister. They are then summarily arrested and sent to the firing squad. The entire film is artfully simple, representative, each shot simply serving to describe an object (thus replacing the object) and to set up its own eradication by another descriptive shot sequence. Characters are stripped of any subjective identity, made into mouthpieces for a variety of political platitudes. The representations of war and the events of war are reduced to simple, theatrical vignettes, encounters between groups of two or three people. For a war film there is no deference to any kind of 'heroic' action *mise-en-scène*. Instead, we are just presented with the squalidness of a firing squad, or a rape, or a looting. The music by

12 Ibid., p.23

Phillipe Arthuys is a repetitive series of variations on martial drum rolls and is not psychologically involving, but does much to maintain the feeling of events taking place inside a highly stylized dramatic and aesthetic vacuum.

A different and more complex film but still with the same sense of characters as objectified ciphers, Lindsay Anderson's *If* (1968), uses the demarcated world of the British boarding school to play out a wish-fulfilment drama of middle-class revolution. A group of three schoolboy protagonists, led by Malcolm McDowell, are subjected to the harsh regimes of school life, eventually appearing to break with it altogether and stage a (possibly fantasized) armed assault on the college chapel during morning service, mowing down the rest of the school. Music plays an important part in *If*, the underrated composer Marc Wilkinson supplying brief musical cues of modern chamber music alongside repeated snatches of a Sanctus from the Missa Lube. On one level the chamber music seems to represent something of the Gothic antiquity of the school itself, at the same time deconstructing the normative musical accompaniment of action sequences with classical crescendos. Both *If* and *Les Carabiniers* use music to partition the different sections of the film. In scenes where music is used to score movement or action it does so in a very arch way, perhaps echoing the allegorical intent of the stories. In *If* much of the music is diegetic, school hymns or the repeated extracts from the Missa Lube (which at one point even seems to emanate from a jukebox), although this is alternated with specially composed music which is used non-diegetically in sequences that operate on a fantasy level. Music becomes a cue for imaginative flights of fancy, but it is music of a particularly sombre and discordant kind. The fantasy sequences in *If* are very often purely optical or sound experiences. They are not personal recollections by individual characters but become objectified fantasies based upon the closed world in which the characters all live. Fantasy in *If* becomes a supra-personal phenomenon, a way of seeing unrelated to past recollection but rather an abstraction of the present, an index of the (romantic) revolutionary instinct. Moments of silence unexpectedly disrupt what appears to be normal sensory-motor action. It is something akin to what the French critic Michel Devillers has called the 'implied dream', in which characters' physical and apparent mental 'movements' become taken over by the shot itself, which seems to move them for us. Space and time seem to become virtual.

This very effective use of music which implies a kind of dream state (where revolutions are born) is brought out powerfully again in Anderson's next film, *O Lucky Man* (1973), where, using a more obviously popular musical style, Alan Price, a well-known songwriter, is seen periodically throughout the film performing the soundtrack in a recording studio with Anderson himself appearing to supervise the recording session. The songs Price performs comment obliquely on the storyline, which is a kind of modern take on the Rake's Progress through a surreal version of contemporary Britain. Music moves the character onwards within a world that is formed and described in the virtual realities of the implied dream.

In symphonic music the contrapuntal moment achieved a new kind of orthodoxy, as music either directly appropriated from or influenced by Stravinsky, Bartok and Charles Ives began to make an appearance in films. Counterpoint in cinema promised a new kind of dissonant freedom, proving that a block or mass of sound could be just as effective as individual notes or chord patterns. Sound masses could be manipulated in terms of their density as well as deployed in different rhythmic and dynamic configurations. Sound blocks are not directly contrapuntal because of the relative insignificance of individual instrument lines, but in the work of György Ligeti, whose *Atmospheres* makes a powerful contribution to Kubrick's *2001* soundtrack, it is possible to hear something of the impact of these kinds of sound masses of varying colour and density, which tend to unfold in macro or large-scale musical rhythm where changes are wrought within the relative durations of differently 'coloured' bands of sounds.

Counterpoint as used in *If* and *Les Carabiniers* actually conferred a great freedom upon the film maker and upon the audience to interpret two stories which are both relatively removed from mainstream narrative techniques. This kind of counterpoint is an asynchronism quite different in intent from that practised by Eisenstein and Prokofiev and an earlier generation of film makers. By appearing to adopt at least the form of conventional canonical musical reference, both Marc Wilkinson's refracted chamber score for *If* and Arthuys' militaristic music for *Les Carabiniers* are carriers of a stridently revolutionary message. In their strong adherence to structural unity both scores do much to 'repair' the disruptive breaks in narrative events that are a marker of the two films' style. There is a great deal of independence between dialogue, music and images in the two films. Music is clearly a structural carrier of messages not explicitly put across in either pictures or dialogue.

In his later 'revolutionary' films, Godard was to abandon the conventional narrative form altogether in favour of a minimalist style that served as a pictorial basis for a newly activated soundtrack that functioned apparently only to carry dialectic. His 1969 film *See You at Mao* is typical in that the picture is often an unchanging, apparently neutral image given significance by the soundtrack – in this case, an exuberant collage of Maoist statements by Western leftists, fragments of songs by the Beatles, radio collages, or a statement by the Women's Liberation Movement which accompanies a sustained shot of a woman's navel. This visually exceptionally uneventful film is perhaps the closest Godard ever came to an experimental revolutionary (in the sense of challenging convention) aesthetic, though it is unclear who his intended audience were since all cinematic involvement for the viewer is lost in a din of didactic harangues and an unending flow of lifeless images. Norman Mailer, himself no stranger to experimental film forms, acknowledged a certain tendency in Godard:

> I think Godard is tiresome. He delights in boring the very people he attracts. That's his trademark. It's like he's saying, 'You're happy. You're enjoying yourselves. You're really enjoying my movie. This must come to an end. Now you'll be bored for a while. You have to pay your price for my movie.'[13]

Vera Chytilová's *Daisies* (1968) broke the mould of social realist comedies that dominated Czech film making of the 1960s. An orgy of visual and aural experimentation, *Daisies* spins a sort of story about two bored young girls who seem to exist outside of any conventional time frame and who stumble through a series of bizarre adventures involving strenuous eating competitions, pie throwing and chance pick-ups by exploitative men which ultimately turn protagonists into victims. The music by Jiri Slitr and Jiri Sust is by turns a speeded-up orchestral dirge, parodying silent film comedy music, and a fragmented jazz score.

WR: Mysteries of the Organism (1971), by the Yugoslavian film maker Dušan Makavejev, is a film composed of a number of quite separate parts taken from a variety of sources, including various kinds of documentary and propaganda films. What begins as a documentary about the German *émigré* sexologist Wilhelm Reich gradually incorporates fictional elements which tell the story of a girl in Yugoslavia who attempts to preach the controversial theories of Reich and to integrate these with her daily life as a member of a Communist society. Aside from a straight biographical study of Reich, Makavejev is concerned to incorporate aspects of Reich's theories of sexual ideology in which the causes of Fascism are revealed to have arisen from distortions and frustrations of the sexual instinct. Throughout this complicated film, the soundtrack comments upon rather than illustrates the screen action, sometimes ironically (as in the alternation of a statement of

13 Norman Mailer, quoted in *The Film Director as Superstar* by Joseph Gelmis (New York: 1970), p. 104

Reich's theories with pro-Communist folk songs over images of a couple making love in a meadow and juxtaposed archive footage of Reich sitting with his first wife in a similar setting). Each element within the film gathers its significance from its context; the Reich documentary and the fictional story seem to represent theory and practice, the two basic determinants of political theory. Makavejev is an intellectual film maker in the same sense that Godard is and he uses dialectical montage to put his points across. Despite this deliberation, *WR* was a film constructed during the post-production process as the director began to formulate connections between seven or eight very disparate sources of material.

Improvements in post-production technology centred on the new generation of sound mixing consoles that had become an essential part of studio apparatus by the early 1970s. Extensive and sophisticated control circuits allowed many different microphone sources to be fed into different and separate channels, each one of which could be separately manipulated. The effective position of the 'sound image' could be controlled through manipulating the proportions of signals from or between any inputs, thus giving an accurate impression of a directed sound source. These new freedoms, which really took off with the advent of multi-track recording in the early 1970s, made possible a new kind of collage for the film maker, revolutionary or not.

Noël Burch's hope for a revolutionary 'open' cinema[14] with the same kind of rhythmic and material freedoms as serial music has taken a long time to translate from the margins to the mainstream, even in this age of media overload. However, the tendency of an increasingly techno-centric cinema over the past twenty years has led film towards a different kind of total cohesion.

The huge improvements in recording technology since the 1960s have completely redefined the musical field in political and economic terms. The marshalling of original sounds during the compositional process has now been replaced by a recording studio that has become an instrument in its own right. Technology is responsible for the tremendous advances taken by all kinds of composition, recording and distribution activities over the past twenty years. New instrumentation and recording techniques have produced new sounds which are unplayable by human musicians; the microtonal worlds of electronic music, the dense drum meshes of Jungle, the reconfigured resystematized sample of, for example, a single note played by Miles Davis reworked into the fabric of a new song in a new style. Adorno's

[14] Noël Burch, 'The Structural Use of Sound', in *Theory of Film Practice* (New York: 1973), p. 99

much-wished-for systematized fragments have become, through sampling and through greater complexity in the basic recording processes, the basis of a whole new way of composing. The romantic ideal of the composer alone, whose musical signature acts as an analogue to the individual heroics of the classical dramatic protagonist, is now severely compromised. The musical mind is no longer an autonomous site of invention, but a conductor of various sonic possibilities unleashed by technology.

Whether these developments were predicted by Adorno as the ultimate regression or whether they will allow music to continue to remain a vital and challenging area of the arts is unclear. It's tempting to suggest that if everyone, through inexpensive technology, has the resources to compose and distribute music easily, then common aesthetic value systems will fragment entirely, thus reducing the impact of music beyond small cliques of devotees. As music and technology coincide with greater sophistication there are signs that music making as a practice and even as a business is devolving from the centre to the margins. The experience of music has become radically more individualized as, increasingly, consumers hear music primarily as a material, recorded object. With more music being recorded than ever before and new distribution channels such as the Internet bypassing the old commercial structures of music distribution, the definitions of commercial and non-commercial music are in flux as never before.

In this sense, then, the film soundtrack through a process of technological fragmentation and merger between film sound and film music has freed itself from the limitations of the old romantic musical ideology. The 'transcendent' romanticism of Erich Korngold has been replaced by the popular abstractions of a new generation of experimenters working very much within the system, but whose music seeks continually to challenge the *status quo*. The soundtrack is now more open than ever before, and as audiences learn to assimilate more and more complex forms of audible information so the experimenters will push the margins even further. The rest of film aesthetics have yet to catch up, since the same kinds of archetypal character relationships that have existed since the start of cinema continue to be played out in the mainstream.

FILM MUSIC AND FILM TIME

Music and film both have a complex relationship to time. Our perceptions of passing time whilst listening to music or watching a film are highly variable, indicating that each exert a powerful impact upon our subjective senses of duration. This realization is, of course, exploited by composers, and more rarely by film makers. Stravinsky distinguished our sense of time passing in music as two different perceptual modes – the real or 'ontological' time in which we hear each note and the 'psychological' time in which we experience the musical piece more elastically and subjectively. Film can be seen in much the same way, yet its particular spell works more on removing us completely from a sense of time passing, and instead places us in what seems like a perpetual present, the permanent sense of now-ness that is the basic characteristic of film narration. The complexities of film time and its similarity to music was discussed as early as 1923:

> [Cinema] will tend more every day to approach music and the dance. The interpenetration, the crossing and the association of movements and cadences already give us the impression that even the most mediocre films unroll in musical space . . . the cinema incorporates time in space. More than this, through the cinema time really becomes a dimension of space.[1]

One of the most articulate film makers to write about the basic ontology of film time was the great Russian director Andrey Tarkovsky. Unlike earlier generations of Russian film makers (particularly Eisenstein and Kuleshov), who saw editing as the main formative process in film, Tarkovsky constructed his films much more within the shot itself:

> The cinema image comes into being during shooting, and exists within the frame. During shooting, therefore, I concentrate on the course of time within the frame, in order to reproduce it and record it. Editing brings together shots which are already

[1] Élie Fauré, *The Art of Cineplastics* (Boston: 1923)

filled with time, and organizes the unified, living structure inherent in the film; and the time that pulsates through the blood vessels of the film, making it alive, is of varying rhythmic pressure.[2]

It is this sense of time passing within the shot rather than the cutting-room trickery that allows a character to cross the world in seconds that bears the closest relationship to music. Tarkovsky's phrase 'rhythmic pressure' is telling, implying that certain kinds of internal movement within a shot have a different impact on our perception of rhythmic time:

The distinctive time running through the shots makes the rhythm of the picture; and rhythm is determined not by the length of the edited pieces, but by the pressure of the time that runs through them . . . Time, imprinted in the frame, dictates the particular editing principle; and the pieces that won't edit – that can't be properly joined – are those which record a radically different kind of time.[3]

The different kinds of movement Tarkovsky describes as 'life processes' are those rhythmic flows which each reveal a different aspect of time passing. This intensely naturalistic conception of film's ontology brings us closest to the kind of descriptions regularly made about musical experience. The manipulation of differing 'rhythmic pressures' is the most basic aspect of musical composition. Subjective musical time (the time spent listening) is phenomenologically denser than ordinary time. At times it can appear to be moving either faster or slower than ordinary lived time.

The French nineteenth-century philosopher Henri Bergson asserted that music did not actually exist 'in time' since it is composed of sequences of single notes which follow each other in time. There is no musical causality as such, one note does not cause the next to happen, yet in a sense the melody exists as a complete entity as soon as we hear the first note. The single notes have a duration in time, but their relation to each other (which generates the sense of melody) lies 'outside' time. Music hints at the non-linear sense of duration that underlines our experience. It is this non-linear duration that is the present tense of film time, and which is what Tarkovsky refers to as his basic raw material from which he must strive to:

create my own, distinctive flow of time, and convey in the shot a sense of its movement – from lazy and soporific to stormy and swift – and to one person it will seem one way, to another, another. Assembly, editing, disturbs the passage of time,

[2] Andrey Tarkovsky, *Sculpting in Time* (London: 1986), p. 114

[3] Ibid., p. 115

interrupts it and simultaneously gives it something new. The distortion of time can be a means of giving it rhythmical expression. Sculpting in time![4]

Music provides a mental continuum to that reality of life which Bergson struggled to capture in words, and which Tarkovsky struggled to capture in his shot compositions. Film time is a doorway into another universe. Perhaps most difficult to swallow is its great central lie of authentic performance. With each movement, each scene rehearsed and shot perhaps twenty times, what we are presented with is the take or version that looked the most 'real', the most spontaneous. Cut together, these approved images appear to inhabit a temporal stream much like our own, but the eerie fourth-dimensionality of their rejected movements, the ones left on the cutting-room floor, threatens our belief in film's present moments.

Film music indexes the perpetual present of film time, since it develops and defines our sense of visual tempo. A silent movie chase sequence accompanied by music played in 3/4 time appears very different from one accompanied by music in 6/8 metre. The sense of relentless rhythm that can be felt for example in a Keystone Cops chase is largely driven by the musical score. This being the silent era, many different scores must have been used but it is likely that they would have had a similar rhythm. The music mimics the accelerated rhythms of the performers' bodies on screen.

Tonal music is 'goal-orientated'. The music track in a typical chase sequence as described above lurches between structurally significant musical events. As we become engrossed the music generates a kind of temporal overlap. Musical and pictorial events anticipate their continuance through a sense of rhythmic overlap between shots.

Our tendency to group sounds together in patterns is a part of our basic physiology. Our experience of melody is more complex since it depends upon us hearing tones arranged within a complex series of rule-like parameters, although one might claim that these rules are also an aspect of our physiology. We tend to anthropomorphize our experience of melody into phrases that draw upon notions of movement. The music 'soars', it 'sweeps', etc. Our experience of music really is inseparable from the felt experience of movement as we hear a melodic cycle. We simply can't help ourselves. Our auditory system evolved from the same part of the brain as that which provides us with spatial information. Our experience of sound or melody is always dependent therefore on the spatial location of the sound source in relation to us as listeners.

[4] Ibid., p. 121

Our perception of musical *Gestalten* is vital to our comprehension of musical events. Rhythmic figurations compete for our attention against the chaotic background 'noise' of everyday distractions. Rhythmic perception is an essential biological asset. By learning to use our bodily movements in more or less rhythmic patterns we expend a minimum of energy and are more physically effective. Yet part and parcel of this is the learned skill to recognize the signals that set off the rhythmic pattern – a readiness to be receptive to such signals. Even without the film image as stimulus, a large part of our rhythmic pleasure in music takes place in the imagination. There is a sense of self-projection, through the sensory cue of hearing, into the more dominant sensory fields of movement and vision. From the perceived rhythm of a given sequence of shots we unconsciously anticipate the length and to some extent the internal structure of succeeding shot sequences. In the case of the chase sequence, once we have understood the basic pattern, we are free to relax and enjoy its predictability. We can impose ourselves into the rhythmic action of the chase.

We instinctively as viewers and as listeners search for a pattern to somehow recognize or complete. The more difficult that pattern is to discern the harder we find it to understand what is happening. The films of Andrey Tarkovsky are complex, slow-moving stories that are rather more like meditations on an underlying theme than dramatic expositions. This raw approach to the depiction of time can often make his films appear boring to an audience used to more conventional ways of story-telling. Tarkovsky's films (like those of Ozu, the Japanese director) are closer to being direct takes on another's consciousness. By this I mean that the films themselves become ontological entities. For the philosopher Gilles Deleuze, cinema was consciousness *par excellence*, personified through the unique style of composition of a few auteurist directors whose 'signature' is so distinctive that they are better compared not only with painters, musicians and architects but also with thinkers:

> Cinema's concepts are not given in cinema . . . Cinema itself is a new practice of images and signs whose theory philosophy must produce as a conceptual practice.[5]

Cinema in the hands of master film makers is constantly pushing towards the formation of new kinds of thought. By retooling our basic sensorium, certain film makers inherently rework some of our deepest held beliefs in wider areas such as psychology or philosophy. Deleuze has written two highly original books on cinema (*Cinema 1* and *Cinema 2*) which, rather than

[5] Gilles Deleuze, *Cinema 2: The Time-Image* (London: 1988), p. 280

seeking to explain cinema and its practices in terms of historical or political processes, describe certain cinematic practices or styles of composition as important innovations in a general genealogy of consciousness. This kind of artistic breakthrough releases the film as a fully fledged artwork from the restraints of its economic and industrial beginning. Exceptional cinema rises above the circumstances of its production and becomes a kind of free-ranging, multi-perspectival yet rigorously material consciousness.

Deleuze claims that the defining condition of nearly all cinema since the Second World War has been its break with the sensory-motor linkage of a cinema based on illustrating movement to tell its stories to one based on time. Time itself becomes visible in the films of the master film makers of the 1950s and beyond. Faced with a growing number of situations to which we no longer have the vocabulary to respond, cinema strives to fill up some of the gaps. Deleuze sees the poverty of communicable experience in the modern era as central to the manufacture by cinematic means of a new kind of artistic sublime.

The time image in cinema can function as sheets of coexistent pasts: for example, the flashbacks of a film such as Orson Welles' *Citizen Kane*, where we jump forwards and backwards in time as the story of Kane (told through the subjective testimonies of those who knew him) and the meaning of his deathbed utterance 'Rosebud' is revealed. Alternatively, the time image can be represented for Deleuze as a simultaneity of past, present and future. Time is foregrounded in a film such as Resnais and Robbe-Grillet's *Last Year at Marienbad* but loses its temporality. Time no longer passes from the present into the past but endures in a multiplicity of possible present moments. As two unnamed characters meet in a baroque hotel, the male character tries to persuade the female character that they met in the same hotel a year earlier and had an affair which has triggered this second meeting. Since both characters' 'versions' are presented in a fragmented and partial manner, any authoritative verification of which version of past, present or future is 'truthful' becomes meaningless, since there is no key with which to decode the story objectively.

These kinds of approach to the temporal aspects of story telling give film a new take on the narrative, since successive action becomes abstracted. Narration now becomes a series of alternative versions of the present distributed between a number of characters. Like Kurosawa's *Rashomon* or Tarantino's *Reservoir Dogs*, the stories told by the characters are 'incompossible'. Taken together they cancel each other out, yet any one account may be 'true'. A complex interweaving of different accounts ('sheets') of the past is no less a time image for Deleuze than a juggling of alternate versions of the present.

In the cinema of the time image described by Deleuze, music becomes especially important since characters come increasingly to resemble feelings rather than having fully sketched-out biographies. Feelings rather than characters are transformed depending on what type of cinematic time they inhabit. This is something like a psychology of pure feelings as opposed to one rooted in characters or individuals. Accordingly, music acts crucially as a navigator of feelings dispossessed from bodies, from biographies.

Music, together with the other elements on the soundtrack, including dialogue, forms a continuum which extends beyond what is seen in the picture. Sound in the form of dialogue continues a conversation after the lights have gone out (e.g. René Clair's *Sous les toits de Paris*, 1930), but sound in the form of music can extend the entire perception of a film (if we follow Deleuze's idea of the cinema in its highest moments as a form of consciousness) making it far more legible. Music in the cinema grounded in the time image is no longer obliged to correspond to the visual image. It is no longer forced to provide either a narrative or an illustrative function, since so much of this function can now be handled by other elements on the soundtrack.

Whereas Eisenstein sought to combine the image and music into a whole which was governed and choreographed by the editing process, thereby forcing one interpretation of rhythmic unity, the ambition now is more to use music to add something to the image that would otherwise be undetected. Composers such as Pierre Jensen, a collaborator of Chabrol and other French New Wave directors, sought to maintain music as a foreign body within the film which nevertheless revealed something not previously legible. Hanns Eisler has also taken up a similar position, denying that there is any movement that can be common to both the visual and the sound fields.

Music in the modern cinema freely moves between the diegetic source that is revealed in the image and the non-diegetic music whose source is never revealed and vice versa. It comes more and more to symbolize the sublime in the most imaginative examples of its use. It literally represents the sublime in Alain Resnais' *L'Amour à mort* (1985), where a man who has briefly 'died' of a heart condition miraculously recovers after a lapse of several minutes only to be forever haunted by his brief encounter with the unnameable. Resnais illustrates his visions simply with black spaces filled by a mysterious falling snow of a few seconds' duration which is tracked by the discordant music of Henze, somehow appearing to bridge the gap between the living and the dead.

THE EMOTIONAL IMPACT OF FILM MUSIC

Why does film music influence our responses to films? It appears to express emotion: certainly films, television, commercials and video games seem to operate on the assumption that it does. At the very least, common sense would say that film music seems to *capture* our emotions. Surely it seems quite straightforward to say that if a given person feels a particular emotion whenever a piece of music is played, then the music is in some way transmitting an emotional message which is responded to by the listener in the appropriate way. But what is it that happens between the signal from the music and the listener's ear?

One response might be to claim that the music is responsible for 'shaping' the emotion in the listener. Yet if music shapes an emotion such as, for example, sadness, then what is the object of that sadness? Sadness in virtually any other context is a powerful emotion directed at something, the object of the emotion, yet music seems to trigger such emotions without providing an object for them. It gives us the feelings, leaving us to grope around for appropriate objects.

Most of the ways in which we discuss music in ordinary language tend to ascribe the reactions we have to the music to the music itself, as if this or that particular piece was melancholic. It may well be that we cannot honestly feel anything other than melancholy when we hear it, but does that mean that the piece itself is expressing the properties of melancholia? This sort of ascription can be problematic. In other areas of aesthetic experience, particularly the visual arts, we do not tend to make this conceptual link in anything like such causal terms. The impact of music is vivid and instantaneous but above all self-directed in a way that the experience of a piece of sculpture or a painting can never be. Music, like film, leads the spectator by the nose through his perception of it. Perception is radically linear, and insight unfolds in direct correlation with the running time of the piece of music or the film itself. The perception of music, like film, takes place through time in a way that an encounter with a painting does not. A painting is perceived at a rate determined by the spectator, beginning with the immediate encounter with the three-dimensional whole. All other subsequent perceptions are subjective orderings by the spectator.

The special perceptive difficulty with music, even more than with film, is to separate out the process of perception itself from the resulting feelings of pleasure (or otherwise). Perhaps we should say that music acts as the 'direct shaping voice'[1] of the emotion, simultaneously arousing and shaping feeling without the mediation of emotional objects. The attachment of our feelings to emotional objects (memories, characters in films, etc.) seems to come after the formation of the feeling itself which music has triggered. Does this mean that music directly arouses core emotions – happiness or sadness? The problem in claiming this is that, without emotional objects, how can we identify what that core emotion is? We can say that the core emotions triggered by music have a common characteristic of intentionality (in other words that they are directed towards something, real or imaginary).

How does this intentionality actually work? In Jack Clayton's superb 1964 film *The Pumpkin Eater*, a lush melancholic score by Georges Delerue is used predominantly to navigate us as spectators through a collage of different time frames which tell the story of a steadily disintegrating marriage. Music is used primarily to lead us towards conclusions about the emotional states of the central characters at specific points in time. For much of the film we are encouraged to sympathize with the central female character, Jo Armitage, whose sense of identity is constantly threatened by her philandering husband. This sympathy is represented by a leitmotif whose languid descent mirrors Jo's recollection of happier times.

Music in *The Pumpkin Eater* shows properties of intentionality in more than one way. The film juggles time frames to show how the central character's relationship changes. Jo is rendered through the music score as a non-speaking narrator who leads us (through first-person close-ups) through various moments from her life. Her melancholic expression frames and signals an optical dissolve which again and again is used to cue the same passage of music from the main score. Music represents her attempt to recall happier times, yet its inherently melancholic quality points to her present distress. On another level the main theme is sometimes broken off mid-phrase by diegetic sources within the picture. Jo's nervous breakdown in a department store is anticipated by the progressive heightening of diegetic sound sources from the scene, eventually to be replaced by the main theme.

[1] Peter Mew, 'The Expression of Emotion in Music', *British Journal of Aesthetics*, vol. 25, Winter 1985, p. 33

As we concentrate on Jo's face, she begins to cry and her sobbing in turn obliterates the theme. At another point, Jo commits adultery with her ex-husband Giles out of revenge on her husband Jake. A variation on the main theme is double-tracked with a lush Spanish guitar as we pan across their bodies and eventually see that the guitar is a record playing in the corner of the room. This complex interweaving between diegetic and non-diegetic elements is an astonishingly vivid evocation of Jo's often needing contact with the external world. She is a character who lives largely in her head, and the main theme that Delerue provides has a penetrating bittersweetness entirely at odds with the sometimes noiseless external world that Jo moves through.

the absence of musical objects

We separate the feelings that a piece of music evokes from the melodic and rhythmic contours we perceive as part of the listening experience. Feelings evoked by music are not the passive moods of satisfaction or disappointment one might have after seeing a painting or meeting an old friend but a more forceful feeling that remains anchored in the reliving of the melodic structure itself. In this process of recollection we are focusing on the structure itself, not the feelings the music evokes, although this may be a part of the experience. There seems to be a strange absence of an object on to which we have projected our feelings.

We offhandedly say that when a feeling is projected on to an object, the object is in some way 'expressive' of that feeling. In music this sort of thing happens all the time. Yet the feelings projected are probably of a fairly low order of intensity, being generalized rather than specific feelings attached to remembered experiences. Someone who was constantly reminded of a traumatic personal event whenever hearing, for example, Mozart's Requiem will never experience that music as expressive of any general class of feelings, since the personal, remembered and internal have displaced any fantasy we might have of identification with external feeling-states that the music's structure may stimulate.

If one were to follow the line of recognition theorists, one might say that the listener notices similarities between musical contours and behavioural features symptomatic of human emotional expressions. With vocal music such an insight might consist of an awareness that a singer must tense their vocal cords to produce a higher note or exert more energy to produce a louder sound. Since vocal experience is common to virtually all of us an unconscious association takes place between the hearing of rising pitch or increasing volume and the sensation of physical tension. So the quality of tension is projected by us into the music which we then interpret as 'tense music'.

The advantage of this particular interpretative theory is that it allows us some latitude as listeners not automatically to feel tense whenever we hear a particular musical structure. Since we are projecting qualities on to the musical experience we are equally able to reserve interpretation voluntarily. The only necessary condition is that the emotive quality should appear to come from the musical object itself. The problem with recognition theory is that it does not appear to hold up for all cases. Beyond vocal music, where there is a fairly obvious correlation between semantic content and expressive capacity, we move into the more problematic realm of instrumental music. Identifying emotional content in instrumental music becomes much more difficult beyond the superficial assignments of happiness or sadness. The subtleties of human emotional response are difficult to assign to musics that are also subtle. Whilst we can be reasonably sure that we feel something when encountering virtually all music, what we can be much less certain of is how to identify those feelings. Whilst this does not necessarily rob music of its expressive content it does pose problems of ascription to recognition theory.

Music is capable of, and indeed usually does succeed in, stimulating emotional responses that lie beyond language itself. Very often we simply cannot put into words what a particular piece has done for us. Possibly it is that we have become as a species over-attuned to semantic or vocal behaviour and have in some sense tuned out our capacity to recognize gestural stimuli. Perhaps the idea of recognition is too narrow and what in fact we should be concentrating on is the experience of sound itself. Many psychologists have equated the subjective feeling of tension with a state of 'activation'. Certainly on a level of animal response, activation would be an appropriate response to an increasingly loud external stimuli which could well be threatening. Whatever the emotional feeling provoked by the musical stimuli, one thing is clear – the feelings stimulated are stimulated by the perception of the changing melodic line; there is a relationship of close causal conjunction.

One might say that certain types of musical responses are experienced as *Gestalten* (indivisible combinations of oscillating tensions and relaxations), which become incorporated through repeated immersion in specific styles of music as feeling-states in themselves. Music was a highly convenient partner to the stutters of the early moving image, precisely because of this ability to trigger feelings objectlessly.

In the same way as there are (perhaps) musical archetypes that govern the form and content of certain musical idioms, within those idioms (particularly functional idioms such as film music or, similarly, Muzak) there are conventional patterns of use. The adoption of these conventions by, for example, a director who uses a well-known suspense theme as a 'temp track' when in the early stages of editing a film plunges film music or rather the users of film music into a circularity. Particularly for composers, temp tracks constitute a problem. Whilst a temp track is supposed to be temporary it very rarely is. Remnants of the feel of the temp track stay with the director and the scene being edited in any case acquires a structural dependency on the chosen music. Frequently the composer is co-opted into producing a virtual carbon copy of the temp track. Temp tracks are useful when a film is going through the early stages of being screened. Usually the assembled audience have some economic or artistic interest in the film and the temp track serves to cushion the film against a silent screening. Temp tracks underline, however, the essential conventionality of much film music practice.

THE IMPACT OF FILM THEORY

Since the late 1940s, film theory in Europe (which really meant France) had been dominated by two figures – André Bazin and Jean Mitry. Bazin was the founding editor of the influential critical journal *Cahiers du cinéma*, which rejigged the context of film criticism by bringing insights from philosophy, literary criticism and psychology into the broad church of writing on film, the majority of which was simply entertainment journalism.

Bazin's theories about cinema were basically 'realist' and arose from his interest in and study of genre. Whilst never having written an overall theory of cinema, he published literally hundreds of articles as well as short books on Orson Welles (1950) and Charlie Chaplin (besides the two-volume *What is Cinema?* in 1959). He saw cinema as being intricately dependent on physical reality, an art form that unfolded and even defined three-dimensional space, and he saw photographic images as mouldings in light, impressions of the objects they are records of. Bazin saw even in the most 'unadorned' (even unedited) film sequences evidence of the uniqueness of the art form of cinema. It was to be regarded as a new sense in its own right.

Jean Mitry's work extended the insights of Bazin in his enormous 1963 *Esthétique et psychologie du cinéma* whilst maintaining a realist platform. Cinematic images were 'analogues' or 'doubles' of the objects they were recordings of. They were not 'signs' to be decoded. Film images were to be regarded as inhabiting their own world, and the film experience a kind of continuum of sensoria assembled by the audience. Mitry dissolved the traditional view that films had some of the same rhythmic properties as music by arguing that it is our ears rather than our eyes that are the dominant rhythmic sensors. The audible experience is much more of a polarity between heard and not heard than the more complex, more nuanced experience of visual perception. A modern analogy would be to compare the sense of hearing as a digital system enacting a basic polarity of 'on-off' (heard/not heard) in response to a sound stimuli whilst the visual senses tend to act more like an analogue system recognizing certain kinds of spatial relationships, similarities.[1] Film rhythm is thus much more dependent upon the content of the image than music, which simply garners its rhythm from tone intermediaries, and in this sense is far more like prose writing than music. Yet Mitry is careful to be clear that the basic elements of cinema are not at all a language, but more a starting point for a quasi-poetic method whereby banal images can be made to express themselves at a higher level. The potency has some superficial similarities (in that it seems to contain a certain consistency of rule and application) to what we normally think of as language. But it is inherently different, and any further analysis of this simulacrum should begin at the level of film poetics. Yet this refuge in poetics and even humanism obliged Mitry to attempt a complete theory of the art form, implicitly rejecting all previous theories in favour of his own, supposedly unifying reach. This highly individualistic approach ran contrary to the currents being felt elsewhere in complementary academic fields. The drift of structuralism with its imperative to point up the similarities between all kinds of linguistic and generative systems necessitated a smaller-scale but more exacting approach to specific issues within film.

Christian Metz's[2] initial work on sign theory ('semiotics') in the early 1960s set a new, more progressive and therefore scientific agenda in film studies. His work has appeared in many forms, and relied heavily on exchanges of ideas with colleagues around the world, whose additional insights were incorporated in Metz's continually evolving project. Semiotics is basically a scientific approach to linguistics in which the central idea was that cinema, no less than other kinds of 'texts', could be opened up for exhaustive analysis through the study and exposure of the art form's hidden codes. These hidden codes were the 'signs' of the film and were taken to constitute the very meaning of cinema. Semiology sought to uncover the laws that made film viewing itself a possibility and then to go beyond this into systematic investigations of the various patterns of signification which are common to, for example, genre films, or the preoccupations of an individual film maker. Metz (and others) took their basic subject to be the various 'channels of information' which mediate our attention when watching a film. These included:

1   the photographic image itself in all its guises
2   any visible text or graphic materials which form a part of the screen image

[1] Dudley Andrew, *The Major Film Theories* (New York: 1979), p. 196

[2] Christian Metz, 'Le Cinéma: langue ou langage?', *Communications*, no. 4, 1964, pp. 52–90

3 recorded speech
4 recorded music
5 other elements on the soundtrack, including sound effects.

Although Metz incorporated a number of concepts borrowed from linguistic theory, he tended to utilize only those terms that were common to all forms of communication theory, terms such as 'code', 'message', 'text', 'structure' and 'paradigm'. At base is the concept of a code, the logical relationship which fosters understanding between sender and recipient.

In his work on the soundtrack of a film, Metz isolates 'aural objects' which he described as the embodiment of the sound source, for example, a girl's scream. The sound of the gunshot itself Metz terms the sound's 'characteristic'. Metz believed that sounds were usually classified according to the aural objects that transmit them rather than by their characteristics, whereas with visual objects the reverse is true. Metz examined the idea of 'off-screen' sound, pointing out that sound cannot evade the screen area since it is either heard or not, despite the fact that sound is more difficult than a visual object to locate spatially. Language itself conceptualized sound in terms of the image, which predominates in nearly all forms of communication. Metz concluded that the perceptual object was a socially constructed unity. As for music, Metz's analysis of the codes of cinema constantly re-emphasize that these codes are self-effacing, always working to foreground the narrative. Diegetic film music remains a hidden code existing uneasily alongside the story in a state of virtual performance.

The problem is that film, and no less film music, is not an isolated system outside of all use in the way that other kinds of ordinary language are. The 'set' of all films ever made is simply too large and full of internal contradictions and inconsistencies ever to be specified by semiology. No one semiology can interrelate the many different kinds of signifier on offer in the film. All that can be done is to look at individual instances of cinema and try to decode the ways in which music has been deployed as an isolated case.

The apparently endless fertility of pop music as a connotative element within a film might be demonstrated by *The Big Chill* (1983), wherein well-known pop songs offer up a variety of ways in which the main characters' demographic and ideological concerns can be profiled. The chain of connotators is potentially endless and will obviously vary with each viewer, as well as with each viewing. The following table covers just some of the possible connotations:

Song	Cue Type	Visual Action	Musical Description
'I Heard it Thru the Grapevine' by Marvin Gaye	Non-diegetic		1968. Classic Motown soul. Powerful, elegant plaintive and emotional. Theme addresses a lost lover, with Gaye the last to find out. Implies a man alone in a community of malicious gossip.
'You can't always Get what You Want' solo organ rendition by Karen	Diegetic	Minister introduces Karen's performance in context of funeral service. Karen performs over montage of guests leaving church.	Elegiac version of Rolling Stones song, played on a small electric organ.
'You can't always Get what You Want' by the Rolling Stones	Non-diegetic	Guests leaving church continued. Montage of different guests driving to reception and arriving at Alex's parents house.	First verse sung in high pitched tones, reminiscent of Bach choir, followed by the Rolling Stones original. An atmosphere that manages to be both majestic and eerily apocalyptic.
'Tell Him' by the Exciters	Non-diegetic	Montage of main characters unpacking suitcases at Sarah and Harold's house. Michael's first moment of attraction to Chloe (Alex's girlfriend).	Up tempo, 1960s girl group bubble gum pop. Lyrics offer girl-to-girl advice on how to hook a man.
'A Whiter Shade of Pale' by Procol Harum	Diegetic	Harold places the song on the record player as the group sit around the living room discussing their professional lives.	Early 1970s progressive rock, slow tempo driven by keyboard organ. Ponderous obscure lyrics full of mockportent.
'Good Lovin' by the Rascals	Non-diegetic and diegetic	Harold, Nick, Chloe and Michael drive out to Alex's old house, Chloe says that she and Alex had great sex the night before he committed suicide, Nick jokes that he 'went out with a bang and not a whimper.'	1966. Garage-style rock reworking of a soul song, shouted vocals, gritty guitar riffs and cascading drums and organ breaks, exuberant and up tempo.
'Ain't Too Proud to Beg' by the Temptations	Diegetic	Harold selects the record (kissing the LP sleeve) and as the record begins, the others all begin to dance around Sarah's kitchen as they clean away the dinner service.	Demonstrates Harold and Sarah's love as Harold leads her around the room in a dance. Unambiguous celebration of togetherness, friendship and life as every character becomes drawn into the dance to a greater or lesser degree.
'Wouldn't it be Nice?' by the Beach Boys	Diegetic	Appears to be from Harold's record player, heard all over house. Transitional shots. Meg and Sam discuss whether Sam would father a child for her, Michael and Nick take Quaaludes downstairs.	Romantic teen fantasy with sophisticated multi-layered harmonies, a sense of Utopian dreaming about an impossible love.
'The Weight' by the Band	Non-diegetic	Montage of 'morning after' scenes, characters sitting in various groups around breakfast table. Karen jealous of Meg and Sam.	1968. Rock and roll, Dylan-esque elegant honky-tonk piano chords and stately harmonies in a song about characters caught up in circumstances beyond their control.
'Bad Moon Rising' by Credence Clearwater Revival	Diegetic	Harold plays the song to Sam as they ride in his car. Sam reveals his concerns about the different sexual propositions he has received during the weekend from Karen and Meg. Joins montage of dinner scene with whole group reading fortune cookies.	1969. Heavier rock treatment of a rockabilly structure, with lyrics alluding to Nixonian politics and disillusionment. Implications of danger and conspiracy in lyrics.
'When a Man Loves a Woman' by Percy Sledge	Diegetic	Montage of group in different rooms of the house. Meg on phone to Sarah's daughter. Sarah realises that Harold should impregnate Meg. Group discussion on why Alex killed himself, Nick's responses reveal his alienation from the others.	1966. Tender soul ballad with sparse instrumental accompaniment, appears to be a celebration of love but ends with Sledge's realization that he must move on after being played for a fool.
'Natural Woman' by Aretha Franklin and 'In the Midnight Hour' by Wilson Pickett	Non-diegetic	Meg and Harold in bedroom about to conceive, Harold tender, Meg nervous. Elsewhere in house, Nick and Chloe and Sam and Karen pair off.	Aretha Franklin sings frankly about independent female sexuality. Pickett swaggers and grooves through an up-tempo percolating dance song unambiguously about sexual conquest.
'I Second that Emotion' by Smokey Robinson and the Miracles	Non-diegetic	The final morning before the characters leave to go their separate ways. Nick sorts through Alex's papers with Chloe, Sam and Karen agree not to sleep together again, Sarah watches Harold running and wakes Meg up in bed.	Soul song about male vulnerability with Robinson calling for 'a lifetime of devotion'. Insistent guitar lines, congas and the crash of tambourines and drums as the singer gets the response he is looking for.

Connotation 1	Connotation 2	Connotation 3
Tragic information spreading through a community of friends, surprise, disbelief and grief, finally acceptance.	Bonds of friendship stretching back to end of 1960s. Contrast between (lost?) youthful idealism, black soul music and this white, middle class group's self evident prosperity.	The 'I' of the song is displaced by the 'we' of the visual sequence, yet all of group are shown to be strongly individualistic, thus 'reclaiming' the personal significance of the song for each one.
Humorous surprise at irreverence of musical performance, understanding of the powerful meanings attached to music by the group of friends, and the ironic significance of the song when played at Alex's funeral.	Locates sense of place in a relaxed (liberal?) community in which the Minister permits such an unusual end to a funeral service. Song implicitly mimics and subverts Gospel tradition of US southern states	
Segue from solo organ performance into original song lends lyrics poignancy hinting at possible motivation for Alex's suicide. Supported by Meg's admission to Nick during journey that she told Alex he was 'wasting his life.'	The Rolling Stones status as 1960s counter-cultural icons, vaguely alluded to by Nick and Meg smoking a joint on the journey.	Slow tempo of song as the funeral motorcade speeds on. Possible association with JFK's motorcade in Dallas in 1963.
The familiar environment of Sarah and Harold's house. The different concerns ('emotional baggage'?) of each character (shown by the contents of their suitcases) – unified by the simple pleasure of an old pop song.	Ritualistic nature of sexual attraction within a group, ironically reversed as the predatory Michael homes in on the simple and unquestioning Chloe.	Up-tempo song leads us out of Act One and into Act Two. Characters and the environment have been established. The simplest of (Utopian) pop songs now signifies that we will see how they have each moved away from this simplicity.
Michael signifies cultural and ideological differences within group by asking Harold if he has any more modern music, Harold indicates he isn't interested in modern music.	Ultimately empty content of lyrics, perhaps for Harold music has no 'meaning' in contrast to Michael for whom music seems more coded. Michael seems keen to escape the 'past' and possibly the specious companionship of the group.	'A Whiter Shade Of Pale' represents the ultimate pretensions of rock manifesting as high art. Comparisons with Martin Scorsese's use of the same song in 'New York Stories' to track artistic temperament of a painter and his stormy personal relationships.
Buddy road movie feel Nick and Michael trade laconic observations. Pauses in song punctuate stops in conversation to comic effect. Male rivals competing for Chloe's attention in subtle ways. Chloe delivers the trump card in the conversation.	Tempo of song accentuates the feeling of motion in Harold's jeep.	
Points up relative levels of inhibition in each of the characters. Nick seems embarrassed, Chloe simply sympathetically (indicating her difference in age and dislocation from the song's impact).		
Meg's wish to find someone to impregnate her during the weekend meets with Sam's possibly shallow rationalization why it would never work.	Flawed romance of many of the Beach Boys' ballads underscores the gap between Meg's hopes and Sam's regrets over the collapse of his marriage.	
Primary connotation would appear to be Meg's disappointment in Sam's refusal to impregnate her, she smokes vigorously, almost appearing to draw equal sustenance from the song as the cigarette.	Most of the characters are hung over from drink or drugs and conversation is frag-mented and confused, the misunderstanding between Meg and Karen over Sam being an example.	
Possibly comic association with Sam's paranoid suspicions of women. Harold attempts to use the song to remind Sam of their old friendship.	Further associations with 1960s counter cultural politics.	
Another aural testament to Sarah and Harold's apparently perfect love. Implications of sacrifices made in the name of love, in this case Sarah 'loaning' Harold to Meg.	Signifies the impossibility for Nick of conventional physical love (due to war injury). Ironically counterpoints Nick's refuge in drugs and careful cultivation of a cynical attitude to life.	
Sex can resolve the wishes and needs of most of the characters. This redemption is represented in musical terms by two strongly contrasted songs about female and male sexuality.		
As the weekend ends, most characters have been through some sort of change, mainly for the better. Whilst the love alluded to in the song is no longer a realistic option, there is at least the reassurance of rich and continuing friendship.	Nick seems at least temporarily to have overcome his alienation and will remain with Chloe. Karen steps back into her mono-tonous marriage but with her eyes wide open, thus re-evaluating the song with a certain 1980s knowingness.	

The whole notion of connotation calls into question any finite reading of the codes of cinema, not least music, and in particular not something as ideologically complex and context-sensitive as pop music. Music in isolation is 'merely' denotative – it is simply 'there', yet when placed alongside pictures, it seems to generate endless chains of connotations which defy semiotic analysis.

Christian Metz attempted to close the gap between the denotative and connotative aspects of the film image/soundtrack by asserting that connotation was itself a form of denotation.[3] This also opens up the question of how different kinds of viewers respond to scenes, since each will 'stop' the connotative process at the point at which the film scene seems to make sense. Connotations cannot be codified in isolation from specific films on view, and from the individual's point of view. By the late 1970s most of those at the forefront of semiotics had abandoned any hope of arriving at a privileged language for film and had retreated to case-study analyses.

Even if one accepts that connotations will vary from film to film, and from viewer to viewer, the fact that we all tend to 'understand' a conventional American horror movie in much the same way does point towards some sort of archetypal rhetorical process operating at the level of mass culture. Rather than seeing film as a language system, perhaps it is more useful to see it as a system of conventions which at some point in the history of cinema were 'figures'. Figuration has been linked by Metz[4] with the concept of metonymy, which in cinema is where a well-known object, for example, a vampire, becomes represented by some sign other than the thing itself, for example, an open coffin filled with earth, a man in a long black cloak, a bat and so forth. This kind of 'shorthand' description could, by incorporating other well-known horror staples, build up into a dictionary of horror devices or figures. The figures are special kinds of metaphor and in cinema the history of the art form might just as well be a history of figuration and its evolution as an industrial history or a history of authorship. Figuration deliberately brings 'dissonance' into film. It clouds the basic denotative process but brings with it a sense of poetics, which in turn adds to and alters the 'dictionary' of figures available to future film makers.

Whilst Metz's critical writings[5] during his attachment to semiology constitute a large and fascinating field (focused mainly on American and

3 Mary Basehart, 'Christian Metz's Theory of Connotation', *Film Criticism* 4, no. 2, 1979, pp. 21–37

4 Christian Metz, *The Imaginary Signifier* (New York: 1974)

5 Christian Metz, *Film Language: A Semiotics of the Cinema* (New York: 1974)

French cinema of the period 1935–55) where just a small part concerns the soundtrack, the enterprise of semiology as a whole failed since the project itself was too ambitious in scale. The almost infinite varieties of signifiers on display in even a single filmed narrative defy an exhaustive analysis of the sort that Metz hoped for. Semiotics focused too closely upon the system of signification, at the expense of a wider understanding of the films it analysed. It predicated an analysis of the conditions for a film's existence over the experience of actually watching a film in its entirety.

ARTHOUSE CINEMA AND CLASSICAL MUSIC

Partly influenced by the 'trickle-down' effect of the new rigours in film theory and the new weightiness of film journalism in France, Britain and the United States, film in the early 1960s was becoming a fully mature art form, pursuing often oblique strategies of story-telling. Andrew Sarris in a 1963 review of *Tom Jones* in *The Village Voice* posited the view that contemporary audiences were torn between their desires for direct story-telling and intellectual guilt for having those desires. As films became more complex in their subjects and treatments, music could be used either as an anchoring point, a touchstone or signification system for the audience or as a departure point in itself, a way to describe hidden motivations and atmospheres undiscoverable visually.

The 'art movie' as we now understand it tends to be defined in terms of its creators, who are regarded as auteurs. Gilles Deleuze defines the cinema that followed the Second World War as in its brightest moments returning to the condition of 'naturalism' found in the silent cinema, which presented us with 'the natural being of man in history or society'.[1] This evolution through the dullness of the early talkies, where the use of sound and music tended to be rather one-dimensional, reaches its zenith in the cinema of a select band of directors whose body of work is so distinctive that they merit the term 'auteur' in the sense of being authors creating an artwork rather than a commercial commodity. Thus the work of directors from the 1950s onwards such as Michelangelo Antonioni, Ingmar Bergman, Alain Resnais, Jean-Luc Godard and Stanley Kubrick becomes readable in the same sense that a musical score is readable – a rich synthesis of sound and image that builds up into a form of art that is more like a form of consciousness, or even a re-creation of philosophical concepts. According to Deleuze, what matters most in an auteurist cinema, whose main concern is the representation of

[1] Gilles Deleuze, *Cinema 2: The Time-Image* (London: 1988), p. 226

temporality itself rather than movement, is the space between the images. The breaking of the chain of associations between montages started by Eisenstein, where spectators are forced to make associations between consecutive pictures, is replaced with a new kind of cinematic technique which isolates pictures for their own sake, co-opting the spectator into a kind of re-enactment of the director's own thought processes. Spectators are forced to find for themselves a connection between often independent images (each of which deframes the previous) rather than be polemically directed by a loaded sequence of montages. Cinema, particularly the kind of auteurist cinema often described as 'arthouse' cinema, has its audiences engaged in solving a puzzle themselves in concert with the film's unfolding. Cinematic images no longer represent the world, but rather rethink the world according to the auteurist directors' own philosophical beliefs and concepts. Given this reinvention of the basic substance of film story-telling, a process of philosophical inquiry rather than of representation of the way the world is, the use of music in arthouse cinema becomes more interesting when one looks at the apparent preference of many auteurs for the classical sources of Mozart, Beethoven and Bach over the commissioning of new music by contemporary composers.

By the mid-1950s, film budgets tended to reach a median point worldwide. Spectacle, the action epic, an area traditionally dominated by the American studios, became less common as film making returned to its cottage-industry roots. Independent producers, whose companies existed solely to produce a single film in many cases, were agile and commercially minded operators who were adept at developing products with a number of co-production partners from a number of countries. In Europe, national film making, particularly in France and Italy, had enjoyed ten years of growing critical attention and the auteurist tag developed by the young critics (and future film makers) of journals such as *Cahiers du cinéma* seemed to fit the artistic rather than the commercial ambitions of many up-and-coming directors and producers. Whilst the early films of those directors mentioned above embrace no single genre, they are attempts to move cinema beyond the simple scenarios of action and re-enactment of the American cinema of the 1940s. At the lowest common denominator, films as different in subject and approach as Antonioni's *L'Avventura* (1959) and Truffaut's *Jules et Jim* (1960) might be said to be attempts to create stories for adult audiences where character and storyline swim in a wider pool of cultural awareness and references than before. On the one hand this may masquerade as a form of modernist self-consciousness not unlike certain conceits of post-modernism, on the other (as in Antonioni's film) it may seek to re-create the attitudes of existentialism. At any rate the auteurist approach (which might be better thought of as a canon, rather than a style) has produced countless films of outstanding beauty and subtlety, and at the same time has proved flexible enough to admit each year new directors of radically different persuasions unified only by their fruitful interaction of sounds, words and images.

Leading film makers of the 1950s, including Fellini, Bergman, Visconti and Buñuel, utilized classical eighteenth-century music as something of a hallmark of quality and a very adult maturity. Despite great strides in critical and theoretical sophistication, cinema in popular reception was still struggling to define itself as an art form to be taken as seriously as, say, theatre or music. This was particularly true of those film works that were themselves adapted from literary sources. Whilst the idea that film was in some way a simulacrum of reality was losing ground to more plastic theories that gave cinema its own special aesthetic status, there was still no popular manifesto that explained cinematic language to its audiences (one might argue that this still remains the case; as Deleuze contends, cinematic concepts in the final analysis can never be fully explained by language). The wide-ranging influence of psychoanalysis helped many commentators, including the philosopher Suzanne Langer,[2] to define the narrative action of film as a kind of 'dream mode', a quasi-scientific metaphysical phenomenon. Yet this did little to explain the kind of cinema being produced in Europe by Bergman and Antonioni which seemed to demand a new generosity of understanding. As Parker Tyler put it in 1969:

> Like painting, film is imagery and has nothing whatever to do with the existence of physical bodies as such. Film, being a time art, requires a much bigger, more complex unit of psychic consciousness to support it than does the still photograph.[3]

What bigger unit of psychic consciousness could there be than the music of Ludwig van Beethoven, Brahms, Mozart or Bach? The symphonic and chamber repertoires of classical music require the immersion of both cognitive and affective capacities as well as the senses themselves, which in the context of a film could threaten to unbalance the other narrative elements. Classical music sources take on a mythic grandeur when added to narrative, and a substantial part of this myth is our recognition of the piece itself. Musical myths are not the same as national myths and after two

[2] Suzanne Langer, *Feeling and Form* (New York: 1952)

[3] Parker Tyler, *Sex, Psyche Etcetera in the Film* (New York: 1909), p. 133

hundred years Mozart is no longer (mythically) a specifically Germanic composer but rather one who somehow has come to represent all of Europe, in some way embodying the Enlightenment. His internationalism has far superseded his national and historical origins, as can be seen in the vehemently anti-Nazi film by Russian director Elem Klimov, *Come and See* (1986), where Mozart seems to stand for the heroism of the Soviet army as the remnants of a band of battle-weary Russian fighters march through a snow-covered forest accompanied by a section of Mozart's Requiem. Mozart has also been used to suggest the 'higher aspects' of mankind in films as diverse as *Out of Africa* (1985), *The Hudsucker Proxy* (1994), *Colonel Chaubert* (1994) and Werner Herzog's *The Enigma of Kaspar Hauser* (1974).

The classical sources used with increasing frequency in films by auteurist directors from the 1950s onwards can be interpreted as defensive measures to underwrite the increasingly complex stories being told, yet they are also the result of a considerable increase in recorded output and the greater availability of the long-playing record, which revolutionized most people's experience of symphonic music. The first few years of the long-playing record saw a rapid increase in interest in previously neglected corners of the concert repertoire: Vivaldi, the Baroque, Bruckner, Berlioz, medieval motets and masses, and the newest twentieth-century music of Mahler, Hindemith, Aaron Copland, Stravinsky and Bartók. This widened the audience's listening experiences, thus elevating still further the status of eighteenth-century composers, whose works now became more subject than ever to individual interpretations by auteur-like conductors and instrumentalists. As Glenn Gould once claimed:

> Recordings deal with concepts through which the past is re-evaluated.[4]

The music of Mozart appeared in key sequences in films as diverse as *Lola* (1961), *The Gospel According to St Matthew* (1966) and *Weekend* (1967), whilst Beethoven could be heard in films by Ingmar Bergman and Jean-Luc Godard. These Enlightenment-era composers were part of a very different world and wrote music for an expanding European middle class, where the central aesthetic concern was in perfecting existing musical forms rather than innovating for innovation's sake. This concern with musical objectivity, clarity and balance lends an interesting status to the music when married to the often serious existential and psychological themes so central to the traditional canon of art cinema. A particularly developed example is Truffaut's character Antoine Doinel, the anti-hero whom we follow as a boy

[4] *The Glenn Gould Reader* (London: 1987), p. 311

from *Les 400 coups* (1958) over six films leading to *L'Amour en fuite* (1978), whose early adolescent rejection by a girl continues to haunt him throughout his life, either explicitly in flashback or implicitly through comparison. Aside from the neo-romantic or pop nostalgic music heard in the films, a darker music tends to track Doinel's inner states, Bach's Suite in D and extracts from Berlioz's *Symphonie Fantastique*.

Jean-Luc Godard had consistently pushed the material possibilities of directly recorded sounds as a narrative device since his début. He deploys sound in *Vivre sa vie* (1962) as if it was just another pictorial element to be landscaped and spatially incorporated within the frame (and just out of the frame). Characters nudge pinball machines or sway to jukebox rhythms which appear on the soundtrack much louder than a 'normal' film sound mix would have allowed, with the interesting effect of signifying that Godard's urban characters are unusually well adjusted to the mechanical background din of their locations. In *Vivre sa vie*, as Royal S. Brown observes,[5] all but a short sequence (used a number of times) by Michel Legrand is diegetic or source music, seen to emanate from radios, passing cars, the immediate environments of the story. With Godard, however, to attempt to isolate the music component from the other material elements on the soundtrack is to miss the rich aural sensorium that cloaked his characters in his mid-1960s films like *Masculin-féminin*, *La Chinoise*, *Contempt* or *Tout va bien*, in particular his pointed use of language as a complex signifying element over and above its status as information provider. Godard appeared to be trying to achieve a level of aural montage that went beyond music and echoed Eisenstein's taxonomies developed for the visual field in the 1920s and 1930s. The voices of characters interlock with musical elements and, as Alan Williams[6] has pointed out, clearly reveal something about the socio-political status of each. Recorded music is used both diegetically and non-diegetically, used for its status as cultural artefact, prefiguring the nostalgic rehabilitation of pop music in the 1970s cinema of Martin Scorsese amongst others. Within one film, pop mingles with Mozart, which mingles with a neo-romantic score by Georges Delerue. Each type of music is accorded its own status, its own logic of incorporation on the soundtrack, thus stratifying the musical world into clearly identifiable bridging moments between high and low culture.

The films of Jean-Marie Straub mark a departure point in 1960s cinema. He was perhaps the first European film maker to experiment formally with

[5] Royal S. Brown, *Overtones and Undertones* (Berkeley: 1994), p. 188

[6] Alan Williams, 'Godard's Use of Sound', in *Film Sound*, eds Elisabeth Weis and John Belton (New York: 1985)

notions derived from considerations of music and cinema as material forms. In *The Chronicle of Anna Magdalena Bach* (1967) the entire structure follows unbroken musical performances of Bach's works in naturalistic settings interspersed with fragmentary 'readings' from his wife's diary. The subject of the film is the representation of music, but also the commodification of music. Whilst the film owes something to the genre of biography, it does not attempt to psychologize its subject. Instead Straub concentrates on the various performative, economic and sociological processes that govern the composer's output to posterity. The actual depiction of performance is an important part of the film and segments from Bach's work are presented unabridged with the camera concentrating on the process of playing itself.

By contrast the music of Bach is used in Ingmar Bergman's *Through a Glass, Darkly* (1962), which explores themes of anomie both physical and metaphysical in the story of a novelist, David, stricken and at the same time vicariously fascinated by the descent of his daughter Karin into schizophrenia. Bergman utilizes hardly any music within the body of the film, although the beginning and end sequences are marked with the melancholic Suite No. 2 for cello by J. S. Bach. Bergman has called this film one of his three 'chamber plays' (the other two being *Winter Light* and *Persona*), a series of contrasting illustrations of moral or spiritual crisis pared down to a small ensemble of actors working in an isolated location. *Through a Glass, Darkly* was filmed on Farö, a small bleak island in the Baltic. The virtual avoidance of music is striking and permits display of the small gestural incidents that Bergman's films are so well known for, but music when it arrives is chilling in its impact. The recording that Bergman uses of the Bach piece is rough and unpolished; we hear clearly the scraping of the bow across the strings, the echoing of accidental strikes against the wood by the soloist. As Karin's final and most serious relapse begins to become apparent, the warming up of the soloist can be heard intermittently on the soundtrack before a few isolated bars are played. This use of rehearsal music to announce the onset of a profound mental collapse is a highly original use of a classical music source. The intricate but flawed patterning of the cello against the dramatic coastline and high-contrast sunlight brilliantly evokes the inappropriateness of Karin's attack when it comes.

In Ken Russell's series of biographical portraits of famous classical composers the emphasis is, unsurprisingly given Russell's reputation, on a highly partisan view of the composers' own psychological processes. Beginning in the mid-1960s with a series of films for the BBC – *The Debussy Film* (1965), a film dedicated to Delius, *A Song of Summer* (1968), and a film about Richard Strauss, *Dance of the Seven Veils* (1969) – Russell moved into cinematic features with a frenetic evocation of Tchaikovsky, *The Music Lovers* (1970), and then two biographies about romantic composers, *Mahler* (1974) and *Lisztomania* (1975). Russell weaves a kind of cinematic pulp psychoanalysis of the composers, bound up in a visual language of excess and surrealistic montage, straining within the envelope of a conventional bio-pic. Many of his techniques used in these films went on directly to influence the language of the music clips from later in the decade.

As films became more associated with the singular vision of their director-creator, it is perhaps not surprising that Bach was used as a primary music source on a number of key films by so-called auteurist directors in the late 1960s. Pasolini's involving study of the life of Christ, *The Gospel According to St Matthew* (1966), used Bach amongst a selection of classical sources including Mozart and Webern that distanced his musical and highly personal conception of the subject a long way away from the commissioned biblical scores of a Hollywood composer such as Alfred Newman. Pasolini approached the story almost in the stylized manner of a silent movie. The acting is not psychologized but rather representational. The human face dominates all other shots in the film, the faces of ordinary Italian peasants rather than actors; this is a life of Christ that emphasizes the impact rather than the personality. The film has in some ways the appearance of amateurism in its jerky sense of editing close-up shots together with rapid zooms into wider shots of crowds or landscapes. Music seems to announce some of the more extreme uses of the zoom, often a crescendo-like phrase from choral works by either Bach or Mozart. A lyrical flute concerto tracks the playing figure of Christ aged about three in a vast, empty landscape, whilst the descent of Herod's soldiers into a village to slaughter all the male infants is accompanied by the discordant strains of Webern.

Perhaps the most striking thing about the soundtrack is its un-sophisticated use of redubbing to emphasize the 'alienation' effect. Birdsong, the sound of various farm animals and wind are often presented as the sole elements of sound in often quite extended shots. Their presence is disconcerting because of their unrealistic effect, which seems to jar against pictures shot almost in a documentary style with hand-held camera and apparently improvised performances. The inclusion of an African spiritual song, 'Motherless Child', at selected points (the attendance of the crowd at Christ's birth and the scene where Christ is baptized) is a daring and highly effective device which unequivocally removes the story from a historical setting and places it on the level of the political.

The incorporation of sacred music into a film is obviously an ideological decision as much as a creative one. Sacred music is far from innocent when used in conjunction with the film image. Much religious music, particularly that of Bach, bears many of the characteristics of an ordering element and, adrift in the shifting fictional universe of his characters, a director may feel a subconscious striving for the kind of order that music can bring to such a universe. The music of the eighteenth century somehow represents for many film makers something of the 'last things' of civilization, a peak of rational human certainty, to be invoked in the face of the unknown. As Gustav Mahler reportedly said:

> In Bach all the vital seeds of music are brought together, like the world in God. Nowhere else has there been such polyphony.[7]

One might think of Kubrick's *2001* (1968) as a highly metaphysical film about future man exploring space and to various degrees losing himself in the process. In Kubrick's film the desire for order is taken to its logical extreme with the imposition of a non-diegetic waltz by Strauss upon a space mission as two spacecraft move silently together in the vastness of space.

Whilst Kubrick for *2001* famously replaced a score by Alex North on grounds of unsuitability with the selections of classical music he had grown attached to as a 'temp track', it is likely that the archetypal influences of his chosen musical sources worked their way into the creative process of decision-making at a relatively early stage. *2001* is very much a film about signs and archetypes. It is only at the end of the film that the sole astronaut seems intuitively to arrive at a decidedly religious picture of the universe, after progressing through a series of cryptograms in the form of cinematic figures, each of which releases a rush of sonorous tones which are like markers for different stages of metaphysical understanding. The most ordered, Strauss's Blue Danube Waltz, tracks the orbiting spacecraft whilst the more ambient sound fields of György Ligeti are clearly used to represent something like 'deep space'. Thanks to the advances in sound recording technology and the widespread commercialization of ambient music over the past five years, these sonic conceits have now been rendered commonplace, but at the time, as Kubrick himself said:

> Don't underestimate the charm of the Blue Danube. Most people of under thirty-five think of it in an objective way, as a beautiful composition. Older people associate it with a Palm Court orchestra or have another unfortunate association and generally,

---

[7] Gustav Mahler, quoted by Andrey Tarkovsky in *Time within Time: The Diaries* (London: 1994), p. 146

therefore, criticize its use in the film. It's hard to find anything better than the Blue Danube for depicting grace and beauty in turning. It also gets about as far away as you can get from the cliché of space music.[8]

Classical music sources of course do not always have the effect on screen that they have when heard in a concert hall or as a recording. The physiological and ideological effects of music are directly dependent upon the cinematic context in which they are presented. In terms of classical music the varying responses of audiences to differing sources are likely, as Kubrick seems to point out, to depend on their specific musical experiences. The dissonance of, say, a Berio or a Boulez may be utterly unlistenable to for somebody whose primary exposure to classical music stopped at the end of the nineteenth century.

Kubrick's musical ear is more eclectic than many other directors' – who else would attempt to put music by Penderecki, Bartók and Ligeti into a horror film as he did for *The Shining*? If composer Leonard Rosenman is to be believed, even Kubrick is fallible on occasion, specifically in the selection of music for *Barry Lyndon* (1975):

Stanley called me on a Monday and said to come to England on Wednesday – the picture was finished. He said he had all the music picked out and all I had to do was arrange it. They told me Stanley worked this way, and, frankly, I wanted a trip to England. I had never done an adaptation before and it gave me a chance to conduct the London Symphony Orchestra with some classical pieces I was interested in. I was under no illusions that I had any creative work to do on the film. I asked him what he had picked out and he said, 'The first thing I want to do is to buy the theme from *The Godfather*.' I said, 'Well, if you're going to do that, tell me now so I can get the first plane out of England.' 'What's wrong with it? It's a very beautiful theme.' I said, 'You're right, but the last time I saw *The Godfather*, it was about gangsters, not eighteenth-century aristocrats.' I listened to all the records he had, and he had picked a saraband which had been recorded with a harpsichord; he had another theme for the dying child, which was from one of Verdi's worst operas. It was as though a psych class had gotten together and said, 'Let's find something that will really repel people.' I told him I couldn't go along with that and suggested I do an arrangement of the tune for strings, continuo, harpsichord and percussion, and see what it sounded like. We tried it with the London Symphony and he fell madly in love with it. I left after having picked out all the music and recorded it there. He then practically made a loop out of the Verdi theme and used it over and over again. If I had known he wanted that much of it, I would have orchestrated some other

[8] Stanley Kubrick, quoted in *The Technique of Film Music* by Roger Manvell and John Hartley (London: 1975), p. 254

variations; there were five charming variations in that piece. When I saw the film I saw this incredibly boring film with all the music I had picked out going over and over again. I thought, 'My God, what a mess!' I was going to refuse the Oscar. The classical music used in the film is much closer to me, because I am a pianist. I was a Bach and Haydn specialist. I picked out about half of it and he picked out about half.[9]

The main evolution in art music this century could be said to be the emancipation of dissonance. The whole concept of dissonance in music takes on a more elastic status when married to moving images. It was Schoenberg who coined the phrase 'emancipation of the dissonance' to describe the chromatic harmonies of his early works. Dissonance carries with it a connotation of 'incompleteness', since the expectation of a musical resolution to a phrase ending in 'consonance' or completeness is thwarted. One might reasonably claim that part of the reason why dissonance or dissonant music can be more widely accepted within a film than in the concert hall or record is that some of the work of pattern completion is undertaken by the image itself, or by other elements on the soundtrack.

The fact that our auditory listening space is directly controlled by loudspeaker placement in the cinema means that our attentiveness to music is precisely controllable in a number of ways. Media traditionally used for recording are now used to play back musical or other auditory materials on the soundtrack. In a sense, the soundtrack, like the image, can be played back any number of times, effectively rendering a medium such as cinema as 'fixed' in time and space as a novel or a painting. Music as a kind of performed work becomes an unstable concept. As films become more 'readable', more like a table of information than an ongoing narrative, music, dialogue and sound effects form a discontinuous whole ever more faithful to the demands of the image but at the same time occupying a separate but equally complex sensorium.

Film incorporates art music formerly from the concert repertoire in ways which directly attack the notion of musical continuity. It becomes extracted. Ends and beginnings are hived off and all that is left is are selected moments, the famous aria or the sound-bite of an adagio such as Albinoni's. Music, particularly 'classical' music in the 1960s, became fetishized as never before, deployed for its immediate emotional power. One might speculate whether this dismemberment of historical music for the purposes of cinema and TV is responsible for the movement towards greater complexity amongst contemporary composers. To psychoanalyse the modern composer, one

[9] Leonard Rosenman, interviewed in *Filmmakers and Filmmaking*, vol. 1 (New York: 1980)

might point up the movements towards greater and greater musical complexity as a defensive strategy to avoid the easy kind of sectarian listening that now characterizes our experiences of 'the classics'.

As classical music became more and more fetishized, and Beethoven's Ninth Symphony gradually came to resemble a set of quotations from Beethoven's Ninth (which by the time *A Clockwork Orange* was released in 1971 it had pre-eminently become), concepts of interpretation on the film's soundtrack seem to have been superseded by fragments from a streamlined performance. The art movie seems to alter one's basic memories of a musical piece, as all spontaneity and surprise are stripped away from the piece by its electronic marriage, fixed and fragmented, to the film's material surface. In a positive sense, of course, this unchanging aural experience can be the source of a rich extra-musical experience but it is just that, an extra-musical experience. Andrzej Wajda sees the impact of classical music in largely negative terms:

> Another discovery has been to superimpose over the picture fragments of classical music. The initial results were charming and impressive. The screen could be filled with ordinary images and insignificant actors. No matter! The harmonies of Bach or Brahms or Vivaldi lent them depth, mystery, and next to such music, the dialogues faded or blurred, the other superfluous noises disappeared altogether. The magic of the old masters reigned supreme. Unfortunately, this bliss lasted for a very short time. All these pictures began to blur into one, as the music swallowed up the personality of the director, the scriptwriter, and the actors, transforming the cinema into a series of pictures illustrating the eternal music.[10]

Sometimes the use of a classical music source seems blindingly obvious, so much so that the impact is reduced. Andrew Sarris, in a 1962 review of Luis Buñuel's *Viridiana* (1961), makes the following claim:

> How a director who seems so disconcertingly obvious can turn out to be so complex is one of the mysteries of the cinema. For example, it seems too symmetrically ironic to synchronize a beggars' orgy with Handel's Messiah. However, Buñuel has never been a champion of background music. He simply does not care enough about his score to seek something more subtle. Yet his indifference to details that more clever directors have mastered only reminds us that ingenuity is no substitute for genius. Buñuel's blend of the real and the surreal, the grotesque and the erotic, the scabrous and the sublime never quite fits into any critical theory.[11]

10 Andrzej Wajda, *Double Vision* (London: 1989), p. 112

11 Andrew Sarris, *Confessions of a Cultist* (New York: 1970), p. 60

Since cinema and recordings are both concerned with the preservation of passing time it is surprising that so little attention has been paid to which recordings of standard pieces from the concert repertoire become incorporated into films. Usually the process is to commission a new recording by one of the major jobbing symphony orchestras yet it is also possible to envision an archaeology of music in which specific versions of particular pieces are used more creatively to represent the film maker's desire for narrative expression. Bergman's careful selection of a flawed performance of Bach for *Through a Glass, Darkly*, or Herzog's featuring of the crackle and hiss of an old Caruso recording in *Fitzcarraldo*, or even David Lynch's careful distortions of Fats Waller in *Eraserhead*, would be examples of this approach.

A common criticism levelled at modern recordings of classical music is that vitality is sometimes sacrificed in favour of a more precise rendering of the musical piece as written. This represents a further abstraction from the milieu of performance. A musical (subjective) sense of time is replaced with an absolute sense of digital time. Michael Chanan claims that the essential plasticity of musical time is lost in many modern recordings:

> In live performance, the ticking of the clock is negated by the pulse of the music and time becomes plastic, suspended between the notes, which constantly alter their tempo and rate of acceleration. This sense of suspended time is not present when music is reproduced mechanically. It continues in this canned form to act upon the human autonomic system, as all music does: it quickens and slows our pulse and our breathing. But in becoming disembodied, the loss of physical presence removes it from the domain of living time. It still affects our temporal experience – it helps to fill it but without the human contact of live performance, the vital element of communion with the musician and the constant play of surprise that this brings.[12]

In extracting classical music to fit the requirements of a measured space of film soundtrack something strange happens to the piece of music. In being excerpted it is almost as if the classical source becomes a different piece of music, something in its own right instead of an extract. Since our normal process of listening is largely about making sense of what we are hearing, according to Leonard Meyer, we form hypotheses or expectations about what is coming up based on what we have heard so far. Our ability in this is related to our familiarity with the style of the music. In performing sections of a work out of context, an excerpt on a soundtrack, there is every possibility that the music is received by the audience in much the same way

12 Michael Chanan, *Repeated Takes* (London: 1995), p. 126

as normal cue music. But the significance of the overall piece is likely to be diluted by being extracted in such a way. This kind of criticism has often been levelled at both films and certain kinds of popular music. It is similar to the position taken up by Virginia Woolf, who felt that film, in adapting literature, in some way threatened it. Writing in the 1950s, by which time traditional culture was under much greater pressure from popular culture than in Woolf's time, Hannah Arendt defends traditional or 'high' culture against the threat of the entertainment industry:

> The entertainment industry is confronted with gargantuan appetites, and since its wares disappear in consumption, it must constantly offer new commodities. In this predicament those who produce for the mass media ransack the entire range of past and present culture in the hope of finding suitable material. This material, however, cannot be offered as it is; it must be prepared and altered in order to become entertaining . . . The danger is precisely that it may become very entertaining indeed.[13]

This seems to be the main objection that can be levelled at the use of classical concert music in a non-diegetic way. However, it seems likely that music even in excerpt can retain at least its emotional significance. Witness the skilful incorporation of Beethoven by Jean-Luc Godard into *Two or Three Things I Know About Her* (1967), *Passion* (1982) and *Prénom Carmen* (1983), or Andrey Tarkovsky's use of the same composer in *Stalker* (1979) or *Nostalgia* (1983) or more recently Steven Spielberg's use of Bach in *Schindler's List* (1993).

No matter how sophisticated the best examples of cinema as an art form become (including its musical sources), the language of film is still thought by many to be transparent and its incorporation of music, particularly historically important music, as tokenism. An important aspect of the problem of film's credibility against the defenders of high culture is that in addition to being an art form, film is also a medium, in the same sense that print is also a medium. Film can be used to record other art forms, in a variety of different styles, including music in performance. There is a sense in which film may record music in an unbroken form, for example, in the recording of a concert, but may not appropriate concert music for its own devices.

In isolating a passage of even a well-known piece of music and pairing it with a dramatic situation which will involve the audience, it seems likely that the audience will be more, rather than less, involved in the appreciation of the passage of music. This seems even more so now in a world that is flooded

13 Hannah Arendt, 'The Entertainment Industry' in 'Society and Culture', *Daedalus*, Spring 1960

with sounds of all kinds from many different sources. Most music that we hear is mediated through a background sea of noises, all of which distract from any kind of direct contact with the piece. In film, everything has been designed to ensure that the music is presented in the most powerful context possible – that is after all why it is being utilized by the film makers. Just as book sales of a classic piece of literature tend to go up following a successful film or television series (witness the 1995 Jane Austen craze in Britain), it seems very likely that successful sales of a soundtrack recording with the excerpted piece of music on it may well stimulate buyers to purchase further pieces by the same composer. For James Fitzpatrick, MD of a specialist film-music record label (Silva Screen):

> The market for any kind of film music, let alone non-US, is very limited. The least important aspect is the actual quality of the music: sales depend by and large on the success of the film. It's not often you have a successful film with a real quality score – movies like *Schindler's List* are a rarity. For specifically British scores the market is tiny. UK sales rarely top 2,000 units, that's the extent of the collector's market in the, UK. However, sales can be drastically increased by having a score that appeals to a much wider public – often using classical favourites – such as *A Room with a View* or *The Madness of King George*.[14]

[14] *Variety*, 22-8 January 1996, p. 81

ELECTRONIC FILM MUSIC AND
MUSICAL UNDERSTANDING

> I can distinguish three ways of composing music nowadays. The first is well known, that of writing music as I do. It continues. A new way has developed through electronic music and the construction of new sound sources for making music by performing it, rather than writing it. And a third way has developed in recording studios, which is similar to the way artists work in their studios to make paintings. Music can be built up layer by layer on recording tape, not to give a performance or to write music, but to appear on a record.[1]

John Cage's comments above from 1987 underline the extreme process of fragmentation that has overtaken music. The advent and development of electronics changed the whole basis of composition, blurring it with performance. Electronic music had been around since the beginning of the century when in 1902 Thaddeus Cahill built the Telharmonium or Dynamophone, which was a combination of Edison dynamos each producing a different sound according to its speed. The resulting electrical output could then be broadcast over telephone lines. The invention of the vacuum tube by Lee Deforest in 1906 allowed these electrical signals to be crudely amplified.

Various modernist composers, such as Ferruccio Busoni and his pupil Edgar Varèse, wrote about the impact of electricity in a variety of obscure music journals and Varèse himself completed a ballet suite, 'Ionization', which used electric elements alongside percussion passages. It was during the 1920s that instruments such as the Theremin and the Ondes Martenot also appeared.

The appearance of the vacuum tube and radiophonic technology opened up the possibility of creating a range of new sounds. The more adventurous modernist composers such as Béla Bartok and Olivier Messiaen were

[1] Interview with John Cage in *Conversing with Cage*, ed. Richard Kostelanetz (New York: 1988)

looking for new instruments suitable for their music and the bizarre architectures of such odd inventions of the 1930s as the Theremin, the Ondes Martenot, the Trautonium and the Hammond Organ provided at least a temporary site for experimentation, Messiaen's incorporation of the shimmering tones of the Theremin into his cosmically inspired *Turangaglia* Symphony being one of the better known results.

Of the above instruments, the Theremin is probably the most celebrated in that it is possibly the only instrument that can be played without actually being touched. There were many imitations but the original was invented by a Russian scientist Lev Theremin partly in order to find a way of 'playing' the electronic signal drones that can be found on the radio frequency in between stations.

The instrument utilizes heterodyning, an emitted signal composed of slightly different frequencies which is 'broadcast' by vertical wire antennae at either end of a box containing the oscillator. The resulting sound is an unearthly but often very pleasant oscillation which was highly fluid and easily directed through the hand movements of the player around the antennae.

The Theremin has been used as a source for sound effects in movies, for instance in *The Day the Earth Stood Still*, as a part of Bernard Herrmann's sparkling score – all discordant pianos and basses with not one but seemingly two Theremins duelling dementedly. From the instrument's introduction as signifier of psychic collapse in Hitchcock's *Spellbound*, Theremins turned up on the soundtracks of many 1950s sci-fi films, presumably symbolizing a kind of alien 'otherness'.

One of the limitations with the Theremin was its lack of pre-set notes or any kind of a keyboard. The French musician Maurice Martenot designed the Ondes Martenot in the 1920s which like the Theremin used hetero-dyning except through pre-set keys on a keyboard, which could create vibrato or glissando effects. The Ondes Martenot was an easier instrument to integrate with conventional orchestras or bands during the 1930s and 1940s. The bulk of its use seems to have been confined to France where its distinctive sound was used by well-known composers such as Honegger, Milhaud and Varèse.

There was a keen interest in manipulating sound, from the basic distortion experiments tried out by Ernst Toch and Paul Hindemith, where gramophone records were spun at different speeds, to the early optical soundtracks of the 1930s film which provided new possibilities for electronic sound synthesis. Oskar Fischinger's sound-on-film experiments where drawn waveforms on the celluloid and other shapes produced sound directly the film was drawn across the sound head during projection.

What these instruments brought to composition as a whole, although this was not obvious at the time, was a different way of thinking about musical notation. Musical evolution is as much a history of musical technology as it is of cultural changes in the listener. There have as in painting always been composers who follow 'lines' as well as those who follow 'colour'. Modern music in the second half of this century has been increasingly an evolution of musical colour, of pitch of musical texture. This is the domain of electronic music, the manipulation of 'blocks' of sound rather than individual melody lines. One might see the development of electronic music this century as pursuing two largely separate areas of experimentation: one was concerned with the emancipation of natural sounds through electronic manipulation, whilst the other's ambition was to create an entirely new range of sounds through the use of electronics.

The association of music and electronic sound effects went through some dramatic developments in the 1940s when Pierre Schaeffer, Pierre Henry and other composers of the Groupe de Recherche de Musique Concrète began experimenting with piecing recorded sounds together in order to make music. These so-called *concrète* sounds weren't simply recorded – they were played backwards, at different speeds, with their attack transients spliced off, scrambled up and processed by various electronic devices, including filters, amplifiers and echo chambers.

A 1954 piece by the German composer Karlheinz Stockhausen (*Studie II*) is entirely electronic and uses aleatory principles (mathematical combinations of the number 5) to construct a dense yet highly ordered composition. The score's notation is literally depicted as a series of contrasted blocks on a variation of manuscript paper. The sheer difference from traditional processes is apparent, as is the painstaking rigour involved in the compositional endeavour. In other works by Stockhausen he manipulated the human voice to great effect; a single child reading from the Book of Daniel in *Song of Children* (1956) seemed to define the spirit of electronic music perfectly, a way to explore language and phonetics through the interface of the human performer. György Ligeti's *Artikulation* (1958) also explored language, although this time an artificial one based upon electronically generated phonemes, themselves modelled on real speech.

By the mid-1960s Bob Moog and Don Buchla had both developed voltage-controlled devices in a modular form and were putting them into the packages that are today called synthesizers. These devices were direct descendants of the technology developed by the *musique concrète* movement. As early as 1956 the influence of this developing technology was heard in the first all-electronic film score, a cult masterpiece created by Louis and Bebe Barron for the MGM film *Forbidden Planet* where the results are much less music than oddly coagulating clusters of electronic sound effects. For the time, these sounds were undoubtedly unique, conjuring up truly alien landscapes and otherworldly terrors. In contrast, the Robby the Robot theme comes across like a coffee percolator bubbling, whilst fluid themes continue with a swimming-pool sequence which combines water droplet effects and powerful glissandi into a whirling kaleidoscope of sound, not unlike an ice-cream van. Dramatic it ain't.

The electronic manipulation of the human voice is perhaps the most direct metaphor of the machine age. The symbolic loss of the creator's voice at the hands of his invention promotes all kinds of dystopian nightmares. Similarly the electronic rendering of the classical canon also seems to provoke a certain unease in some people. Iconoclast Wendy (née Walter) Carlos's free-form Moog-assisted Bach interpretations (*Switched on Bach*) from 1968 or the outstanding score to *A Clockwork Orange* (1971), which freely mixed electronica with fragments of Purcell, Beethoven, Rossini and Elgar, were spearheading a new form of recording star in the commercial marketplace.

Switched on Bach pretty much defined the terms by which the synthesizer is judged. Its controversy stems from the paucity of its resources, two people in a studio conjuring up orchestral sounds. There were many symphony musicians and musicians' guilds who saw the synthesizer as a way of automating music. With hindsight, of course, it is easy to see that the synthesizer was not doing anything of the kind. The kind of synthesized scores built up by Wendy Carlos and her producer Rachel Elkind for either *A Clockwork Orange* or *Tron* (1982) are painstakingly constructed, with every line individually played by Carlos, who often recorded one note at a time. To make the first generation of synthesizers sound expressive was no easy task, as Wendy Carlos described:

> The quality of discipline we impose on the results that we come up with on the synthesizer is very high because the instrument is so lacking in any really interesting timbre. Whatever anyone tells you, it's just a simple Fourier waveform that just has a simply related harmonic overtone series, and no matter what you do you can never hide that. Therefore it's a little bit more boring, I think, to listen to any of these individual notes. And because of that any deviation shows up more clearly than it

would on a physical instrument, where there are other things happening that somewhat blur the periodicity.[2]

Many of the criticisms that the first generation of electronic film scores in the 1970s attracted were because they were bad scores rather than the way in which the music was produced. Those that were praised, such as Gil Melle's 1970 electronic score to *The Andromeda Strain* (1971), worked because they utilized the unique aspects of the sounds of electronica. Obviously science fiction was an attractive environment for synthesized soundtracks. All the symbolism inherent in the electronic sound could be served up as an intentional marker for the audience on what kind of sci-fi future they could expect. To what extent the ominous aspects of electronica have been collectively understood by mass cinema audiences is unclear; certainly there seem to be the same kind of associations for many people with the 'darker' tones of the synthesizer as there were with the traditionally 'frightening' registers on instruments such as the violin or cello. The darker tones of electronica are inextricably linked to their amplification. This is one of the defining features of modern music – that what *is* is increasingly what is *amplified* rather than what is played.

Electronic film music blurred the dividing line between music and sound effects and even dialogue. One might claim that film music's function was always to integrate other elements on the soundtrack, but with the incorporation of the synthesized score (and in the 1980s the MIDI-based sampler technologies) the soundtrack became seamless. Music tracked not only significant dialogue or action but smaller minutiae that most audiences were not even aware of.

The huge upswing in composers working with electronic scoring equipment from the mid-1980s is largely a result of the technology offering up a cheaper way for composers to work in a climate of low-budget films. In an industry which is often very influenced by the latest trends going on in popular music it isn't so surprising that the synthesizer caught on so quickly. When combined with a contemporary (read pop- or rock-influenced) rhythm section the results can be an interesting mix between the breadth and cinematic feel of synthesized elements of a symphony orchestra and the driving innovative live sound of the rhythm players. Giorgio Moroder's *American Gigolo* (1980) score is a great example of successfully combining the raw urban feel of a synth score with live bass and drums.

On a much grander scale, Hans Zimmer has in recent years almost

[2] *Keyboard*, December 1979, p. 126

completely blurred the distinction between the electronic and the orchestral. Beginning his film soundtrack career almost entirely based around the clever manipulation of keyboards, Zimmer's palette has since broadened to include large-scale orchestral elements, although he remains unafraid to sample in order to generate the musical effects that he wants. On a score such as *Black Rain* (1990) it is difficult to know what one is actually hearing, electronic or acoustic instruments.

Bernard Herrmann maintained from his days scoring radio dramas that the musical cue could be reduced to a cellular unit, perhaps as little as three or five seconds long, a musical length unlikely to be noticed by an audience engrossed in a film. However, it has a vital structural significance as a transition agent precisely because of its short duration: it used to chime precisely with dialogue and/or special effects. Its effectiveness comes from its flexibility; it is highly cellular and adaptable. In film terms this cellular conception of musical cueing can be seen in the opening of *The Magnificent Ambersons*, where the familiar Welles' waltz motif is used to signify time passing as we catch up with the present through a highly articulated series of montages which introduce us to the Amberson family and to their peculiar influence on the small town in which they have lived through the years. Small transitional devices such as harp glissandi, unexpected key changes or musical underscoring of dialogue which cuts off in mid-cadence are all ways in which Herrmann finds an auditory equivalent to the spatial pyrotechnics of Welles' dazzling opening to the film.

There are some similarities here to the musical conceptions possible through electronic scoring. Synthesized music is, of course, minutely capable of cellular direction. At the most fundamental level, the basic waveform, the sound itself and the basic building block of all electronically produced music, can be almost endlessly refined to produce a variety of timbres. Musical pitch can be transposed through the synthesizer itself or from the sequencer unit that controls playback. Perhaps the most original aspect of synthesizer scoring is its ability to 'glide' continuously from one note to another combined with the VCF or voltage filter, which allows the composer to emphasize almost any aspect of an original sound by omitting frequencies above or below a certain level. This minute sensitivity allows a soundtrack sequence to be precisely mapped by the composer in a way far more difficult without digital technology.

The downside is that the articulation process between a composer and the technology interface (usually a synthesist who handles much of the programming) becomes more complex. Maurice Jarre has complained about the difficulties resulting from the almost limitless choices offered to a composer by electronic music. This problem is not likely to be solved by simpler-to-use interfaces, but by a greater understanding of how to use electronic instruments dramatically.

At their most effective one might view the early electronic scores as extended song pieces running in various reprised and remixed versions throughout the soundtrack. This would be the case with three Giorgio Moroder scores, *American Gigolo* (1980), *Cat People* (1982) and to a lesser degree *Midnight Express* (1978). The commercial packaging of these films necessitates a stand-out song by a name artist on the soundtrack: in *Cat People*'s case, David Bowie singing 'Putting Out Fire' and in *American Gigolo* Debbie Harry singing 'Call Me'. In atmosphere much of the subsequent music in the films does not deviate very far from the pacing and feel of the title song; although the impact resembles a classical score, it is simply that the sounds are electronic. Maintaining in the cue music the rhythmic and textural feel of a strong title song lends weight to both the title song and the contemporary feel that was needed. Harald Faltermeyer pulled off a similar success in *Beverly Hills Cop* (1984).

The tendency in electronic music as in the rest of film music is to reduce musical cues to the level of sounds and to allow the resulting interplay to provide the emotional atmosphere. It is a debatable point whether the experience of hearing music is the same kind of experience as that of hearing sounds. Do we emotionally interpret certain sounds in the same way? To reconcile these two kinds of experience is perhaps the challenge of new music.

John Carpenter was one of the first film makers fully to explore the possibilities of electronic scoring for his numerous sci-fi and horror movies. As a film maker he is unusual in that he also composes, and his distinctively minimalist electronic scores for films such as *Halloween* (1978) stand in direct contrast to the traditional musical *gestus* of the horror movie. Basically just chords and textures, *Halloween* takes a raw, unadorned synthesizer palette and fashions a kind of electronic *Tubular Bells* but with plenty of the traditional horror genre musical progressions. This musical process is simple but effective.

One of Carpenter's long-time collaborators is composer and sound designer Alan Howarth, a veteran of electronic instruments, and one of the first to begin to explore the impact that programmable synthesizers would have on the process of sound creation and recording. It wasn't until around 1979 that machines such as the Prophet 5 enabled composers actually to store for future retrieval sounds that they had created. Until this point one was stuck with the capacity simply to produce sound that had to be recorded at the same time. The innovation of programmable synthesizers made a profound difference to the types of sounds that composers were able to record. The main appreciable difference was a greater tendency to explore the textures of sound rather than simple melody lines and the slow movement towards electronic underscoring began. As both a sound designer and a composer, Howarth was able to judge precisely the layering effects of sound effects created for the film *Star Trek: The Motion Picture* (1979), alongside suggested music cues from composer James Horner.

Ryuichi Sakamoto is a musician, sometime film star and producer from a techno-pop background who embodies many of the vices and virtues of the modern composer with hands in many projects. A founding member of Japan's Yellow Magic Orchestra, one of the first wholly electronic bands, Sakamoto has both anticipated and extended in small ways most of the musical ripples of the past fifteen years. His compositional style is hard-edged, often relying on percussive effects as a basic emolement, then building with chords, bass parts and keyboards. Sakamoto's film music has been surprisingly varied, ranging from the sweet melodies of *Merry Christmas, Mr Lawrence* (1984) to the more martial *The Last Emperor* (1987) and the epic *The Sheltering Sky* (1990). His film music can sometimes come across as over-analytical, a trait shared by some of his performance work. His score to *The Handmaid's Tale* (1990) is the musical vision of the film's future dystopian society, and the coldness in the score goes some way towards capturing this. A basic electronic underscore of chordal figures is supplemented by koto, flute and piano, played either together or solo, which soften the synthesized passages. Sakamoto tends not to use melody a great deal, preferring to experiment with tonal variations that in places suggest rather than provide melody as in the strikingly elegant music for Oliver Stone's television series *Wild Palms* (1993).

the electronic manipulation of sound

Electronic music has a huge capacity subtly to manipulate the perceptual properties of sounds. All sounds are sensory objects, a stimulus we react to, but the perceptual properties of a sound are what we measure our musical or auditory experience by. The difficulty of discussing electronic scores is that the basic tools for understanding the musical experience are themselves obscured by the blurred distinction between electronic sound and electronic music. The American musicologist Leonard Meyer[3] has categorized three different ways in which listeners form hypotheses about pieces of music. It is the process of hypothesis forming which Meyer believes is fundamental to musical understanding. These hypotheses can fairly be called types of musical 'meaning'. There are 'hypothetical' meanings which are the musical events one hears as part of what we believe is an incomplete pattern and expect to be completed with the next sequence, there are 'evident' meanings which are confirmations of those initial hypotheses; and then there are 'determinate' meanings which, most importantly, one assesses in retrospect, 'timeless in memory' once the music is over. These processes of hypothesis forming, which Meyer suggests are central to the experiencing of sounds as music, happen when the listener has an understanding of the style in which the music is composed. Only the kinds of event which can be understood from the basis of hypothetical and evident meanings can be classified as purely musical and described in the special language of musical analysis.

This narrow definition of musical events may threaten the musical status of much recent electronic film scoring, with its reliance on dislocated sounds strung together often with the logic of sound effects rather than freely associative music. Meyer's definition would not seem to admit the more expressive qualities of music, a particularly important part of the impact of electronic scoring. Nor would it seem to allow listeners to form aural expectations of anything other than 'purely musical' events.

The complex soundscape of *Apocalypse Now* (1979) has an electronic score by Carmine Coppola which is 'musical' only on a fairly banal level. Yet the primitive slabs of electronic sound that mark the geographical and psychological journey into the heart of darkness are highly expressive. Blocks of electronic atmosphere act as a carrying device for a painstakingly detailed sound mix by Walter Murch which uses sounds in an almost musical way effectively to transverse both time and space as Captain Willard's first-person narration leads us into the story:

> At the very beginning of the film, Captain Willard is in a hotel room in Saigon. He wakes up and looks out of the window, and what you hear are the off-screen policeman's traffic whistle, the car horns, motorbikes, the little fly buzzing in the windowpane, etc. Then he sits down on the bed and starts talking, in narration, about how his heart is really in the jungle and he can't stand being cooped up in this hotel room. Gradually, what happens is that all of those street sounds turn into jungle

3 Leonard Meyer, *Emotion and Meaning in Music* (Chicago: 1965), p. 37

sounds: the whistle of the policeman turns into a cricket; the car horns turn into different kinds of birds; and the fly turns into a mosquito. You are watching Willard sitting in his hotel room, but what you are hearing is a very strong jungle background. One reality is exchanged for another. The thread that links them is the fact that although his body is in Saigon, his mind is in the jungle. That's what Willard really wants to get back to. By gradually making that shift you've presented the audience with a dual reality which, on the face of it, is absurd, but one which nevertheless gets at the dilemma of this particular character.[4]

Apocalypse Now is a milestone in production sound mixing, and with its use of music as sound effect and sound effect as music it points the way forward to possible future uses of electronic sound production. Expressiveness on the modern soundtrack is not so much a question about musicality or even about musical expression but more about structural effectiveness. The ability to combine elements in a perceptually expressive form is the unique contribution of electronic music. These expressive properties combine and modify what Meyer refers to as the 'purely musical' properties and offer a new way of experiencing music, a new way of perceiving structure.

Ben Burtt, sound effects designer on *Star Wars* (1977), created most of the sounds used in the film from scratch using a synthesizer for the first time:

I was hired to work on the picture about two years before it was released. That's unusual. Most soundtracks are done within a few weeks' time, near the end of production. But sound effects are largely responsible for lending a film like *Star Wars* its credibility, so in this case they were given a lot of thought right from the beginning. With the synthesizer I could start from nothing and just build up tones, and see in the process what it was that made them different from each other. It was very exciting, I got very analytical about sound because of my contact with the synthesizer. It provides a very discrete means of creating textures.[5]

With the rich and diverse textures of electronic music comes an ambiguity of musical meaning which undermines many of film music's basic conventions. In isolation such music or sound flows can create ambiguous feelings in the audience since it can't be coded in terms of simple pitch or rhythmic structure. However, whilst much electronic music does not tap

[4] Frank Paine, 'Sound Mixing and *Apocalypse Now*: An Interview with Walter Murch', *University Film Association Journal*, 33, no. 4, 1981

[5] *Keyboard*, February 1978, p. 238

into the basic cognitive drives in the way that a romantic melody played by an orchestra might, there is much that achieves the same impact whilst managing to avoid the traditional rhythmic frameworks on which so much acoustic music depends.

When amplified in a cinema, electronic or electro-acoustic music creates an illusion of placement, as if it emanates from somewhere in the centre of the screen. The feeling of space, even of some kind of musical landscape, is one of the most commonly used analogies in describing electronic music, which seems to extend our musical perceptions beyond the traditional musical parameters.

Denis Smalley talks about 'source bonding' to describe our natural tendency to try and relate sounds to supposed sources and causes, and to relate sounds to each other through apparent shared or associated origins. We tend to try to interpret certain kinds of abstract sounds in terms of what kind of human activity we believe caused them (which to an extent challenges the functionality of sound effects, whose primary purpose is to create illusion). Our experience as listeners to a variety of musical instruments, including electronic ones, is based on a subtle cultural conditioning process which has been in operation since our first conscious experiences.

Electronic music, particularly away from the context of a film soundtrack, is sometimes felt to be too strict to justify concentrated listening. In an interesting recent paper John Young suggests that:

> Abstraction is a measure of the psychological distance between a sound which displays a source-cause ambiguity and a surmised source-cause model . . . As soon as the sounds are articulated in a tangible three-dimensional spatial field, an important aspect of environmental reality has been analogized . . . Although a sound itself may not be specifically from a particular environmental or cultural source, it may nevertheless serve to define a realistic acoustic space and behave as though it were a physical entity.[6]

These 'distances' then are analogous to concepts such as harmonic distance in more conventional musical forms; we use this information to overlay a pattern or structure to the music. It is this that makes the piece appreciable.

As cinema amplification becomes more and more 'realistic', in effect surrounding the audience with sounds which seem to be precisely anchored

[6] John Young, 'The Extended Environment', Proceedings of the 1994 International Computer Music Conference (San Francisco: International Computer Music Association)

in a kind of sonic virtual reality, the capacity of film music, particularly music of an electronic kind, to manipulate audiences' emotions will increase dramatically. The placing of loudspeaker systems in cinemas (and increasingly in 'home cinema' systems) is constantly being refined, creating a seamless world of sound. The most obvious spatial oppositions in sound are those sounds that appear to come from 'in front', that is from the screen itself, and those sounds which, more alarmingly, seem to come from 'behind' our seated position in the cinema. Similarly, sounds placed at 'left' hand and 'right' hand to the audience seem to suggest oppositional forces, whilst sounds heard as 'close up' tend to encourage a kind of participation and those 'further away' tend to leave us as observers. Speed of apparent sonic 'movement' also does much to influence our appreciation of the sound space we are in. Faster motions tends to convey more energy, slower movements passivity. Regularities may lead to mechanistic associations whilst angular jabbing movements might suggest hesitancy.

These everyday preconceptions about smooth electronic sound serve to carve out a basic grammar of how that music is often used in much the same way as harmonic and rhythmic forms serve to demarcate more traditional forms of music. The listening conditions of the new kinds of film music exemplified in the work of composers such as Simon Fisher Turner or even Hans Zimmer become a much more crucial part of the musical-sound landscape's impact on the audience. This impact is now primarily determined by loudspeaker placement in the auditoriums, but equally important is the evolution in audience tolerance for the virtual sound fields of minimally chordal music and sound effects characteristic of modern cinema.

THE STATE OF THINGS

Peter Bogdanovich's *The Last Picture Show* (1971) contains a nice metaphor for cinema's losing battle with television. The usher of a small-town cinema puts the popcorn machine to rest for the last time after showing *Red River* to an audience of just three people, blaming television for the demise of a theatre that had once been the pulse of the town. The same story was being played out across the world as cinemas lost their audiences in ever growing numbers.

The 1970s were the first decade where the back catalogue of film history, resurrected through television, made an impact on contemporary film-making style. Whereas other art forms seemed subject to at least some aspect of the filtering system that the philosopher David Hume called 'the test of time', cinema through its enforced afterlife on television, through bulk-buy deals between the television networks and the studios, downloaded the best and worst of itself to a mass audience. Everything rose to the surface of the television screen. There was little discrimination in what was shown on the television networks and the most forgettable B-movies received an undeserved transfusion of new life.

Worse still, movies were segmented for commercials. Apart from the indignity of commercial breaks there was also the technical process that reduced an image down to television size, often dispensing with up to twenty per cent of the image. Those films whose screen size and ratio signified cinema at its most spectacular in the 1950s were the ones that suffered the most when finally squeezed on to videotape. Films by such visually literate directors as Satyajit Ray or even Orson Welles did not translate well to the small screen. More successful was the vast middle ground, as Pauline Kael has suggested, of mediocre movies that offered up undemanding plots, not too melodramatic, not too obviously foreign.

The apparent wilderness of television land seems to be reflected in a dearth of quality film scores, if David Raksin is to be believed in a 1974 article he wrote for *Film Music Notebook*.[1] Blaming in equal parts a movement away from symphonic scoring on grounds of cost and a misplaced belief in the commercial power of a pop-driven soundtrack, he says:

> It is one thing to appreciate the freshness and *naïveté* of pop music and quite another to accept it as inevitable no matter what the subject at hand. And still another to realize that the choice is often made for reasons that have little to do with the film itself. One: to sell recordings and incidentally to garner publicity for the picture. Two: to appeal to the 'demographically defined' audience, which is a symbolic unit conceived as an object of condescension. Three: because so many directors and producers, having acquired their skills and reputations at the price of becoming elderly, suddenly find themselves aliens in the land of the young; tormented by fear of not being 'with it', they are tragically susceptible to the brain-washing of Music Biz types.[2]

Just a few years after writing that article, Raksin was to have one of his finest scores thrown out of an American television series about nuclear holocaust, *The Day After* (1983), because the director, Nicholas Meyer, did not want his audience's emotions manipulated by music in the face of such serious subject matter. Raksin complained bitterly, after seeing his threnody for the film's final scenes bring tears to the eyes of television executives who saw early screenings:

> I said, why don't you save yourself a lot of trouble and the network a lot of money – you should have forgotten about both the camera and the music! The moment you do something that makes some kind of a mark, it alters the balance of the scene. If it alters it for the good, that's wonderful. If it doesn't that's a shame. We can't be right all the time. But we're much more often right than we are wrong, because we not only know our own profession, we know theirs.[3]

Whilst Raksin's complaints about a generally philistine attitude towards music in the American film industry were certainly accurate, some very impressive film music was written throughout the 1970s. One might think of the highly effective musical score of *Badlands* (1973), a début film by Terrence Malick which was scored by George Tipton. Malick's other film, *Days of Heaven* (1978), has a magnificent score by Ennio Morricone which also incorporated pieces by Saint-Saëns. Both films define their story

---

[1] David Raksin. 'Whatever Became of Movie Music?', *Film Music Notebook*, Fall 1974

[2] Ibid., p. 23

[3] *Soundtrack*, vol. 9, no. 6, December 1990, p. 31

though the voice-over narration of a young female who tells a powerful story against the panoramic backdrop of the American landscape, serenaded musically by a sparser and more melancholic version of the Americana of Aaron Copland.

Some of the best-known scores of the 1970s were Nino Rota's stunning pieces for Francis Ford Coppola's *The Godfather* (1972) and, to a lesser extent, *The Godfather Part II* (1974). In these films which are both a critique of capitalism as well as sprawling family sagas, music acts as a touchstone for the old simplicity of the Sicily now left behind and as a powerful marshalling agent knitting together a very large cast of characters and defining their emotional and filial allegiances. In the sequel, Coppola utilizes the age-old technique of cross-cutting between different time frames to contrast the rise of the young Vito Corleone with the moral fall of his son Michael. A similar polarity is enacted in Rota's score. In the famous baptism sequence near the end of *The Godfather*, J. S. Bach's music is used in a particularly inventive way to bridge a complicated series of cross-cuts that show the young Michael being baptized at the same time as his father's men are carrying out assassinations of members of a rival family. Using a solo organ for much of the sequence, with the sonorous voice of the priest speaking in Latin, Rota ingeniously arranges the timing of his chosen Bach sequence to mimic the silent film suspense scoring conventions as a sustained chord illustrates each of the five murders carried out during Michael's baptism. The impact is simple and, as Royal S. Brown points out, the connotation is clear:

> The cross-cutting in *The Godfather*'s baptism sequence leaves no doubt as to the metaphorical level of power into which Michael Corleone is 'born' via his orchestrated executions of the heads of the five Mafia families.[4]

As Brown goes on to point out, in Coppola's third Godfather film, *The Godfather Part III* (1990), the climactic sequence is marked off by another cross-choreographed massacre, this time to the more secular strains of a Mascagni opera, although for this sequence Coppola sets up a musical duel which plays the opera against a funeral theme reincorporated from the first *Godfather* movie:

> At points both musics are heard simultaneously in a counterpoint of two distinct entire scores. Further emphasizing the closed-off, god-like world of incest and inevitability to which Michael has ascended.[5]

---

4 Royal S. Brown, *Overtones and Undertones* (Berkeley: 1994), p. 81
5 Ibid.

Active since the 1940s as a film composer, Nino Rota was still working with Fellini in the 1970s until his death in 1979. His melancholic score to Fellini's *Amarcord* is a sentimental but wholly characteristic piece with inventive arrangements for a small orchestra. Nino Rota and Ennio Morricone were undoubtedly the most successful Italian composers of this century. That both should have chosen to make film their primary arena of work says much about the fragmentation of the Italian concert-hall environment since the Second World War. Rota's trademark was the ritornello, a galloping rhythm that seems to bend in upon itself, and in Rota's hand that musical device became a precision tool through which to access our experience of passing time. In Fellini's and Coppola's circuses of on-screen personalities, Rota's music gives those characters life. Rota's arrangements gave the keyboard a touchstone quality; it became a medium of interpolation, purveying fragments of melodies that are as recognizable as a nursery rhyme, with the easy appeal of a vaudeville song. Rota's music dredges up a musical haunting that is rooted in our earliest experiences of melody. His themes linger on as linear sketches of ideas taken from reservoirs perhaps quite outside music, and there remains something at the centre of his themes that is always unreachable, a buried musical archetype. Rota provides in both the *Godfather* films and in his many scores for Fellini a legacy of feelings in search of objects, the 'props' of character and location. Rota's music seems to be more *about* nostalgia than it is genuinely nostalgic. His 1964 concert work *Concerto for Strings* takes as inspiration the formal divisions of a much earlier musical era: Preludio, Scherzo, Aria and Finale. His music is harmonically very direct, a lucid, tonal and enticing repeated motif, and it is this quality which made him a perfect partner for complex film makers such as Fellini and Coppola. Rota's music acted as a translator, taking all that was difficult in a maze of images and communities and making them simple, universalizing them.

Some of the best uses of pre-existing music during the decade came from the films of independent directors such as Martin Scorsese, whose fable-like portraits of New York life, *Mean Streets* (1973), *Taxi Driver* (1976) and *Raging Bull* (1980), were some of the best American films ever made. Scorsese's instincts as a director are clearly influenced by the classical style of film making from the 1940s and 1950s but no less by the French New Wave style of the 1950s. Scorsese integrates music into his films with a rare sophistication, whether it be American and Italian popular songs for *Mean Streets*, *film noir*ish bombast from the Bernard Herrmann-scored *Taxi Driver* or the lush orchestral and operatic sweep of *Raging Bull*. Music becomes a jumping-off point in time in a Scorsese film, a moment of transcendence in an otherwise very realistic urban setting. One recalls music sequences as non-diegetic glimpses into not only character psychology but also the collective social fabric of emigrant Italian-American communities. The music itself often has a cheap disposability, but when it appears to break with the other elements on the soundtrack, as it does so often in these three films, it takes on an otherworldly, almost religious significance.

In the pop-scored universe of *Mean Streets*, the big beat sound of the 1960s fills the air. Taking his cue from the earlier underground oeuvre of Kenneth Anger, whose riotous assembly of pop and camp introduced the three-minute single to the soundtrack as part of a grammatology of style rather than simple commercial appeal, Scorsese takes the process one stage further by liberating through its casual deployment against a background of violence the epic from the banal bubble-gum narrative of a typical Phil Spector song. These layered, atmospheric songs are laden with complex social coding reflecting Johnny Boy (Robert De Niro), who personifies a blown-away hipster cool, swaggering oblivious into a bar tracked by the Stones' 'Jumping Jack Flash', dancing ecstatically in celebration of his own imminent destruction on the hood of a car to Smokey Robinson's 'Mickey's Monkey'. Where one might argue that the Stones' song mirrors Johnny Boy, to some extent this explicit possibility of musical identification is nowhere else really followed up on in *Mean Streets*. Most pop soundtracks are made up of simple dance songs that do not appear to offer any direct connotations to the on-screen characters of the drama. However, the pop music of *Mean Streets* (and most of Scorsese's early films, e.g. *Who's That Knocking at My Door?*, 1968) is so well chosen that individual songs by artists as different as the Rolling Stones, the Ronettes and Smokey Robinson gel together into a sound field that perfectly captures the everyday living resonance of pop. Music of this kind in *Mean Streets* is a transforming element, that immediately recognizable Phil Spector drum sound acting as a catalyst to the movement of the characters through a crowded visual space. Music navigates them, rounds them and above all defines character. The central visual motifs to which pop acts as a Greek chorus most effectively tend to be journeys of one kind or another, by foot, by car or through overheard music to another scene. Music presents a world through which the audience is moved, a world of hypocrisy and claustrophobic community bordered at the edges by an almost religious praise of salvation – the salvation encapsulated in the sugary innocence of a pop song.

In *Taxi Driver* (1976) Scorsese adopts a darker musical tone bordering on the *noir*ish and utilizes a brilliant original score by Bernard Herrmann (Scorsese had apparently told Herrmann he wanted 'New York Gothic'), which portrays the extreme psychological states experienced by the protagonist Travis Bickle. In a series of hallucinatory voyages into urban hell, Herrmann sustains a mood of brittle yet sensuous indistinctness. The music seems to snake in upon itself, muted trumpets and snare sounds and the relentless ticking bass like a bomb about to detonate. Music mirrors both character and the oppression of a city gone out of control. Through an impressionistic style of photography the streets of New York seem literally to bleed off the screen, rain-streaked splashes of abstract colour and reflected light. Herrmann's music mirrors this abstraction in the composer's sparsest, most menacing and, as it turned out, final score of his career. By turns tender and even romantic in its jazz-inspired love themes, the music is grouped into a series of quite separate movements, each a unitary marker of the film's darkening mood as Travis Bickle finally goes over the edge into psychotic madness. The music that accompanies the climactic ending even features harp arpeggios, as the camera roams over the resulting carnage. In the closing moments Herrmann recycles something very like the 'madness' motif from his earlier score to Hitchcock's *Psycho* (1960), yet here the effect is even more chilling, since throughout the film one identifies much more closely with the moral outrage of Travis Bickle than the oedipal twist that is Norman Bates.

Raging Bull (1980) follows the career of boxer Jake La Motta over twenty years from his beginnings as a promising neighbourhood fighter in the 1940s to his subsequent extended bask as a washed-up night-club entertainer in the 1960s. Perhaps more than in any other film, music here is used to stop time, to step outside the narrative frame and to observe an Italian-American society in the process of extinguishing itself. The glamour of Little Italy with its elaborate hierarchies of gangsters, girls and priests is contrasted with the day-to-day-hell of La Motta's wife as she is swiftly transformed from a teenage bombshell into a harried and beaten wife, married to the psychotically jealous boxer. This is a society isolated from the rest of America. Its extended codes of family constitute the beginning and the end of the law. Scorsese uses opera music by Mascagni, very much the kind of repertoire that would have played in the community theatres of fifty to eighty years ago. He appears to be drawing and commenting upon the instinct for nostalgia that is characteristic of societies on the verge of eclipse or absorption into a more anonymously American identity. Everything is coated in a luminous black and white photography and in virtually every scene of public life the influence of the street photographers such as Cartier-Bresson or Weegee is present. Music replaces the absent photographer's flashbulb in *Raging Bull*; the film is full of moments of everyday transcendence, filmed in slow motion, all extraneous sound muted except for the music, an odd combination of the familiar *Cavalleria Rusticana* and Robbie Robertson's incidental music. La Motta's home movies unfold as a series of leisure-time cavalcades lent a certain dignity by the opera's main overture, which elegantly coats an extended sequence which carries us forwards some five years in La Motta's life. Perhaps the most stylized sequences are those in the ring itself, where sound becomes highly directional and subjective, 'heard' on the soundtrack as if from inside the boxers' heads. The drawing of breath, the crunching sound of blow by blow impacts and the unexpected rush of the crowd's applause make *Raging Bull* a highly visceral experience.

Gangsters step out of cars or up to tables in night-club scenes in high-contrast, monochromatic slow motion, casually dropping a cigarette, self-consciously checking their appearance: it is all highly fetishistic and is tracked by an odd approximation of overheard dance-hall jazz. Smaller, muted and more distorted, as if from a radio, Robbie Robertson's music montages might best be understood as a kind of collage. The notion of the musical overheard as the locus of time and place has always been an important part of Scorsese's overall technique. Particularly in *Mean Streets* and *Raging Bull*, this is a significant part of the films' conjuring of community, whilst in *Taxi Driver* the music overheard is the banal disco blaring from a television as Travis Bickle sinks into isolation.

the new composing establishment

The whole idea of the film hero and a heroic turn of musical phrase had evaporated by the 1970s. The Italian and Spanish 'spaghetti Westerns' of the 1960s had turned the traditional Western frontiersman into a haunted, amoral outsider and the music of these films had literally fragmented the traditionally Appalachian sonorities of an Elmer Bernstein or even a Franz Waxman into shards of cacophonous sound effects. The influence of the avant-garde composers of the 1950s and 1960s was now noticeable within even mainstream Hollywood film.

By the early 1970s the A-list of Hollywood composers was made up largely of new names, arrangers and songwriters who had emerged during the stripped-down 1960s. Whilst one might argue that there was a slow return to symphonic arrangements in the 1970s it was a new generation of composers weaned on, amongst other things, jazz and television that were now trying their hands at film scoring for a mass audience.

Foremost amongst this new generation was Jerry Fielding, whose long apprenticeship in television (*Star Trek* amongst other projects) had made him a highly versatile composer and arranger used to working on varied assignments with tight deadlines. His style tended to be rather dark and foreboding, and his writing for brass, even if orchestral, showed up his jazz tastes and arranging background. He could range from being highly melodic to chaotically dissonant, and his musical technique of spotting action cues was quite distinctive, choosing to accent action cues in a very original way. His Mexican-inspired work on *The Wild Bunch* (1969) and *The Mechanic* (1972) was highly distinguished. He also turned in some very sophisticated adaptations of Mahler for *The Gambler* (1974) and wrote some effective action themes for two of the Clint Eastwood Dirty Harry films, *The Enforcer* (1976) and *The Gauntlet* (1977).

Lalo Schifrin, an Argentine-born composer, was first a jazz pianist of some renown before scoring films. He was also a skilled jazz arranger, turning in some of the best mod-jazz scores of the 1960s, such as *The Cincinnati Kid* (1965) and *Bullitt* (1969). Schifrin, like Fielding, has enjoyed a long association with Clint Eastwood and has also scored several of the Dirty Harry movies.

John Williams is a rather more traditional composer, at ease with the large orchestral styles of the Golden Age of film music, and he has one of the highest profiles in American film music. Like many other composers, Williams came up through television but also through low-budget 1960s comedies such as *How to Steal a Million* (1966) and *A Guide for the Married Man* (1967), where he was turning out formulaic 1960s pop tunes. It was not until the 1970s and an early involvement in a long cycle of action and adventure films that Williams turned to the late-romantic idiom which now characterizes his work. One might argue that his celebrity is due more to the films he has scored rather than the scores themselves, which whilst stirring enough are hard to single out as distinctively his own since they are so varied, due in part to Williams' frequent use of a variety of different orchestrators and arrangers. He scored some of the biggest box-office hits of the 1970s, including *The Poseidon Adventure* (1972), *The Towering Inferno* (1974), *Earthquake* (1974), *Jaws* (1975), *Star Wars* (1977), *Close Encounters of the Third Kind* (1977) and *Raiders of the Lost Ark* (1981). *Jaws* remains

Williams' best-known score, primarily because of the distinctively menacing cue signifying the approach of the shark. In a film whose visual and story-telling technique is so grounded in foreshadowing, Williams' music is the perfect complement. Interestingly, musical foreshadowing is not used to mislead the audience, as is so often the case in horror scoring – a false alarm in which two boys terrorize a beach with a rubber shark goes out unscored. Music serves to warn the audience of the shark's impending presence, a measure both of Spielberg's confidence as a film maker and Williams' ability to manipulate musical expectation and anticipation without actually betraying the audience's trust.

Again, in *Close Encounters of the Third Kind*, a single musical motif is allowed to carry a good deal of the foreshadowing. It is actually used as the musical code by which the alien visitors make contact with earth. The theme exists both non-diegetically and diegetically, apparently passing into various characters in the film as they come into contact with the aliens in one way or another. Williams' subsequent work on the *Star Wars* franchises for George Lucas have been credited with resurrecting the symphonic score. *Star Wars* does use some very conventional scoring techniques, clearly delineated character themes and a lot of lush woodwind arrangements. In retrospect it was a surprising choice:

> One would think that faced with the limitlessness of space and the multiplicity of life forms Williams would explode with ideas. But in composing the sound to go with the future, Williams doesn't look to any of the 'avant-garde' composers like Varèse or Cage . . . Instead Williams looks to the major-key flourishes of Wagner . . . and Tchaikovsky . . . and the swashbuckling *Captain Blood* and *Adventures of Robin Hood* soundtracks of Erich Wolfgang Korngold.[6]

Williams essays his themes in large type. The *Star Wars* main theme is unambiguously heroic, the Darth Vader theme from *Return of the Jedi* is a classic 'baddie' signature, whilst the diminutive Ewok creatures get a playful, energetic duet between oboes and recorders. However, Williams also experiments with polytonality in the *Star Wars* main theme and improvised rhythms in passages from *Close Encounters of the Third Kind*. This allows him to hit a variety of rhythmic effects without losing the strong primary accents in his writing.

In foregrounding the symphonic score, Williams is siding with tradition, but his very tight working schedules mean that he works extensively with orchestrators. In general his scores tend to sustain the narrative, focusing on

---

[6] Greg Oatis, *Cinefantastique*, quoted in *Settling the Score* by Kathryn Kalinak (Madison: 1993), p. 184

the moments of spectacle rather than the story itself. Melody is used expressively and almost always tonally. Williams has claimed that his science-fiction scoring used traditional classical orchestration and timbre in order to provide a marker of familiarity in the alien worlds shown on screen.

A modern composer with a very different view on musically representing science-fiction themes on screen is Jerry Goldsmith, whose entry into mainstream film scoring dates from the early 1960s, when he introduced a variety of new atonal techniques, most notably in his breakthrough score for *Planet of the Apes* (1968).

Much of Goldsmith's work can be characterized as skilful underscoring rather than grand thematic musical statements in the style of an earlier generation of composers. Goldsmith more than any of the A-list composers working in the United States today has used atonal elements to fashion a unique musical voice. The roots of his approach lie as far back as his score to *Freud* (1962), which built extensively on themes of suspense carried by woodwinds and string tremolos.

His score for *Planet of the Apes* shows great subtlety and restraint. It uses a conventional orchestra and the studio techniques of reverb and overlay in post-production. For the opening chase sequence, a stepping rhythm sets up a solo oboe backed by sporadic crashes of bongos and brass, tolling chimes and a walking bassline. Goldsmith will very often choose not to score rather than to score if he believes that a greater dramatic impact can be arrived at. One might think of the final scenes in the film where a nearly buried Statue of Liberty sticks out of the deserted beach as a last signal of human civilization.

In *Planet of the Apes*, Goldsmith supplies an almost monothematic score. His lean orchestrations do not seem to contain any easily identifiable musical motifs or even melodies. With a difficult form such as serial music which foregrounds system over musical effect, cinema may be the best environment in which to try to develop the genre. Goldsmith is hard to pin down musically but his compositional instincts seem to be closest to serialism. In a 1969 interview with the BBC he claimed:

> I have a strange versatility, I can do pop, jazz, I do romantic. But personally in my
> own genre I am a serialist, a serial composer.[7]

The real resonance of the *Planet of the Apes* score is generated by the percussion sections, where Goldsmith utilized exotica such as conch shells

[7] John Caps, 'Serial Music of Jerry Goldsmith', *Film Music Notebook*, no. 1, 1976, p. 27

and metal baking tins. The overall feel is unsurprisingly primal, but also futuristic and alienated. The effectiveness comes from its clever contrast with the more orthodox orchestral instruments. Some of the syncopated rhythmic sections are reminiscent of passages from Stravinsky's *Rite of Spring*. In placing the alienating effects, including reverb and some electronics, near the bottom of the orchestral palette, Goldsmith maximizes the contrast between atonal and tonal elements, combined with studio-generated effects. Individual themes range from martial (cue music for an attack on a village by mounted gorilla soldiers) to poignant, as different musical textures take us through an ape society as stratified and as flawed as our own.

In *The Illustrated Man* (1969), a supernatural, apocalyptic collection of short stories centred around a tattooed man, Goldsmith utilizes a number of differing arrangements of a folk song first heard at the beginning of the film. Beginning with harp and oboe the song develops a chamber accompaniment. The song reappears throughout the film in different guises, even in versions for synthesizer, sitar and clarinet. Appropriately enough for a film that takes place in three different dimensions of time, *The Illustrated Man* uses a number of tension-building strategies to build up to the sustained five-minute piece of scoring near the end of the film when crescendos of strings and a repetitive tugging harp and rhythmic clarinet pattern weave a high tensile washboard of drama and emotion.

Atonal or twelve-tone music has still not been used extensively for film scores. If the various music discussion groups on the Internet are anything to go by, many composers object to atonality in films because it is likely to alienate the majority of audiences. Yet this does not address music's ability in film to go beneath the surface of the listening experience and trigger emotional responses. Atonal passages have the ability precisely to structure and focus dramatic action in a musical way without having to adhere to the normal tonal and temporal relationships. As Bernard Herrmann discovered, once freed from the tyranny of the romantic melody line, music can be broken down into tiny clusters and can therefore be manipulated and placed within the film much more precisely. Atonal music's scarcity so far has much to do with the composer's (and almost certainly producer's) reluctance to break with a long-established musical genealogy of drama and emotion. Goldsmith has frequently attempted to cross boundaries in his compositional inventiveness and his style often seems to border on minimalist:

My preference is that music be used as sparingly as possible. If there is a constant use of music, it becomes like white sound, your ear eventually tunes out those frequencies.[8]

More obviously a straight-ahead *film noir*, Roman Polanski's *Chinatown* (1975) had one of Jerry Goldsmith's better piano-driven scores, although the film is full of suitably 1940s-influenced trumpet colour. The main theme is oddly unresolved, suggesting the traditional mainstay of *noir* psychology, alienation.

Goldsmith's score for *The Omen* (1976) is a brilliant experiment with liturgical choir music, complete with some ominously sparse passages of bells, piano and strangely atonal chants. The story of a satanic child born into a wealthy American family plays off the demonology attached to certain kinds of religious ritual, and Goldsmith created a score which stands as an analogue of a new kind of more sophisticated horror movie. The traditional textures of the liturgical mass are subtly undermined by polytonal, moaning string glisses. The score certainly has the atmosphere of a twelve-tone piece in places but there is not a strict compositional system in force.

Goldsmith's most recognizable trait is a thin, angular, unsentimental sound with clear counterpoints in which changes in instrumentation alter the whole fabric of a passage. If anything his music of the 1970s, particularly the more daring scores such as that for *The Omen*, bring to mind Stravinsky. If Wagner might be said to be the patron saint of the classical American film score then Stravinsky stands as wicked uncle to those few examples of deviations from the musical norm. For *The Omen* score, Goldsmith utilized a large orchestra and choir, with wind instruments arranged in pairs: flutes, oboes, clarinets, bassoons, French horns, trumpets and trombones. However, it is the string section with its sharp jabbing style that produces the sinister associations, along with an inventive gallery of effects, including vocal glissandos for a choir of forty.

Whilst Goldsmith is an original composer, there are influences from Bernard Herrmann in his approach if not his musical style. By the 1970s Herrmann's complex, almost surgical approach to scoring was adopted by many of the younger composers as a way partly of escaping having to write for orchestra. This in itself was partly a question of economics but also marks a growing confidence with the kind of musical shorthand that audiences could recognize for its effect, not solely because of its direct emotional power but also because of the familiarity of convention.

[8] Roy M. Prendergast, *Film Music: A Neglected Art* (New York: 1975), p. 158

Despite something of a return to the large-scale symphonic ambitions of the Golden Era of film music, the 1970s were not an easy time for many film composers. The average allotted preparation time now given to a composer working on an assignment had fallen dramatically since the 1950s, when a composer such as Elmer Bernstein could spend ten weeks scoring The *Magnificent Seven*. In an era dominated by the commercial tie-in, composers found work in a new genre, the medium- to high-budget action movies, begun in the 1970s with the 'disaster' movies of producers such as Irwin Allen. These tightly scripted stories run strictly against the clock, with a protagonist or group of people trapped in a given situation such as burning office blocks, sunken passenger liners or sudden earthquakes. To these dramas John Williams brought a symphonic sophistication (but a musical conservatism) which has become the blueprint for action movies ever since.

Carter Burwell, a contemporary composer with a number of scores for Coen Brothers films such as *Blood Simple* (1984), *Miller's Crossing* (1990), *Barton Fink* (1991) and *The Hudsucker Proxy* (1994), is working within a film music tradition initiated by Miklós Rózsa's *film noir* scores of the 1940s but he brings to his assignments a sensitivity to the wider elements on the soundtrack that makes their often very expansive and dramatic scores consistently melodically and texturally interesting. In *Barton Fink*, for example, the protagonist, a writer with a chronic case of writer's block, sinks into paranoia holed up in a 1940s Hollywood cockroach-infested hotel peopled by a garish circus of freakish characters. As his world grows increasingly interior, his language seems to fail him and words are replaced by sounds, with every noise amplified, echoed and distorted. The score showcases all these possibilities whilst providing a taut underscoring of the protagonist's increasingly shaky grip on reality and increasingly dangerous relationship with the bizarre Charlie Meadows (John Goodman), who promises to 'show him the life of the mind'. In the twilight world of the Coen Brothers' films, characters are reduced to trademark gestures and phrases, an extreme stylization that requires music to provide accents not only of movement but of a scene's basic style. The score to *Miller's Crossing* is a hauntingly memorable variation on Irish folk ballads given a symphonic breadth despite the highly abbreviated length of many of the individual cues, some lasting just a few seconds.

Danny Elfman is a very successful young composer who came into film music, like so many others, from a rock background, leading the critically acclaimed Los Angeles band Oingo Boingo in the mid-1980s. He is completely self-taught as a composer and extremely eclectic in his range of styles, running the gamut from wild classicism (*Pee-Wee's Big Adventure*, 1985, and *Big Top Pee-Wee*, 1988) to some slick modern jazz-blues scoring for *Midnight Run* (1988), to the dramatic fantasy worlds of *Beetlejuice* (1987) and *Nightbreed* (1990), to the massive symphonic scores he wrote for *Batman* (1989), *Dick Tracy* (1990) and *Darkman* (1990). Influenced primarily by Bernard Herrmann, with some of the whimsical touches of Nino Rota, Elfman's tastes are suitably eclectic for a high-profile mainstream Hollywood career that has covered a wide variety of film genres. His *Batman* soundtrack was the only instrumental soundtrack to break into *Billboard*'s Top Ten, in tenth place for the year of the film's release (although the simultaneously released Prince soundtrack of songs written around the time of the singer's two actual contributions to the film made third place). Having also written cartoon music (for, amongst other things, Fox's *The Simpsons* series), Elfman tends to write the emotional mood of a scene large. When Pee-Wee Herman is happy, Elfman's score renders him deliriously happy, when the Beetlejuice character becomes ever more playfully twisted, Elfman adopts some Stravinsky-like dancing violins in a minor key to emphasize these qualities.

The *Batman* and *Dick Tracy* soundtracks are probably Elfman's creative high point to date. *Batman*'s score envelops the brutalist architecture of the Gotham City set, coating what is visually a very dark film with correspondingly dark and brooding underscores, relieved by the main hero theme, which is a triumphant march figure with a lot of percussive colour matched with heroic horn timbres. *Dick Tracy* is a much warmer, more varied set of Gershwin-inspired romantic themes and melodies in miniature, most lasting no longer than thirty seconds or so in the film. As in *Batman*, Elfman's music competes with songs by Madonna and in many cases actually segues with those songs. Although *Dick Tracy* is set in the 1940s, most of the music could be situated in any era after that, with the exception of the main romantic theme for *Tess*, which is much more period-orientated.

Alan Silvestri has scored, amongst other things, *Romancing the Stone* (1980), *Back to the Future* (1984), *Who Framed Roger Rabbit?* (1988), *The Abyss* (1989) and *Predator* (1990). A very rhythmically aware composer, like so many of his contemporaries he comes from a rock background. His score for *Back to the Future* is a grandiose symphonic collection which still managed to fit well alongside the considerable amount of pop-tinged 1950s source music that is heard in the film. The two elements, instrumental and lyrical music, reinforce each other to create a strong sense of time and place. Beginning with a grand overture to suggest the present-day size of

Mayberry, the small town where the hero lives in the present day, the score manages sympathetically to cover the town's diminishing size as the hero travels back in time twenty years. Most of the environment is covered by the source music, primarily heard diegetically, but as the film goes on Silvestri's score becomes more closely linked to the concept of time travel itself, making what is actually a fairly modest film seem much bigger. The score for *The Predator* mixes a large symphony orchestra with electronic interfaces like the Synclavier, which is a keyboard set-up which locks into a video time-code and allows the composer to record cue sketches whilst watching the sequence at the same time, a great tool for capturing spontaneous ideas. *The Predator* carries a mix of military-style themes, complete with drum rolls given an unusual texture by an electronic underlay which accentuates and extends the bass elements in the score. In *Who Framed Roger Rabbit?* the challenge for Silvestri was to avoid straightforward cartoon music complete with Mickey-Mousing, but to create a rich tonal wash which could at the same time incorporate the manic unpredictability of cartoon characters alongside the more developed themes for the main characters, some of whom also happen to be animated. Silvestri's solution was to combine a five-piece jazz band with a symphonic orchestra and the two elements segue in and out of each other throughout the film, leading to a very dynamic unpredictability.

Howard Shore's subtle and restrained score for *Silence of the Lambs* (1990) is unusual in its adroit use of what would traditionally be called action themes within the thriller genre. Shore supplied nearly sixty minutes of music for the film and, although the music in isolation is neither particularly dramatic nor distinctive, it works superbly well within the film and is a great example of the modern approach to scoring thrillers. Shore is a long-time associate of Canadian director David Cronenberg and has scored most of his mainstream films (*The Brood*, (1979), *Scanners*, (1980), *Videodrome*, (1982), *Dead Ringers*, (1988), and *The Naked Lunch*, (1991). Shore generally tries to bury his music in the fabric of the film he is scoring. The music in *Dead Ringers* (a 'body horror'), for example, is barely noticeable but in fact tracks nearly forty-five minutes of the film, written as a monochromatic background score for a small horn and string section with just the occasional use of woodwinds, mainly as solos. With the *Silence of the Lambs* score, again the approach is monochromatic, flowing textures without much counterpoint but still managing to cue some effectively chilling action sequences.

The bulk of the successful modern American composers are writing large-scale symphonic soundtracks, a rediscovery owed at least in part to the ambitious scores created by Jerry Goldsmith and John Williams in the early and mid-1970s. That this style has stuck and proved popular with producers is evidence enough that the 'big' score is synonymous in many producers' minds with a high-impact movie. For the (not inconsiderable) cost of a few days in the recording studio with, say, a seventy-five-piece orchestra the music produced can bolster the emotional impact of otherwise unexceptional films. It's not hard to fathom that in the era of event movies, populated by A-list stars, where budgets have swelled to an average of around $50m nobody wants to take a step back into the kind of subdued, spare writing that was popular in the late 1960s. Composers such as John Barry, whose first successes tended towards the tight, small arrangements that characterized much of the Bond music, have followed suit with often disappointing results. Barry's score to *Dances with Wolves* (1990) is simply orchestrated and many of the cues are equally simply repeated throughout the film. Barry is primarily a melody writer and this can give his scores a spontaneity that other composers lack, but much of his work since the late 1970s has tended to favour leisurely arrangements which, combined with a highly melodic line, can come across as rather shallow, lacking the orchestral depth of, say, Elmer Bernstein. Clearly influenced by Copland, particularly in the use of trumpet, the score covers three basic melodies (which in a three-hour film is arguably not enough).

Outside the United States, film music in Europe, particularly since the 1980s, has been dominated by a few moderately well-known composers, but even these names are stars within a tiny universe, at least in terms of a presence within the recorded soundtrack marketplace. Francesca Campi, president of Rome-based film music record label CAM, agrees:

> It's difficult for non-US film composers to break beyond their local market unless they're an established name or a film becomes an international hit. No one ever talks much about the composer if the film is a flop, no matter how good the score. A good example is Luis Bacalov's score for *The Postman* [*Il Postino*] which we issued; the film's international success, much more than the music itself, has been a major help with sales of the soundtrack CD, especially in the United States.[9]

The most successful European composers (in terms of soundtrack CD sales) tend to associate themselves closely with the work of a small group of auteurist directors. One might think of French composer Gabriel Yared's creative partnership with Jean-Jacques Beineix during the 1980s (*Moon in*

---

[9] *Variety*, 22–8 January 1996, p. 80

the Gutter, Betty Blue, IP5), but also his involvement with some popular and quintessentially French films such as *Tatie Danielle* (1991) and the adaptation of Margaret Duras' *The Lovers* (1991). There is also Patrick Doyle's almost exclusive musical association with Kenneth Branagh's films (*Henry V, Much Ado About Nothing, Mary Shelley's Frankenstein* and *Hamlet*) and Nicola Piovani's scores for films by the Taviani brothers (*Kaos, Good Morning Babylon* and *Night Sun*) as well as a previous period of scoring some of Fellini's last films after the death of long-time associate Nino Rota (*Ginger and Fred, Intervista*).

Germany's Jurgen Knieper is one of the more in-demand musical voices within European cinema. His work with Wim Wenders on films such as *The State of Things* (1982) and *Wings of Desire* (1988), as well as a superb score for Helena Sanders-Brahms' *Germany, Pale Mother* (1980), has established his spare, melancholic, somewhat academic style through basic synthesizer shadings combined with delicate string overlays. In collaborations with Wenders, Knieper's music is often packaged amongst an eclectic selection of contemporary rock music. Fellow countryman Hanns Werner Henze has also been a distinctive presence in the new German cinema with some intensely brooding and complex scores for films such as *Young Törless* (1966), *The Lost Honour of Katharina Blum* (1975) and *L'Amour a mort* (1985).

Eric Serra, like his contemporary Gabriel Yared, has written music for some of the more post-modern French films of the 1980s and 1990s. Serra has worked most notably on Luc Besson's films from *L'Avant-dernier* (1983) and *Subway* (1985) through to *The Big Blue* (1988), one of the most popular soundtrack releases in French history, selling over two million copies. His most inventive score is the synthesized doomily atmospheric music to Luc Besson's *Nikita* (1990). Percussion-dominated, Serra's scores have a strong rock influence and incorporate many electronic effects, particularly in his use of the guitar as a major coloration tool fed through an assortment of effects pedals. Accessible and self-consciously *modern*, Serra's soundtracks are neither particularly surprising nor experimental, but as an analogue to the slick highly graphic cinema of Luc Besson they function effectively enough.

Michael Nyman is one of the best-known film music composers, although he has also written a considerable number of concert and opera works. Born in London in 1944, he has studied both music and musicology and spent the early part of his working life as a practising critic for newspapers including the *Observer, The Spectator* and the *New Statesman*. His success has come primarily through his film scores for Peter Greenaway – *The Draughtsman's Contract* (1982), *A Zed and Two Noughts* (1985), *Drowning by Numbers* (1988), *The Cook, the Thief, His Wife and Her Lover* (1989) and *Prospero's Books* (1991) – although he has also composed music for Jane Campion's film *The Piano* (1993) and Christopher Hampton's *Carrington* (1995).

Nyman's music is rich in rhythm. In many of the collaborations with Greenaway, the music came first and scenes in the film were then shot to the musical tempo. In the stylized, late-seventeenth-century setting of *The Draughtsman's Contract*, Nyman incorporates and reworks Purcell, or rather a memory of Purcell, as the basic musical identity, whilst avoiding historical pastiche, inserting some typically Nymanesque developments upon small extracts of Purcell, almost deconstructing the original and then piecing it back together again through a filter of 1970s-style minimalism and process music, and even including rock elements. In this score can be found many of Nyman's most recognizable features as a composer: a concern with repeatable, variable harmonic structures, and an acute sensitivity to the organizational, systemic and temporal concerns which distinguish Peter Greenaway's films. In *The Cook, the Thief, His Wife and Her Lover* the musical flavour is appropriately funereal for a film which explores the implicit links between the food chain and capitalistic greed in a bizarre allegory of Britain in the Thatcher era. In Nyman's preference for musically antiquated structures (with a post-modernist overlay) there are parallels with Greenaway's own enthusiasms for pre-modern paintings, coded references to which make frequent appearances in the distinctly Jacobean *The Cook, the Thief, His Wife and Her Lover*. *Prospero's Books* is a radical reassembly of Shakespeare's *The Tempest* by Greenaway for which Nyman contributes a beguiling mix of Shakespearean songs set to some very contemporary music and in some cases performed diegetically (such as the Masque sequence). Nyman's recent work for other directors has opened up sides of him as a composer that remained hidden in the colder climes of Greenaway's films. His score to *The Piano* sold fairly well as a soundtrack release but was critically mauled. Nyman injected more characterization into this score for a mid-nineteenth-century story about a woman and daughter transplanted to a remote New Zealand community. The main character, Ada, is a mute whose Scottish upbringing and love of piano playing are drastically out of step with her present surroundings. Nyman uses Scottish folk and popular songs as the basis for the score, which since Ada herself is a piano player is heard both diegetically in its keyboard incarnation and non-diegetically in its orchestral passages. The emotional, rolling melodies function as a substitute for Ada's speech, her music being 'like a mood that passes through you . . . a sound that creeps into you, and therefore incorporate an expressiveness rare in Nyman's film work. Nyman's music for *Carrington* is probably his strongest and also the most character-based, and was actually composed after the film was completed. As is becoming more usual with Nyman, musical interest centres on the contrast between the rigid organizational structure of the music and the emotional strength it embodies. The music in *Carrington* is unmistakably English in its matching of precision and passion and in passages is vaguely reminiscent of Vaughan Williams, as it sits alongside pieces by Schubert as well as some trad jazz.

In Europe, far less money is spent by producers on either the recording or the marketing of a soundtrack than in the United States. In one sense, the commercial pressures of producing music that is destined for the CD racks is less acute. However, as the need for European producers to recoup money from their films from more and more sources increases, this is likely to change. Even if it does, and more European film scores adopt a mix of commercially viable song releases alongside their diegetic music, it seems probable that European films will preserve an innovative edge, both in the images and ideas they deal with and the musical illustration of those ideas. It seems that there remain basic aesthetic differences between the film cultures of the United States and Europe. It can even be seen in music videos, where American-made video clips tend to concentrate much more upon the straightforward illustration of musical performance whereas European-produced music videos tend to be more abstract in their visual treatment of the music. The far higher budgets of American music clips are often outweighed by the creativity of European music video directors and designers, as Pete Chambers of leading UK music video producers, Partizan, claims:

> American music promos are much more in-your-face performance videos. They're great at what they do, but I think we're less gullible over here. We're not fooled by long hair and Spandex trousers, there's a bit more depth.[10]

There are analogues to this rather unimaginative approach to illustrating music in some of the most banal American youth movies of recent years, where the metaphor of performance is eclipsed by the non-narrative digressions first established in television series such as *Miami Vice*. This is not at all to claim that in some way American cinema is less rich than European – the industry that created *Waterworld* (1995) or *Bad Boys* (1995)

[10] Ibid. p. 86

also created Woody Allen, John Cassavetes, Orson Welles and countless others. It is more that in its position of global dominance, American cinema automatically off-loads the best and worst of itself to audiences in many countries that are deprived of real alternatives due to the poverty (primarily economic rather than aesthetic) of their own national industries.

As film becomes more global, paradoxically national cultural identities matter more. Universally popular stories can, and often do, originate on the margins of mainstream culture, and where the mainstream is over-whelmingly English-language-based, other cultures will need to develop films that both transcend their own countries and yet emphatically embody their countries' cultural values and signs. The basic dramatic structure of three acts and a climax shows no signs of retreating from the films from all over the world that break out of their own national cultures to achieve international success. The films of Spielberg and the plays of Beckett use the same dramatic tools; it is simply the way in which those tools are used that is different. It is the differences but also the commonalities between films and other works of art that make their greatness and their dramatic effectiveness. European directors are likely to continue to make identifiably European films rather than to imitate the film cultures of the United States. The world of film is so varied now that to try to circumscribe the possibilities for music's integration in the future is next to impossible. Radical pluralism in style and content will be more than ever the anti-aesthetic of cinema over the next ten to twenty years, with both film and music heavily integrated in a game of chance encounters.

A TENTATIVE CONCLUSION

Noël Burch's concept of an open cinema is probably closer to being fulfilled today than ever, although this situation has arisen primarily through the availability of technology rather than a quantum leap in our appreciation of film aesthetics. Since the introduction of the Sony portapak in 1965, video technology has progressively redefined the basic grammars of film construction. Whether actually shot on videotape or not, the aesthetics of videotape, the most basic being ease of manipulation and accessibility, have become a watermark for the film makers' pursuit of new images. Michelangelo Antonioni's early experiment with a film shot for cinema on videotape, *The Oberwald Mystery* (1980), has largely been forgotten and has been displaced by the more high-profile and semantically loaded diegeses of Oliver Stone's *JFK* (1991) or *Natural Born Killers* (1994), which ultimately undermine any attempt to derive a singular interpretation. Clearly much of their impact is drawn from the ways in which they trigger subconscious anxieties about surveillance and voyeurism in the audience.

Video has spawned a cinematic culture of endless manipulation of the image. Contemporary films are composed largely in post-production, where video technologies reduce everything to a digital stream of numbers rather than analogue records of real phenomena. Digital editing systems allow for endless permutations of experimentation with virtually any constituent part of the image or soundtrack, and not least the music. Robert Zemeckis' extensive collaborations with Industrial Light and Magic, a leading post-production effects company, on *Forrest Gump* (1994) illustrates how sophisticated digital 'retouching' of an image can become, creating illusion within what is basically a realist film.

Through vastly more sensitive sound recording and re-recording systems, music, dialogue and sound effects are gradually moving towards an integration. As the British composer Simon Fisher Turner observes:

The whole sound, music and FX side of films has moved on so much since I started in 1986. Final dubs and remixes are far more complex. They can take months now. We laid the music for *Caravaggio* [Derek Jarman, 1986] in just three days. The technology has changed everything. Very hi-fi![1]

The introduction of digital technology into the post-production process may yet prove to be one of the most significant impacts technology has made on the basic narrative techniques of film. The decision-making process becomes almost infinitely pliable, in terms of arranging elements on the soundtrack and to a lesser degree in the picture. Users are allowed random access to footage, which can then be edited and viewed in real time. For film, this allows an editor and a director to view potential changes in a sequence without needing mercilessly to butcher the original film. With industry standard machines, for example, Lightworks, Avid, Montage and EMC2, currently retailing for as little as $30,000, such technology is within the reach of individual editors and directors. The leading manufacturers are now producing special editions of their products aimed at film editors, such as Avid's the Film Composer and Lucasfilm's Edit Droid. The larger and more complex the post-production work to be done the more effective digital technology becomes, which presumably explains why Hollywood studios were amongst the first to embrace it with such enthusiasm.

Just as picture storage and access have become more flexible so has sound and music. The Audiofile system, produced by AMS Neve, for example, is a fast and flexible hard-disk-based digital audio recording and editing system which allows multi-track replay, and can considerably speed up the time-consuming process of 'track laying' (the placing on to the soundtrack of edited pieces of the soundtrack). This can particularly help in difficult post-production situations such as the producer's decision during the editing of *Greystoke* (1984) to replace actress Andie MacDowell's entire voice track with a new revoice by Glenn Close because he was not happy with MacDowell's performance. This technique, known as automated dialogue replacement (ADR), can be particularly effective in foreign-language dubbing, producing a better-quality dub in less time than the old linear systems. Increasingly, digital post-production facilities are networked constellations of companies located in different countries and connected via fibre-optic ISDN lines which permit the light-speed transfer of digitized, compressed signals across band widths big enough to transfer a high-quality full Dolby music track across the world in a split second. Steve Cook of

[1] Simon Fisher Turner, interview, February 1996

343

post-production company Magmasters in London is optimistic about the impact of digital post-production technology:

> The potential is enormous. For example, Charles Dance, who is based in London, is working on a film that's having post-production work done in California. The producer, director and editor went into our studios in Burbank while Charles Dance came to our London studio to do some ADR. We had two video tapes, one here and one in LA, and we were sending not only Charles Dance's voice and the duplexed comments from the producer, side by side, but time-coded as well, so the VTR's could sync up and the director could actually watch Charles Dance revoice himself.[2]

Others are less optimistic, not least because of the impact on labour. A 1995 article in *Variety* documented moves by a group of Motion Picture Editors' Guild members to investigate deteriorating working conditions in the post-production industry. Compressed working schedules and long editing sessions are the result of a mistaken belief by producers and studios that digital processes can cut post-production time down to the point where they can begin to save a lot of money in the overall budget. There is a trend towards using multiple editors on a project, again in order to cut down the post-production schedule, where it is cheaper for a producer to hire a group of editors on a short schedule than to let one editor work on a longer schedule.

The whole interface between sound design and music has become blurred with the widespread take-up of digital audio technology. Electronic sound design has made enormous progress in the last ten years as sound moves ever more towards being an 'experience' in a film rather than simply a source, and now seems to rival music in its impact. The close integration of music and sound is not in itself new, although in the musical collages composed by Simon Fisher Turner and others the barriers between the two often break down completely. Some Japanese films of the 1950s integrated sound and music particularly successfully and one can also look at films by Jean-Luc Godard and Alain Robbe-Grillet, both of whom worked with the sound engineer turned composer Michel Fano. These early films established an alternative aesthetic to the Hollywood tradition that gave music a far more central position in the creation of narrative diegesis. Andrew Glen is a prominent British music editor who also works with sound design:

> The distinction between FX and music is becoming blurred, largely, I suppose, because the technology, the composer and FX editor are increasingly the same. However, on a particular project, the two roles continue generally to be performed by

2 *Screen International*, 22 April 1994, p. 16

two or more different individuals. There is usually not enough communication and interaction between the sound effects editor and the composer. It's often limited to a query about the key of a church bell effect an editor intends using in a particular scene. Where such communication is established, or at least where one is aware of the other's intentions, the results can be stunning. Let me give an example. Hans Zimmer is one of the more 'sound effects aware' composers. On the film *Paperhouse* he had the benefit of hearing the final sound effects mix before he composed his score. During a crash scene he was able to score round the siren of a departing ambulance and then continue its modulation musically hence creating a very interesting integration of music and effects. His score for *Black Rain*, for example, went even further, featuring heavy use of rumbles and unusual, bold atmospheres as part of the music.

I recently had a pleasing experience working on a film series for British television. This was on *Cold Lazarus*, the last work by the late English playwright Dennis Potter. The score by Chris Gunning was very big by TV standards, featuring the London Symphony Orchestra. I was responsible for sound effects. The series was set in the future and the plot revolved heavily around the technology of the time. The sound effects were vital in helping to enhance the futuristic visuals and make them believable, yet I knew that whatever effects I offered up had to blend and enhance, or at least be inoffensive alongside, this very grand (and expensive) score. Such was the schedule, I was able to get hold of the master tapes of the score a few days before the final mix and play it alongside my sound effects sequences in the cutting room. I then tuned my various beeps, hums, rumbles, etc. such that they would at times harmonize and blend with the score but then where dramatically appropriate would clash to create an uncomfortable atmosphere. This might seem an obvious course of action but it is often not possible due to the scheduling of the typical film mix where sound effects' premixing might be occurring before the music is even recorded. Furthermore, it is only recently that the technology – non-linear editing systems – has been readily available in the typical film cutting room to play the music and all the sound effects in sync and at the right pitch.[3]

Technology increasingly affects the way in which the composer approaches the task. Probably the most significant impact of electronic technologies is that they allow the composer to create on the same instrument for which he is composing. This largely does away with the need to understand musical transcription systems and opens up the field to composers with little or no theoretical background in music. With certain combinations of musical technology, the composer does not even need to be a musician skilled in a particular instrument, hence perhaps the increasing

3 Andrew Glen, interview, May 1996

involvement of directors in the creation of their film's musical textures. The trend is towards simplicity of musical idea and towards the creation of an atmosphere rather than the creation of a musical work. The synthesizer's unique coloration fills up a lot of space on the soundtrack and limits both the need and the space for musical complexity.

Maurice Jarre's score for *Witness* (1985) used a group of up to ten synthesists whom he recorded working on sections of the score on the same stage at the same time. Each synthesist brought their own unique instrumental colour and texture to the sessions and Jarre treated the set-up as if he was conducting a chamber ensemble, choosing not to MIDI together the different musicians but to let each find their own atmospheric space within the ensemble.

It would, however, be a mistake to think that the current state of film music is due solely to the popularity of certain kinds of instruments or technological platforms. Bruce Broughton, an American composer, offers the following perspective:

> Where I see film music heading has nothing to do with instrumentation. It's heading towards a reliance less on the traditional elements of music and more on the use of sound for its own sake. I personally do not understand this great interest in contemporary film music, because I find most of it is unsatisfying as music. As one friend complained to me recently, many film scores sound as though they are mostly just chords. This is to my mind a result of an unintentional collaboration with studio marketing (temp tracks), nervous film makers making talky, effects-laden films and keyboard players thrust suddenly into the role as hot composer with their cool and unusual synth sounds. The orchestral writing, when it exists, is generally a transcription from a composer's keyboard doodling, improvised whilst viewing the video version of his work print. The synth tracks are prepared and the orchestra is laid on top. Like any method, of itself it is a benign process and not necessarily indicative of a lack of creativity. But in the hands of composers who rely not on musical ideas but on musical sounds, the process takes on a certain musical sameness or familiarity. However, in all fairness, this seems to be a direction that contemporary music is taking as well.[4]

Three-act story-telling remains the conventional form of mainstream cinema and, in the majority of cases, the use of music remains unchanged from cinema's earliest beginnings. As Caryl Flinn[5] states, given the ease of

[4] Bruce Broughton, interview, March 1996

[5] Caryl Flinn, *Strains of Utopia* (Princeton: 1993), p. 151

access to new music now afforded by global distribution systems, modern
audiences are still more likely to hear an extract of Mozart or Beethoven
woven into the soundtrack of a new film than music by contemporary
composers. This despite the fact that the basic substance and practice of
music has changed and is being changed by technology faster than ever
before. Composition is no longer a specialized activity, since musical
language has become subsumed into the digital language of computing. The
assembly language of turntable artists, as Brian Eno describes them,
'squeezing Cezanne from the tube, rather than vermilion', has in turn
reactivated the sense of music as a continuum, a living history that defeats
final packaging.

The composer John Adams observes:

> Stylistic things can come and go but technology is here to stay. I've always thought
> that technology precedes artistic invention, that the electric guitar was invented
> before rock'n'roll . . . The tape recorder suggested lots of the compositional routines
> that minimalists and various other composers thought up. No one would have
> thought of creating musical structures by tight repetition of the same material had it
> not been for the tape recorder.[6]

Music, and film music in particular, could be better understood by both
writers and musicians and therefore more creatively explored if more was
understood about the effects of its sound within a film. In music education,
music theory is usually isolated from musical history, resulting in intuitions
about music that are rooted in pitch structures rather than more culturally
accessible elements such as tone-colour, melody or rhythm. Many
nineteenth- and twentieth-century harmonic concepts are no longer
applicable to modern music. Notation is not, in itself, music, it is an analogy
which developed to teach music-theoretical concepts. Music does not
consist of 'musical works', isolated from each other and from their cultural
contexts, nor is music simply the structural organization of pitches within
a given piece. The performance aspect of music shows the composer to be
at best a co-creator of his music alongside other musicians. The more
interesting moves in contemporary music theory are interdisciplinary,[7] but
these are substantially outweighed by the more traditional emphases on
autonomist-formalist research. As Claire Detels makes clear:

[6] John Adams, quoted by John L. Walters, 'On Phonography', *Times Literary Supplement*, 26 April 1996, p. 10

[7] See, for example, Nicholas Cook, *A Guide to Musical Analysis* (New York: 1987), and Mary Louise Serafine and
Wayne Slawson, 'Interdisciplinary Directions in Music Theory', *Music Theory Spectrum*, 11, 1989, pp. 74–83

As a consequence of the isolation, music receives little or no discussion in general humanities and social science courses and curricula which otherwise benefit from interdisciplinary integration. The same omission occurs in cultural criticism; that is, music is omitted from discussion in cases where it is obviously relevant, such as film reviews, or mentioned only superficially. In the case of many films, omitting critical consideration of the music is not unlike analysing *Tristan and Isolde* without discussion of Wagner and his musical style. Nonetheless, it happens all the time.[8]

The sound of music remains theoretically isolated from the various cultural meanings, historical and sociological, that are assigned to it. Because of this separation, our cultural understanding of music remains partial. Yet we are all listeners to music, and it is the listening experience that needs to be more closely understood, making people rather than pieces of music the centre of the musical universe.

---

8 Claire Detels, 'Autonomist/Formalist Aesthetics, Music Theory, and Soft Boundaries', *Journal of Aesthetics and Art Criticism*, Winter 1994

INDEX